Breaking into Information Security
Crafting a Custom Career Path to Get the Job You Really Want

Breaking into Information Security
Crafting a Custom Career Path to Get the Job You Really Want

Josh More

Anthony J. Stieber

Chris Liu

Technical Editor: Beth Friedman

AMSTERDAM • BOSTON • HEIDELBERG • LONDON
NEW YORK • OXFORD • PARIS • SAN DIEGO
SAN FRANCISCO • SINGAPORE • SYDNEY • TOKYO

Syngress is an Imprint of Elsevier

Acquiring Editor: Chris Katsaropoulos
Editorial Project Manager: Anna Valutkevich
Project Manager: Priya Kumaraguruparan
Designer: Matthew Limbert

Syngress is an imprint of Elsevier
225 Wyman Street, Waltham, MA 02451, USA

British Library Cataloguing-in-Publication Data
A catalogue record for this book is available from the British Library

Library of Congress Cataloging-in-Publication Data
A catalog record for this book is available from the Library of Congress

ISBN: 978-0-12-800783-9

For information on all Syngress publications
visit our website at store.elsevier.com/Syngress

Working together
to grow libraries in
developing countries

www.elsevier.com • www.bookaid.org

Contents

Author Biographies

JOSH MORE

Josh More started Eyra Security after spending more than 15 years in IT. He holds multiple security and technical certifications and serves in a leadership position on several security-focused groups. When taking a break from reducing IT and security risks for his company's customers, Josh enjoys reading, cooking, and photography.

ANTHONY J. STIEBER

Anthony J. Stieber has spent over 20 years in academia, banks, retail, information security, and insurance; designed enterprise security architectures; installed military and commercial firewalls; engineered medical diagnostic systems; reverse-engineered Internet stores; encrypted data warehouses; provided expertise for legal cases; spoken at international cryptography conferences; broken encrypted storage systems; studied as an apprentice locksmith; and became a published writer and recently a book co-author.

CHRIS LIU

Chris Liu has over 20 years of information technology experience, a CISSP, CISM, and no idea how he ended up where is. He has been a help desk technician, network administrator, quality assurance engineer, release manager, IT manager, instructor, developer, consultant, and product development manager, and is currently an information security professional. He is proof that careers sometimes only make sense in retrospect.

Acknowledgments

Many people helped us with the book; family and friends provided support and understanding for the many nights, evenings, and weekends we each worked on the book.

We are particularly grateful to all of those who contributed the information security stories in the book, and regret those we couldn't include:

Travis Abrams, Jim Chan, David Henning, Michael Huber, Heather Kohls, Mak Kolybabi, Joshua Marpet, John Meyers, Stephen Northcutt, Greg Sullivan, Jimmy Vo, Alan Waggoner

We support free and open-source software and its communities and believe it is critical to information security. GNU Emacs, GNU/Linux Knoppix, LibreOffice, Mozilla Firefox, Perl, VIM, and much other free open-source software were used in the production of this book.

INTRODUCTION

INTRODUCTION

This book was written by three people with three vastly different experiences in information security. The book has been influenced by everyone with whom we've worked and by every book and article we've read. So this book is from the information security community. This book has illustrative stories of over a dozen people, describing their own information security stories. The number of people involved in this book is too many to count and goes well beyond those listed on the cover and in the Acknowledgments.

Information security is constantly changing, and we expect this book will also change to keep pace. The second edition will involve even more people and cover even more topics. We don't know what the third or even fourth editions will cover.

It is our aim that this book will grow, not just with our own careers, but yours as well. With that in mind, as you read this book, please feel free to tell us what has been important to you so we can include it in the next edition.

As authors of a community book, we feel that it is important that the book not only be from the community but also be part of the community. As such, we have earmarked a portion of the royalties of this book to be donated to the Hackers for Charity nonprofit organization.

WHO SHOULD READ THIS BOOK

This book is for anyone changing roles into or within the security community. While it will likely be of more interest to people trying to break into entry level information security, the book is written so that you may break into any role, not just at the beginning of your career. Whether you're just getting started as a security analyst or are becoming a penetration testing lead in charge of your team, there should be something in this book of interest to you.

HOW TO READ THIS BOOK

This book is a survey of the information security job market and community, not a direct path to success. Information security and technology changes quickly, so any direct advice given will quickly go out-of-date. Instead, we propose a different way of thinking about your career.

Careers often follow a path of three phases or "tiers" in which you first spend most of your time learning, then spend a large amount of your time doing what you've learned, and then you may focus on teaching others. This book follows these three tiers with a Learn/Do/Teach approach. While any one role will likely involve all three tiers, the proportions of Learn/Do/Teach will change as you progress.

To read this book, read the "core" of each first, going through Models, then Learn, then Do, then Teach. Each has descriptions of several information security roles. Feel free to jump around and read what the different roles involve. Once you know what work you want to do, consider which roles earlier in the process appeal to you the most. This should help you to create your own custom career path, which will both be more rewarding and more likely to succeed than anything any of us could lay out for you. For many people, career paths are dynamic, and change as roles or jobs change.

As you progress through your information security journey, keep your goals in mind, but also keep in mind that your goals may change. Both your goals and your environment determine the path your career will take. It may be that this path will not lead you to your new goals, so pay attention as things change and adjust accordingly.

CAUTION

Ethics and Career

The cautions in this book aren't just because you could be responsible for lost or damaged data, but also because you could lose your job and damage your career. You are responsible for your life, and your career is part of your life. You are responsible for your own career, and you are responsible for using your own judgment. Ethics matter in information security; any poor ethics and bad judgment will make a lot of trouble for yourself and others in your current or future jobs.

There is no guarantee that the path you choose will work for you, so if you find yourself at a dead end, consider other options. If you keep building your skills and remain persistent, you can get where you want to go.

This book provides a framework for thinking about your career. Careers move forward in fits and starts, so be prepared to fail fast, recover fast, and start over in another role as you move to where you want to go. This book is not a hard-and-fast guide, rather it is a steady and slow career guide. Your career will probably not be like any of ours, or anyone else's. If you see a path we didn't define, consider it, if it works for you, or doesn't, share it with the community and us. As the stories in the book show, there is no single true path to success.

NOTES FROM THE AUTHORS

We are three authors attempting to speak with one voice. It was not always possible; but where we had conflicts, we worked them out together. But there is also value in us each speaking individually.

WHY COMMUNITY? — JOSH MORE

Information security is a losing game. Our adversaries — the attackers — are better-funded than we defenders, and they have more time to cause problems than we have to fix them. This will not change. Throughout history, the cycle of attack and defense arms race has been built on the premise of "good enough." A wooden shield is a good enough defense until your enemies get metal lances and longbows. A stone castle wall is a good enough defense until your enemies get siege engines (or helicopters).

The fact is, someone is always going to lose because once we get to war, it's too late for a win-win situation. And with every win, the attackers are going to get a little bit better. They are tuning their tools and techniques every day, while far too many of us defenders are spending our time just catching-up. In order to survive, we have to learn as quickly as they do, and the only way to do that is to share knowledge.

This is what community is about. Our community is not perfect; but we are getting better at sharing. When I started, companies were loath to admit that they had experienced an attack, much less were breached. Today, we're seeing reports of major data breaches monthly. The more we talk about what everybody faces, the better we can work together. Knowing what we're thinking does give attackers an edge. However, on balance, the boost we get from sharing knowledge is greater than the increase in our risk.

And really, that's what it is about. As an information security professional, your job is about balancing risk. However, you will almost never be the sole decision maker. You will explain the risks as you see them and you'll have to understand those who see them differently. To win these battles and increase your chances of surviving the constant war, you'll need help. After you read this book, talk about your ideas with your local security groups, on mailing lists and blogs, and at conferences. Seek out those who disagree with you and learn how they think. Give feedback, so we can all improve.

This even applies to book authors. This book is written by three people with collectively over 50 years of experience in the industry. But still, we're just three. We've asked for help from a handful of others, but we're also asking for help from you. If you help us help others, we all get better. If we get better faster than the attackers, we can improve everyone's defense.

SECURE THINKING? — ANTHONY J. STIEBER

The biggest difference I have seen in being good at security, not just information security, is an attitude, a mindset, to think in ways that others don't. This isn't about being smart, imaginative, educated, technically skilled, or experienced, although those can help. I have met too many smart, imaginative, educated, technically skilled, and experienced people who can't imagine security problems. They are neither stupid nor ignorant, and they are very good at other things; but they aren't very good at security. Unfortunately, some of them are in the security industry.

For example, it doesn't occur to them that their system will be attacked by someone as smart, educated, and experienced as themselves. Perhaps this is an innate goodness in them, or a lack of empathy for someone else's goals. Successful defending means being able to think at least a little like the attacker, ideally before the attacker does. This doesn't require superhuman thinking, the ability to predict the future, or being a bad person—it just means thinking enough like an attacker *before* getting attacked.

If you can think about what an attacker might do at the same time you are trying to defend, you'll be better at security than those who can't.

Some defenders, such as security researchers and penetration testers, go further and even act like attackers. If you can think about two different and incompatible ideas at the same time, if you can ask that next question, if you have the empathy to think like an attacker, but have the sympathy to not be an attacker, then you can break into information security. Everything else you can learn, and teach others so they can do security better. If you can do this, then security could be right for you.

Empathize with your adversaries, and defeat them anyway.

IS SECURITY RIGHT FOR ME? — CHRIS LIU

As an instructor who has taught security both to college students and professionals, I have found that many people are interested in being information security professionals. Unfortunately, not as many people are interested in learning *how* to be a security professional. What do I mean by this? Simple: There are no shortcuts. You must get down and dirty with technical information. You need to become intimately familiar with bits and bytes that are boring and challenging at the same time. You need to be comfortable—very comfortable—with things not working the way you expect.

I have generally been able to spot those who will do well with security by the presence of a single attitude. Do they want to learn as much as they possibly can? Are they willing to explore stray paths and dead ends, but use those to learn from their mistakes? Or do they ask the question that gives it all away: "Do I need to know this for the test?"

Yes, hacking is cool. Being able to attack websites is neat. But being able to actually analyze a disparate set of data, and develop a cohesive vision of the target takes time, patience, and the ability to think outside the box. If a probe gives you an unexpected response, you need to be able to analyze that information and use it to create a new probe. If you can only run by the script, you will never get to the cool stuff.

Things are always going wrong when you are doing security. The script that worked the last time to attack a web server doesn't work this time, even though it should. Well, you think it should. But you weren't aware that this new client had a slightly different configuration that made this attack entirely irrelevant. Are you able to look at a long list of failed attempts and go, "Well, at least I know this won't work here," and develop a new strategy?

Are you able to learn, while you are doing? Are you able to teach while you are learning? If you can, then security could be the right fit for you.

If not, you may discover that security is more frustrating than cool for you.

TERMINOLOGY

Cyber, Hacking, and Information Security Growing Pains

Information security is a young and immature field, even the term "discipline" can't really be applied yet, and the term "profession" is still debatable. Just being paid to do something doesn't make it a profession, it also has to get done properly, and right now information security is often not even done. Information security also has many common terms without commonly accepted meanings or are highly ambiguous. Some terms and some meanings are even controversial. The meanings of ordinary words like "defect," "exploit," "threat," "vulnerability," and "weakness," are still argued about. Some words are particularly controversial and are information security sub-culture shibboleths that will mark the speaker. For example, within some groups the word "hacker" means "computer criminal," in other groups it means "computer genius," and in other groups it means both.

Another common word is "cyber" and may mean "computers, the Internet, and command and control systems in general" or it can mean "I don't know I'm ignorant about computers or security". Cyber can also mean almost nothing.

To avoid the ambiguity of these words and others we've avoided them, except when used by others in context.

MODELS

0.2

MODELS

> "Essentially, all models are wrong, but some are useful."
>
> — George E. P. Box

Humanity has acquired more knowledge than can fit in a single human brain. To help us understand what's going on, we continuously abstract concepts into other concepts. For example, most people don't need to know the differences between an Adirondack, a Bofinger, and a caquetoire. For everyday life, the abstract concept of "chair" will suffice. We do the same in information security. Networking is abstracted with the seven-layer OSI model, the four-layer TCP/IP model, or just a single "is it working?" layer on which other even higher layers are placed.

The point of a model is to simplify the world and make it more understandable. Albert Einstein is often quoted as saying "Make it as simple as possible, but no simpler." What Einstein actually wrote in the journal *Philosophy of Science* was:

> "It can scarcely be denied that the supreme goal of all theory is to make the irreducible basic elements as simple and as few as possible without having to surrender the adequate representation of a single datum of experience."

The fact that Einstein chose to keep his lesson on simplification rather complex indicates the type of people who typically read the journal *Philosophy of Science* in the early 01930s. This book is aimed at a somewhat different crowd. We will primarily use the model: Learn/Do/Teach.

TIME MANAGEMENT

Five Digit Years

As this book is about time management and taking the long term view, we have adopted the practice of The Long Now Foundation of writing years with five-digit dates. While we do not realistically believe that much of this book will be applicable past the year 09999 — information security changes rather quickly, after all — we do feel that deliberately thinking in a longer term that most people are used to will help you to realize the importance of taking the long view as you plan your information security career.

> **NOTE**
>
> References and URLs
>
> Full references for many items mentioned in this book, such as Albert Einstein's article in *Philosophy of Science*, can be found in the "Appendix: People & Quotes". Others references are in broad categories in roughly the order as presented in the book, such as Security Models and Time Management.

LEARN/DO/TEACH

The Learn/Do/Teach model is adapted from the medical community. The core idea is that you learn significantly better if, after the initial learning, you actively apply it. Then, after you've demonstrated understanding, you teach someone else. This gives you the opportunity to learn without causing harm, and provides a chain of knowledge stretching from generation to generation.

This book is organized similarly. The first section, Learn, is about the importance of learning and lists common entry-level information security jobs in which you typically learn the basics. Entry-level jobs are seldom fun, but only by using them to acquire a firm background can you expect to gain the experience needed to excel at higher levels. To use your experience from other jobs in information security you can perform "lateral" moves into the Do and Teach sections of the model.

The Do section of the model introduces the importance of getting your hands dirty, literally and figuratively. It lists common mid-career jobs and discusses how there can be gaps between formal "book learning" and "the school of hard knocks" on the job. We do not prefer one option over the other but those who understand the theoretical underpinnings and then also get deep experience tend to be more successful. The point is to maximize the amount of skill you gain in a specific amount of time. Thus, if you first Learn, then Do, you can gain a significant amount of demonstrable skill. These are the roles on which a business succeeds or fails, and that put you at the heart of information security. Many people are happy working these sorts of jobs for their entire career.

The Teach section brings it together. To close the loop and pass the learning to the next generation, you give back to the community through teaching. Teaching helps solidify your thinking and makes learning new things more efficient. As with the Do section, there are lateral paths to jump into the Teach of information security. The jobs listed in the Teach section include commonly accepted senior level jobs. However, what distinguishes Teach from Do is that each of these jobs has a teaching component where you are expected to help your colleagues improve over time.

Finally, there is a section on Boosting. This section is separate because it is optional, but has highly recommended suggestions for bootstrapping skills on your own time. Boosting defeats the "experience needed to get experience" trap and shows how to use the Learn/Do/Teach cycle outside of work to rapidly gain the skills needed to make that leap to your desired job.

INFORMATION SECURITY MODELS

Other information security models are also used in this book. These are not core such as Learn/Do/Teach but they are commonly used in information security.

(ISC)² COMMON BODY OF KNOWLEDGE DOMAINS

The International Information Systems Security Certification Consortium or (ISC)² is best known for its stewardship of the Certified Information Security Systems Professional (CISSP) certification. This certification tests on what (ISC)² calls the CISSP Common Body of Knowledge (CBK). The CBK is organized into domains which are "buckets" of information security knowledge concentrations which form the (ISC)² view of a well-rounded security practitioner. In 02015 the ten domains were reorganized into eight domains but with the same information: Security and Risk Management, Asset Security, Security Engineering, Communication and Network Security, Identity and Access Management, Security Assessment and Testing, Security Operations, Software Development Security. See the Appendix: Models for details.

The CISSP CBK approach involves several domains of study that may not necessarily apply to your specific job or interests. As such, this approach may be considered too broad for some individuals. The CISSP is generally considered "broad but shallow" which is well suited for generalists who can consult specialists, but not as well suited for those same specialists.

CIA TRIAD

A simple approach to information security is the CIA triad which has the three qualities of confidentiality, integrity and availability. Sometimes this is called ACI to avoid confusion.

- **Confidentiality**—Is the quality that only those who need access to or knowledge of the data will have either. Many reports you see of people intruding on networks involves a loss or breakdown of confidentiality. Lost laptops, poor database and web site access controls, insecure email, and weak cryptography are common ways to lose confidentiality. Examples include medical record and credit card exposure. Common terms for confidentiality loss include data breach, data theft, exposure, leak, and piracy.
- **Integrity**—Is the quality of how trustworthy the system or the data within the system is—in other words, how confident you are that the system will respond as it should and that it has not been tampered with. No access controls, poor web site access controls, and weak cryptography are common ways to lose integrity. Examples include incomplete or wrong medical records and ATM skimmers. Common terms for integrity loss include data corruption, defacement, modification, subversion and tampering.
- **Availability**—As you might expect, describes how available the system is. This idea comes from such fields as health care, where unavailable information, such as a heart-rate monitor, may result in someone's death, or financial systems, where lost transaction data means lost money. No data backups, equipment failure, no redundancy, and unexpected load are common ways to lose availability. Hard disk drive crashes, failed backups, power outage, and very high and aggressively low popularity are common ways to lose availability. Common terms for availability loss include business continuity loss, data destruction or loss, outage and denial-of-service. A denial-of-service (DoS) attack is specifically against availability by an adversary. Good security detects, prevents, and withstands DoS attacks. Conversely, if a security feature protects a system by preventing anyone from accessing

it, it creates a low availability regardless of the "good" or "bad" status of the individuals using it.

All of the CIA triad qualities can be adversely affected by merely accident and natural disasters, not just deliberate actions by an adversary. This does not lessen their status as information security concerns. In addition adversaries can take advantage of accidents and disasters and make them worse.

It is useful to rank the three CIA triad qualities in order of importance which will vary. Some environments have mostly equally balanced requirements, but others will be biased toward or away from one or two.

The CIA triad approach makes some security issues very simple to explain and helps determine which quality to prioritize. Health care often prioritizes availability, finance requires integrity, and defense organizations tend to focus on confidentiality. The CIA triad is a powerful tool for thinking about information security, but like all models, it is limited.

PARKERIAN HEXAD

In 01998, Donn B. Parker proposed a different way of looking at information security. This approach doubles the number of qualities from the CIA triad, thus squaring the number of possibilities, but it is not as difficult to work with as the eight domains of the (ISC)2 Common Body of Knowledge (CBK). The variables are:

- **Confidentiality**—As in the CIA triad.
- **Possession or Control**—Covers situations where a data element or system escapes the scope of controls placed around it. It may or may not involve a compromise of Confidentiality, but simply knowing that it has escaped allows you to treat it as "tainted" until verified as unaccessed or altered.
- **Integrity**—As described in the CIA triad.
- **Authenticity**—Covers the creation of data or systems. Possession or Control focuses on potential losses of Confidentiality, but Authenticity focuses on potential losses of Integrity. If you prove a trusted system as being authentic, it may be necessary to create additional controls around it.
- **Availability**—As described in the CIA triad.
- **Utility**—To disclose a bias on the part of the authors, Utility is a critical aspect to security that most models miss. Utility combines the concepts of usefulness and usability. Some security features fail "closed," making it difficult or impossible for anyone to access the system. In such scenarios, Utility is zero and this can overwhelm any other issues at play, although it may very well be secure in that it is inaccessible. Utility can also be considered a measure of usability. Some security controls are extremely restrictive and users actively work against them to get their work done. Since security involves a mix of both technology and people, building an understanding of how people respond is critical to your model. An unusable system won't be used and security that isn't used isn't secure at all.

SANS LEARNING FAMILIES

SANS is one of the best security training companies in the world, and offers dozens of different training classes. As with many academic approaches to learning, SANS groups the classes into categories. This approach is similar to the families discussed earlier. As of October 02015, the classes break down into several categories with some overlap between each:

- Cyber Defense—general information security covering the basics and and more advanced use of common defensive tools such as firewalls, anti-virus, monitoring, auditing, and system hardening.
- System Administration—focuses on information security for the operating system administrator.
- Digital Forensic Investigations and Media Exploitation—catching concerns after they've been exploited. This can involve reverse-engineering malware and carving memory and disk to obtain evidence. In short, forensics focuses on determining what happened, so appropriate plans can be made to address any issues.
- Penetration Testing—using and creating tools to break into live wired and wireless networks, web applications, mobile devices.
- Incident Response—often combined with Digital Forensics to form DFIR, this is near-real-time and real-time response to attack using forensics, reverse engineering, and any and all of the other tools available in the other categories.
- Management—for people who are responsible for the business as a whole. This category of security learning involves understanding things at a very high level, so appropriate decisions can be made.
- Secure Software Development—all aspects of development, regardless of language. Many developers have a different approach to security, and this category is aimed at catching security issues earlier, as the sooner you find an issue, the cheaper it is to fix.
- Intrusion Analysis—after the fact analysis including defensive techniques used elsewhere and forensics.
- Cyber Guardian—a high level subset of Cyber Defense.
- Audit and Legal—focus on specific issues around standards, regulations, and other things that people are required to do from a security perspective so people can demonstrate compliance.
- Industrial Control Systems—industrial control systems (ICS) and supervisory, control and data acquisition (SCADA) systems fit in here.

JOB REQUIREMENTS

The existing models represent the daily cycle of attack/defense very well and can also be used to discuss security issues in general at a very high level. However, they do not work well for personal career growth. These models are based mostly around Doing and not Learning or Teaching. This makes sense, since most businesses are focused around getting things done. Getting things done directly affects productivity and profit, which is what matters to businesses.

Individuals, however, care about more. We care about doing better, and we also care about understanding better, making people's lives better, doing things differently, and doing different things. A straightforward model doesn't capture the inherent "squishiness" of human nature. We need something different.

So let's look at getting hired.

A detailed look at being hired is available in Josh More's book dedicated to this topic: *Job Reconnaissance: Using Hacking Skills to Win the Job Hunt Game* also published by Syngress. We will not repeat all that material, though you may wish to read it for yourself. As a summary, consider why an organization hires someone. In general, people are hired to solve a problem. In for-profit businesses, they are often hired because the product of their work can be sold for more than it costs to generate. In nonprofit organizations, people are often hired because their presence helps organizations achieve goals better and more cost effectively than without them.

With that in mind, consider two otherwise identical candidates. Both have no higher education, but one has a certification and the other does not. Odds are the one with certification will get the first offer. Now consider two new candidates. Both have college degrees, but one has taken the time to explore something and has written and published a detailed HOWTO document about it. Again, who do you think will get the job?

Fundamentally, proving yourself the best option in the job market is like proving yourself the best anywhere else. You have to stand out, in a positive way. Often, the smallest differences will make surprisingly large impacts. A single project can set you apart in a field of people that haven't bothered to do a project. In a slate of people without degrees, having a degree of any sort will matter. However, against a slate of people with degrees, a degree that matches your selected field is far more important. So:

Table 0.2.1

A person with...	Wins over a person with...
No degree, but with certifications	No degree
A general degree	No degree, but with certifications
A focused degree	A general degree
A focused degree and certifications	A focused degree
A personal recommendation from a mentor	A focused degree and certifications
An interesting project to discuss	A personal recommendation from a mentor
Experience in the "good old boys" club	An interesting project to discuss
An interesting project they have led	Experience in the "good old boys" club
An awesome life story	An interesting project they have led

Clearly, this is extremely subjective and based on the limited experience of the authors, with job experience in a specific region of the world. This model also loses the intricacies of different types of degrees (associate, bachelor's, master's, doctorate) and ignores differences in people's interview skills. Instead we can model this as people accumulate points for each thing they've done. So:

Table 0.2.2

Experience	Points
Certification	1 certification = 5 points 2 certifications = 7 points 3+ certifications = 9 points
Degree	Associate = 20 points Bachelor's = 30 points Master's = 35–50 points, depending on job PhD = -10–100 points, depending on job
Personal recommendation from a mentor	Mentor not known to interviewer = 10 points Mentor known to interviewer = 30 points Mentor is the interviewer = 300 points
An interesting project to discuss	1 project = 20 points 2 projects = 30 points 3+ projects = 40 points
Experience in the "good old boys" club	Mentor not in the club = − 10 to 10 points, depending Mentor in the club = 50 points
An interesting project they have led	1 project = 40 points 2 projects = 60 points 3+ projects = 80 points
An awesome life story	Story not pertinent to job = 20 points Story pertinent to job = 100–200 points

As you can see, having an awesome life story can trump pretty much everything here. Even if you may not be able to do the job as well as someone else, if those hiring you think you're awesome and want to work with you, you'll be considered the "best" for the job. If they think this, the hiring company will find some way to ignore requirements like degrees and certifications. You may have to get a degree or certification after you get the job, but you'll have broken in, and that's the goal. Some organizations will also support you in getting a degree or certification by paying for tuition, books, or exam fees.

Our job hiring model assumes there are common job types, and details those jobs, their requirements, and a rough path you may follow into the job you want. Ideally, you'll also create an awesome life story so maintain your story narrative as you move through your career. But having an awesome life is only half of it. The other half is that you must be able to tell your story.

This book will help you to find your new opportunities, maximize the outcome of each, and help you tell your story.

A NOTE ON EXPERIENCE — JOSH MORE

When I was young, being turned down for an ideal job because I lacked experience was both humiliating and angering. After all, I was smart and driven. I had the magic degree that was supposed to open doors. Running the whole "need experience to get experience" game was intensely frustrating.

Then, years went by and I found myself in the position of interviewing others. And I've got to tell you, the kids with degrees but no experience were arrogant idiots who had no idea how the real world worked. I hoped they'd get some experience because they'd be good after that, but I didn't want to be the one to break them in.

One way to get the experience you need to get a job that requires experience is to ignore the 40-hour cap on what you "should" be doing. *Should* is one of the biggest career killers there is. If all of your competitors get caught in the "should trap" and you avoid it, you automatically land in a position above them. For example, you could work 40 hours per week, and learn 10 more hours a week on your own time, and get a basic entry-level job. Then add projects to your resume so at the next career leap, you have more experience than everyone else who only put in 40 hours a week. This allows you to take advantage of demand for experience. If you're still in school, devote a specific time each week as well as time on school breaks towards developing the skills you need to give you a definite edge over everyone that doesn't. Identify your limitations and work on them until they no longer damage you, then focus where you can excel.

DEGREES

This book assumes that a degree is a bachelor's degree in the US collegiate system, with between three and five years of study with an emphasis in a specific field. The US also has associate degrees, which are usually two years of study, typically in more hands-on fields. US advanced degrees include master's degrees of usually two to four years, law degrees of two years, and doctorates which are usually six years or more.

The two-year associate degree typically fulfills a prerequisite toward a specific type of job, and are usually only offered by community and vocational colleges. Such degrees are useful when competing against high school graduates without training. Associate degrees also give you useful theoretical underpinnings for your intended field. Typical associate degrees that are useful in information security are in networking or system administration. Associate degrees are relatively cheap to get and can be attained fairly quickly. Degree programs for working adults on evenings and weekends are often for associate degrees. Beware of low quality associate degree programs and schools, don't trust the schools' own marketing, guarantees, or claims of successful graduates find your own contacts of current students and graduates, ask your mentor, and current and future employers about both good and bad schools.

Bachelor's degrees come in several flavors, but generally involve four years of study for a wider understanding for your subject matter as well as study outside of that area. A degree in physics, for example, will likely involve one or two classes each in math and physics for eight semesters. A degree in computer science would typically combine math and programming. There is also an expectation that you spend one to two classes each semester in unrelated disciplines such as literature, history, or psychology. The idea is that, by the end of your program, you have a more well-rounded understanding of the world and, along the way, have picked up the techniques you need to talk to people outside of your field.

Advanced degrees can involve between two and twelve years of study after your bachelor's degree, as you focus deeper on a specific issue in your selected field. Some very specific jobs require these degrees but, increasingly, they are seen as a liability outside of dedicated academic or research-focused fields.

No one can see the future. The more narrowly you focus, the more you risk getting it wrong. If you guess wrong with an associate degree, you're out two years of your life, and tuition. If you guess wrong with a PhD, you could lose a decade. However, if you guess right, you could land your perfect job and keep it for life. It's a high-risk, high-stakes game.

Many people reading this book will have a bachelor's degree (or equivalent) or be working on it. Such a degree will give you an edge over everyone who doesn't have one, but also doesn't require quite as much time or money as an advanced degree. The cost of advanced degrees is rising, and their relevance is being questioned more, so it is likely that we'll be seeing fewer of these in the information security market. Master's degrees in information security are uncommon and not well tested yet in the market. However, at the time of this writing, they are becoming more popular so unlike other advanced degrees, we expect we'll be seeing more of them.

A bachelor's degree tells a hiring manager that you've managed to stay focused and work within a system for four whole years. It says that you can get things done and won't cause trouble in the company. That's what matters to them. Many don't even care what field your degree is in. However, you can demonstrate these things without a degree once you've put in enough work elsewhere, but it may be more difficult to get that work and it may take longer than an associate or bachelor's degree.

Degrees typically only open the first few doors in your career. Not having a degree will make it harder to get some jobs, but when you have around 10 years, experience, you'll find that not having one will matter less and less to what you want to do. If you develop a pattern of doing awesome things and are known in relevant communities, lacking a degree may not matter at all.

CERTIFICATIONS

Certifications are sometimes viewed as a cheaper alternative to a degree, usually both in time and financial cost. They show that you've learned something and, if you work hard, that you can do something with what you've learned. Some certifications are more rigorous than others. The Offensive Security Certified Professional (OSCP) certification involves hands-on work attacking test systems to verify that you can actually perform a penetration test. Others, like the $(ISC)^2$ CISSP exam, are multiple-choice exams with required minimum years of information experience.

There are two challenges around certifications—which to get first and which to get last. A lot of people, once they get a certification, feel the need to acquire more. For more hiring managers, the first certification is much more important than the fourth certification. More certifications may add to your personal growth—and you may choose to let one certification expire and replace it with a more advanced one. However, generally speaking, more than three certifications are going to cost you more time and money than they'll add to your earning power. Certifications can also be perceived as negatives by experienced information security professionals who have personally experienced poor certification standards.

Part of the problem is that certifications are nearly always pass/fail for minimum requirements. Some feel that time and money spent on certification and yearly maintenance is better spent on practical work experience and study which go beyond any certification. It's not unusual for experienced information security professionals to allow their certifications to lapse. Some of them think so little of information security certifications that they don't approve of using certifications anywhere except as an otherwise useless but necessary evil to get through HR departments. They won't mention their certifications, omit certifications from their business cards, don't put them in job requirements if they can, and would prefer if others did the same. But this is a personal decision and the right choice is up to you.

Only a handful of certifications are considered requirements in the industry, and which ones change over time. These certifications are generally not the most respected by actual information security practitioners. This seeming paradox is created by the economics of certification. Human Resources (HR) departments may require a particular certification, but HR departments don't know much outside of HR, especially in information technology and information security.

Large organizations like the US Department of Defense use certification as a standard of entry, and select one that their current employees in those roles can pass. So it must provide assurance, but also it must be possible to pass certification, otherwise it is not useful for those who accept certifications. The certification must also be well-enough known that the exam can be taken at any location that the organization has people. Ideally, it will also be vetted by a third party, such as the US ANSI or another standards organization. All of these requirements are expensive for the certification agency, so the certifications must also attract enough applicants that the certification fees cover the cost of the program. All of these requirements result in a market environment in which the best-known certifications are weakened (to increase passing rates). Some of the inexpensive certifications are extremely easy to pass, as they have to increase the number of applicants to cover the cost of managing the program. Thus, less-well-known, but more highly respected certifications are created in response to the belief that certifications "aren't what they used to be," as people want their certification to be something they can be proud of.

So how do you choose a certification? In our experience, your first certification should directly apply to your new job. A good listing of door-opening certifications can be seen on the US Department of Defense's Approved 8570 Baseline for different roles reproduced below with roles **in bold**:

Table 0.2.3

IAT Level I	IAT Level II	IAT Level III		
A + -CE	GSEC	CISA		
Network+ CE	Security+ CE	CISSP (or associate)		
SSCP	SSCP	GCIH		
	CCNA-Security	GCED		
		CASP		
IAM Level I	IAM Level II	IAM Level III		
	CAP			
	GSLC			
CAP	CISM	GSLC		
GSLC	CASP	CISM		
Security+ CE	CISSP (or associate)	CISSP (or associate)		
IASAE I	IASAE II	IASAE III		
CISSP (or associate)	CISSP (or associate)			
CASP	CASP	CISSP - ISSEP		
CSSLP	CSSLP	CISSP - ISSAP		
CNDSP Analyst	**CNDSP Infrastructure Support**	**CNDSP Incident Responder**	**CNDSP Auditor**	**CNDSP Manager**
		GCIH		
GCIA	SSCP	CSIH	CISA	CISSP-ISSMP
CEH	CEH	CEH	GSNA	CISM
GCIH		GCFA	CEH	

As you can see, (ISC)^2 CISSP, EC CEH, CompTIA Security+ CE, and SANS GCIH are fairly popular certifications across the board, so these might be good choices for your first certification. They're well-known and likely won't work against you. They are not, however, technically equivalent. If you go to the specific certification outlines and training agendas, you'll see that they cover entirely different things. See the Appendix: Certifications for URLs.

But, if these certifications are equivalent from a hiring perspective, it makes sense to pick the one that will teach you the most and cost the least time and money. A good method of selecting which certification is best is to look at how much you'll learn. The more learning you do for a certificate the more valuable it will be over the long term, not because the certification itself has that much intrinsic value, but because the certification learning process will be with you for the rest of your life.

As an example to measure the personal value of a certification, compare the SANS GCIH to the EC CEH. In the two tables below, the certification objectives are placed one-per-line and a subjective guess is made as to how much new material would be learned in that area. For example, a developer reviewing the list might already have detailed understanding as to what a buffer overflow is and score it low at 10%. However, a network administrator might not know much about buffer overflows and score it high at 80%.

Once both certification lists have been scored, average the scores for how much new learning would be involved with each certification. In the examples below, we are assuming a skilled but moderately inexperienced person is comparing the two certifications.

Table 0.2.4

SANS GCIH New Learning for Skilled but Moderately Inexperienced	
	% New Material
Backdoors & Trojan Horses	80
Buffer Overflows	80
Covering Tracks: Networks	80
Covering Tracks: Systems	80
Denial of Service Attacks	10
Exploiting Systems using Netcat	50
Format String Attacks	80
Incident Handling Overview and Preparation	80
Incident Handling Phase 2 Identification	70
Incident Handling Phase 3 Containment	50
Incident Handling: Recovering and Improving Capabilities	50
IP Address Spoofing	80
Network Sniffing	10
Password Attacks	40
Reconnaissance	50
Rootkits	30
Scanning: Host Discovery	20
Scanning: Network and Application Vulnerability scanning and tools	40
Scanning: Network Devices (Firewall rules determination, fragmentation, and IDS/IPS evasion)	40
Scanning: Service Discovery	40
Session Hijacking, Tools and Defenses	80
Types of Incidents	70
Virtual Machine Attacks	90
Web Application Attacks	80
Worms, Bots & Bot-Nets	60
Average new material:	**57.6**

Table 0.2.5

EC CEH Learning for Skilled but Moderately Inexperienced	
	% New Material
Introduction to Ethical Hacking	10
Footprinting and Reconnaissance	50
Scanning Networks	20
Enumeration	50
System Hacking	80
Trojans and Backdoors	60
Viruses and Worms	60
Sniffers	10
Social Engineering	50
Denial of Service	10
Session Hijacking	80
Hijacking Webservers	80
Hijacking Web Applications	80
SQL Injection	70
Hacking Wireless Networks	70
Evading IDS, Firewalls and Honeypots	80
Buffer Overflow	80
Cryptography	40
Penetration Testing	50
Average new material:	**54.2**

For this person, the SANS GCIH certification at 57.6% new material is a somewhat better choice from a learning perspective compared to the EC CEH at 54.2% new material. But this is just an example. A simpler approach would just count the number of new enough items. What is "new enough" is also subjective, but using 60% or less has similar results: SANS GCIH is 13 and EC CEH is 11. Note that these numbers are just examples and would always be subjective and dependent upon each person.

A deeper but still subjective approach would review a complete study guide for each certification and measure new material by the number or percentage of pages, paragraphs or lines of new material. A short cut would only look for new material in the glossary or index. If practice certification exams are available for free or cheap, then take them, and whichever score is lowest determines the certification to pursue. Again, the goal is to learn, not to accumulate certifications.

If money is limited and you have to pay for it yourself, it may be wise to compare the certifications in terms of total dollars. Include exam preparation costs, the exam cost itself, any travel or time off needed to take the exam, and certification maintenance costs. Some certifications have effective maintenance costs of hundreds of US dollars a year. Some exams are only infrequently offered in some cities requiring possibly expensive travel. Others have reduced costs for retaking after a failing score.

There are three ways to pursue certification: class, self-study, or directly challenging the exam.

Table 0.2.6

SANS GCIH vs EC CEH Costs				
	Price	**Percent New Learning**	**Cost of Knowledge**	**Wasted Money**
EC CEH—Exam Only	$600	54.2%	$325.20	$274.80
EC CEH—Courseware + Exam	$825 + $600	54.2%	$772.35	$652.65
EC CEH—Class + Exam	$2,895 + $600	54.2%	$1,894.29	$1,600.71
SANS GCIH—Exam Only	$600	57.6%	$345.60	$254.40
SANS GCIH—Courseware + Exam	Not Available	Not Available	Not Available	Not Available
SANS GCIH—Class + Exam	$5,095 + $600	57.6%	$3,280.32	$2,414.68

Here, by calculating the amount of the money you're spending that goes only towards new knowledge (percent times price), you can determine cost of knowledge. You can then subtract this number from the total price to determine whether that is the best use for such money. The wasted money—money spent to learn things you likely already know—is the measure of how valuable the certification is to you. Clearly, if the person in this example thinks they can study on their own without purchasing the courseware, taking the GCIH in the Exam Only mode is the best way to go. However, if they need a class, perhaps the CEH class is a preferable option, given that it wastes almost $800 less than the GCIH option.

How these numbers break down will vary drastically based on the specific certifications you are comparing and your specific skill level in each. In some cases, such as defending a job you already have, you might already know the majority of what you'll be tested on, so new knowledge is low. If the price is low enough, it may be worth doing just to keep your job, even though most of it would fall under "wasted money," If, however, you want a challenge, it may be worth it to pursue a much more highly priced advanced certification, because the wasted money count is low, so most of your spending will go toward new learning.

In general, many people get their first certification in a way that is as easy as possible, simply to get that edge over otherwise comparable people. Subsequent certifications tend to be far more challenging; the direct financial effect is minimal compared to the joy of learning and the increased effectiveness gained.

STRIKING A BALANCE

In the end, you need to strike a balance. By considering where you actually are, you can decide how much effort it is worth to try to do more. This may involve investing time in your education, projects to boost your experience, or studying for certifications. As you get older, you will likely find more of your time going into interesting projects rather than education and certification, which provide diminishing returns for experienced professionals.

However, you will likely go through a period in your life where it's tempting to go for more and more schooling. After all, most of us spend 16 to 20 years of our lives in school. That's the safe option. If you graduate and don't immediately find a job that you "deserve" and are tempted to go to grad school or pursue another degree, consider whether you actually need it, or whether you're just discovering that the real world is harder than you were led to believe. Many information security professionals have considered advanced degrees. However, as shown in some of the stories included throughout this book, many information security professionals have found successful, useful, and rewarding careers without them. Sometimes you just have to roll up your sleeves and get to work.

It won't be easy. There will be pain and frustration. That's part of life.

However, information security has more pain and frustration than some other fields. Your organization's adversaries are well-funded by criminals and/or nation-states. Your bosses and customers don't understand the issues, and you will not have enough time and money to build the solutions you want. However, if you can get past this—something we've learned by experience—you can find yourself making real differences in people's lives and getting paid well to do it.

For us, it's worth it. If you think that applies to you, read on.

MODEL FAILURES

BARRIERS

> "The map is not the territory"
>
> — **Alfred Korzybski**

Models are imperfect representations of reality. Problems can arise when you measure your progress against the abstract perfection that's inherent in the model you are using. This book uses a generic approach to gaining or improving employment within the information security industry. It will work in some environments, but will fail (sometimes spectacularly) in others. In general, though, working from a solid model will help you to identify and overcome barriers you may experience in the working world.

You can deal with barriers to the job you want by pushing through them or by subverting them within the system. Different barriers require different approaches.

BARRIER ENERGY

The first barrier you are likely to encounter is that of energy. Getting a new job isn't easy, especially in a field new to you. It's hard to work for an uncertain outcome. It's possible to expend too much effort for too little reward. Progress isn't straightforward, so each thing you do gives you a new or better tool to use in working toward your goal, and perhaps gets you one step closer. Success is not guaranteed. You're building skills, not checking off items on a guaranteed plan. There *are* no guaranteed plans; failure itself is learning, so gain energy from learning, and don't lose it from failure. Once you've started, it's often easier to keep going.

In the field of chemistry, there is a concept called "activation energy." This concept holds that some chemical reactions require a certain amount of starting energy to happen. A good example is that of combustion. A puddle of pure alcohol will just sit there evaporating to nothing. However, if you apply a flame, something rather different will happen—it will ignite. The same is true, metaphorically speaking, with doing the outside work needed to get a new job. Many people have trouble just sitting down and doing what they feel needs to be done. Often, the hardest tasks are shifted to the bottom of the "to do" list. Thus, you may find yourself organizing your digital music collection three times to avoid cleaning out the garage, or cleaning out the garage instead of looking for a new job. With learning tasks, a "hard" task tends to be one that involves more learning than others.

You may find that learning a brand-new skill is much harder than improving those you already have. Improving current skills is great if you want to move further up in your current job. It's not as good if you want to transfer into a different field. If you find yourself constantly putting off tasks because you're tired or because of something else that must be done, you may need to apply a large amount of activation energy to get yourself started or you need a catalyst. For example, as we worked on this book, in fact, there were some tasks that were just too hard for us to do individually. Instead, we set aside specific "sprint" days, where we'd hold one another accountable and push through the barriers blocking us.

A common task catalyst is the dedicated work day and dedicated work area. If you can afford the time, reserve four to eight hours and plan to do nothing but focus on your required task during that time. A dedicated work area and equipment is often helpful and sometimes required for security work. Don't include work area setup or tear down in that time period. Instead, do it ahead of time so you can immediately start work when the clock starts.

Minimize distractions:

Block out your schedule ahead of time and let people know so they won't interrupt you during dedicated time.

If your work space has a door, close it, if there's a window with distractions, block it.

Silence your phone, alarm clocks, and any other devices, including turning off vibrate. It may be easiest to turn them off, put them into airplane mode, or put them out of sight but where you'll easily find them again. There are apps for that.

If it's noisy, use ordinary, cheap, readily available ear plugs. Don't use ordinary ear phones which if turned to high volume to mask noise will also damage your hearing. Noise canceling ear phones help, but cannot block all noise, especially voices, will cost more, and are yet another technological distraction.

If you need to listen while working consider instead *noise isolating* earbuds, also known as canal phones or in-ear monitors (IEM), which seal inside the ear canal and passively block outside noise and sound. The cost is comparable to good ear phones but with much better isolation, especially with custom fitting by a professional audiologist.

Block visual distractions by running applications in full screen mode, especially text editors and word processors. Turn off task bars and notification areas. If you have multiple displays, but don't need them, turn them off.

For deep concentration avoid any background noise because any sound, even soothing music, is distracting.

If you don't need the Internet to accomplish your task, turn it off. If you think you do need the Internet, seriously reconsider and instead make a list of what you need and do it later. Defer your procrastination. If you find yourself constantly going to different social media sites, consider using web filtering to temporarily block those sites, or unplug and disconnect during this time. The goal is to focus and take less time to get into the deep concentration need for thoughtful work. If you are trying to light a puddle of alcohol on fire, a flame applied for a few seconds is more effective than shining a heat lamp for several hours. If you have an energy problem, focus the energy you do have as much as you can and you're much more likely to solve it.

This focusing limited energy is like borrowing from the future. You may find that the technique works well, so you do it over and over again, only to find that eventually it stops working for you. The problem is that you can't create energy from nothing. When you think you're being productive by cutting out all distractions, you are also likely cutting out those activities that allow you to rest and regain energy for the next round. If you start getting sick or extremely tired, you may just need to take some time off from the focused tasks to recover. If you don't, you risk burning out completely and losing focus for months.

However, most of the barriers you'll encounter will be external to you. These cannot be addressed by simply buckling down and pushing your way through. Most are surmountable, but you have to question whether they are worth fighting. What follows is an incomplete list of barriers that you may encounter on your way to your information security dream job.

HUMAN RESOURCES

Many organizations have a Human Resources (HR) department. HR is supposed to keep the organization out of legal trouble, handle interpersonal conflicts, and, to varying degrees, manage benefits. Many such departments also become involved in the hiring process. This typically happens because there are a lot of time-consuming steps involved in hiring someone, and it makes economic sense to move those tasks off the plates of the hiring managers, so they can manage people. However, it often results in a situation in which you have people unfamiliar with the actual job performing the initial filter for candidates. This trend within business is largely responsible for the "you need experience to get experience" trap.

Dealing with this barrier is particularly difficult if you are trying to move into a job you've never done before. HR personnel tend to follow the old "no one ever got fired for buying IBM or Microsoft" approach to decision making. If you look like a risk, you'll be passed over for the safer choice. Thus, you have two options. You can repackage yourself to look safer. This involves spending more time developing a work history in related fields, probably by doing additional work on a volunteer basis. However, the second option is more likely to be successful— bypass them altogether.

By taking the bypass approach, you find a way to meet the hiring managers directly and get far enough along in the process that by the time you meet HR, you've already been approved, avoiding the whole appraisal process. There are many ways to do this, most of which are detailed in Josh More's book *Job Reconnaissance*, also published by Syngress.

OLD BOYS' CLUB, RACISM, AND SEXISM

The phrase "old boys' club" refers to the tendency of people to want to work with people just like them. It brings up images of old white men sitting in private clubs smoking cigars and giving favors to their friends. However, the attitude itself is universal. Fundamentally, most people want to work with those who are like themselves or those they have worked with before, regardless of other differences. It's more comfortable. However, evidence strongly suggests that more diverse workplaces are more effective, more successful and more profitable. Pointing this out, of course, may get you kicked out of the club.

Whether the tendency to prefer their own type applies to previous employment, race, sex, or class, the first decision is always going to be the same. Will you be comfortable in a job where you have to either try to blend in or constantly fight the status quo? It's okay to not want to do either. That means that the organization isn't a good fit for you and that you're not a good fit for them. Find one of their competitors, add diversity there, and out compete the other firm.

If, however, you decide you want to try to blend in, learn the cultural markers. This is easier to do in some cases than others. In the United States, an individual who appears to be white, male, and reasonably (but not overly) educated will have a lot more options than someone who presents otherwise.

If you're comfortable hiding aspects of who you are from your co-workers, at least initially, that may make it easier to find a job. People with different political opinions, belief systems, sexual orientations, and gender expressions from the majority can often find reasonable employment and later, as they prove themselves an asset to the organization, slowly let more of their personality out. The cost to this approach is possibly never being fully comfortable in that workplace. It should also be noted that some people will simply not be able to blend in to all environments. Some environments won't be compatible with all people, you can learn how to speak and act in different ways and become familiar enough with specific interests to blend in.

There are increasingly more jobs where little to no physical presence is required, sometimes called full-time telecommuting or 100% telecommuting. This is common enough in the open source communities and some organizations that are conferences just so people can physically meet. These events are usually not mandatory, with most work still done remotely and over the Internet.

If you are a natural fighter, odds are that you've been doing it for a very long time. You probably had to fight your way through school and any previous job experience. It is unlikely we can give you any advice on how to fight that isn't insulting. The techniques you use to combat racism and sexism in the workplace will be uniquely personal and vary with your environment. So, instead of tips on how to fight, we instead suggest that you consider these things:

1. Security is about protecting others. If an organization recognizes and values that, you can find common ground in common protection. If it does not, the job will be undervalued. If you are personally undervalued because of irrelevant personal details, and are doing an undervalued job, think strongly on why you want to do it. It may be a great stepping stone, but it is very unlikely to ever become the job of your dreams.
2. Business is about making money. Most people in a high position in business recognize this, and the belief in the almighty dollar can trump other prejudices. As with protection, if the company can make more money with you than they can make without you, you have your "in" into the business.
3. An organization's mission is about accomplishing goals. Sadly, nonprofit organizations can be some of the most racist, sexist, and otherwise badly functioning organizations out there, largely because there is no counterbalancing profit motive. Nonprofits can also be some of the best places to work, for the same reason. If you can show that an organization can accomplish its goals better with you than without you, you better overcome these barriers.

These three points can get other people to fight for you. In a hiring situation, there may be a group of people influencing the decision, but usually only one person making it. If that person is on your side, they can fight for you. If they're not, but enough people are on your side, you may find yourself with a job offer anyway. This indirect fighting is far more likely to succeed than any sort of direct fighting.

Direct fights, such as involving the law, are expensive and less likely to work. Even if you do succeed with such a tactic, you'll always be known as the person who sued your way into the job. Once you get the job, continue the fight to keep it, advance, and to change the culture. Join organizations and community groups such as those listed in the Appendix, and discuss ways to improve acceptance and increase diversity.

Remember, at this phase of your professional development, your primary focus is on overcoming the barrier to entry, not fighting the constant uphill battle for universal equality. That fight can wait until you're in the door.

CORPORATE CULTURE

An organization's corporate culture is something you may never understand fully, and almost certainly will not understand before working there. There are many books on corporate culture that may be worth reading, especially those for a particular company where you wish to work. Instead, we want to explore how corporate culture can prevent a job offer. Some companies have unique, unusual cultures that may be difficult to understand. Particularly notable organizations will have articles and books written about them; look for them and read them as part of your job reconnaissance. Current employees may be able to help, but ex-employees, part-time employees, and contractors who have experience outside the organization may be better able to explain the culture.

Sports Culture

In an organization with a sports culture, most employees will have played a sport in school or college. Sports metaphors will be used in most meetings. Everyone will have a favorite team and, most times, it will be the same local professional or college team. There will be an overall belief that, when asked, you should "be a team player" and "take one for the team." You may be expected to work late nights or weekends or even be publicly called out in a meeting so the business can save an important client relationship.

If you are a person who would fit into such a culture, none of this sounds bad. If, however, you were never one of the "jocks" or "athletic supporters" (somewhat likely if you're reading a book on information security careers), it may sound awful. However, if you still want to work in such an organization, you have to get in the door. To overcome this barrier, check out the Facebook and Twitter accounts of the people who work there. Figure out what sports they talk about and which sports teams are involved. Pick one team and learn the names of the important players. Go to YouTube and watch the highlights of some games. Learn the rules for the game and review the last few years of results. Don't lie, don't pose, don't pretend to be a fan—the goal is be inoffensive, culturally sensitive, informed, and not give a blank stare when they make some sports reference. When asked about it, answer truthfully, such as "I don't really follow sports much, I've just seen some <team> games." This approach can help you blend in without lying or otherwise being dishonest.

This same approach can work for other corporate cultural interests, see below. You might even find a new interest yourself.

Education

Most organizations have one or more base education levels. Many small businesses expect everyone to have a college degree. Some startups involve everyone having a master's degree or even a PhD, while others are made up of current college students or college drop-outs. Many large companies expect employees to have at least a high school degree. These are, however, just basic expectations and not every organization will fit the pattern. What will fit, however, is the overall expectation that you be able to communicate on the same level as the rest of the team. Generally speaking, the more educated a person is, the more abstractly they speak.

Cultures centered around people with less education tend to be more focused on day-to-day issues and less on the long-term goals. If you don't fit such an organization's model and still want to work there, you need to explain how you will make their day-to-day work easier. Find out what they don't like to do and make it clear that you don't mind doing that and perhaps you can improve the process. Cultures focused around greater levels of education will tend to speak more strategically. They want to achieve big dreams and by focusing on that you can blend in even if you don't have the expected degrees.

An exception to these "high" and "low" education-based organizations is that of artistic organizations which tend to be far more accepting and less focused on general education. The artistic part of an organization may be most of the company, or a sub-group such as marketing, or information technology. Some of these organizations have a high number of people interested in art, books, and film. Some interests are general, others are highly specific. Within information technology groups, science fiction fandom and computer gaming are common. However, if you—for example—mistake Star Wars for Star Trek, the response can be brutal. These organizations follow a basic educational path except that you are expected to be highly educated in the specific form of art that is preferred by the group.

Like a sports culture, you need not be an expert; just familiarize yourself enough with the core interest to be able to talk about it reasonably and also know when to admit your ignorance. If you need cultural references, Wikipedia is excellent for nearly all popular areas, even sports.

Military

Organizations made up of mostly ex-military personnel exist within the information security community. These tend to come in two types.

The first type consists of people who think the military had it right and are trying to run their organization like a military unit. These are the no nonsense highly driven people you often see depicted in war movies. You may think they're just a stereotype, but they do exist and some people thrive in that culture. If you have not served in the military, you will likely not fit in, regardless of how hard you try. Having served in a different military service or different country's military may also be a problem—not only is the culture going to be at least somewhat different, but it may even be antagonistic even if from the same country. For example the rivalry between the US Army and the US Navy is notorious.

The second type have a militaristic preference, but employ a number of those who have never served in the military. These organizations share a common background that is stronger than that of education or sports, but are more welcoming. You may encounter some terse speech and intolerance for mistakes, and a militaristic chain of command, but in general, these organizations are very goal-oriented and can be great places to work. If you wish to work for one of these, it really helps to appreciate the work that the military has done. If you have negative opinions about recent military involvements, it is generally best not to express them; you hear them expressed by someone who has actually served. Even then, be careful to keep criticisms to those who sent the military to war and not to those who actually fought. Militaries are not democracies, and neither enlistees or draftees get much choice in how they serve.

Academia and Health Care

Academia is, oddly, both extremely similar to and the exact opposite of militaristic cultures. Academic institutions are structured such that the most educated people, professors and doctors, are at the top and everything done by the organization exists to support them. This structure exists in healthcare, universities, and other organizations started by those doctors and professors. They are every bit as idealistic and driven as the military-based cultures, but lack a team focus. In academia, it is very much "everyone for themselves." Sure, you can make great friendships, but don't expect anyone to put themselves in figurative harm's way to help you. This is very different from a military organization, where putting yourself in literal harm's way for your team is part of the training and often part of the experience. Fortunately there is much less physical harm in academia, although the fighting may not be any less fierce.

To break into an academic culture, be prepared to defend yourself intellectually. Any time you need, not just want, to point out that someone is wrong, have the proof and be willing to enter a debate, using the scientific method where possible, because your opponent will also. If you can play the game without making those in power look bad or directly telling them no, you're in. Note that intellectualism and scientific method by name or by practice will not work in some other environments. It may not be understood, or worse, understood to be academic and consequently derided.

AGE

Ageism isn't talked about nearly as much as sexism or racism, but as the world's population gets older, the issues are growing. Older people tend to be more expensive employees because of their accumulated salary and compensation requirements and increased experience. This isn't exactly ageism but if a company can hire someone for half the cost of someone else, and believes them to be otherwise equivalent, of course they're going to go with the less expensive candidate, who will probably be younger and have less experience. The trick here is to make it clear that you're better than the other candidates (or be willing to work for less). Use the techniques discussed in Chapter 4.0 "Boosting" of this book, also see the branding suggestions in Josh More's book *Job Reconnaissance*.

Ageism can also work the other way: younger people may be wrongly assumed to lack the skills or experience to do the job simply because they are younger. Such assumptions are as ageist as assuming older people can't learn new skills or know new technologies.

To combat straight-up ageism, you must demonstrate that you can do the job. Information security isn't like working in a warehouse. If your brain works, you can do the work, even if your body is older. If you leverage your skills and experience and show that you can out think your competition, you should be able to get through the door. Some people report successfully using blending techniques as mentioned above.

TIER 1—LEARN

LEARN/DO/TEACH

> "In theory there is no difference between theory and practice. In practice there is."
> — **Jan L. A. van de Snepscheut**

The key to this book and, we believe, to life in general, is the concept of Learn/Do/Teach. This concept was first developed in the medical field, where medical students first learn a medical procedure, then do the same procedure while guided by someone experienced, then teach a less experienced student the same procedure. Experiencing a concept directly multiple times from multiple perspectives results in better understanding and retention.

Unless you are extremely unusual, the first time you learn something, you are unlikely to learn it in any great detail. You may understand it roughly, but it is unlikely that you understand it well enough to have any level of mastery. Once you start doing something with it, however, you can rapidly find where your understanding fails. When theory meets reality, reality always wins, and it will be common for you to discover where the initial theory omitted some details. The more time you spend in Do, the greater you refine your understanding. Finally, in the Teach phase of learning, you get someone else through the Learn step. This further enhances your understanding, as you find areas where other people's understanding comes into conflict with yours, and you resolve the conflict by better understanding them and the material.

WHY LEARNING MATTERS

Learning is critical in a career. At one time, perhaps, people could do the same job every day for a lifetime and not have to learn anything new. However, so long as there is someone or something that will do the same work for cheaper, you are forced to improve, or learn a completely new job. Over time and at quantity, this tendency toward continual improvement sets person against person, company against company, and nation against nation. Fundamentally, the best Learners (as they become Doers, then Teachers) drive the economy ahead.

Traditional jobs are going away. It is important, however, to understand what "going away" means. The Earth is a closed system. We can't lose a significant number of jobs any more than we can lose a significant amount of water. While a small amount of either may vanish over time, this amount is negligible. Instead, when people speak of "lost jobs," what they mean is "structural unemployment" where society either perceives less value for that particular work or there is a less costly way to achieve the same work. In the former, odds are that something has replaced it and things that used to be valuable simply no longer are. If jobs are "lost" during this process, they invariably reappear somewhere else in the economy.

For example, aluminum is now used for disposable, single-use beverage cans used to be a precious metal. As an example of conspicuous consumption, Napoleon III reserved a prized set of aluminum cutlery for special guests at banquets, while less-favored guests used gold knives and forks. However, cheap industrial scale bauxite ore refining, and mass production, made and anything made from it cheap. The latter case, however, is often tied to competition.

None of this means that in the case of a job shift, skills will be transferable. Quite to the contrary. In the same way that Earth is a closed system and species that cannot compete die out, skills that are no longer needed, due to improvements in technology or changes in what the market demands, will similarly die out. The trick is to constantly be adding new skills so when this, inevitably, happens, you are not effected as much as others.

This is a book about information security. It will, by necessity, occasionally drift into the philosophical, but fundamentally, we assume that you are reading this because you want to get into the field. Within information security, the good news is that, unlike elevator operators, ballast heavers, and scutchers, most jobs in information security are unlikely to go away because of technological advancement. However, specific jobs tied to particular vendors or very specific technology are subject to the fashions of the industry and organizations. An elevator operator who could only operate an Otis and not a Schindler or General Electric would have had a difficult time. The trick is to aim toward the general, while still being specific enough to be of value to prospective employers. The more specific you are, the more value you have to an employer. However, the trade-off is that such a career is limited. As technology advances, common tasks get automated, both in terms of attack and defense. So from a strategic perspective, it is better to focus on specific threats and automate their defense than to focus on an entire class of attacks that could eventually be managed by a standalone appliance.

Attackers and defenders are in an arms race. An attacker finds a vulnerability and creates an attack to exploit it. A defender may detect this attack, and if the defender is not completely destroyed, then recovers and implements a countermeasure, so the attacker is driven towards a new attack or even counter-countermeasure—repeating and moving ever faster with each cycle. This cycle affects all attackers and defenders and results in an ever-changing environment where advantages change moment to moment.

WHY LEARNING MATTERS TO YOU

Attaching yourself to a specific technology or even a specific area of compliance is short-sighted. If your chosen technology is proven to be ineffective, you may find yourself at a dead end—both unable to find more work in your field and unable to find time or money to learn something new.

This is why learning is critical to you. Only by constantly learning can you keep in front of the wave as old technologies drown in the marketplace and sink into disuse. Also, only through learning can you determine what new areas might exist in the future and position yourself to leap onto the new technology platform as your old one dies.

You can make a good living with older technologies. However, as those technologies become common, it results in job market crowding, which can drive down salaries and even result in unemployment due to too many people being available for a specific job.

By focusing less on specific technologies and more on learning, you become nimble, leaping from platform to platform as the market changes.

WHY LEARNING MATTERS TO COMPANIES

Learning is also critical to companies. Since the attackers are constantly learning and creating a new deluge of attacks, defenders must respond. An organization must decide whether to learn or to hire. When one organization learns and uses that knowledge to protect others, it basically functions as a product or service. However, products are easily analyzed and attackers put a disproportionate amount of effort into finding flaws. After all, if one product can be shown to be flawed, all organizations protected by that product are vulnerable.

A company is in the same situation you are. By connecting itself directly to a specific product, it faces the risk of that product eroding over time and leaving it vulnerable. However, by not doing that, it has less time to devote to targeting its customer base, resulting in lower profit margins.

By focusing more on learning, companies can take greater advantage of new technologies, either to improve efficiencies (costs) or to gain advantage (value).

HOW TO LEARN

There are many ways to learn within information security. As is common in technical fields, there are many who function well as self-learners. These people learn best from books, videos, or tech articles. Others learn better when being guided, either by taking classes or under direct mentoring of another. There are learning opportunities both online and offline. The key, once you identify what you need to learn, is to identify how you best learn and maximize your use of time.

Identifying what you need to learn is what the rest of this book is about. How to learn how *you* need to learn, however, is addressed here.

The first step is to identify how much you need to learn before it can be called "done." Few people are used to thinking this way, as school was highly structured and much learning after that worked under a model of "poke at things until they work, then stop." This is a perfectly functional model for learning about many things, but it doesn't serve you well when it comes to security. Security professionals talk a lot about the idea that people either have a security mindset or they don't—that security thinking is somehow inherent to a person. This is not necessarily the case.

In truth, thinking about security involves not just understanding how things are built, but also how they break, how they can be broken by people deliberately, and what other people would gain by breaking things. Thus, one way to measure how much learning is necessary is when you can answer the following questions:

- Do I understand why it works the way it does?
- Do I understand at least three ways it can fail?
- Can I list at least three ways someone else can benefit if it fails?

One approach to learning is to keep at a subject until these questions are answered. That gives you a minimum bound for learning. However, some things are harder to learn than others, so it may be helpful to place a maximum bound as well. First, decide the worth of what you learn in hours of your time. If it's only worth one hour then set a timer or alarm clock for one hour ahead. If you can answer the above questions in an hour, great. If you can't, then stop after an hour, since you already decided that it's not worth the cost to learn it. Don't fall into the trap of sunk costs, where even more is spent because so much was already spent.

MENTORS

A mentor is someone who can suggest, guide, and advise. There are many kinds of mentors, and a person can have more than one mentor. Even mentors will have mentors. A career mentor helps with the career path, such as what skills to develop, and what certifications, if any, to pursue. A skills mentor helps with the particular skills. Technical skills mentoring is important, but social/soft skills mentoring can be even more important, especially for the technically minded. Good social skills and soft skills will elevate the technically minded far above those who lack these skills.

Corporate and industry culture mentors can be very different. Corporate culture can vary considerably. Industries also have cultures which will be common in companies in that industry. Mentors can help with navigating the difficult aspects of these cultures. This means that a mentor from a different company but in the same industry can as useful, or even more than a mentor in the same company. The outside mentor can provide the perspective that all companies in the industry are alike in some way, or not, as it may happen.

A particularly experienced mentor may also provide direct longer-term instruction as part of a master/apprenticeship. Although the master/apprentice terms are somewhat archaic, the old traditional concept is coming back in some industries as an alternative to both formal, structured education and informal, unstructured on-the-job training. Traditional apprenticeships consisted of on-the-job-training under a master and would last for several years. At the end of the training the apprentice would become a journeyman who would typically leave the master and set up their own business. An all-too-common tradition was abuse of the apprentice by the master — having the apprentice be involved in work, but not involved in learning new skills, thus protecting the master's livelihood. Although modern-day formal apprenticeships are rare, the shorter term unpaid and often exploitative internships are common, should the opportunity arise, prospective employees should be aware of their rights.

Finding a Mentor

Some professional organizations and some companies have formal mentoring programs. If your organization or company doesn't have a mentoring program, consider starting one. Management support is particularly helpful here, but informal mentoring can still work and may be a natural extension of a work-related relationship. Mentoring programs may also be available through local young professional groups and trade associations.

A mentor needn't be in the same company or even the same industry. Local clubs, meetups, social networks, and other gatherings can be a place to meet a mentor. See the Appendix: Community for more details. Once found, identify how you will work together and what each of you will get out of the relationship. Some people work best with a face-to-face meeting each month. Others can work fine via email, telephone, or social media. In identifying the purpose of the mentoring, try to be more specific than "I want to learn from you." Set goals, such as a 20% salary increase within two years, achieving a specific certification or job title, or even just laying out a general road map to get you where you want to go. Everyone works better with goals.

Being a Mentor

Mentors are similar but not identical to teachers or tutors; see the Teach chapter for more information on being mentor.

CLASSES

Classes work in a similar way as mentorship, but money has to be factored in as well as time. When you take a class, you must expend both time and money. Perhaps you have an employer willing to pay and you can discount the money aspect somewhat, but it is still going to take time. If you really want to break into a new job, you have to consider how much learning you can get for your time and financial resources.

One way to do this is to assign an estimate for the value of learning. Learning something new could result in a new job at more pay and greater happiness, or just reduce the stress you find in your current job. Before you invest in a class, consider first if there is any other way to learn what you need to learn. Then, figure out how well you will learn that way. Only then can you make a decision as to whether or not that approach makes sense.

Fortunately, legitimate classes provide an agenda or syllabus. Much in the same way we measured learning for certifications, we can measure classes for learning. As merely an example, let's look at an old but representative version of SEC401 from the SANS Institute. This is one of the classic starter classes for getting into information security via a training/certification approach. The syllabus for day 4 is listed below:

SEC401 Syllabus—Day 4	
Network fundamentals • Network types (LANs, WANs) • Network topologies • Ethernet, token ring • ATM, ISDN, X.25 • Wiring • Network devices • Voice Over IP (VOIP) IP concepts • Packets and addresses • IP service ports • IP protocols • TCP • UDP • ICMP • DNS • IP behavior • TCPdump • Recognizing and understanding	• UDP • ICMP • UDP Behavior IOS and router filters • Routers • IOS • Routing • Routing protocols • Access control lists Physical security • Facility requirements • Technical controls • Environmental issues • Personal safety • Physical security threats • Elements of physical security

(Continued)

Cryptography	PGP
• Need for cryptography • Types of encryption • Symmetric • Asymmetric • Hash • Ciphers • Digital substitution • Algorithms • Real-world cryptosystems • Crypto attacks • VPNs • Types of remote access • PKI • Digital certificates • Key escrow • Steganography • Types • Applications • Detection	• Installing and using PGP • Signing data and what it means • Key management • Key servers Wireless • Common protocols • Common topologies • Misconceptions • Security issues • Securing wireless Operations security • Legal requirements • Administrative management • Individual accountability • Need to know • Privileged operations • Control types • Operation controls • Reporting

To assess the value of this class to you, score each item by how well you already know it and how you perceive its market value. Create a score list as seen below. Assume that the maximum any skill may be worth is $100 and the minimum is $0. The "Learning" column is a percentage of what's left to learn. For example, if you feel that you know 80% of VoIP, then you have 20% left to learn. This approach may not be completely fair but, as a rule of thumb, if you have no idea what's left to learn, just score a column as half value, such as $50 or 50% learning and be done. But if you don't know what a term means, assume $100 or 100% learning value in that item.

Learning Objective	Value	Learning	Learning Objective	Value	Learning
Network types and topologies			Symmetric Cryptography		
VOIP			Asymmetric Cryptography		
TCP, UDP, ICMP			Hashing		
DNS			VPNs		
TCPdump			PKI		
Routing Protocols			Steganography		
Physical Security			PGP		
Technical Controls			Wireless		
			Legal Issues		

For illustrative purposes, let's assume two different people are going through the exercise. Azal has been working in technology for a while, specifically in the networking area. Day 1 is likely to be review for him. Morgaine is just graduating college with an degree in mathematics. She is experienced in academic cryptography, but little else.

Here is Azal's estimate:

Learning Objective	Value	Learning	Learning Objective	Value	Learning
Network types and topologies	$50	0%	Symmetric Cryptography	$50	100%
VOIP	$75	20%	Asymmetric Cryptography	$50	100%
TCP, UDP, ICMP	$100	20%	Hashing	$75	100%
DNS	$100	50%	VPNs	$100	25%
TCPdump	$25	20%	PKI	$50	100%
Routing Protocols	$90	50%	Steganography	$50	100%
Physical Security	$20	75%	PGP	$50	100%
Technical Controls	$75	50%	Wireless	$75	25%
			Legal Issues	$25	50%

And here is Morgaine's:

Learning Objective	Value	Learning	Learning Objective	Value	Learning
Network types and topologies	$100	100%	Symmetric Cryptography	$100	10%
VOIP	$50	100%	Asymmetric Cryptography	$100	10%
TCP, UDP, ICMP	$70	100%	Hashing	$100	10%
DNS	$100	100%	VPNs	$75	80%
TCPdump	$50	100%	PKI	$100	20%
Routing Protocols	$50	100%	Steganography	$50	50%
Physical Security	$50	100%	PGP	$100	50%
Technical Controls	$50	100%	Wireless	$100	100%
			Legal Issues	$100	100%

Azal and Morgaine scored both value and learning differently. When estimating a market value for a skill, you're going to score what you already know higher simply because it's more familiar. If you're concerned with accuracy, have others review your estimates to bring the value more in line with reality. Your perceived percentage left to learn will also have a familiarity bias. Beginners often feel that the more they know, the less they have to learn. With experts, this tendency reverses itself as the more they know, the more they know there is to learn. Correcting for these biases is less critical if you are using the tool to choose which class to take or whether to learn on your own.

To calculate the value of a class, simply multiply each value by the amount left to learn and tally up the total score card. In this example, Azal estimates that days 1 and 4 would be worth $618.75 to him and Morgaine estimates them to be worth $905.00 to her. Suppose this class cost $750.00 (not true, but since we're just looking at two days from a six-day class, it's a reasonable simplification). Azal would not get as much out of it as he'd be paying, so he should look at other classes or other modes of learning. Morgaine would clearly get the value of the class plus $155 more and should thus consider it.

For other classes, the approach is the same: just run through this exercise for every class that interests you and passes a basic quality check. The one that has the highest value to cost ratio is the one you should consider first. Although the value numbers you've assigned are arbitrary, if the same arbitrary values are used consistently, the relative values of the classes will still be correct.

SELF-STUDY

The other classic method to bootstrap learning is to go through self-study. While it is often the cheapest and fastest way to learn, self-study can be difficult if you have problems focusing, completing, and limiting interruptions. To be successful at self-study, you must be able to set a plan and stick to it. A common failure mode for this style of learning is to lose time doing things that do not advance your goal. When learning in a class environment, the instructor is responsible for the structure of setting your goals and helping you maintain your forward progress. Without an instructor, you are on your own.

Many books and recorded lectures are available for much of information security, from which you can get some structure. Most "learn on your own" books and recorded lectures function much like a class, where you are presumed to start with a certain level of knowledge and gain more understanding with each portion that you complete. At the end, it is expected, you have complete knowledge and are done. However, unlike traditional classes, this approach has at best only self-assessment tests and quizzes, so you don't know what you've actually learned. This mode of self-study requires more rigor and self-honesty to be successful.

Not all learning materials, books, and recorded lectures will be useful to you, or worthwhile in general. Read reviews, check sources, ask around, especially your mentor, and fact check the material before investing much time or money.

Information technology and information security computer aided training/instruction (CAT/CAI) is almost uniformly poor. If you have free access, give it a try, especially for introductory topics, but seriously reconsider paying any money for it. However, if you have skills in curriculum development, and authoring tools then good information security CAT/CAI would be a valuable contribution to the community. See the Chapter 4.1 "Boosting—Author" and Chapter 4.7 "Boosting—Community Support" chapters.

If you are not taking a class-based approach to your learning, it is still wise to lay out a rough plan. You may know what you want to learn. This should help you design a "final exam" so you can verify what you learned. The goal may be something technical, such as setting up an Apache web server to perform a specific goal. It may be nontechnical, such as writing a report or paper for someone else to read. It may even be externally measured, such as passing a certification exam. Only by having a goal in mind, and a means of testing, can you truly call what you're doing self-study.

To be highly successful (as defined by learning a large amount in a relatively short period of time), you also have to track your days and weeks of study. These metrics help keep you from following dead-ends and tangents into areas that matter little to your end goal. One way to do this is to break apart your learning process into smaller pieces. Each piece should be roughly the same size—about a day's or a week's worth of work. Each piece should also have a set test at the end, so you can verify that you learned it sufficiently well to move along to the next item. Once you have your agenda down, you can start the self-study process.

PROJECTS/EXPERIMENTATION

If self-study doesn't work for you, either because you have difficulty learning that way or because you face constant interruption, you may learn best by doing. Many people learn best by blending the Learn and Do phases. However, if you learn by doing, your first work will necessarily be incomplete and flawed. The old programmer's adage of "write one to throw away" really applies well here, so plan to do more Learning and Doing.

Fundamentally, the issue is that people often learn best through mistakes. We typically learn from the mistakes of others; we're hard-wired for story, and stories of wild successes and massive failures are what stick with us. However, if we're blazing new ground or have to learn on our own, we must make our own mistakes.

There's nothing wrong with this. Scientific studies have shown that there is a measurement, called Error Positivity (EP), that shows how well people learn from mistakes. Those that have higher EP tend to learn more and better than those that do not. Since high EP correlates to positive attitude and a willingness to work but does not correlate to intelligence, there is a theory that this is why, over time, competent hard workers outperform their more intelligent but less hard-working competition.

However, if your learning process was built out of a series of mistakes, it's likely to not be sufficiently stable to build upon. In technology in general, we tend to build something until it works and then move on. This makes sense because it's a lot easier to determine when a thing is functional than when it is secure. However, if you want to break into the information security field, you have to build things that work, but also break them until you understand how they fail. This is a very different process and, as you're learning, can be dangerous because by definition you don't know what you're doing.

People who learn best by doing often do it while working for someone else. This may be on-the-job learning or learning done on your own but involving work-related systems. This may be work done when volunteering for nonprofit groups or open-source communities. But learning while doing is a risk to your company, to your customers, to your friends and to yourself.

Stop and ask yourself, "What did I learn from this?" and "How can what I built harm others?" and "How do I prevent harm?" Apply the answers to these questions and fix the mistakes you made as you went. In some cases, this may require a complete rebuild; in others, it may involve leveraging other skills you have to harden the environment that people will be using.

However you decide to minimize the risk to you and others, remember that security is about protection. It's also about helping some people achieve their goals, while limiting attackers' options. However, at the end of the day, if what you did doesn't improve the protection of someone else, you can't claim that it was security-related work.

BREAKING DOWN TO BREAK IN

The rest of this book focuses on specific jobs, roles, and tasks that are common in the information security industry. Each section within the Learning tier details a specific entry-level job—what it's like and how to get into it. We will detail not only the duties of the job, but also how and why the job might be less than enjoyable. Entry-level jobs are by definition stepping stones to something greater, but where you go is often a reflection of where you have been, so jobs that you hate will taint every job after as you'll be following a path based on work you dislike. Some paths will not be worthy of your goals.

To get where you want to go, you need to know where you are and what additional skills you need to acquire to get there. There is always more than one way to do something, and that is true for career management as well. You'll find some jobs to be dead-ends, where it feels as though there is no way forward. Jobs based on dying technologies may result in your feeling as if the market has dried up.

Remember, however, that your actual job is not reviewing firewall logs or deploying patches. It's protecting people. So long as you keep that in mind, you will find other ways to protect people. Maybe it will be with a new technology. Maybe it will be replacing the legacy technology in which you are currently an expert with newer technology. Maybe it will be something nontechnical, and you'll move into management.

As long as people are cheap, lazy, or stupid, you'll have work. The trick—the only trick, really—is not to be cheap, lazy, or stupid yourself. Fortunately, the opposites: thrift, hard work, and intelligence also provide work, and will usually be more pleasant. Learn about new technologies. Invest in and develop new skills. Hold yourself to high standards. Constantly improve. And, finally, always test your understanding. Do all these things with each job and, as you move through your career, you'll find the job you want and how to get it.

TIER 1—LOG REVIEWER

1.1

INTRODUCTION

"Once is happenstance. Twice is coincidence. The third time it's enemy action."
— **Auric Goldfinger in** *Goldfinger* **by Ian Fleming, 01959**

The log reviewer role involves a periodic review of files that store critical data about what happens within your environment. These logs typically originate from applications or from devices like firewalls or servers. In more mature organizations, the logs will likely be stored centrally in a Security Information and Event Management (SIEM) system. These logs typically contain an ongoing description of what the system is currently doing—indicating whether the system started up properly, which specific events occurred, what problems were encountered, what failed, and finally whether the system shut down properly.

In many organizations, this role is entry-level and may be filled by untrained individuals or those in a junior role in system or network administration. In larger organizations, this is a full-time job that may be one of the roles in a dedicated team. In very well-developed security organizations, this team may be dedicated to a centralized (politically, if not physically) Security Operations Center (SOC) continuous 24/7/366 real-time monitoring and response. A well-developed information security organization will have a full staffed SOC with enough log reviewers to allow all critical security logs to be reviewed for all operating hours. Although "SOC" is a common information security term, it is not universal, and even very large organizations may not have a SOC by that name, or any single unit that does SOC functions. A network operations center (NOC) may include some SOC functions. In these cases, the term "SOC" represents the job functions, if not the organizational unit itself. It also represents a possible opportunity for an ambitious and resourceful person who could create a SOC where none previously existed. Lacking a SOC is also an opportunity for attackers and represents a risk to the organization.

At a technical level, most people never interact with logs or even know they exist. Logging is often an afterthought, even with information security systems. However, the logs can be a valuable way to troubleshoot a system, both during an incident and after the fact.

There tend to be two types of logs: debugging/informational and security. Information logs are used to track application behavior and troubleshoot; most developers and system administrators are used to working with them. Security logs are different. These logs store critical information about system use, such as when people log in and out of systems, when people fail to log in successfully, and what data access attempts fail or succeed based on access controls. These logs, such as audit logs and security event logs, can provide a great deal of information about security issues on a system, which is why attackers often alter or remove logs to hide and destroy evidence. Network security logs in particular can track which websites people visit and what sorts of network applications they run.

The job of a log reviewer is to ensure that any indications of attacks are detected and responded to within a reasonable amount of time where "reasonable" can include immediately. Logs need to be regularly reviewed, perhaps even in real-time. In addition, log reviewers may be responsible for managing and protecting logs so they are not not viewed by unauthorized people or modified in any way. The job can be boring, but it is also absolutely essential.

HOW TO BREAK IN

Log reviewing is often extremely boring, so it's often the first thing offloaded onto new or junior staff. Though logs are often dull, they can hide gems. It can be interesting to trace a 20-year-old bug as you analyze network traffic from one system to another to identify why a particular log entry keeps recurring.

Reviewing logs can be hazardous. You may discover information you shouldn't know, such as possible acquisition targets, just from seeing the browsing habits of senior managers. You may discover activities that shouldn't be occurring, such as employees selling illegal items or browsing to online gambling sites. Of course, you may also identify indications of compromise (IOC) in the attack's killchain that can help your organization get in front of an attack and determine how best to respond.

The role requires being trustworthy enough to not snoop where you shouldn't, but also intelligent enough to see and investigate things that look odd, or hinky. This is a great opportunity to learn. How you break in will depend on the sort of business you wish to target.

An otherwise fully staffed SOC may have positions available for those that start out in log reviewing. A SOC may require employees to have backgrounds in the systems they monitor, including non-security systems. These may include systems that support business operations, software development, system administration, accounting, customer support, and even marketing. Working in these areas can bring useful skills, knowledge, and business contacts to a SOC. Your experience in these non-security areas and understanding the technical underpinnings for how these systems function can help land your job in the SOC.

Smaller firms will not have a SOC, but log review is still required. This may be part-time and involve reviewing each system individually or looking at centralized SIEM log reports. If there isn't a centralized SIEM, your best way to break into the role is to spend some time implementing a central SIEM logging system and then tune it. If you are starting from scratch, look at the Security Onion, a free Linux-based system created and supported by Doug Burks. See the Appendix: Tools for details.

HAZARD WARNING

Policy Compliance

Activities such as setting up a centralized log service, any kind of monitoring, or any kind of server may have serious policy or political issues, and as mentioned above, moral issues. Make sure that such activities are within policy, within your job description, and known of and approved by your management in writing. Management approval needs to include conflict of interest resolution for monitoring of co-workers and direct management..

In a small organization a centralized SIEM system can be implemented on old hardware that may be lying around and, as you turn on the SIEM and tune it, you will find many internal activities that would be of interest to your boss. Tuning any alerts that occur may involve touching many different systems and implementing changes to things like web filtering and MS-Windows log settings, and removing unnecessary services on numerous servers.

If you wish to move to a new company in such a role, you will need experience. You can gain such experience from implementing a SIEM on your own, perhaps at a nonprofit or school near you, or your own home environment if you can't get approval elsewhere. This not only gives you the skill you need to get over the "need experience to get experience" hump, but also gives you an excellent story to tell in interviews.

HOW TO IMPROVE YOUR SKILLS

The contents of security logs can be highly counterintuitive. A sternly worded log warning message about dangerous activity could be an indication of compromise (IOC) or be a completely normal, but misleading, entry. Simply by looking at logs, real-time, or historical, a log reviewer will begin to understand what is common and what is not. Note that commonly occurring activities may actually be quite dangerous—just because it's frequent doesn't mean it should be occurring. Log reviewers learn the difference both for the general case, and for the specific environment they are reviewing. Context is critical.

By comparing log activity with known events, and by comparing logs of different systems, the log reviewer can start to build the skill of understanding the environment. A seasoned Log Reviewer will understand what a particular log entry really means, and if it's normal and innocuous, or subtle warning of serious security issues.

There are several areas in which you can grow your skills as a log reviewer.

The first, and most obvious, is tuning the logs within the logging system. Whether you're just using a standard syslog server or a much more complex enterprise log management system the system will need tuning. A tuned security logging system will log everything that is needed, log nothing that is not needed, and alarm, alert, and/or merely warn where needed. Every time a new server comes online or a major upgrade is installed, the logging system will detune and the logs will become "chatty." The trick behind tuning is to make a choice as to whether to adjust the source of the logs or the target.

For example, the log source may be a server that is running in debug mode because a developer needed some information, perhaps a lot more information. This mode is seldom turned off, but just resetting the log level to "informational" may reduce the logging to a more manageable level.

At the log target side, you may find that every Monday morning a legacy system sends ten thousand otherwise innocuous packets that trigger an alert. Legacy systems are notoriously difficult to change, but once you know why something is happening, if you can't stop it from happening, you can instead adjust the alerting system so that it knows that the problem isn't serious and shouldn't alert.

Another way to grow your skills as a log reviewer is to look at any custom logs that a developer may have implemented. These logs may contain extremely sensitive data, such as passwords or Social Security numbers, so you could get involved with developing a tokenization or masking system so the sensitive data is not compromised, but the logs remain useful. This is also an opportunity to learn software development and further expand business contacts.

Yet another way to grow your skills is to expand your logging capabilities. Many organizations are either running a central log collector or a network-based monitor. Usually only larger and more mature organizations do both. Expanding from network utilization and service monitoring to alerting on security events is often a very easy step to take. Implementing a log parsing and alerting system is also often something you can do to improve your position.

Finally, integrating trusted alerts into your ticketing system can improve efficiency and demonstrates a solid understanding of your environment.

RECOGNIZING WHEN YOU'RE STUCK

Security logs usually have recurring patterns, both short- and long-term, ranging from seconds to months. Some environments can take years to really understand, due to seasonal and yearly fluctuations. Although computers don't have seasons, the systems they are a part of, such as retail businesses, schools, and sports, can be directly affected by seasons.

Organizations often consider log review to be a low priority task not requiring a dedicated person or team. In these cases, log review might be even ignored and replaced by other tasks considered more urgent. This is an opportunity to move over to these other areas full-time. An organization that doesn't consider security log review and monitoring important is quite possibly an organization to learn from and then leave behind. Some organizations do consider security log review important enough to do consistently, but the organization may still not provide an advancement path.

After you've been through a few seasons of logs review you should have been able to grow your skills as mentioned above, but if not, then it may be time to move on.

HOW TO GET OUT

Log Reviewer may bring skills and knowledge into new areas. For example, by focusing on particular issues, a Log Reviewer may have valuable insight into Coding/Development, Patch Management, System Administration, and Network Administration. In some organizations Log Review may be so important that it requires a Subject Matter Expert.

This deep knowledge can be used to more quickly evaluate events and issues, and to start automating log review tasks.

1. Do: In a quiet, low-threat environment, a log reviewer may be able to quickly determine that no issues exist for the moment, so they can start growing skills in related areas.
2. Do: Partially automate the log review task with simple filters (Chapter 1.4 Coder/Developer).
3. Do: Fully automate with more complicated filters and custom code and reports (Chapter 1.4 Coder/Developer).
4. Learn: Dig deeper and learn more about the logs; notify what systems produce those logs (Chapter 1.5 System Administrator).
5. Teach: Find non-security issues in the logs and notify and help others in the organization (Chapter 1.9 Quality Tester).
6. Teach others how to be a log reviewer, as someone else will have to do it when you leave (Chapter 3.0 Teach, Mentoring section).

7. Volunteer at work or do personal activity for specific tasks outside of pure log review (Chapter 4.0 Boosting).
8. Write an article, or do a presentation on what you've done, learned, and taught.
9. Advance: Automate log review to the point you are no longer needed. Your new job, perhaps at a new company, won't be log reviewer, but instead will be a multi-classed log automation specialist, which combines log review and coder/developer and quite possibly adds system administrator and network administrator.

CRITICAL WARNINGS

Unlike many information security roles, the stress level of a Log Reviewer is simultaneously and paradoxically both high and low. Commonly described as "long periods of boredom punctuated by moments of sheer terror," the life of a Log Reviewer will have its up and downs. Most environments are relatively low in terms of threats, and most threats are not subtle, so the stress is usually low. However, one anomalous event may occur that will spur further investigation, causing stress levels to spike to extremely high levels. That the high stress can occur at any time without warning is itself stressful.

Log Reviewer can be a dead-end job and should be avoided by those who don't have the circumstances, patience, or discipline to benefit from its strong learning opportunities and potentially long wait for advancement.

Table 1.1 Role at a Glance—Log Reviewer

Hours	Travel	Stress Level	Creativity	Flexibility	Stability
0.5–8 hours/day	Usually none	Generally low	Low	High	High
General job duties	Reviewing logs. Writing log filter rules. Fulfilling log research requests.				
Learning	High – Reviewing the logs for an entire organization covers all aspects of their operations. You can learn about how firewalls work from the firewall logs and these logs potentially contain the details of all Internet access by everyone in the organization and details on everything on the Internet that connects to that organization. Anti-virus logs contain details on what malware the organization encounters and how users react to it. As you troubleshoot issues, you may find yourself learning about servers, networking systems and vulnerability management. The learning opportunity in this role is very high, but you will likely have to push your way into the learning as the role is often also culturally isolated and time limited.				
Advancement	Typically, people advance into the role as an entry level position or laterally from junior System Administrator or Network Administrator. Expect to advance to Security Assessment, Risk Assessment, and especially Incident Responder. Log Review can also serve as critical experience for Incident Responder, Security Architect, Security Consultant, or Security Management.				
	Culturally, most organizations will provide little in the way of formal advancement paths for Log Reviewers. If you serve within a centralized Security Operations Center (SOC), you may be able to become a team manager, but generally speaking, you will have to either change employers or petition a superior to move out of the role.				

1.2 TIER 1—PATCH MANAGEMENT

INTRODUCTION

> "All programmers are optimists."
>
> — **Fredrick P. Brooks, Jr.**

Patch management is a component of configuration management where you are responsible for ensuring that patches are applied to computers as directed by a company's policies and procedures. Generally, when a patch is released, individuals in Vulnerability Management roles will identify the urgency of releasing the patch based on the vulnerabilities it addresses and the systems to which it applies. Once the patches that need to be released are identified, those in Patch Management are responsible for ensuring that the patches are tested before release, if possible, and then applying the patches to the appropriate systems.

Depending on the devices being patched, various tools may be used to manage the process, such as Microsoft's System Center Configuration Manager (SCCM) and SolarWinds Patch Manager. You may be responsible for a single platform (such as those workstations running Microsoft Windows) or multiple platforms.

This is the type of job that can be very monotonous in its duties but, if you take some initiative, it can provide you with many opportunities for learning.

HOW TO BREAK IN

Though technical skills are important, being well-organized and comfortable following set procedures is at least as important for this role. If there are no available mentors you will need a clear understanding of the organization's platform and environment. Other organizations may have mentors who will train you into the role if you are able to demonstrate solid general technical skills.

In some organizations, this role can be used as an entry point into the IT field. There are many standardized tasks, and the primary job responsibilities are to monitor, document, and report, so interns or other entry-level people may be assigned this work under close supervision. People who are already enrolled in or have graduated from a computer-related degree program are often given preference, since it demonstrates an existing level of general technical skills.

For non-intern positions, showing how you provided support as a volunteer, or helped patch computers at a local nonprofit, are ways you can demonstrate experience in this area.

HOW TO IMPROVE YOUR SKILLS

Some people view patch management as a dry and boring field, but if you are willing to put in some extra effort it can be hugely beneficial for learning about the information security field. Nearly every patch addresses some form of security vulnerability—something that either has been, or could be, used to infiltrate systems.

Take the time, either at work or on your own, to deeply examine the patch and the vulnerabilities they address; they are a great repository of security knowledge. Understand not only the specific vulnerability that is being addressed, but the class of vulnerabilities it falls under, what causes the vulnerabilities, and how to prevent them. Learning the difference between a buffer overflow and SQL injection is important for the security professional. Early on, it is unlikely that you will be able to do so for every patch, but as you go on and develop your knowledge, it will become easier and easier. This same technique is used by penetration testers and security researchers to develop attacks against un-patched systems and to develop brand new attacks. Patches often only fix a specific vulnerability, not the class of vulnerabilities.

As you get better at understanding what sorts of attacks a patch prevents, you will also become better at implementing such attacks yourself, should you wish to eventually move into active auditing and penetration testing of systems.

Similarly, one of the key concepts of security is understanding that security is not about technical solutions addressing technical problems; security is about reducing risk to a level with which the business is comfortable. Take the time to learn why some patches are critical to your organization and others are not and you will learn the business drivers for security. Learn the different reasons that may make one buffer overflow patch critical for immediate installation, outside of the normal patch schedule, while another patch can easily be installed in the regular patch schedule, or not at all.

Well-run organizations will have processes for testing patches before their rollout. Take advantage of the fact that these processes have already been set up to learn about them. Identify the key characteristics of your organization's processes, and work to learn enough about them that you could implement your own elsewhere, should it become necessary.

Finally, take the time to learn about your organization's platform and environment.

RECOGNIZING WHEN YOU'RE STUCK

- You dread Patch Tuesday.
- You fear Exploit Wednesday even more.
- You don't care if that patch really did get applied.
- You don't get a sense of job satisfaction from having the best-patched environment you can manage.

HOW TO GET OUT

These roles are common at large organizations, so if you are looking to stay in the same role, you will usually be able to find a similar role elsewhere. Server Administration roles could be an advancement opportunity, as could a Security Coordinator role. If your organization splits patch management by platform, this could be an opportunity to switch platforms and retain your patch management experience. Alternatively, if your organization splits patches by internal organization structure this can be an opportunity to change job role and retain your platform experience. Other organizations split patches between servers and clients, or operating system and applications. There is no one best way, only what works for that organization.

If you have taken the time to learn deeply about security throughout your time in Patch Management, then advancement to Vulnerability Management, Auditor, or Security Assessment, depending on the skills that you have developed along the way, may be possible.

CRITICAL WARNINGS

If you are in this role too long, you will have a hard time leaving it. Patch management is often underfunded. Ideally, this role would involve you building your skills and automating patch processes within a test or lab environment. Then, when you have enough skills to be useful elsewhere, you get promoted and another person would come in and take over your role.

Sadly, this is often not the case. Many organizations don't have test environments. All production environments should have dedicated and safe test and experimentation environments. Patches can break a system, make it unstable, or take away key functionality. Sometimes key functionality is a security vulnerability and therefore a required feature! If an organization is not willing to spend the time and money to address these risks, you should be wary of staying there too long, as they are not supportive of helping your efforts to improve things.

Also, since it is an entry-level role, you should be working to get out of this role in one to three years. The organization and team you end up in will have a significant impact on your ability to grow. If you are left in your cube, only asked to perform your tasks, and never provided opportunities for cross-training and growth, that is another sign that the company is not serious and you probably need to plan to build skills on your own so you can move on to a better job sooner rather than later.

Table 1.2 Role at a Glance—Patch Management

Hours	Travel	Stress Level	Creativity	Flexibility	Stability
8 hours/day Overtime	Low to None	Low	Low	Low	High
General job duties	Testing patches on non-production systems. Setting up systems for automatic distribution of patches. Documenting the application of patches.				
Learning	Medium High. Leverage platform skill to security management skills. Leverage security skill to platform skills. Get exposed to vulnerability management and incident response. Many opportunities for the driven individual. Can be effectively avoided if you so desire, but don't do that.				
Advancement	Vulnerability Management, Auditor, Security Assessment or Incident Responder, depending on the skills that you have developed along the way.				

TIER 1—HELP DESK

INTRODUCTION

> "Don't Panic."
>
> — **Douglas Adams**

The Help Desk is a common part of larger information technology environments. It provides a single physical place, phone number, email address, or other communications channel for what are typically the most basic and least experienced information technology people in the company. Consequently, it's one of the most likely places an inexperienced person will start.

The help desk is where a "people person" is appreciated, but not always valued.

Some organizations separate the information security help desks from the information technology help desks, while others combine the functions. Either approach affords a good way to break into information security for someone with limited skills or experience. If you have a choice, the information security help desk might be a better place to start. But since information security is as much about the technology as about the security, an information technology help desk could also be a good start.

Consider these differences when choosing between a job at an information security help desk and an information technology help desk: Talk to people who work specifically in those areas in those organizations, talk to both your potential co-workers and your potential management. Find out how technical each is, how much flexibility in the job exists, and what you can learn, and where you can advance.

The stress level associated with this job is highly dependent upon the stress level of the incoming requests. For example, a help desk for a data recovery company may have highly stressed customers, so much that some data recovery companies provide specialized data loss bereavement counselors. Additional stress comes from help desk operators having limited to no ability to fix systemic problems, which will be highly stressful when there are many systemic problems.

Pay is usually hourly; work hours can be highly variable, and may include working nights, weekends, and holidays, yet still be part time and seasonal. Overtime is rare.

Help Desk employees usually operate in fixed shifts, but not necessarily as part of regular 8-hour days. Hourly employees are often limited to 40 hours a week or less, while seasonal variations, and extended operating hours may result in irregular hours, but which may provide high work hour flexibility to help desk operators.

Work flexibility is usually stable, but some organizations have seasonal workforce fluctuations. The Help Desk tends to be the largest group with the lowest seniority and least experienced staff, which may result in less stability.

Help Desk duties tend to be boring, with the same types of recurring customer problems—sometimes exactly the same problems, which becomes tedious, and possibly also stressful. The most interesting problems can't be solved at the lowest help desk tier and are moved up the chain to more experienced staff.

HOW TO BREAK IN

Help Desk is an entry-level position, and so is often a new hire position, perhaps an internship. However, in some cases it may be a horizontal movement from a non-technical or non-IT position. Non-technology companies may provide this horizontal movement for those who are interested in help desk jobs, and may also provide training. Someone with some basic technical skills but not enough to get hired directly may gain both experience and business contacts by becoming the local "computer person" that people go to before they call the official Help Desk. In some environments they can immediately provide better support because Corporate Help Desk employees are unfortunately notorious for providing poor service, with long waits, poor people skills, or irrelevant advice. Becoming the local technical "go to" person can develop from any non-technical position; such a person has the advantage of already knowing the organization.

HOW TO IMPROVE YOUR SKILLS

Most help desks have frequently asked questions and problems. Not all help desks have detailed and up to date documentation for those questions and problems. Some have no documentation, or even training. Either way, it's an opportunity to Learn/Do/Teach. Read the documentation, if any. Ask questions. Research and get the answers to your own questions and those asked of you. Document and solve problems. Update and write new documentation using what you've learned. Teach what you know to your co-workers and your customers. If you're starting from nothing then as you take calls, do metrics, take note of how long calls last, and what the most frequent problems and questions are. Set up a documentation environment; share with your co-workers.

In some cases a technology company may put senior people on help desk duty to supplement staff. These are opportunities for you to learn from experienced people and develop professional relationships. The help desk environment can be a highly structured and stressful one, with limited time to do anything but take calls and resolve trouble tickets. If this is the case, use this as an opportunity to ask others, senior or not, how they learned to cope with the environment. If it is not, you should cultivate relationships outside of the organization and build a team of people of which you can ask general questions. You will have to be careful not to let slip sensitive information, but a well selected team of colleagues can be very helpful.

RECOGNIZING WHEN YOU'RE STUCK

An organization is stuck when the same problems keep recurring which could be fixed with a better product or at least better documentation. A good Help Desk environment treats help desk tickets, resolved or not, as information for making better products and services. If the organization isn't learning from this, and you as a help desk operator aren't either, it's time to move on.

If you're learning and becoming a senior person, but you haven't had at least a minor promotion or had your hard work acknowledged in six months to a year of starting, it might be time to move on. Either the organization is using you for cheap labor, or you aren't working out in that environment. This doesn't mean you aren't suited for help desk, rather that that particular work situation may not be good for anyone, or only for certain people. Many people choose to move out of the help desk environment when the opportunity arises.

If you find yourself well suited to the role, you may find yourself promoted to Help Desk Lead and, eventually, into management. This is not a way to break in to information security, but it can be a very satisfying career nonetheless.

HOW TO GET OUT

Entry level Help Desk is close to the bottommost tier in the support structure, just above the end user. They are the ones who directly handle calls and requests, while more skilled or experienced help desk people will often be moved up to a higher tier. Each tier hands off work they cannot complete to the next higher tier. To move up a tier doesn't mean being able to handle all incoming requests without having to pass on to the next tier; it means being referred by others who are at a lower tier.

Table 1.3 Role at a Glance—Help Desk

Hours	Travel	Stress Level	Creativity	Flexibility	Stability
20–40 hours/day, variable	Usually none, although may have different job sites in the same area.	Variable	Low	High	High
General job duties	Directly answering the phone. Responding to email. Working trouble tickets.				
Learning	Variable. Help Desk operators may have a formal training program, either on the job, or a classroom type environment. Supervisors are often also trainers, and sometimes even mentor-like. Every incoming request could be a learning opportunity and will be for the new help desk operator. However, over time, perhaps quickly, the learning opportunities tend to drop and the same nearly identical requests keep arriving.				
Advancement	Help Desks can vary significantly. In larger environments the Help Desk supervisor positions may be available as a growth position. The Help Desk may have significant internal and external turn-over, which can be an opportunity for the new help desk operator to stay and retain.				
	In some organizations they are considered the menial labor of the information technology organization. However the Help Desk can be an entry level position for an information technology career. Some organizations integrate the Help Desk and use it to find and feed talent into the entire support organization. A good organization will see talented and hardworking operators and want to retain them. In not so good organizations a help desk operator will have to figure this out on their own.				

1.3.1 TIER 1—HELP DESK— STORY

JIM CHAN

I started my IT career in 01999 by attending Brown Institute in Mendota Heights. I finished their program with an A+ certification and landed a desktop support job at Target Corporation. During a hardware refresh project for the Finance executives, my boss asked me to work with the Information Security team to ensure the drives were erased properly. Target Corporation is huge on mentorship programs and development plans. I checked with my boss to see if I could schedule an informational interview with someone on the InfoSec team. My boss gave me the name of the Compliance and Monitoring manager and I scheduled an informational interview. During this informational interview, the Compliance and Monitoring manager said that they have an internship program. My current boss approved, and the internship program was a one-day-a-week shadow and Q&A session with various members of the Information Security team. This is where I learned an overview of IDS, Forensics, Architecture, Identity Management, etc. At the same time, I started attending night school to finish up my bachelor's degree. After finishing the internship program, there were no openings in the Information Security team. I continued the mentorship meetings and started attending open weekly "cryptolunch" lunch meetings with the Information Security team. After a few months, my mentor informed me of an entry-level user access management position on the Information Security team. I had finished my bachelor's degree before the opening came about, applied, interviewed, and got hired on.

The interpersonal relationships I developed through the internship program, having a bachelor's degree completed, and proactively getting involved with Information Security tasks and projects were the biggest contributors to breaking into the field.

TIER 1—CODER/DEVELOPER 1.4

INTRODUCTION

> "What I really need is a droid who understands the binary language of moisture vaporators."
>
> — **Uncle Owen**

Everyone who worked with computers was once expected to program them. Now it is common for people to work in information technology without learning any programming languages at all. In this section we will discuss those few remaining people who start out in the development world and then wish to break into information security.

If you are approaching information security from this perspective, you should have some familiarity with programming languages. Once you get in, you may find yourself reviewing existing code for security concerns. You may be creating brand-new programs or extending old ones. You may have a bridge role between non-security developers and the information security teams. Most information security roles involve some sort of bridging, but few roles bridge more different worlds than between non-security developers and information security.

This bridge role role will probably be at most 75% development and the rest discussions, explanations, and meetings. You should expect to gain deep skills in languages and to get very good at understanding how other people communicate, identifying application and business model issues, and prioritizing tasks.

HOW TO BREAK IN—PRELIMINARIES

Typically this role involves first knowing one language very well. A common but bad practice is that good security coder/developers must know a little bit about many different languages. Commonly chosen languages include: C, C ++, Java, Javascript, Perl, Python, and Ruby. Knowing a little about each means your work will be poor in all of them.

There are no shortcuts to learning, and this applies to learning programming languages just as much as other subjects. Perhaps you spend one month learning Perl. Then, when you hit limitations to the language, you spend a month learning Python. As you dig into security scripts, you learn some Ruby. Later, you may create modules to get your code to run efficiently, which means two to three months learning C and another two months in learning C ++. In a year of learning, you've learned only part of six to eight languages but none of them very well, and perhaps not well at all. In a worst case, you may only be able to write bad but otherwise useful code only by using all of the languages you know, instead of using the one language that would be best suited for the task. This is worse than the feared "spaghetti code," it's random layered pasta code.

Contrast this approach with the "learn one language very well, then move on" approach. The better you know your first language, the easier it is to pick up similar ones. Consider how much easier it is for English speakers to learn French and Italian after having thoroughly learned Spanish. The grammar, vocabulary, and logical structures of the latter languages are all similar, so picking up the differences is easier than learning any one of them from scratch. The same applies to programming. Once you learn one programming language thoroughly, you can use that knowledge to understand other programming languages. Documentation is easier to understand, because you've picked up the vocabulary around the language and can find what you need much more quickly. Troubleshooting code also becomes easier because you can quickly create proof-of-concept functions in first language to identify whether the issue is related to a bug or fundamental misunderstanding.

In general, you should start with the language you know best and spend upwards of six to eight months learning it as well as you possibly can. If you learn best from books (likely, as you're reading this one), read one or two beginner books, three to four intermediate books, and at least one advanced book. Select books with exercises to do, and never skip the exercises. The goal isn't to just read the book, the goal is to learn, and completing the exercises is your proof to yourself that you learned. The completed exercises are also a valuable reference for yourself and can be part of the portfolio you can present to prospective employers. A good example of book learning is the approach of Perl book publisher O'Reilly and Associates. If you start with *Learning Perl*, then move on to *Programming Perl*, *Mastering Regular Expressions*, and *Perl Best Practices*, then wrap up with *Advanced Perl*, you can jump from beginner to master in very short order. See the Appendix on Perl for details. Once you've mastered one language, you can pick up any intermediate book on C, Python, or Ruby and bootstrap yourself to an experienced level very quickly.

The same approach applies if you're learning from online materials, videos, or a classroom. Make sure that, before every new lesson, you understand the previous lesson as much as you can to minimize time lost to misunderstanding.

HOW TO BREAK IN—BEYOND THE BASICS

Once you have your basic skills down, it's time to leverage them and move in an information security direction. One common method is to join the team as a code assessor. These jobs are frequently advertised; in large companies they should be easy to find. In smaller organizations and some development teams, you may find a hybrid developer/security team lead role. For both of these, the basic approach is to apply for the position and then do well in the interview. This is, of course, easier said than done.

If you want to help a company start a development security practice, you have to come across as an expert. For this, it may help to develop some additional skill via one of the "boosting" paths near the end of the book. In general, working on a code similar to your target environment will do more for you than anything else. If you're targeting a company with legacy Microsoft ASP.NET code that it's converting into Java, you can quickly develop some experience. Find an older orphaned project written in ASP.NET that still has some legitimate value in terms of business logic on Microsoft's CodePlex. com, SourceForge.net, or similar open source hosting site. Then port it over to Java, documenting what you did and why you did it. This builds your portfolio and will give you the type of story you'll want to talk about in the interview, greatly increasing your chances of landing the job. Increasingly developer resumes are their open source code repositories.

Unfortunately, most hiring firms are obsessed with specific languages, and if you don't have what they want, you'll be rejected. If you follow the above advice and know one language very well, you should be able to pick up your new target language very quickly. This can help you turn an industrial disadvantage into an advantage, since if they're discriminating against you for not having the target skills, they'll be doing the same to everyone else. If you can develop the target skills quickly, you can move into a much smaller pool of applicants.

There are a lot of programmers out there. The number of those programmers that know information security is considerably smaller. If you can target a specific language at an organization where you want to work, you've cut the smaller pool into a tiny fraction, and increased your chances. For specific uncommon languages like Haskell and Smalltalk, you may be down to a pool of one—which means you get to name your price for the job.

HOW TO IMPROVE YOUR SKILLS

Once you have the job, you'll have to stay on top of things. Unlike other information security jobs, you can't just stay on top of security events and new tools. You also have to watch for code libraries. A very common failing for developers is to use an older library and also fail to keep it up-to-date. This allows security vulnerabilities and incompatibility to creep into a code base that is completely isolated from any actively developed code. Thus, there are several vectors along which you will need to grow:

1. New languages—There is a tendency in development teams to use the newest or sexiest languages. This is part optimization, part planned obsolescence, but mostly fad and fashion. The optimization is related to the tendency, when learning a new language, to know the flaws of what you've been using but not yet encounter the flaws of the new language. Many shifts between Java and Microsoft.NET, MS-Windows and Linux, and Perl, Python, Ruby and Microsoft PowerShell are due to this "grass is greener" tendency. Your job, as a security expert, is to remain familiar enough with operating systems and languages to advise on the hidden information security costs of changing.
2. Defending against laziness—There is a saying that all programmers are lazy. The truth is that programmers want to program; they get into the field because they enjoy creating, but hate repetition. Programmers love automating, but hate what can't be automated. So programmers tend toward more enjoyable tasks like writing new code, learning new languages, but ignore other critical tasks like updating libraries and refactoring code to address noncritical flaws. They especially avoid documentation and development work needed to support fundamental infrastructure changes. Your job will be to advocate important security changes without alienating the team or being an irritant.
3. Ongoing analysis—Just as developers tend towards laziness, you must combat that tendency within yourself. You will need to create a schedule and stick to it, so activities such as pre-release code scans, team code reviews, and library assessment continue to be done properly. You also need to find and use as appropriate new security tools. For example, when input fuzzing was new a different fuzzer was released about once a month. Each tested for different issues, so each fuzzer

could have been run against each application, with each run resulting in more known security issues that would need to be prioritized for the future. The same idea applies to automated code scanners, vulnerability testers, and web application firewalls.

4. Programming—You must continue to improve your development skills. This can mean attending user group meetings, hackathons, and "code camps" within the community, going to official training, conducting your own training, or simply exploring a new area of the language. Many developers have achieved truly excellent levels by simply reviewing a different operator or function every single day, so that eventually they become world-class experts in the language.

RECOGNIZING WHEN YOU'RE STUCK

The most common place to get stuck in a coder/developer job is when the business stops valuing your contributions. In economic recessions, security is often the first to go as companies refocus their development efforts on adding features to attract new customers.

Though it sounds like a long time, you may find it takes a year or two to address the easiest findings. Some people make their entire careers moving from company to company, just working on this low hanging fruit. Others stay after the first set, and focus on next issues. Then there are the architects that typically come through last and address high-strategy issues such as framework and infrastructure changes, after which the first set of people is needed again. That the architects are involved last is one of the many ongoing issues in information security. Learn which phase you prefer, so you can identify when these corporate shifts happen and move to the next company.

You can also identify when you're stuck if you spend several months just addressing one class of issue in the code base. While there are some systems that need a year's worth of work to mitigate SQL injection issues, most developers choose to implement a global input validator and make sure that all classes of input types are handled there. The same approach can apply to other common validation issues, such as cross site scripting, request forgery, and the less common injection attack types like LDAP. If you spend too much time addressing a single class of flaw, it often indicates that your organization is operating in a break/fix mode and not making strategic progress. If you can't remove issues in the code faster than the other developers are putting them in, it's probably time to leave.

HOW TO GET OUT

There are many levels of work for a coder/developer. If you stay in this area, you may find a career's worth of work. However, if you want to shift focus, you can find an easy jump to system and network administration, as those roles are often made a lot easier with some scripting. At a more advanced level, programming skills will be useful in penetration testing and quality assurance. If you focus on code assessments, you can find a place on an assessment team focusing on internal code at various companies or departments.

Just as you improve your skills before you get your specific coder/developer job, you can do the same thing when jumping into another role. Find out what languages are likely to be needed in your future job and spend some time at your current job learning them. Again, once you have the basics down, you can pick up the new languages or frameworks you're going to need surprisingly quickly.

CRITICAL WARNINGS

The biggest risk you take as a developer is getting caught in a dead-end job as an application expert. New developers are often given legacy projects that are painful to learn and even more painful to maintain. If you excel at this kind of work, it is likely that you will never get anything else. It's important to be involved in an organization's future rather than its past. Although there is more risk of failing on new ventures, there are also more learning opportunities. By pursuing the future, you are much less likely to get trapped where you don't learn anything new, but also feel you can't move because you're indispensable where you are.

- "Premature optimization is the root of all evil." – Donald Knuth
- What to expect: Occasional bouts of boredom and frustration adding spice to a daily work life that involves repeated tasks and time-driven goals.
- As you develop code: Remember that people other than you will have to work with it later, including your future self, so make sure the design, algorithms and paradigms are understandable by others and that your choices and reasoning are documented.

Combat laziness: Experiment with "code katas" and self-driven language exploration to maximize your professional development and avoid falling into ruts.

Table 1.4 Role at a Glance—Coder-Developer

Hours	Travel	Stress Level	Creativity	Flexibility	Stability
8–12 hours/day	Usually none	Low	High	Low	High
General job duties	Application design, working out requirements, writing specification, coding from specifications, documentation, some project management, and a lot of debugging and troubleshooting.				
Learning	This role has a great deal of learning potential, if you wish to pursue it. It is also sadly easy to get caught in a rut when you "take a break" because learning is hard. However, if you dig into it, you can learn how the internal structure of specific languages will constrain the thinking of developers, which in turn affects how different security layers can be implemented. Diving deeper, you can learn about memory management and gain a deeper understanding as to how memory protections function on a modern operating system. Looking laterally, as you use different libraries, you will learn how those libraries both speed development and restrict future options. Learning opportunities in this role is very high, but you'll have to drive yourself through the process as there will be few formal options available to you.				
Advancement	Typically, people advance into the role as an entry level position or laterally from System Administrator and Network Administrator. From this role, people can expect to advance to Security Assessment and Penetration Testing. These skills are particularly useful if you ever wish to get into custom exploit development, Security Architect, Security Consultant or Security Management. Culturally, most organizations will provide little in the way of formal advancement paths. You can realistically expect to move towards a team lead position if you stay in this role, eventually moving into manager. You can also find a lot of flexibility to move around within large organizations, as the development process will help you to familiarize yourself with the business logic in numerous departments.				

1.5 TIER 1—SYSTEM ADMINISTRATOR

INTRODUCTION

"You can be replaced by a small shell script."

— Bill Hassell

There are a many variations in the job of System Administrator. The flexibility of this job is generally dependent on the size of the organization you are working for. In some organizations, your job would be to keep a small handful of servers patched and troubleshoot them when they act up. In other organizations, you may be responsible for all the servers and, as needed, the workstations. Smaller organizations may require you to also involve yourself in networking and vendor review.

There are also two approaches to how one conducts system administration: reactive and proactive. While there is a spectrum on how you work within each approach, the two approaches are sufficiently different as to warrant separate discussion.

REACTIVE SYSTEM ADMINISTRATION

Reactive system administration is the most common approach to the work and is also known as "constant fire fighting." Many organizations have enough problems that you can be kept extremely busy moving from figurative fire to figurative fire. You may be required to quickly build new systems for a project team that only recently thought to involve the infrastructure team in their activities. You may have to apply emergency patches to address vulnerability assessments and penetration tests. You will also have to troubleshoot why systems suddenly stop working, schedule emergency reboots, and build replacement systems for failing hardware. While failing hardware is much less of a problem in these days of virtual environments, it does still occur.

As a reactive system administrator, your goal will be to make things a little bit better every day. But your ultimate goal is to become a proactive system administrator. This is done by implementing more proactive processes and the supporting technology. However, you will seldom be given the time to do so, so expect a lot of additional work in the evenings and on weekends. When I (Josh More) was working such a role, a very effective strategy was to work a Sunday through Thursday week, which opened up Sundays for patching, research, and implementing new projects.

PROACTIVE SYSTEM ADMINISTRATION

Proactive system administration is becoming more popular in companies following Agile principles and in mature service firms. In these roles, your job is to create server templates from which new systems may be built, run automated management infrastructure (such as patching, monitoring and configuration management), and create scripts to automate common tasks. A lot of proactive administration involves monitoring scripts. Typical monitoring scripts start from a centralized system that simply checks for open ports on a periodic basis. However, in a true proactive environment, these scripts will evolve over time and start to model the actual business logic. This level of monitoring may move toward an operationally focused quality assurance team, but in most organizations it's part of system administration.

As a proactive system administrator, your goal will be to automate as much of your job as possible. This will involve creating and administrating the systems that administrate other systems. Tools like Microsoft's SCCM and WSUS are common, as are open source configuration management tools like Puppet. There are also many organization-specific proprietary tools that are used in this space. These jobs tend to become boring if you fail to continuously strive for better monitoring. However, going after better and better monitoring may eventually cause conflict with developers and network administrators, so you need to work carefully with such groups and not cause political issues.

A LITTLE BIT OF PROGRAMMING

System administration is not a programming role, but learning a little bit of programming can be extremely helpful. Modern Microsoft Windows systems often have PowerShell installed, which can be used to provide far more detail about system internals than more traditional methods of monitoring such as WMI and SNMP. Linux and UNIX systems have typically more language options, although Bash, Perl, and Python are the most common. While you do not have to be an expert in any of these languages, reaching the intermediate level will save you a great deal of time on your daily tasks and help you understand how such systems work internally.

HOW TO BREAK IN

System Administration jobs are the next easiest to get after Help Desk. Organizations often face a lack of system administrators as their current set of admins improve their skills and move on to different jobs or as the organization grows to require more systems. Breaking into such a role often requires a few basic skills and the ability to demonstrate that you can patch systems without causing unexpected problems. More advanced levels within the role would require you to demonstrate your ability to predict which changes would and would not be likely to cause problems and obtain the buy-in from affected business units.

If you're starting without any of those skills, it would be wise to develop skills with monitoring and management tools. Do a search on LinkedIn for your target company and look at the resumes of people who used to work there. Their skill lists will give you an idea as to what technologies they use. If they use open-source technologies, download a copy of Oracle VirtualBox or other virtual machine environment and build a small test environment so you can try out the tools. Document your learning process in a series of blogs and, if you can find a problem that others have had (by looking on forums), write a short post on how to resolve it. That will set you above the others competing for the same job.

If your target firm uses proprietary technologies like Microsoft Windows and management tools, its more difficult. If you can afford it, consider purchasing a year of the Microsoft Developer Network (MSDN) Operating Systems subscription. It's a bit expensive, but much cheaper than purchasing the software separately and it gives you licenses and download rights for all current Microsoft operating systems. From there, you can build any pure Microsoft environment you need. Then, if your target uses other management tools, try to sign up for a free 30-day trial with those vendors to familiarize yourself with the technology. This won't be as good as real experience, but it's much more than what the average job applicant does, so it should give you an edge.

HOW TO IMPROVE YOUR SKILLS

The most critical thing you can do to improve your skills is to invest in time management and metrics. Use a stopwatch or timer to track short tasks; use a diary or calendar to track longer tasks. System administration is about managing your time. Any daily work task that takes five minutes will cost over 20 hours a year, or over half of a work week. Even if it takes 20 hours to automate that daily five minute task, the automation will break-even in a year. Once automated, those hours can be used for other tasks.

Invest in time management to get dividends of more time. The better you understand how you spend the details of your day, the better you'll be able to determine where to focus your automation efforts.

Once you've identified where your time goes, you should review each task you do and ask yourself these two questions:

1. Does this involve so little thinking that it can happen automatically?
2. What does success look like and is there a way to write my script so that if the success condition isn't met what are the consequences: can the changes be undone automatically or I am alerted right away?

If you approach your skill growth in this way, you can develop rapidly and in ways that directly help your employer. From there, it's a matter of understanding your systems to the maximum extent possible. If you learn well from books, Microsoft Press books are very good explorations of Microsoft systems internals. For Linux systems, study them component by component, spend a month exploring the Apache web server, then a month exploring Apache modules like ModSecurity. One component per month is a good rule of thumb, but if you are extremely dependent on one component, such as Apache Tomcat or JBoss, spend more time.

Develop your skills at home in directions you'd like to go but that cannot yet be justified at work. If you are the local expert in a particular tool, the more valuable you become and the more chances you'll have to learn further.

RECOGNIZING WHEN YOU'RE STUCK

People typically get stuck in system administration roles when they or their employers are resistant to automation. By embracing automation, numerous options open up for other fields. If, however, you find yourself unable to automate for any reason and doing exactly the same thing day to day, week to week, and month to month, you may grow bored and your work will suffer.

As with log review, if you are successful with automation, you'll have time to invest in skill growth for other areas. If you enjoy development, you could look into coding monitoring scripts that mimic the way a user uses your systems. You can also do counter-coding and code repeating attack scripts to ensure that a system change doesn't inadvertently disable a security layer. Set up an internal wiki and start documenting; then, at a later date, tie that into your monitoring script so the documentation is automatically kept up-to-date. If your team does not have a good log review practice, you can look into addressing automated log review through system alerting, or adding a log management appliance to your system inventory.

Any of these skills will help boost your understanding of the field and increase your capabilities both on and off the job.

HOW TO GET OUT

Leaving a system administration job is easy. Once you have such a job under your belt, finding others like it is remarkably simple. There's almost always a need in the market, so there is a lot of movement within the system administration world. However, moving from system administration to a more security-focused job can be challenging. Hopefully, you used the time in the job to automate much of your environment so that, by now, you are skilled in at least one scripting language. This will help if you wish to refocus on the attack side of the industry and move into penetration testing.

Outside of attack, analysis is one of the better areas to move into, as your experience with systems will make it far easier to assess and remove false positives. Common analysis roles include Security Assessment, Risk Assessment, and Auditing. Also, if it turns out that you enjoy system administration and wish to continue the same sort of work, but more of a focus on security, you may wish to consider taking a Vulnerability Management role.

Any of these roles will be relatively easy leaps from where you find yourself after a few years of system administration.

CRITICAL WARNINGS

The biggest warning about system administration is that you will spend most of your days deep in the internals of live production systems. If you make a mistake, it could directly affect your company's profitability. In some industries, such as healthcare, it could have a direct impact on people's lives. The trite advice is "don't screw up," but this misses the great importance of the Learning stage of your career. If you don't screw up, you'll never learn. The trick is finding a way to screw up without causing huge problems for the organization or your career.

One common way to address this concern is to build a staging environment where you test everything before production. Some organizations do not provide funding for such an environment, and many of those that do will refuse to fund the systems needed to keep the staging environment completely synchronized with production. If you find an organization that wants you to do system administration but will not give you what is required to do it safely, and is, at the same time, very risk-averse, you may wish to pursue employment elsewhere.

- What to expect: System administration is boring work for lazy people, but exciting with many technical and social challenges for self-driven experimentalists.
- As you manage systems: Small changes may cause significant and critical problems within the environment. Expect sudden spikes of stress without warning mixed with long-ranging quiet periods. Also expect a significant amount of evening and weekend work and sometimes holidays, as many systems can't be worked on during the day.
- Combat laziness: Use automation everywhere you can to keep the boredom of your job from giving you a sense of complacency.

Table 1.5 Role at a Glance—Systems Administrator

Hours	Travel	Stress Level	Creativity	Flexibility	Stability
8–12 hours/day	Usually none	Low to High	Low to High	Low to High	High
General job duties	Resolving escalated trouble tickets. Troubleshooting. Writing documentation. Writing scripts. Backup and restoration. Specifying, reviewing, testing, installing new software and hardware. Patch management. Future platform planning, budgeting.				
Learning	Some – This job can be what you make of it. If you are very self driven, learning opportunities will abound. However, this is also a job in which many people feel comfortable "coasting" – going through life doing only the bare minimum needed to keep their job. If you approach it as per the latter, you will likely never get good enough to leap from system administration to security. However, if you're overly driven, you may make the "coasters" look bad, which could have political ramifications for you. As you learn, pay attention to who gives resistance to your ideas, why they say they are resisting and why they might actually be resisting. In general, if you can structure a safe test of a new process or technology and your ideas are still rejected, there may be an internal political issue that you don't know about.				
Advancement	From Network Administrator or Log Reviewer – Typically into an entry level position or laterally. Advancement or lateral move to Network Administrator, Security Assessment, Risk Assessment, Incident Responder, Auditor and Vulnerability Manager. It can also serve as critical experience for Security Architect, Security Consultant or Security Management. If you work with patching, you may be able to move to Vulnerability Manager or to a leadership role within the systems team. However, it is more likely that you will have to either change employers or petition a superior to move out of the role.				

TIER 1— SYSTEM ADMINISTRATOR STORY

1.5.1

ALAN WAGGONER

My InfoSec story is not terribly interesting. In reality, it relates directly to my current position. Therefore, I took the initiative and used one week of my vacation time, paid for a Novell IntraNetWare 4.11 Administration class, and a hotel for a week. After completing the course, I paid for the certification test myself and became a CNA (Certified Novell Administrator). When a position opened up in the IT department I was able to demonstrate my personal commitment to earning the position.

A few years later, I took the position I currently hold (it was a one-person IT department at the time). I continue to do my best to keep up-to-date with current technologies and trends with a combination of reading, webinars/webcasts, and professional training. You can never stop learning when you hold an IT/security position. If you do, you quickly become irrelevant. Keeping an open mind and being able to be flexible is very important if you want to be successful. Also, like it or not, politics plays an important role if you want to procure funding for your projects and get management approval for your policy recommendations. The soft skills of person-to-person interactions can sometimes be just as important as the technical skills, so do not ignore bettering yourself in this regard as well.

I currently hold GSEC, GSLC, and GCED certifications from GIAC. I am active with the monthly OUCH! newsletter, and have contributed to the scripts for Securing the Human training videos. I have participated in the SANS open advisory board. I am also qualified as a SANS mentor, although I have not had the opportunity to mentor a class yet.

1.6 TIER 1—NETWORK ADMINISTRATOR

INTRODUCTION

> "Never underestimate the bandwidth of a station wagon full of tapes hurtling down the highway."
> — **Andrew S. Tanenbaum**

A Network Administrator's specific job duties will vary based on the size and structure of the organization it is in. The focus will be on the transport infrastructure (routers, switches, firewalls, and wireless access points) used by the organization. In some cases, cable plant and network wiring will also be part of your job. In smaller organizations, there will often be additional job duties assisting with servers or even end-user workstations.

NETWORKING ROLE

In many organizations, especially larger ones, a Network Architect provides the high-level guidance for the enterprise network. A Network Engineer defines the specific configuration for each of the different pieces of hardware, and the Network Administrator makes day-to-day changes necessary to meet the business needs. For example, when a new computer is set up, as a Network Administrator you would be responsible for ensuring that the physical network port that computer will be connected to is configured appropriately. When a new application server is being set up, you would be responsible for modifying the access control lists (ACLs) on the firewall that are necessary for clients to be able to access this machine. Some organizations have dedicated network security staff just for firewalls.

In smaller organizations the Network Administrator may perform all of the above roles.

HOW TO BREAK IN

Breaking into networking varies by organization. Many organizations look for certifications such as a CCNA (Cisco Certified Network Associate) or less commonly a JNCIA–Junos (Juniper Networks Certified Associate Junos) as evidence of your skill set. There are many books and courses out there on getting network credentials. If you have a specific organization in mind before you start working toward your credential, check job skill requirements to focus your studies. Check the job postings of that organization, and search on-line forums for that organization's email addresses. Ask around at user group meetings. Keep in mind that if you have strong demonstrable skills in one platform, many organizations will view that as adequate for moving to another platform. However, if you already have the skills on the platform they are using, you are a stronger candidate. For large organizations where you must get past an HR screen, a certification is often mandatory, unless you know a hiring manager well. If you can convince the manager that you have either the necessary skills or learning aptitude to succeed in the field, that may be enough to get you a position.

The most common mistake people make when working for their credential is focusing exclusively on what it takes to pass the test, rather than learning the material. Just because you can make it past the HR screen is no guarantee of success in the interview or on the job. Also, these are the skills that are providing the foundation of your security knowledge for breaking into the security field. Don't take short-cuts in getting certifications.

If coursework or self-study is not the best option, help desk roles at smaller organizations will often provide the opportunity to learn networking skills. Smaller organizations cannot afford dedicated help desk personnel so they will often be asked to assist beyond simply assisting end-users, and this may give you the opportunity to learn networking skills. For example, basic help desk troubleshooting may include network diagnostics down to the physical cable plant and network infrastructure layers.

HOW TO IMPROVE YOUR SKILLS

This role provides multiple ways to improve your skills. Whenever you are working under the direction of a more advanced role (such as a Network Engineer or Architect), take any opportunity you have to learn the reasoning behind their decisions. Do not be surprised to discover that sometimes the decision is business- or risk-based, rather than purely technical.

As you are going through your own job duties Evaluate why you are doing them for the organization. Are your tasks being done the most effective and efficient way possible? If not, can you identify an underlying business driver (such as a compliance requirement) that requires this way of doing business? This evaluation process, and understanding the business drivers for your role, will make you more effective in advanced roles. If this process is not required, develop an alternate, more efficient, method. Whether it is implemented or not, the processes involved will help develop your skill sets both technical and non-technical.

To grow your skills through courses and certifications, many vendors have certification tracks to advance your skills and career. Some vendors provide online labs in which to learn. If not create a lab network at home using used equipment from online auction sites to practice and study for these exams.

RECOGNIZING WHEN YOU'RE STUCK

If you do not advance, either formally or informally, within a few years, then you are likely starting to become stuck in this role. If three years into the job your duties match those you did after being on the job three months, then you are likely stuck and need to figure out how to best extricate yourself from the situation.

HOW TO GET OUT

Moving from one Network Administration role to another Network Administration role is generally easy. Having gained the experience, you are now much more attractive to other employers. If you enjoy networking, and have advanced your skills, moving up to a Network Engineer role is often an option. If being in networking is not for you, then often lateral moves into System Administration, Security Coordinator, or Coder/Developer are possible, depending on what other skills you have.

The key to getting out from your current situation are the skills you have developed while you were in the role. Did you work with your company's compliance team to develop auditing procedures? Did you develop techniques for automating changes using scripting languages? Did you run a standard scan developed by the security team after you made firewall changes? Those types of experiences will help provide opportunities for advancement into other roles.

CRITICAL WARNINGS

Organizations that do not provide any means to test changes on non-production systems are worrisome. While few will be able to have an exact duplicate of their production system in their test labs, good organizations will have labs for testing system upgrades and significant configuration changes. If you do not have the opportunity to learn, either through interactions with more advanced peers, or through experimentation in a test lab, then future advancement will be more difficult.

If you find yourself only doing exactly what you are told, without taking any time to investigate the environment or improve your skills, then you are very likely going to stagnate in this role and should consider lateral moves into areas involving tasks that you find more engaging.

Table 1.6 Role at a Glance—Network Administrator

Hours	Travel	Stress Level	Creativity	Flexibility	Stability
8–12 hours/day, after hours	Varies, often none	Generally Low with spikes	Generally Low	Low	High
General job duties	Making standard changes to network equipment based on predefined procedures.				
Learning	Can be high in the right organization. Some environments require creativity.				
Advancement	Many opportunities are available for those that take the time to advance their skill sets. Advancement may require changing employers, but advancement can occur within the same organization. If you stay in networking, you can advance to Network Engineer and from there to Network Architect (varying levels of Subject Matter Expert).				
	For those who move into more security focused roles, potential moves into Vulnerability Management, Risk Assessment, or Incident Responder may be possible depending on the skills you have developed while working in this role, and the organization.				

TIER 1—NETWORK ADMINISTRATOR

1.6.1

DAVID HENNING

My undergrad degree is in biology. I was even enrolled in a PhD program for molecular biology when I realized I needed a dramatic and risky career change. I was able to build enough skills to switch into sysadmin work during the dot-com boom of the late 01990s.

I had been working about two years as a sysadmin in Texas when I got my break to get into Info-Sec. I had connections in DC through my existing job in Texas, which got my resume in front of my eventual boss who was looking for an assistant to do firewall admin and other work.

I was looking to move to the DC area. I'd had other interviews that hadn't worked out but in 01998 the job market was in my favor. Once at the job in DC, I was able to get support from management to attend SANS in Baltimore. I was able to volunteer time helping their IDNet demo where IDS vendors would plug in and show their product. This led to selecting a particular vendor for our first IDS at my job. From there, our group moved out to start up a security consulting and 24×7 monitoring group. I had an opportunity to work with some well-known folks in the industry that were part of the attrition.org site.

Then we all got unceremoniously bought and laid off by a bigger company. That hellacious story is too long to cover here but serves as a great learning experience. I was lucky again, had a neighbor move in next door to me who worked for another small consulting and monitoring shop. I worked for them for two years before getting tired of life on the road and found my current position where I'm going on 10 years. During that time I've continued to grow my skills, attend conferences, etc.

Maybe the best thing I've learned is not just the direction I think I want to go but also the directions I didn't want to go. Attending conferences and getting time to sit in small groups with the biggest names in the industry showed me aspects of pen testing, code development, and vulnerability discovery, which made me decide that was not going to be a successful path for my personal career. I currently manage a team of 3 analysts for an internal SOC.

TIER 1—SECURITY COORDINATOR

1.7

INTRODUCTION

The role of Security Coordinator is broad; in some organizations, it is several distinct but closely related positions. Other titles that overlap this role include Security Analyst, Security Consultant, Security Facilitator, Security Liaison, Security Officer, Security Planner, Security Manager. For any of these names, "Security" can be replaced by or supplemented with "Risk," for a similar but risk- rather than security-focused role.

Security Coordinator is a full-time job, but project and management responsibilities in some organizations may require significantly more time. The Security Coordinator role is highly dependent upon the organization and bureaucracy of an organization and itself is part of that bureaucracy, but it can also be the point of flexibility within the security process.

Some organizations tightly define the Security Coordinator role, and the security policy may prevent them from performing some types of security or technical tasks.

Actual responsibilities will vary, but may include a mix of business analyst, project manager, document writer/editor, technician, engineer, architect, security/risk assessment, vendor relations, auditor, and even investigator. A Security Coordinator may perform these other roles or work directly or consume the deliverables of these specializations.

These roles usually have no direct reports or subordinates, even if they have the words "management" or "officer" in their titles. However, some organizations will directly or indirectly assign legal sign-off responsibility to the Security Coordinator so stress can be high.

Depending upon the organization's culture, geographic distribution, and specific responsibilities, travel can range from none to 100% based on the project and management aspects of the role and the wide range of expertise that may need to be consulted.

Some organizations combine information security and physical security in this role. Although integrated physical/information security is still unusual, it's a long term trend and can be an excellent way to cross over to the other side of security.

Security Coordinator can be a stepping stone to higher levels of management, or into any of the security or technical areas that touch this role in a particular organization.

HOW TO BREAK IN

In some organizations, Security Coordinator is a natural progression and even promotion from non-security and non-technical roles. For example, the Security Coordinator may be required to be very knowledgeable about the organization, which may preclude a deep security or technical background; if so, they will have to depend upon others for this expertise. In this case, having good management skills and expressing an interest in security can be enough to get started. Note that organizations with non-technical Security Coordinators may not value security as a career. Other organizations may expect a general specialist who can do everything, or at least try.

HOW TO IMPROVE YOUR SKILLS

All of the other roles are places for a Security Coordinator can learn.

Good writing skills are important for both writing and reviewing security documents, policies, procedures, security assessments.

Understand the roles of each of the different people have who work with the Security Coordinator.

Be able to possibly perform the tasks of at least one of the people who work with the Security Coordinator.

RECOGNIZING WHEN YOU'RE STUCK

Security Coordinators usually have to work with the existing security infrastructure. They may have little to no authority to change policy, purchase or implement new technologies, or accept risk. When these or other limitations of the role become frustrating, it may be time to look for new jobs and develop the applicable skills to address these issues.

HOW TO GET OUT

Because the Security Coordinator can be in the middle of the security process, there can be clear places to move on, both in lateral moves to peer roles and promotions to roles in technology, policy, and management. Because the Security Coordinator role can vary significantly, simply getting a new job at a new organization can make all the difference and be a way to grow.

Table 1.7 Role at a Glance—Security Coordinator

Hours	Travel	Stress Level	Creativity	Flexibility	Stability
8–10 hours/day	None to High	Medium to High	Low to High	Low	High
General job duties	Scheduling/running meetings and follow-up. Project management. Writing reports. Analysis. Budgeting.				
Learning	Whether an organization which requires the knowledge, or provides a team of experts, there is a wide range of things to learn.				
Advancement	Security Coordinator can be a stepping stone to higher levels of management, or into any of the security or technical areas that touch this role in a particular organization.				

1.8 TIER 1—TRAINER-EDUCATOR

INTRODUCTION

> *"Educational* refers to the process, not the object. Although, come to think of it, some of my teachers could easily have been replaced by a cheeseburger."
>
> **— Terry Pratchett**

A Trainer-Educator is not an information security-specific role, but is particularly important in information security. Basic information technology skills are now so widespread and expected that most organizations do not bother teaching these skills. However, even basic information security awareness is frequently not known at all, and information security technical skills even less so. This is one of several reasons why information security is still immature, and is even getting worse. The Trainer-Educator is on the front-line to make information security better.

A Trainer-Educator may have a full-time job elsewhere and do training and educating as a second part-time job during evenings and weekends. A trainer-educator may also have another, possibly non-technical job. Travel time may be over weekends to allow for full work weeks of training. There may involve a lot of travel, even 100%, as it's usually more efficient for one person to travel to meet with multiple students. Although distance learning is becoming more common it still lacks the advantages of meeting face to face.

Stress levels are highly variable and depend upon management, resources, travel, and students.

Stability can be high, as some organizations and industries have mandatory yearly training requirements. But being only yearly may mean frequent travel to get to the students. Information security is constantly changing, so the need for teaching remains constant.

There can be a place for creativity, depending upon flexibility in developing course materials. Requirements can range from completely fixed legally mandated training materials that can't be altered or deviated from, while others give complete flexibility even in the same organization.

Flexibility can be limited due to fixed recurring class schedules.

Trainer-Educators may have very limited opportunity for advancement, as most organizations have small education departments. Dedicated training organizations may have more advancement possibilities. There is opportunity for the specialized Trainer-Educator independent security consultant.

HOW TO BREAK IN

The Trainer-Educator is well-established in information technology, but tends to exist in organizations dedicated to training and education. A background in training and education is a plus, but technical skills are required to work in any related job beyond basic end user instruction. Most information security Trainer-Educators have a technical background but spend part of their time doing training and education, typically in colleges and universities, and sometimes corporate training centers.

As with the Help Desk role, there is often an opportunity to get into the Trainer-Educator role by being the local "computer tutor" in the organization. Unlike the local "computer person" who fixes the computer and moves on, the "computer tutor" helps end users understand what went wrong and instructs them how to fix it in the future. This usually takes more time at first, but in the end can result in less time total spent fixing problems.

HOW TO IMPROVE YOUR SKILLS

What to learn depends on where you came from and where you want to go.

Trainer-Educators who got there by teaching users to avoid future problems may have good technical skills, but no formal training in how to train people. A common approach is one-on-one tutoring sessions. These can be very rewarding and effective for the one student and Trainer-Educator, but they are time-inefficient. With no other training, a computer tutor can attempt to develop the experience of these learning sessions into simple written course material, a video, or—with more technical knowledge—a website or automated course material.

Educator-Trainers from non-technical academic backgrounds have skills and experience in the learning and teaching process, but not the technical material. They may have to rely upon existing training material and fixed class plans. They can benefit from learning the underpinnings of what they teach—not just the material they use now, but more advanced material their students may later learn in more advanced classes taught by others. If they have Educator-Trainer co-workers they may be able to learn from them as teachers or mentors. All of the other sections in this book are also material to learn for the non-technical person or non-security technical person who wants move on to understanding more technical material.

RECOGNIZING WHEN YOU'RE STUCK

You're stuck when you dread facing a class with the same old material and you can't or aren't allowed to change it.

You're stuck when you can't see anything new in what you're teaching or what the students are asking in class.

If you're the local "computer tutor" person, you may get stuck as the "computer person" who only fixes the problems and can't get people to learn for themselves. If you're stuck here you could go elsewhere as elsewhere as a help desk engineer, network administrator or systems administrator depending upon your skills.

You're stuck when the Learn/Do/Teach cycle stops and there is no more learning, no new doing, no new teaching.

HOW TO GET OUT

If you grow tired of training others, see if there's something else you can train them to do. A lot of people who enjoy teaching wind up teaching forever and symptoms of burnout are often more about the topic you're working with and not the role itself. So see if there is anything new you could teach, if you have the option to build courseware or write books to rejuvenate your career and re-energize yourself.

If, after doing this, you decide that you still wish to move on, you should be well suited to any job involving team leadership or management.

Table 1.8 Role at a Glance—Trainer-Educator

Hours	Travel	Stress Level	Creativity	Flexibility	Stability
8–12 hours/day and after hours	None to High	Low to High	Low to High	Low	High
General job duties	Creating course materials: slide decks, presentation scripts, coordinating subject matter experts,				
Learning	Even a completely knowledgeable Trainer-Educator will learn a lot from students. A good organization will expect and provide for the training and education of Trainer/Educators.				
Advancement	May have very limited advancement as most organizations have small education departments. A dedicated training organization may have more advancement available.				

TIER 1—TRAINER-EDUCATOR

1.8.1

STEPHEN NORTHCUTT

Stephen Northcutt was a network designer for the Department of Defense. The primary tool he used in 01986 was Autocad hosted on a Sun 3 workstation, since it was much faster than a tricked-out Windows system on a 386 chip with a graphics accelerator. One day, after lunch, he was grinding some coffee beans to caffeine up, for a really complex design problem. He looked over and noticed the disk access LED on his workstation was blinking furiously. Odd! He was grinding coffee beans, not pushing his workstation around. He typed "ps" and learned his workstation was compiling software. He realized he had been hacked; there was a flaw in sendmail. Stephen felt violated and decided to switch careers to security. He wrote the Shadow IDS, and later joined SANS as an instructor, author, and manager. He retired as a SANS instructor on December 14, 02013, after logging 1.5 million miles on United Airlines, plus flights on other airlines as well.

1.9 TIER 1—QUALITY TESTER

INTRODUCTION

> "Quality is job 1.1"
>
> **— unknown**

Creating complex but still functional software is very difficult. The process to accomplish this has developed several names, such as quality testing, quality assurance, quality management, and more. Although software testing is, in effect, done by everyone who encounters that software, the formal role of quality tester is common in software engineering organizations. A quality tester's qualifications can be as simple as being the end user of the software in question, recognize flaws found and sufficiently document them. Consequently even those who otherwise lack technical skills might not merely be quality testers, they could even be excellent quality testers.

A Quality Tester can have a range from low to high technical skills. At the low end, a quality tester merely has to know how to use the software in question. This may involve highly specific and technical skills in the operation of that software. A Quality Tester doesn't have to know how the software works, or even how to write software; the critical skills for a Quality Tester are being able to consistently cause software to break and communicate to those who can then attempt to fix the problem. Hence there are opportunities for both the highly, and not so highly, technically skilled. In both cases, reproducibility and communications skills are important. If a flaw cannot be reproduced then any attempted fixes themselves cannot be tested.

Software quality testers need sufficient technical skill to operate the software and know when something has gone wrong. For some software this can be very technical and very specialized. Additionally, the tester needs good communication skills to describe what was done and what happened, so it can be reproduced by a software engineer. Most software development environment organizations have some way for end users to file bug reports. Although it may not result in a job, taking an active although unpaid role in quality testing is a way to gain experience. Some organizations will solicit external users for beta testing before a production release, typically for no compensation other than early access to products, and sometimes by getting a free or discounted commercial product.

HOW TO BREAK IN

Some organizations make heavy use of internal alpha testing, sometimes known as "dogfooding" as in "eating your own dog food." Where dogfooding is in place, there may be an expectation that all employees are part of the quality testing process. Dogfooding may also be part of the organization's culture to use it's own products and services in which case it may actually lower quality by being blinded to the competition and ordinary users.

Some amount of quality testing is often an expected part of a coding/programming job, but dedicated quality testers typically work full time. If other software development staff work long hours, it's likely that the same will be expected of quality testers.

Quality testing stress levels tend to reflect that of the rest of the software development organization, and team and management expectation. Organizations that emphasize high-quality products may stress quality testers as much or more than software engineers. Organizations that have less concern for quality may stress quality testers who want to do high-quality jobs.

Quality testing may be considered an adjunct to software engineering, either as a pathway to it, or out of it and into other areas; or quality testing may be a separate organization.

Creativity is critical to producing test cases, both in general and in detail. Even a small test item, such as "Application starts correctly," can be subject to a wide range of subtle failures.

Some organizations expect all software engineers and even other technical or even non-technical areas to engage in quality testing. A separate Quality Testing role may not exist.

Some organizations use Quality Tester as a junior position within a software engineering department, where there may be quick advancement to the primary goal of the department of software engineering. Other organizations have dedicated departments for quality testing, where advancement is through generalization, specialization, or management.

HOW TO IMPROVE YOUR SKILLS

The core qualities of a quality tester are:

- Understanding the software.
- Reproducibility
- Communication

As a Quality Tester you can become an expert user of the system, which itself may be valuable. If its not a skill you can take to other jobs, how you learned to become an expert user is itself a powerful skill. Going beyond understanding as a user can involve reading the design documents, talking with the developers, and reading and understanding the source code. If possible, talk to end users about what they do and how they use the system. Join a user group for the system, and the tools you use or could use. Read about not just your organization's products, but others as well. Learn the operating system and programming languages used for the system. If those programming languages aren't suitable for test automation, learn a language that is suitable.

Reproducibility is critical in quality testing, if you can't reproduce a problem, you may not be able to prove it exists. Study the scientific method. Learn about control and experimental groups, and why changing only one variable at a time is crucial. Precision, and your own software engineer skills to automate tests are important.

Communication skills are needed to read and completely understand requirements to be tested, writing test cases based on requirements, writing test scripts, both manual and automatic, and writing test reports which explain what was done are required.

RECOGNIZING WHEN YOU'RE STUCK

A dedicated quality tester may be stuck when the system to be tested itself is stuck. If it's not improving, if the same flaws keep showing up, if you've completely automated testing, and have nothing more to learn, if you could do the software engineer's job, but they won't let you, it's time to move on.

HOW TO GET OUT

Security product quality testing is similar to and sometimes identical to penetration testing. In some organizations, they are even the same group or will have clearly identified paths. A lateral move may be possible into pen tester, or perhaps a promotion into pen test lead. In other organizations Coder-Developer may be the normal career path. Depending upon the systems tested other roles may also be suitable such as System Administrator or Network Administrator.

Table 1.9 Role at a Glance—Quality Tester

Hours	Travel	Stress Level	Creativity	Flexibility	Stability
8–12 hours/day after hours	Low	Varies	High	High	Varies
General job duties	Writing test plans and contributing to software engineering process scheduling. Reviewing and troubleshooting test results. Reading source code. Detailed troubleshooting reports and possibly writing and submitting source code changes.				
Learning	A Quality Tester doesn't require a software engineering background, but will benefit greatly, and in becoming an experienced QA person, will understanding in many aspects of software engineering.				
Advancement	Some organizations use Quality Tester as a junior position within a software engineering department where they may be quick advancement to the primary goal of the department of software engineering. Other organizations have dedicated departments for quality testing where advancement is through generalization, specialization, or management.				

TIER 1—QUALITY TESTER STORY

1.9.1

MAK KOLYBABI

I think if I had a defining moment it would be back in high school (probably 01999/02000). My girlfriend back then spent all her time on a Perl-based CGI webchat called Socko.net. Why didn't she just use IRC like a normal geek, I'll never know. This chat was run by another couple of kids our age somewhere in the USA. Anyways, the security on this thing was atrocious. I'd hang out on the chat to spend time with her—she lived across the city—but instead of actively talking, I'd spend my time poking at the chat itself, out of boredom.

The code for the chat was forked from something called JellyBeanz http://www.mindreader.com/chat/chat.cgib, and was very naive: no databases only files, minimal session management, poor anti-XSS, but this was all before I knew what a database was, to be honest. What I did know was HTML, QBasic, and Perl.

One day, the admins of the chat decided to add in session management code, but they did it completely wrong: you would be given a session ID when you first viewed the login page, but the site never associated an IP or username or any kind of state to the session ID. I explained the mistake to the admins, but was told that it wasn't considered a problem. So I wrote an HTML file with a <form> in it that had two <input> boxes: one for the username that you wanted to be on Socko.net, and the other for a valid session ID harvested from the login page.

I then showed this HTML file to one of my friends, who refers to himself even today as The Designated Asshole of any group he's part of. He then dedicated something like a week of his life— I think it was Christmas or summer vacation, so he was on his computer every waking moment—to round-the-clock trolling of this chat. Every time a user—even an admin—logged onto Socko.net, he was waiting and would use the HTML file to become them, change their nickname to SAXON <number>, which would boot them from the session, and then /kick them with the reason "stupid".

The end result of that week was that the admins bulletproofed their session management code, banned my asshole friend from the chat (deservedly), and I learned the importance of providing a PoC with bug reports and **not** sharing information with asshole script kiddies.

1.a TIER 1—SUBJECT MATTER SPECIALIST

INTRODUCTION

> "A *philosopher* is a person who knows less and less about more and more, until he knows nothing about everything. A *scientist* is a person who knows more and more about less and less, until he knows everything about nothing."
>
> **— John Ziman**

A subject matter specialist is knowledgeable, skilled, and educated in some area. The area is not necessarily specific to information security but may instead be specific to information security in a particular area or vice versa. A specialist might be knowledgeable in information security applied to a particular industry. For example, financial services, health, medical, manufacturing, and retail are each quite different, but each typically uses identical information security technologies but applied in different ways.

Subject matter specialist hours can be long due to the work needed to maintain the specialization and being the only person who can do the job. The subject matter specialist may end up traveling a lot, possibly on short notice, for the same reasons.

Stress can be low because the job is well-understood and well-managed, or can be high due to high expectations and work load. Good management can make all the difference.

Stability can be high because no one else can do the job. However, some kinds of expertise age quickly and thus can also be unstable. For example, web application development knowledge can very quickly become out-of-date due to changing fashions and fads in languages, frameworks, and application servers.

HOW TO BREAK IN

Becoming a specialist is easy but time consuming: just know and admit to knowing more about an area than anyone else in the organization. Unless it's part of your current job, you'll have to do this learning separate from work. In the IT industry, there is a strong bias toward new tools and technologies, but most real work is done by legacy systems. Trying to be a specialist in the very latest technology can work, but not only does it require constantly keeping up-to-date, there may also be competition with the rest of the organization. For a very small subject area, this is easy: just find something that is so obscure that no one knows or even wants to know anything about it. However, if no one wants to know it, the information might not be particularly useful, and thus would be difficult to get paid for knowing it. But just because no one wants to know something doesn't mean it's not worth knowing. For example, in an organization dominated by a single vendor or technology, the organizational culture may look down upon any alternative vendors or technologies. Outside the organization, knowledge of these vendors or technologies may be nothing special, but within the organization such specialized knowledge could be the path to distinction despite being looked down upon. Choose your specialization carefully.

An overlooked, or unpopular area could be desperate for a specialist. A specialty might not be technology, but instead be a different part of the company, a geographic region, or even a particular work schedule. For example the finance department with a special COBOL environment that no other IT people want to admit even exists; backwater field offices that lack prestige; highly unpopular overnight, third shift, weekend, and holiday operations.

A useful amount of knowledge and skill usually takes quite a while to learn. But there are some areas where there are so few true experts that it takes little effort to become a relative expert. Finding these areas either within your organization or outside, is itself specialized knowledge. If you and others can't find the specialized knowledge in an organization, consider becoming the meta-specialist, the specialist who finds and knows the other specialists.

Some specializations are highly dependent upon the organization. For example, retailers often need people who know the Payment Card Industry Data Security Standards (PCI-DSS). It could be a particular information technology, an information security domain, technique, requirement, or an industry. In some organizations, information security is itself a candidate for subject matter specialist.

Consider how a specialization may fit your goals. Learn about that area and see if it's a fit for you. Find subject matter specialist or even better a subject matter specialist (SME) inside or outside your organization. Find a mentor/master. See the "How to Learn" section in this chapter for more details.

Learn from an existing specialist or expert in the organization. Determine what existing subject matter specialists or SMEs the organization may have. An organization chart, HR career path documentation, and the organizations mission, goals, and other direction can help. See Josh More's book *Job Reconnaissance* for more details. If there isn't a specialist or SME already, this is an opportunity to become that person.

Some organizations are too small, or have a corporate culture that favors generalists; they will not benefit enough from or will not appreciate a subject matter specialist. Some organizations can't afford the resource costs of specialist, even taking into account the benefits.

Find an area in the organization that has no subject matter specialist, but for which the organization has a use. Any of the job areas in this book are suitable for being a specialist, although these areas are broad enough that few organizations won't already have people who already are, or are becoming specialists—but if it's open, it will need to be filled, so take that opportunity. Usually, however, more specialization is needed. A specialist could specialize by industry, technology, vendor, or technique, or be performance-focused.

HOW TO IMPROVE YOUR SKILLS

Growing as a specialist can be by depth or breadth, or both. A specialist who goes for particular depth will learn even more about a smaller detailed area. For example, a database management administrator specialist (DBA specialist) is usually already a specialist in a particular database, so the next step might be another function of databases, such as security. However, security can itself be divided into further areas, such as Confidentiality, Integrity, and Availability. DBA specialists usually already have some attention paid to Availability, but can go deeper to High Availability, or further still to Fault Tolerant. This level of detail also usually requires special hardware, so that is a further specialization. At some depth, going wide again may be the right choice. This is highly dependent upon the organization, and future job direction.

Specialists may not have the opportunities to do hands-on work, but that's how they originally learned, so it can be important to go out of the way to Do. A Coder-Developer specialist could decide to port older code to a different language. Such porting doesn't have to be strictly a learning exercise with proficiency in both languages. It can also result in a useful product that is easier to maintain. Use your existing knowledge and keep it current by applying it in new ways. The DBA specialist may decide to build an entire database environment from scratch, using current practices. This should be easy for a DBA, but if it's been a while, things may have changed.

Specialists have a lot to offer, and Teaching others even a fraction of their expertise can be valuable. This can be done through personal instruction, mentoring, documentation, and cross-training. A Quality Tester specialist can Teach someone else, perhaps even in another role, such as Patch Management, to do regression testing of a patch and troubleshoot problems.

RECOGNIZING WHEN YOU'RE STUCK

It's best to recognize before becoming stuck, as specialists tend to be valued in their area but may not have sufficient qualifications to transition to another area and be as well-regarded, and thus comparably paid. Particularly bad is staying in one area long enough to become specialist merely by default, but without sufficient skills to go elsewhere.

HOW TO GET OUT

Some organizations may allow a subject matter specialist to move laterally, where aspects of their experience can be applied in new ways. For example, a database performance specialist might move into database security, or a backup and recovery specialist might get into forensics. Doing well in a specialization may also provide the credentials to go into a completely different area.

A specialist might move up to Subject Matter Expert (SME), see Tier 3, in the same specialty, this might otherwise be the same work but also might have to be at another organization.

Table 1.a Role at a Glance—Subject Matter Specialist

Hours	Travel	Stress Level	Creativity	Flexibility	Stability
8–12 hours/day after hours	Varies None to High	Low to High	High	Medium	High
General job duties	Research. Documentation. Mentoring Teaching				
Learning	The SME can be by definition limited in learning as there may be little more to learn. Although, few areas so small and so well known that there is truly nothing more to learn.				
Advancement	An obvious next step is Subject Matter Expert (SME), if that position is already filled then keep learning from the SME. If you can't learn any more in that position but can't get promoted to SME, consider Chapter 4.0 Boosting especially in your subject matter area to prepare for new opportunites. Also consider lateral moves to a complementary position within Tier 1, or leverage your subject matter knowledge to Tier 2.				

TIER 2.0—DO

2.0

DOING

> "Life can only be understood backwards, but it must be lived fowards."
>
> **— Søren Kierkegaard**

The second tier of Learn/Do/Teach is, unsurprisingly, actually doing things. From a career perspective, if you never do anything, you don't have a career. Without a career, you can't prove yourself to prospective hiring managers, and the opportunity will instead go to those who can prove themselves. More importantly, if that learning is not applied, you will never know if you're right. Learning builds upon learning, and if you build knowledge on the top of faulty knowledge, the entire construction can fall down at the worst time.

By focusing on actually doing things, either with work or personal projects, you'll get feedback on incorrect assumptions. For example, bad network routing has immediate feedback; traffic simply will not flow. But in general, a defense cannot be tested until it meets an adversary, so you may wish to build adversary-style testing into your Do process. This will be easier for some topics than others, but the more you test as you go, the less time you'll spend going down dead ends.

TEST-DRIVEN DEVELOPMENT/SPRINTING

Developers often start with basic requirements such as "Application A must have feature B." This is easy to do when application A has few features. However, the more functionality you add to an application, the more you risk breaking an existing feature. To reduce the chances of this happening, some developers have embraced a concept called "test-driven development." With this approach, each application is assigned a suite of tests that must pass for the code to be accepted for any further development to occur. This can be applied to the Doing phase, although the particular testing technologies may not apply outside of the development world—but the core idea is the same.

When you are working on anything new, it is very likely that you don't understand it as well as you think you do. Verify your knowledge and skills later by creating a list of goals first. Such a list makes it easier to stay on track, to know when you've accomplished your goals, and know when you haven't.

This approach can be adapted into the time-based sprint method. The tasks needed to reach a goal are separated into sprints, with each sprint taking a fraction of the total time spent reaching a goal.

Between each sprint is a break to rest, test, review the past sprint, and to plan future sprints. Although some goals can be reached with a single sprint, this has several disadvantages. If the goal isn't reached, the time needed to accomplish the goal was wasted. Worse, it probably isn't clear when and where any problems occurred.

If, instead, the time spent is divided into multiple sprints, and each sprint is followed by a test, then when a test fails, it's clear when there is a problem. Once the problem is resolved, another sprint may begin.

By moving from Learning to Doing, your path constricts somewhat, but to greater advantage. Using sprints may feel awkward at first, but over time, you can get a lot more done in a lot less time by using a time clock. Start by building a small list of goals to accomplish in a day. At the end of the day, refer to your list to see which ones you got done. Then, as you improve at it, try the same thing for half a day, an hour, or 15 -minutes.

As you get better at these sprints, you'll be learning more quickly, but also creating work that is useful to others as each sprint is linked to a desired feature. This puts you in the position of building a portfolio to show others, as well as creating a group of hopefully grateful users. Both of these improve your leverage when trying to move into another job. It's important to track this over time, because, unlike other fields, information security is necessarily a multidisciplinary world.

INFORMATION SECURITY AND SILOS

The word "silo" is used a lot in business to indicate that a person or team is stuck in their area of expertise, and is unable to work with other people in other fields. In technology, for example, it is common for someone who has learned how to code in Java to avoid working with .Net. It's common for someone who works on the help desk to resist working with the server team, even if working together would allow both teams to solve a problem more quickly.

This tendency is, in part, due to corporate structures that tie salaries and bonuses to measurements that do not support cross-disciplinary work. However, it is also true that many people just get uncomfortable when forced to look at things in different ways. However, as an information security professional, you must resist this. To be successful over an entire career, you must know the basics of many different disciplines, such as being a database administrator, programmer, or project manager.

In the professional world, if you focus on a single skill group, you can get extremely good at it. If you don't specialize, you're unlikely to ever get as good at any given one as you would if that's all you did. A lot of people are singularly focused. After all, if you have to solve a COBOL problem, you want the best person in the lead. However, there isn't a lot of COBOL left, nor other very large but otherwise uncomplicated problems. In a world with blending boundaries and increasing complexity, you need to know a little about a lot instead of the other way around.

In the era we called Y2K (ironically brought about due to abbreviation of a date field), programmers with high skill levels in COBOL and other legacy systems were in high demand. However, Y2K was solved, and since then, there's been little for those legacy experts to do other than sit around and reminisce about the olden days. Large critical problems aside, it's often safer to hedge your bets and build a varied set of skills. That way, if the really big problems are solved or become irrelevant, you can still find work and continue to advance in your career.

This is particularly true for the information security field. In just the last decade, information security has moved from mostly firewalls and anti-virus to include patch management, log review, server hardening, workstation hardening, honeypot design and management, programming, compliance analysis, user training, penetration testing, social engineering, and so on. We've also lost the need, generally speaking, to manage Windows NT, Windows 2000, SGI IRIX, HP-UX, HP MPE, PR1MEOS, and the like. Those, so to speak, have died of old age.

Information security has largely become a multidisciplinary field. There will always be room for the best penetration testers, social engineers, and cryptographers in the world. The problem is, they're the best in the world, and to compete with them, you must also be the best in the world. But since people learn from doing, those people at the top tend to remain at the top because they get the most chances to practice their skills. So, not only is it hard to get the skills you need, it's also hard to get the experience to prove it. If you're aiming to displace those at the top, you face a very hard challenge to exceed their skills. The answer to this is to maximize your skills.

SKILLS

If we assume that any skill can be grown, the concept of boosting skills applies in the same way as boosting your career. Consider an approach if you want to become reasonably competent with firewalls, starting at zero, knowing nothing of networking. A reasonable breakdown of skill boosting may be:

1. Learn the network protocols including IP, TCP, UDP, and ICMP, where they're used and generally how they work and how they're vulnerable.
2. Learn basic IP routing and how IP subnets work and how to attack them.
3. Understand the different ways that firewalls can terminate and block connections and their limitations.
4. Create and implement a basic firewall policy that is aware of internal targets and also maps allowed connections.
5. Troubleshoot and attack a basic but otherwise unknown to you firewall policy.
6. Troubleshoot and attack an advanced but otherwise unknown to your firewall policy.
7. Migrate an advanced firewall policy from one type of firewall to another.
8. Attack and bypass basic and advanced firewall policies.
9. Defend against the previous attacks.

There is no maximum level. You can always learn something in greater detail, but every advance will take more effort. It could take a lot of effort to reach level 7 in the above list, but if there's no need for you to gain that particular skill, it may be wiser to invest that time in something easier to obtain, such as a patch management skill boost. Balance generalist and specialist skills with your current and future job requirements.

A common rule of thumb is that it takes 10,000 hours to become an expert in a subject. This is, of course, a gross oversimplification of the research; but since it suits our purposes, we're going to promote the concept. Thus, if you worked on something for just two hours each evening, it would take just over 13 years to become an expert. If you really focused and did four hours each evening and eight hours each weekend, you could get it done in half that time. Still, more than six years is a long time to wait, and by then that expertise might no longer be relevant.

Instead, focus along the easier paths. It's just as hard to find an expert in carrier-grade Cisco switch security as it is to find someone who is decently skilled in firewalls *and* Linux *and* patch management *and* social engineering. However, it might only take 1,000 hours in each of these areas to reach a level of "good enough." It can take less than a year to put in this kind of time, and you get to use that skill immediately. Spreading effort and skills around means greater employability sooner. For example, only carriers need carrier-grade Cisco switch security, but nearly all companies need at least one or more skills in firewalls, Linux, patch management, and social engineering.

THE RISK OF A MULTIDISCIPLINARY APPROACH

You'll probably be rather upset with yourself if after twenty years you had only basic skills in twenty different areas. While it is true that there aren't that many jobs for an expert in carrier-grade Cisco switch security, it is also true that it's hard to find jobs for someone who is competent but not expert in twenty different areas. To succeed, you must hit a happy medium for the job you want.

There are many career planning books on the market. Most of them say trite things like "you can't expect anyone to plan your career for you but you," "remember, the key is hard work and hard work is the key," and "those who fail to plan, plan to fail." While these sayings are true, the approaches they explore are woefully incomplete, especially in an emerging and highly technical industry. Instead, here are our two trite rules about careers:

1. Careers only ever make sense in hindsight. What you did in the past will make the most sense in the future.
2. Don't let Rule One make you stupid. Do what makes most sense when you're doing it.

We've structured this book in terms of jobs and job families. The Learning section jobs are generally entry-level ones. Once you've done an entry-level job or two, you're ready to move up. It's easier to move within a job family, but with some effort it is also possible to move into a higher-level job within another job family.

Story is key. There is no point in doing work to advance yourself if you can't tell your story. In almost all cases, a well-told but otherwise unimpressive accomplishment wins against a poorly told but impressive accomplishment. As you move through your career collecting projects and experience points, think about how you'll tell these projects' stories. Once you start thinking about your performance and how it affects others, you'll massively improve your ability to capitalize on your accomplishments. This allows you to treat your career, and therefore your path in information security, as a series of building blocks.

It is unreasonable to expect to become a team lead in penetration testing with absolutely no experience. However, there are many paths to such a job. For example, a log analyst may get a system administrator job doing server hardening. This may be followed by vulnerability analysis, then junior penetration testing demonstrating the vulnerabilities. Doing penetration testing for a while may result in a promotion to a team lead position. Another common path is to start in the help desk, go through organization layers, and become senior or supervisor help desk worker. This experience in understanding how people use systems can branch out into social engineering and eventually help penetration testing teams. Yet another approach is from development. Many developers start out extending and maintaining legacy systems. Over time, they write more and more code and develop ever-more-intricate applications. This experience primes them for application analysis, which allows an "in" into penetration testing.

Each of these examples shows a process of learning, and at certain points you have to tell a good story to achieve the next tier. In other words, it looks much like this:

Table 2.0.1 Information Security Career Paths

Standard Path	Help Desk Path	Developer Path
Log analysis	Help desk	Maintenance programming
Server hardening	Subject matter expert	Project development
Vulnerability analysis	Help desk supervisor	Product development
Penetration testing, junior	*Social engineering assistant*	Product management
Penetration testing, team lead	Social engineering, team lead	*Application security analysis*
	Penetration testing, team lead	Penetration testing, team lead

The turning points are at the steps *in bold italics*, where you must successfully tell the story of your previous achievements to convince someone to let you make the lateral move into the role you want. It's likely but not certain that some of these moves will be in different organizations or even different industries. Promotions and raises are often easiest and best obtained by changing employers. Few employers grow and change in the same way as their employees.

OTHER CAREER PATHS

A lateral career path will take you outside your main field into something else. There are more ways to get into information security than we can cover in this book. Instead, we'll explore just nine different lateral paths here in Chapter 2.0 Do and five more in Chapter 3.0 Teach.

The first nine lateral paths are Physical Security, the Military, Law Enforcement, Legal, Sales, Project Management, Non-IT Engineering, Accounting, and Business Analysis. Each of these fields has its own way of thinking and will give you insights that people with more traditional paths won't have. Some of these fields of thought will work against you, but others will be extremely valuable.

For example in the military, there are things you Do and Don't Do not found in the private sector. Many military workers function more "by the book" than those in the private sector. This experience can result in more efficient operational practice, especially since "the book" may be an actual book of required formal processes and procedures. However, it can also cause problems when the book has to be written or revised as is common in information security. Militaries often depend upon empowered, strong, and decisive leadership to overcome issues like this, but this is often lacking in the private sector. Many people leaving a job doing military log analytics may consider their co-workers in a civilian Security Operations Center (SOC) as sloppy with inconsistent process and poor discipline. Start-up entrepreneurial environments promote an element of creativity often lacking in military circles.

What you Learn is reinforced by what you Do, so if you take a lateral path, put some careful thought into how you want your thinking to change and what you want to keep. Consider that your thinking about this will itself be biased by what you've Learned and Done, and may also need to change.

Each of these paths will be explored in greater detail in the chapter assigned to it.

BOOSTER PATHS

Building experience is hard and takes time, but there's only so much time in a day. While you can maximize your Learning and Doing time by focusing on one thing at a time and minimizing distraction, there is a practical limit to how much you can work.

The phrase "work/life balance" is popular today. However, if you want a job, your competition consists of people all along the work/life balance spectrum. If you want to win, you have to have Learned more and Done more than anyone else and be good at talking about it. To reach this level, you must have worked longer or harder at work or on your own time. If you don't want to wait to break in, you must plan and execute projects on your own time.

In other words, you need a boost. A boost path is a carefully chosen project that will reward you both in the present and in the future, for example, working as an author, a developer, an evangelist, a researcher, or a community supporter. This is because evening and weekend work tends to be better-defined and result in a higher experience-to-time ratio than your day job, where you also have to attend meetings, answer ignorant questions, and fight fires. It may also be much more enjoyable. Beware of conflict-of-interest issues between work and home. Some organizations have very specific rules on doing work at home, using work resources for personal use, or using personal resources for work.

Chapter 4.0 Boosting discusses this in greater detail.

HOW TO DO

We've talked a lot about the importance of Doing and what to Do, but not much on how to Do things. There are at least as many ways to do a thing as there are people on the planet; some are more right than others, and at least some of them are simply wrong. However, there are some fairly common issues that can get in your way as you try to get things done. There are various tips and tricks to dealing with such things. Many people seem, in the course of their careers, to discover the concept of time management and be astonished at their ability to suddenly be highly productive. This is not a time/work management book, so we'll trust in your ability to use an Internet search engine (and the Appendix of this book) if you need detailed help with that. Instead, we'll briefly discuss how to maximize the Do portion of your career in different ways.

DOING AT WORK

If you're like most people, most things you'll be doing will be for your primary employer. When you're new to the work, there won't be much to this, as you'll be told what to do and, if you're lucky, when to have it done. Sometimes your work will be more collaborative as you try to solve problems. As you gain experience, though, more and more of your work will be self-driven, and you may even find yourself telling others what to do. To maximize your experience, you have to know how your workplace functions.

Broadly there are two kinds of organizations: "do what I say" and "help me solve this problem."

Governments, militaries, law enforcement, prisons, manufacturing, retail, K-12 elementary schools, and other authoritarian organizations tend to be "do what I say" organizations.

Colleges, universities, museums, research institutions, and some nonprofits tend to be "help me solve this problem" organizations.

If you work in a "do what I say" sort of organization, think about the business importance of what you're doing. If you don't understand why it's important, then ask—but not at the beginning. Bosses in "do what I say" organizations seldom reward questioning. If you ask questions as you go and actively solicit feedback at the end, your work will improve faster and you can avoid this career-limiting move.

If you are working in a "help me solve this problem" organization, though, ask questions first. In these organizations, try to understand and discuss the problem as much as you can at the beginning, but be aware that some problems can't be understood until you experience them. Try to identify what's known, what's unknown, and what simply can't be known yet. Then, discuss with your co-workers on ways to identify what can't be known, and build a series of small explorations into the project plan. Most people don't do this, but if you do, you can not only rise above them but also maximize your experience gain.

If you are self-guided then create projects that help your organization where you get interesting stories you can tell later. By working within your job description, but constantly pushing the envelope, you can gain more experience both in doing things and in convincing others why they matter. This will make your leap into your next job easier.

Finally, if you are guiding the work of others, remember that each of them will be in one of the above categories. If they try to work without an understanding of why what they're doing matters, help them to understand. If they try to go off on their own, make sure to pull them back in so their assigned work that you are guiding them in gets accomplished. Ideally, you will both work together to achieve both your goals. If, however, this cannot be done, determine that their new goals are not incompatible with yours.

In the end, the work you do for your employer will be limited in both scope and Learn/Do potential. It may be necessary, but most tasks that are high in learning aren't cost-effective from a business perspective. Also, cost-effective tasks are often less interesting from a storytelling perspective than work done for other reasons. However, some organizations value cost-effectiveness and saving money can be a story all by itself, so pick your stories accordingly. You can generally learn more Doing things on your own time.

DOING ON YOUR OWN TIME

Working on your own time trades structure for flexibility. In a work environment, the structure you need is often provided for you. When you work on your own, you can easily get distracted, go down dead ends, and fail to polish the work once you're done. If you want to be successful, you have to keep yourself under control.

Start each project you do on your own with a fairly clear idea of what you're doing and why you're doing it. Some tasks never really end, but this helps you to identify when you're done, that you've done enough so you can get to the next task. Remember, it's okay to do something just to learn about it. However, if you can take it the extra step where it helps out someone else, you've turned it into a story. Having someone to help also sets a particular goal and provides someone to evaluate your work. Set aside a recurring time to do the work, or least think and plan about it. Having someone to help can also help set a schedule. Daily, weekly, or biweekly recurring times can work well. More frequent sessions mean less time to forget what happened in the previous session, but may require shorter sessions. Longer sessions may be more efficient, with less average overhead in starting and ending a session. Experiment and learn what works best for you.

It's tempting to only focus on the fun part of the work. However, the reason it's the fun part is probably because you already know how to do it. Learning is painful. Doing something while you're learning about it is even more painful. Fitness coaches have it right when they say to "embrace the pain" or "no pain, no gain." Only by doing what you don't know will you learn what you need and do what's worth doing. Remembering the goal will help to keep you on track, but preparing yourself for pain and frustration will help even more.

Anyone watching kids grow up will see a series of changes that are all prefaced with frustration and anger. When you learned to talk, you probably didn't just leap straight into complete sentences. When you learned to walk, you probably fell down a lot. The first time you went to school, learned to drive, went on a date, moved to a new place...each milestone is scary, frustrating and hard. This doesn't stop as we get older, we just get better at masking our pain when we talk to others. As adults, we get to feel the same pain we always have, but now we compare ourselves to people who seem to have it all so easy, making things even harder.

Remember that it's hard for everyone. All experts were once beginners. Your co-workers whose jobs you covet didn't always know what they know now. The trolls on the Internet who specialize in making beginners feel stupid are often unwilling to put in the amount of work needed to get where you want to go, and soon you'll surpass them.

When doing work on your own, your biggest enemy is yourself. The storytelling model goes both ways. While you're working toward being able to tell other people "I'm awesome," you may be telling yourself "I'm not awesome." The one true trick of being able to be productive while learning and doing things that are entirely new is to be aware of your internal monologue and add "...yet."

Yes, you don't have the job you want ... yet. You're not an expert ...yet. You're not awesome ...yet. But you will be.

WORKING WITH OTHERS

It is likely that some of the work you'll be doing will involve working with others. In general, remember that each person has their own motivation. Many people are driven by money and only Do things when compensated. Some people work to make a difference in the world, and others, to increase their social status.

You must keep your goal in mind when working with others within a Learn/Do/Teach model. When you're Learning, are the others helping you or hindering you? If they're Teaching and you're still Learning, there may well be a good match. The same applies if reversed. Similarly, if you're both Learning or Teaching at the same time, you can discuss each others' ideas to make progress.

If all of you are Doing, consider whether or not you will get in each other's way. It is common when working collaboratively for each person to take the work that is easiest for themselves. This gets the work done as quickly as possible, but it also drastically weakens your stories and entrenches your current position, hindering your ability to move forward. Similarly, if you are Doing and someone else is Learning or Teaching, you may find them working toward understanding while you are working toward storytelling. This will not work well, and you may find yourselves fighting. The following chart shows these interactions:

Table 2.0.2 Learn/Do/Teach Interaction

	Learn	**Do**	**Teach**
Learn	yes	-	yes
Do	-	maybe	-
Teach	yes	-	yes

Basically, Learning and Teaching are compatible with one another, because they are education-focused tasks. Doing is only compatible with Doing, and even then you have to be careful. This is a cause of poor on the job training. When one person is trying to understand or get another person to understand, but that person only wants to get things done, there will be conflict.

Thus, when you have to work with others, consider where they are with respect to the project and see if their position and yours are compatible.

MAKING MISTAKES MATTERS

Doing work means making mistakes. This shouldn't come as a surprise. After all, you are translating theoretical knowledge into practical knowledge. Anything that you didn't understand completely will eventually result in an error. It is better to fail fast, before bad knowledge is applied for the long term. And yet, in an environment where a boss views *your* time as *their* money, any mistake feels to them like money lost. This puts a lot of pressure on people and, in effect, slows down the learning process—which, ironically, costs the bosses more money.

WHY MISTAKES MATTER

Fundamentally, a mistake shows you where you misunderstood something, so you can correct it. The faster you make mistakes, the faster you learn. It's that simple.

As an example, when one is writing a nonfiction book, one is expected to use a certain type of language. One is not supposed to be emotional. One is not supposed to swear. Violating this rule is frowned upon by editors and publishers. However, this is an emotional topic and one, I (Josh More) feel must be addressed emotionally. So, in the plainest language I can use...

Mistakes. Suck.

Many of us are perfectionists. Many of us are extremely intelligent. We know what we want and we know what we have to do to get it. After all, that is why you bought this book. Perhaps you're upset when you see other people getting the jobs you want. Perhaps you want to prove yourself or bring home more money. Perhaps you just want to do something more interesting. The key word here is "want." Wanting hurts. The more you want, the more pain you'll feel. Odds are that you are living with a constant level of emotional pain. It's not the same as living with a chronic disease like fibromyalgia or rheumatoid arthritis. However, it does mean that you have a certain threshold of pain that you just deal with every day.

Each mistake you make and internalize adds to that.

If you move from Learning to Doing at your maximum speed, at some point, you will exceed your limit. You will break. Your projects will fail or stall and you'll get stuck. This is, fundamentally, how humans work. And, in fact, the more superhuman you think you are (a common issue in IT and information security), the worse you'll break. It's like driving along a mountain road. The faster you go, the more likely you are to drive off a cliff. The exact people we want in this industry, smarter people, have this vulnerability—the more they know, the more multidisciplinary they are, the more comfortable they are driving quickly...the more catastrophically they will flame out. And in so doing, they'll learn their breaking point and what happens when they do, but it's much better to learn before crashing.

Unless you take the time to recover from and understand your mistakes, each one you make gets you closer to your breaking point.

THE VIOLENCE INHERENT IN THE SYSTEM

Information security is dangerous, but we don't like to talk about it. There are different types of Internet crimes. In commercial information security, we mostly think about adversaries as malware authors who are after our money or data. In education, the adversaries are often the institution's students. In the military, adversaries are foreign countries. The truth is that our attackers are all of these, and more. When you're first investigating an incident, the people who created the issue could be any of:

- A technical competitor, employed to steal your data.
- A technical activist, motivated to attack your infrastructure for ideological reasons.
- A technical thief, living off of what they can steal.
- A kid who doesn't know what they're doing.
- A kid who does know what they're doing, but doesn't care.
- A criminal, working for an organized crime syndicate.
- A warrior, working for a military organization.
- Someone you haven't even considered.

There is never a single response that is appropriate to the entire range of adversaries. This is one of the first areas where you can make a mistake. When you make assumptions about an adversary, you run the risk of the wrong response either from yourself or from them. If you're from a finance background and move to education, you should know that it's not appropriate to call the state police on a student who is exploring the network. However, that's not what your gut will tell you. Your gut "knows" who your enemy is, and will drive you emotionally, not rationally.

You can often pick up on things intuitively, resulting in a much faster analysis. The best analysts can't really explain why they think as they do. Sometimes things just feel "hinky" or just wrong. Know when you're operating intuitively and when you're operating rationally. This allows you to use your entire gamut of responses, from rescue to discussion to lawsuits to jail to military action, as appropriate.

WARNING

Violent Risks

While we hope that you are never engaged in physical violence, be aware that such a response is possible for militaries and organized crime syndicates. Know that we live in a world where attacks over the Internet can be digital, emotional, and physical. Some adversaries have killed. Some victims have died, either by their own hand or that of another. If you're going to play the game, understand what you may be called upon to do, and understand your limits before you must meet them.

As you shift from Learning to Doing, slow down. Realize that everything you try has a risk of failure, and think about the consequences of such a failure. Security is not about blocking the bad guys or taking control. Security is about protecting. The instant you take a risk that puts those you are protecting at risk, you're no longer a security practitioner. You become the enemy.

TIER 2—PEN TESTER

INTRODUCTION

> "Men rise from one ambition to another: first, they seek to secure themselves against attack, and then they attack others."
>
> — **Niccolo Machiavelli**

Pen, or penetration tester. Getting paid to hack other people's systems. To many people, this is the dream job that attracts them to the information security field. The idea of getting paid to behave as a criminal is very enticing.

But it is hard. You must have strong technical skills. The minimum level of knowledge includes at least an understanding of networking, Microsoft Windows and Linux operating systems, Microsoft IIS, Apache, Tomcat, and nginx web and application servers, many testing tools including Metasploit, Nmap, BurpSuite, among others, and script writing. You will also need decent communication and social skills.

This list may seem daunting, but these are the skills the criminals possess. When pen testing an organization, one must be able to breach its technologies. Without a strong breadth of skills, your marketability and utility will be limited.

While pen tests used to be exclusively technical, social engineering has become an expected component of penetration tests. Being comfortable making phone calls, talking your way into buildings, or otherwise acting in various roles is required.

Beyond the technical, you will be expected to have other skills. After the pen testing you must provide understandable reports. This requires good writing and perhaps presentation skills, attention to detail, and a willingness to do the necessary drudge work. All reports should have non-technical executive summaries, but sometimes entire reports need to be written for and understandable by non-technical staff.

Most of pen testers are found at consulting companies; however, as regulations and standards increasingly require penetration tests, more and more organizations are adding internal pen testing teams.

HOW TO BREAK IN

The path varies, but the core process is generally the same: first develop general technical skills, then develop security knowledge, then develop pen testing skills. It's possible to break into systems with no technical skills or security knowledge, by using free and commercial tools and scripts. Someone with this minimal skill level is called a "script-kiddie," because they are so inexperienced they can only run the scripts, but not read them, understand, or write new scripts.

Technical skills can be developed through the Tier 1 jobs in Chapter 1.0 Learn. The key is to develop the breadth of technical skills required for pen testing. If you only understand networking, then exploiting a Windows IIS web server will be challenging. If you only understand Windows and its platform, doing initial reconnaissance is going to be challenging, because customers will expect you to be able to break into any system. If you don't know a system, you will be doing them a disservice if you imply they are secure just because you happen to be ignorant.

Take advantage of any opportunity you have to gain breadth of technical skills.

While developing technical skills improve your security knowledge. Understand not only the technical components of security, but the overarching security concepts that drive the security decisions in your organization.

HOW TO IMPROVE YOUR SKILLS

As security advances, more and more tasks are automated, and new tasks enter pen testing. Network reconnaissance used to be an entirely manual process; then tools such as Nmap semi-automated the process, and testers' knowledge went from understanding less about network scanning (although some knowledge is still required), and more to understanding the tools.

This type of growth is continuous within the realm of pen testing. One of the best ways to improve your skills is to learn how to automate as many tasks as possible, leaving you able to focus on other areas during the pen test.

RECOGNIZING WHEN YOU'RE STUCK

Pen testing requires running forward merely to stay in place. New vulnerabilities are discovered daily, and must be incorporated into your testing frameworks. If you find yourself relying on older exploits, or older tools, then you are quickly working your way to irrelevance. If you are hearing about vulnerabilities from non-pen testers, then you are probably falling behind.

HOW TO GET OUT

The breadth of technical skills you have as a Pen Tester provides opportunities to move back into technically oriented roles (such as the various Systems Administration or engineering roles), should that direction be of interest. Similarly, moving to a role such as Security Architect (defense), Pen Test lead (management), Risk Assessment (less technical), or Auditor (business-focus) are possibilities. The key for any move is to emphasize how the skills you have developed will be appropriate in your new role.

Table 2.1 Role at a Glance—Pen Tester

Hours	Travel	Stress Level	Creativity	Flexibility	Stability
8–16/day	Low–High	Med–High	Moderate–High	Moderate	Moderate
General job duties	This job consists of performing scans, identifying vulnerabilities, performing social engineering and generating post-test reports. Along the way, you may find yourself creating new exploits, doing research and presenting at conferences. Basically, you have be able to keep pace with the attackers, which means doing what they do. When on engagements, you will need to work at odd hours, and frequently work long days in order to ensure appropriate testing is in place. Travel is low for internal team-based roles, high when working for a consulting company. International travel is common in this role. There is added stress. Did you find everything? What if someone comes in immediately after you? What if someone was already in, and you didn't find the way in that they did? Be prepared to have these questions floating around in your head. The high level of technical expertise required makes this somewhat stable. However, as pen-tests may be optional for some organizations, that does make the demand somewhat economy dependent.				
Learning	Learning is required in order to stay relevant in this role. You will be able to learn from both your peers and general research in preparation for each engagement.				
Advancement	Demonstrated technical and leadership abilities will present opportunities in other roles.				

2.2 TIER 2—VULNERABILITY MANAGEMENT

INTRODUCTION

> "vulnerabilities arise at the boundary between two protection technologies"
>
> **— Ross Anderson**

The Vulnerability Manager works closely with other information security roles to determine, often in real time, the risk of any and all vulnerabilities that exist in an organization or a particular environment. Real-time response can be critical, as there may be a very limited time to understand, create, test, and deploy any solution before a vulnerability is actively exploited. In the case of zero-day attacks, the vulnerability is already being exploited against production systems. However, there is opportunity to engage in mitigation before the attacks occur by understanding higher level weaknesses. A vulnerability manager must balance the risks of continuing to operate vulnerable systems, even as they might be under attack, against the risks of shutting down systems and no longer being able to operate as an organization. As a role, vulnerability management may not be a dedicated position but instead be part of other positions up or down the management chain.

HOW TO BREAK IN

Vulnerability Management is, in a sense, a specialization of change management. However, it is focused on making a change that moves a vulnerability from a risk to an addressed issue—one that has been patched, mitigated, or is no longer a concern because the organization has already taken action.

The Vulnerability Manager can be a natural outgrowth from other management roles, such as Patch Management or Security Coordinator, and may be part of or a promotion from senior System Administrator, Network Administrator, Coder-Developer, Security Consultant, Security Facilitator, Security Assessment, Risk Assessment, or senior Incident Responder positions. Each of these positions feeds information to and works with vulnerability managers, providing a bigger picture of the issues of new, current, and past vulnerabilities to determine security posture and actions for the organization.

If there is no formal vulnerability management structure, any person in the positions listed above can step up when a new vulnerability is announced and take on the responsibility of collecting, organization, understanding, and suggesting mitigation paths for the organization. Many people did this with well-publicized vulnerabilities in the years 02014 and 02015 such as HeartBleed and ShellShock. One of the simplest tasks is to set up the first meeting, write the first memo, or take the first stance on next steps. However, follow-through is critical, both for the organization, and also to maintain momentum of change to get the vulnerability addressed and resolved.

There are opportunities from many other positions to become the informal vulnerability manager.

Each of these roles and positions feeds information into and receives information from a vulnerability manager. In doing so, these roles could grow into a vulnerability manager position:

Patch management may be the first to know of the vulnerability, through a patch release or notice if there is no patch. A patch is very often the only solution to a vulnerability, so such experience is critical to understanding the limitations of patching, including minimum time, risks of patches, and required outages.

System Administrators and **Network Administrators** are on the front line in dealing with vulnerabilities, including configuration changes that can avoid and perhaps prevent a vulnerability. They also contribute their own take on patch management.

Coder-Developers may be involved with the creation of a patch for the organization's own software. They can be the first to know of vulnerabilities and may also provide a patch or update at the same time.

Quality Testers and **Quality Assurance** provide input on risks of applying patches or configuration changes, the results of quality testing and assurances processes, the risks of not using such processes, and how the vulnerability can be prevented in the future. In some cases, they are the first to know of vulnerabilities.

Security Assessment provides input on the current known state of the environment and how the new vulnerabilities impact it. Then, after configurations changes and patches are completed, they follow up by checking for the same and any new vulnerabilities.

Risk Assessment brings all the risks together and provides input on what risks can be taken by the organization, which then goes to the coordinating vulnerability manager.

Incident Responders and **Log Reviewers** may be the very first to encounter the results of an attack such as from a zero-day vulnerability, and provide critical information for vulnerability management as to the current status.

Log Reviewers may provide information on what happened in past but previously undetected attacks.

HOW TO IMPROVE YOUR SKILLS

Every new vulnerability presents a new learning experience. When you deconstruct a vulnerability, you will often find it is made of many different issues, each one of which requiring study and analysis. The worst vulnerabilities tend to be from very different sources. For example, the top vulnerability of one week might be entirely client-based and not affect servers at all. Another might server only and have no effect on workstations.

Vulnerabilities are often the results of a failure of imagination, so understanding, managing, and fixing them requires creativity. For example, vulnerabilities often follow one another in an informal release cycle with creative thinking on the part of attackers helping to predict new vulnerabilities in the same class.

Research your environment and your industry, know what threats your organization faces both in terms of technology, your competition, and your customers' expectations.

Your organization's response should reflect it's goals and risk acceptance.

Communications is critical in an incident. All organizations will have incidents so effective and frequent internal and external communication can make the difference.

If your organization doesn't already have security architects doing long-term planning, this can be an opportunity for you to grow into that position. Be able to write a quick-to-read and yet easily understood summary of the vulnerability, how it affects the organization, what the organization should do, and what the consequences are if the organization does nothing.

RECOGNIZING WHEN YOU'RE STUCK

Are you doing everything you should but haven't been able to get the organization out of fire-fighting mode? Is each new vulnerability yet another crisis? Is your organization's vulnerability management process non-existent? Is there any prospect for a formal vulnerability management process? Does your organization have a formal process, but it's no longer improving?

Unless you thrive on fire-fighting and continual crisis management with no end in sight (some people do), then you may be stuck.

The stuck vulnerability manager may not even realize they are stuck in the position, since it is a synthesis of different roles. Being stuck means not being able to do the official job, and yet not being able to grow into a dedicated vulnerability manager.

HOW TO GET OUT

Vulnerability Manager may not exist as a dedicated position; consequently, it's possible to get stuck and have no way to get out because no one, even the person in the role, knows they're doing this role. If the role doesn't formally exist within the organization, it needs to be formally recognized. Once the role is realized, and the past work appreciated, then the formal role can be created.

To get out requires that the person stuck in the role realize it, and present it as a formal role in the organization and get it funded at least as a part-time role formally assigned to their position. In some organizations, this would automatically require that the role be assigned to a different person because the existing person already has a job; in others it could be a way to grow into a dedicated full-time position.

At the top of the management hierarchy, such as the Chief Information Security Officer (CISO), a vulnerability manager might be personally responsible for information security in the organization. Although this can be a stable position, there are well known examples of even a CISO, by title or not, leaving an organization because of a failure in vulnerability management. In some cases, as the top vulnerability manager in the organization, the Chief Information Officer (CIO) was fired, resigned, or otherwise left to pursue new opportunities.

Table 2.2 Role at a Glance—Vulnerability Management

Hours	Travel	Stress Level	Creativity	Flexibility	Stability
8/day	Low	Varies	Moderate	Low	High
General job duties	This includes managing configurations, software engineering where applicable, iterative testing and tuning. Stress can be high, especially when significant vulnerabilities are known. It's not unusual for this role and those this role works with to require overtime, weekend, and holiday work. This is usually the time available to mitigate vulnerabilities.				
Learning	Every new vulnerability is a new learning experience. Most vulnerabilities are a mix of issues and so there will usually be a lot to learn each time. The worst vulnerabilities that come up, perhaps even on a weekly basis, tend to be from very different sources. For example, the top vulnerability of one week might be completely client based with no server component with no mitigation or risk anywhere but on client systems. Another vulnerability might be entirely server based and similarly not have any client vulnerability. Some vulnerabilities are very vendor specific, while others cut across vendors due to common code or common design defects.				
Advancement	This is a management track role and can lead to any management roles, but especially within information security. It can lead to any of the other information security management positions. This position can grow into the Chief Information Security Officer (CISO) or higher if it doesn't exist.				

2.3 TIER 2—SECURITY ASSESSOR

INTRODUCTION

When approaching information security, one must remember that not every solution works for every company. A large organization may be able to bring in a team to do a full penetration test, including testing physical controls, compliance with policy (social engineering), and detailed analysis of legacy systems. The cost for this type of single test could easily outstrip the entire annual profits of a small company. Specialists are needed to fill this gap and help a small company understand its security profile while helping it identify and evaluate the steps required to protect its infrastructure.

Doing Security Assessment requires a different approach than pen testing. The Security Assessor is working from the perspective of the attacker; rather, their process involves more discussion and interaction with the organization.

To help explain this role, here is an example engagement.

The Security Assessor is brought in by a small organization to review its security controls. During the initial kickoff meeting, they discuss the specific goals that they hope to achieve. In this example, the goal will be to build a general profile of the adequacy of the security around the main infrastructure: network, servers, and end-user computers.

Using this as a basis, the assessor would then begin asking questions of those responsible for this infrastructure. Depending on the size of the organization, this could be a single individual or a small team. The assessor would identify the controls in place around the network. For example, they would determine whether default usernames and passwords have been changed, if systems are patched regularly, and if the configurations used are appropriate for the environment. Questions regarding how end-user machines are configured and if any malware protection software is installed will also be important for determining the company's overall profile.

After talking to the technical team, the assessor will discuss policies and procedures with HR. Is the technical team notified of staff departures so that accounts can be disabled? Are there policies in place to protect the company regarding appropriate use of the equipment? The organization's industry and requirements to meet various regulations and standards will influence the questions that must be examined and discussed.

After gathering all of this information, the Security Assessor would produce an analysis report describing the findings and recommendations as to how to address any shortfalls that were found.

This role requires a wide range of technical and business skills. The ability to understand a wide range of equipment and operating systems is required to perform a complete and thorough analysis of the client's security profile.

HOW TO BREAK IN

Because of the breadth of skills required to perform these assessments, the Security Assessor must have gained knowledge in a wide range of technical and business areas. Working as a Wildcard, as described in Chapter 2.7, is a good way to develop these skills due to its generalist nature. Similarly, if you move between roles such as Network Administrator and System Administrator, this can provide similar breadth of expertise.

Since this is a consulting role, having some form of security certification may be required. It is significantly easier to sell the skills of a consultant to a client when they have some level of certification. A CISSP from (ISC)^2 or a CompTIA Advanced Security Practitioner can demonstrate security expertise. Other certifications from GIAC or ISACA are appropriate as well. Which will be required will depend upon the market you are in and your target audience.

HOW TO IMPROVE YOUR SKILLS

This role provides many opportunities for growth in its regular job duties. Since no one can know every piece of equipment or software that an organization may have, you will often have to learn about the site's infrastructure while on the job. Some of this investigation will need to be done after hours, or at least not in front of the client, as they will expect a certain level of expertise. Because of this, work weeks of well over 40 hours are common.

Depending on the direction you wish to move your career, you will want to advance your skills in those areas while doing assessments. If you wish to move into auditing, then improving the questions asked, your ability to ask questions and process answers, and your work with the individuals will be important. If you wish to move into more technical roles such as pen testing, then diving more deeply into the technical facets of the assessment will be an area of growth for you.

RECOGNIZING WHEN YOU'RE STUCK

If you really enjoy working with the smaller clients and using a wide breadth of skills, then this may be an end role for you. However, many people view this as a stepping stone role to a more advanced security position. If you intend to advance your career, staying in the role for more than a few years may be indicative of being stuck in the role. If you are not advancing your skills and getting more advanced assessment opportunities, or worse, getting simpler ones, that is indicative of it being time to look at your next career change.

HOW TO GET OUT

Depending on how you have advanced your skills, a move to Pen Test or Auditor could be a logical step for a Security Assessor. For more lateral moves, moving to Risk Assessment, Vulnerability Management, or Wildcard are options, even if you have not advanced your skills while in this role.

Table 2.3 Role at a Glance—Security Assessor

Hours	Travel	Stress Level	Creativity	Flexibility	Stability
8 + /day	High	Moderate	Moderate	Low	Low
General job duties	Evaluating a small organization's security profile. Providing reports to clients. As a consultant you will be under pressure to ensure that you have enough billable hours, while the clients will be trying to get as much as possible from you during your engagement. Because each organization will vary, you will need to adjust your questions and evaluations based on what you observe, rather than exclusively following a script. You will be tied to the client's calendar, and working to ensure that you get the necessary billable hours a week. As these types of assessments are often optional for small organizations, the demand will vary depending upon current economic conditions.				
Learning	Lots of opportunity to learn through the job duties, if you are willing to leverage some time after hours during your engagements.				
Advancement	The experience gained through this type of position can be used to move into a wide range of positions for the properly motivated.				

TIER 2—RISK ASSESSOR

INTRODUCTION

The Risk Assessor, as part of Risk Management, is responsible for assessing the overall risk profile of an organization's IT systems. Every system is associated with some level of risk. It is the job of the Risk Assessor to determine how large an impact a security compromise would have upon an organization, and work with Vulnerability Management to mitigate risks to a company-acceptable level. The organization may or may not know what systems are the most important. That may sound unreasonable, but without going through the process of analyzing the overall risk profile of an organization's systems, the company may not realize its level of dependence. It is not uncommon, for example, to find a dependency on a single system that is running out of sight, hidden under the desk of a developer.

While the specific tasks that are used to identify an organization's risk vary based on the framework used, they all have the same ultimate goal of identifying the impact to the company, should a system be compromised. The most commonly accepted categories for ways in which a system may be compromised include losses of confidentiality (sensitive data is no longer controlled), integrity (data has been inappropriately manipulated), and availability (a system is no longer available to use).

The nature of that risk will vary from organization to organization. For an online retailer, keeping the website up and running (ensuring availability) may be the highest priority. For an insurance company, keeping patients' medical records secure (ensuring confidentiality) may be the highest priority. It is important to understand that the importance of a system is not a technical decision, but a business decision.

Once the impact on the organization has been determined, the possible threats must be identified. Which is more likely to take down your system: a hurricane, an Internet denial-of-service attack, or some other threat? Each threat has its own distinct set of mitigations (or controls) that reduce the damage to the organization. Understanding which mitigations are the most likely to work, most cost-effective to implement, or least damaging to the organization will determine the order in which the controls are implemented.

HOW TO BREAK IN

Risk Assessment involves understanding not only the business, but also the systems that the organization uses. Being able to spend time talking to a business manager about the costs of potential loss (how much will it cost the company per minute when the website is down) and then talk to the technical people (such Vulnerability Management) about implementation costs will be key skills for this role.

Many Auditor skills are also used in Risk Assessment. Auditors tend to focus on standards or regulations, such as PCI-DSS, US Health Insurance Portability and Accountability Act (HIPAA), or US Children's Online Privacy Protection Act (COPPA). Risk Assessors tend to focus on business needs. If those in Audit are comfortable determining relevant standards they are evaluating systems against, then they are well set for a move into Risk Assessment, should they so desire.

There are certifications, such as the ISACA Certified in Risk and Information Systems Control (CRISC), that may be required by some organizations; however, being able to relate your current experience to the job tasks of identifying risks and being able to recommend/investigate controls will often be more important.

HOW TO IMPROVE YOUR SKILLS

This type of role requires growth simply to keep pace. Business drivers change. New threats emerge. New vulnerabilities are discovered. New controls become available. Maintaining your knowledge of the current state of the business is required to continuously do your job effectively. The advantage of the growth associated with this role is that it can position you well for other positions, should you be interested in changing.

RECOGNIZING WHEN YOU'RE STUCK

If your role as risk assessor is one where you are a check box in some process—"ensure risk assessment done"—rather than an integral part of a business development, then you are in an organization that does not value this role. This type of role should be a dynamically engaged one within the company.

On the personal side, if you find that you are not taking the time to seek out as much information as possible as part of the process, or only working with the minimum amount of information necessary to do a perfunctory review, then you are not engaged in your role, and should investigate other positions. Consider either a different role or changing the organization for which you are working.

HOW TO GET OUT

This is a growth role as more organizations move to risk-based analysis for the implementation of controls. Frameworks such as the US NIST SP-800 document series are becoming standard in the US government for security design and implementation. As such, your opportunities in other organizations should be plentiful.

Table 2.4 Role at a Glance—Risk Assessment

Hours	Travel	Stress Level	Creativity	Flexibility	Stability
8/day	Varies	Moderate	Low	Low	High
General job duties	Performing risk assessments. Analyzing available controls. Developing risk reports. Travel will vary based on whether the risk assessor is a consultant or working for a specific organization. The need to work with a wide range of people within the organization, especially business managers who view your job as a necessary (or unnecessary) component of their job will make this job stressful. Explaining to technical people that while a technical control is indeed very exciting, but does not meet a business need can also be challenging at times.				
Learning	This position requires constant learning in order to stay abreast of the current risks.				
Advancement	Many opportunities. Potential for moves into management positions such as CISO, chief privacy officer (CPO) or similar is potential. Those with exceptional technical skills have the potential to move into Pen-Testing and Security Architect. Most other roles in this tier will be available if you develop your skills in that direction.				

2.5 TIER 2—AUDITOR

INTRODUCTION

> "Sed quis custodiet ipsos custodes?"
>
> — **Juvenal**

In some ways, the role of an Auditor is simply to ensure that an organization is doing what it is supposed to—either according to an outside standard, or its own policies and procedures. Though simple in concept, in practice it requires a range of skills, including attention to detail, the ability to work with a wide range of abilities, and the ability to understand the underlying areas that the auditor is responsible for auditing.

There are two general categories in which Auditors can be grouped: internal (those employed by the organization) and external (those employed by an outside firm or from a regulating body).

Internal auditors are responsible for finding problems as soon as possible. During system development, they help internal groups understand what they will be looking for after the system goes live, helping to ensure that systems that are developed will meet the standards. In many cases, after running internal audits, they will provide suggestions as to how to address the issues that they find.

External auditors that are hired by a company are usually responsible for certifying that an organization is meeting a certain standard. For example, an organization may be required to be certified as an ISO-27001 organization to be eligible as a supplier in certain industries. The company will contract with an organization that is accredited to do ISO-27001 audits, which will supply the auditors to do the evaluation. In some cases, auditing organizations also have consulting divisions that can provide services to help ensure that an organization will meet the required standard.

External auditors from regulating bodies such as the US FDA or US FDIC are solely responsible for ensuring that an organization is meeting the regulatory standards that agency is responsible for enforcing. Depending on the regulatory body they represent, they may not provide remediation recommendations. They do, however, expect responses back describing how the issues will be addressed.

When embarking upon an audit, the first step is to identify what you are auditing against. Is the audit to ensure compliance with PCI-DSS, or is it to confirm that an organization is actually at Level 4 of the Carnegie-Mellon University Software Engineering Institute Capability Maturity Model (CMU SEI CMM)? Each standard has a different area of focus, and the auditor must be familiar with the underlying standard. Within a given standard are certain expectations for performance. For example, Level 3 of the CMM includes an expectation that processes are documented and established. However, the exact implementation for how those processes are documented and managed can vary and still be acceptable within the model. The Auditor must be capable of determining whether or not the required characteristics are present within the company that is the target of the audit. While the Auditor may have guidance documents to use to look at, it is key that they can actually comprehend both the standard and the system under audit.

One thing to be aware of as an Auditor is that you will rarely be directly involved in the development process. While you may be asked to help provide guidance, Auditors are not responsible for the actual development themselves. Because of this, those who have a desire to be builders should not enter this role, and instead investigate Engineering, Architect, or Subject Matter Expert roles instead.

HOW TO BREAK IN

There are many paths to auditing, but a common component is solid understanding of the areas being audited. If you are auditing a company's financial statement, you need to understand accounting principles. If you are auditing a company's security controls, you need understand the security concepts associated with information systems. This will likely involve a great deal of reading. Auditing the PCI-DSS, for example, will involve being intimately familiar with over 200 different audit points and understanding them from both the implementation and auditing guidance documents. Additionally, you have to be familiar with over 20 different support documents. Auditing US HIPAA is similar in scope, but auditing against ISO and US NIST standards and guidelines could well involve referencing ten times as much documentation.

Auditing is a two-way process, involving both the group doing the auditing and the group being audited. Because of this, you can gain experience by being part of the team that is responsible for responding to audits. As a Vulnerability Manager, Risk Assessor, or Quality Assurance Engineer, you may be asked to be part of an audit response team. Go through enough audits, and you will be familiar enough with the process to become an auditor yourself. In this case, the most common transition is to a role on an internal audit team, especially within the same organization in which you have been working to respond to audits.

There are IT audit certifications (such as CISA from ISACA, Systems and Network Auditor from GIAC, and CIA from The Institute of Internal Auditors). Each has its own set of requirements regarding tests and previous experience. Which one will work best will depend upon your circumstances. For example, if you can show your audit experience as an IT Manager or other role that includes auditing, then a CISA or CIA may be appropriate for you. If you have no experience, then the SANS GIAC: Systems and Network Auditor certification may be a way to differentiate yourself from other candidates with no certifications. Some positions, especially those with companies that provide audit services, will require certification.

HOW TO IMPROVE YOUR SKILLS

The more standards you can audit against, the more valuable you are. If there are opportunities to be part of teams that are doing different audit types, take advantage of them. Some audits (for example, CMU SEI CMMI or PCI-DSS) require specific certifications. Take advantage of any opportunity that may present itself to get those certifications.

As an internal auditor, become a part of development teams where auditors help ensure that new development meets the appropriate standards. Also work with other departments within the organization to identify not just which standards the organization is held to today, but which ones are anticipated for the future. Being able to provide guidance for projects so they will hit multiple audit areas will be highly valuable in terms of future career growth.

RECOGNIZING WHEN YOU'RE STUCK

If you are an internal auditor and are not involved in the process of helping develop systems, and the opportunity exists within your group, ask yourself why. If it is because you have no interest in expanding skills or learning about new technologies, then you are stuck. If you are not keeping up with the new standards as they come out, that could lead to the point where your skills are not relevant any more, and you need to think about your career path.

HOW TO GET OUT

There are many opportunities to move to other organizations, as the demand for auditors is growing. If you are no longer interested in Auditing, a move to management, Risk Assessment, Vulnerability Management, or Quality Assurance is reasonable, depending on the other skills that you have.

Table 2.5 Role at a Glance—Auditor

Hours	Travel	Stress Level	Creativity	Flexibility	Stability
8 + /day	Varies	Moderate	Low	Low	High
General job duties	Running audits against standards. Recommending remediations for issues found (as an internal auditor). If you work as a consultant, remote engagements can be significantly more than 40 hours/week. Similarly with travel, if you are a consultant, expect high level of travel. As an internal auditor, travel level will often be low. Your job is to find where people are not doing what they should be. As such, your presence is rarely something that people look forward to, and the interactions may be stressful.				
Learning	Many opportunities. You will need to learn about standards. As you audit companies, you will learn something new in each audit.				
Advancement	Potential advancement to management (CISO, CPO). Lateral moves to Risk Assessment, Vulnerability Management or Quality Assurance are available as well.				

TIER 2—INCIDENT RESPONDER

INTRODUCTION

> "Months of boredom punctuated by moments of terror."
>
> **— New York Times**

The title of Incident Responder brings to mind images of chemical spills, earthquakes, tornado damage or other natural disaster. While there can be dramatic security incidents, day-to-day incident response is much less glamorous but still essential.

While an incident is going on, one must be able to collect and analyze the data that is being generated by the systems that the attacker may have compromised.

When collecting data that may be used in a legal case, maintaining an impeccable chain of custody is required to ensure legal admissibility. You must understand the process of collecting the data, making forensic copies (so that you do not alter evidence), and then analyzing the data collected to be able to understand the scope of the incident.

In situations where maintenance of evidence is not required, the focus will be on analysis of data. The business priorities will dictate whether or not the collection of evidence is expected.

Analyzing forensic evidence requires a range of skills, and can be an interesting and challenging security role.

If you are dealing with a skilled attacker, they may hide data through the use of steganography—the process of hiding information within another file, such as an image file. This makes exfiltration, getting the data out of the organization and past data loss prevention systems, easier. Similarly, attackers often delete data after they leave. Being able to analyze a hard drive to identify and extract deleted files is an important skill to have.

Beyond hard drive analysis, there are additional skills that are important for an Incident Responder. The process of network forensics, where you analyze network traffic and log data to determine the characteristics of an attack, is becoming a larger component of incident response. The use of virtual machines in the analysis of malware and systems is also becoming increasingly important. It used to be that when you had a computer you needed to analyze, you would have to find a similar computer to run the acquired forensic image. Now, a virtual machine makes the need to find a similar model no longer necessary.

HOW TO BREAK IN

The tasks of collecting and analyzing forensic data require a level of specialized knowledge that requires study and training. This knowledge can be gained through self-study, assisting others in your organization, or formal training. There are certification programs, as well as Associate degrees in Information Security, which include Digital Forensics as a component of the coursework.

The certification or degree, in combination with a demonstrated technical ability in some other technical role, will often be enough to get a lower-level Incident Responder position. For an advanced position, extensive network and system knowledge is necessary. You may be able to find an organization that would be willing to train you if you can demonstrate solid general technical skills, as well as an excellent attention to detail.

HOW TO IMPROVE YOUR SKILLS

How you improve will depend upon what skills you entered with. You never start with a full set of Incident Response skills. If you start strong with forensic collection skills, work to expand your analysis skills. As new technologies enter the market, you will need to learn how to analyze data that is stored using them (analysis of a solid state hard drive is different than analysis of a magnetic plate hard drive). Understanding the techniques that attackers use to hide their tracks will be necessary so that you do not miss them. As these techniques are continually changing, this provides you with an opportunity for continuous growth and improvement.

Similarly, the tools used for forensic analysis are continually changing, it is important to stay up-to-date with the new tools and how they can assist you in your job duties.

Beyond forensics, most incident response teams are composed of individuals who have additional responsibilities outside of incident response, such as Systems and Network Engineers. When working with them, learn as much as you can about their areas of expertise so you can expand your knowledge.

RECOGNIZING WHEN YOU'RE STUCK

As with most of these positions, the clearest sign that you are stuck is that you are not expanding your skill set. However, unlike some positions where maintaining the status quo may be adequate to continue being employed, as an Incident Responder, failure to update your skill set continuously could be a slow path to irrelevance and unemployment. Improving your skills is critical in this type of position, and if you are not in a position that allows you to do so, or have no interest in doing so, then you need to find an alternative position.

HOW TO GET OUT

The skills that you develop—being able to maintain a strong attention to detail and the ability to be very precise in your work—will, with the right organization, allow you the opportunity to move to similar roles, such as Security Assessment, Vulnerability Management, Risk Assessment, or Auditor.

Table 2.6 Role at a Glance—Incident Responder

Hours	Travel	Stress Level	Creativity	Flexibility	Stability
Varies	Varies	Varies	Low–Moderate	Low	Moderate
General job duties	Forensic analysis of storage media and network traffic. Travel level will be dependent upon whether or not you are a consultant, or working for a single organization. Forensic analysis requires the ability to think about the possibilities associated with a task, but standard procedures are often required in certain situations. As you do not get to dictate when you are attacked, your flexibility is highly limited. Stress will be high during the active attack, lower when doing background tasks.				
Learning	Learning is an essential component to maintain your jobs skills for this role.				
Advancement	Within the same tier to Security Assessment, Vulnerability Management, Risk Assessment or Auditor. Potential advancement to Security Consultant or Security Management.				

2.6.1 TIER 2—INCIDENT RESPONDER—STORY

JOHN MEYERS

My name is John Meyers and I currently work for Hewlett Packard as an Incident Response/Forensic Specialist. I am part of a team that investigates computer security incidents for HP's trade clients. Information Security is my third career, and ten years ago I did not think I would be working Incident Response for one of the largest IT companies in the world.

Ten years ago, I was working as an Industrial Electronics Technician for a consumer goods manufacturer. Due to an acquisition, the plant I worked at was slated to be shut down. Since the company was moving manufacturing out of the US, I was eligible for retraining under a Pennsylvania Jobs program. I decided to take advantage of retraining and went back to school at the local community college. I enrolled in the Associate Degree Program in Information Systems, Network & PC.

While in school, I got a part-time job working in the College's IT department. It was a valuable experience for me and also gave me real-world experience in addition to the education. Because I worked in the IT department I got to know the faculty. One of the instructors was a SANS alumnus and this was the first time I heard about the SANS Institute. This was when I first became interested in Information Security.

I graduated in May of 02005 and in July 02005 I started work at a nonprofit in a help desk/System Administrator role. My interest in security led me to take the SANS course Introduction to Information Security. I received my GISF certification in March of 02006. I had been a subscriber to the SANS newsletter and one day I received an email from SANS that they were going to have a local mentor teach the SANS Hacker Exploits, Techniques, and Incident Handling class in Pittsburgh the summer of 02006. This was an opportunity I could not pass up, and I signed up for the class.

The class was great and I earned my GCIH certification in October 02006. After that, I brought what I learned about security from SANS back to my job. I started looking for ways to improve the security of the network I administered. Some of the changes I made were to standardize the builds of the PCs, install an IDS system, and implement Software Restrictions Policies.

All of this just whet my appetite for security. I taught myself Linux in my free time at home and played around with the tools I learned about in the SANS Hacker Exploits class like Metaspoit and Nessus. I got involved with SANS Mentor Program. Basically I tried to learn skills that would lead to some kind of Incident Handler job.

I finally got an opportunity to work for a managed security services company called Solutionary in January 02010. I would be working in their Security Operations Center. While at Solutionary I took every opportunity to learn new skills. Eventually I worked my way up to shift lead.

Then I saw an ad for my dream job, Incident Response at HP. I applied and was hired in January of 02011. Now I get to work with some of the most talented people I know on some of the most complex problems in Information Security. Being an Incident Responder for lots of large companies, HP's clients, provides a breadth of experience that is invaluable.

Well, that is my story. I went from losing my job as an electronics technician to working Incident Response for HP in eight and a half years. It was a lot of hard work, self-education, and luck. I'm sure I took the road less traveled to get to where I am, but I'm here now and having a good time.

2.7 TIER 2—WILDCARD

INTRODUCTION

> "Specialization is for insects."
>
> **— Robert A. Heinlein**

As a Wildcard, Jack of All Trades (JoAT), or Go-To Technical Person you may be the only technical person at a small organization and if not the only such person, you may still be responsible for all technical architecture. The Wildcard is responsible for all of the technical architecture at a small company. From servers to phone system, website to end-user computers, it is your responsibility.

This type of position has three main job responsibilities: end-user support, current system maintenance, and infrastructure improvements. The ratio of the three will vary greatly from organization to organization and from day to day. If malware gets loose within the network, the Wildcard will be spending time fixing machines. When patches come out, system maintenance will be the focus. When the chief financial officer (CFO) wants new accounting software, that will take up a large fraction of the available time.

More than any other role, each day brings new challenges in many areas. You will need to be comfortable working alone, without any other experts to turn to within the organization. To meet the crises face on, you must be able to research solutions on the Internet and fully leverage your own problem-solving skills.

Since this position frequently exists at small companies and nonprofits where money may be limited, your biggest challenge will frequently be the budget. More often than not, you will not have the option of solving problems by spending money. Your creativity and knowledge will be required to keep the organization running. However, this has advantages as well. The approval process is usually simple, involving only a single person (owner or business manager). Additionally, many of the projects selected will be ones that you designed and developed. Rather than being handed a specification and told to build it, you get to design the specification and then implement it, but using little or no money.

To succeed in this role, you must be a self-starter and able to work independently.

HOW TO BREAK IN

These roles often grow out of another position within the organization. When the company was too small to support a dedicated full-time technical person, you were the person people turned to when things went wrong. You were able to support the company a bit at a time, and as the role grew, you grew with it.

For those situations where you would be coming into an existing role, the key is going to be to demonstrate as wide a range of relevant skills as possible, along with the ability to learn new skills. If you have a role that only has a few skills, work on getting certifications and other credentials in other areas to demonstrate a breadth of skills.

HOW TO IMPROVE YOUR SKILLS

This role is a classic "learn by doing" role. You will be learning by solving the new problems that arise, building new infrastructure, and helping others as their needs change. Because you are the only one with technical expertise at the organization, you will be able to drive many projects to improve the infrastructure, but probably not at the same time. Additionally, as you will be working with everyone in the company, you will develop a level of understanding about many non-technical components as to how that business is run—knowledge and skills that have value in future roles.

RECOGNIZING WHEN YOU'RE STUCK

If you spend no time working to improve the infrastructure, you are in danger of being stuck in this role, with your skill set stagnating. Even if your company cannot afford to pay for any more infrastructure, you should be able to investigate free solutions for ways to improve the organization.

HOW TO GET OUT

This role can be used as a stepping stone to a wide range of other technical roles at larger organizations. Larger organizations tend to look for specialists rather than generalists such as the Wildcard, so you will need to demonstrate a depth of understanding in a specific technology or, if you can make it past the HR screen, the ability to learn rapidly to meet the specific needs of the organization.

Table 2.7 Role at a Glance—Wildcard

Hours	Travel	Stress Level	Creativity	Flexibility	Stability
8+/day	Low	Varies	High	Moderate	Moderate
General job duties	Everything technical related. Help desk, server management, network management, website management, and anything else that seems like it should be your job. There will be periodic after hours work so as to not disrupt the work of others during system upgrades. Since you are the go-to expert, you will get to devise the solutions to the problems that arise. Creativity will be a key skill because your budget will be smaller than in a large corporation. The stress level will be very dependent upon the company, work load, and your supervisor. This can be a dream job with enough to keep you busy, but not enough to be overwhelming, a job that is boring in general, or a one where one person really should be three people. In some environments you will have rigid hours or regulations that you must work within, but in many others you will have a high degree of flexibility, as long as you get the job done. Stability is generally high as the company will be completely dependent upon you for their technical needs. However, since this is usually at a small company, the stability of the company will be the most important factor in the position's stability.				
Learning	High. If something new comes up, you will have to learn how to deal with it, rather than turn to the other expert in house.				
Advancement	Few options within the same company. The opportunities to advance will not be within the same company, but when you want to move on to be more specialized at a larger company.				

2.7.1 TIER 2—WILDCARD— STORY

TRAVIS ABRAMS

Like most people in InfoSec, I started out in IT. I started out managing desktops for a large law firm; we had over 3,000 desktops. I took on the responsibility of managing the anti-virus for the desktops, because no one else wanted to do it, among other tasks. This was 01997 and we had no central management console, so I would email the weekly DAT file to users and ask them to click on it! It was absurd then and even more so today. We were asking users to run the executable in their email from us but not click on files from anyone else!

One day, I was walking out of my work area into the main hallway at the same time the CIO walked out of his office. I am not sure he even knew my name. I was the first one he saw and he said, "Hey, I just got a call and someone said there is something wrong with our training website. Go fix it." It turned out the site had been defaced and I had to argue with the site owner that we had to take it offline, patch it, and them put it back up. It took time to convince them this was the only way to correctly fix it but I was successful.

After this I was known as the security guy. The organization recognized the need for security and invested in training for me. I was able to convince them of the need for a centrally managed AV solution, regular vulnerability assessments, etc. A few years later I was officially given the title of Security Manager, which was a first for this organization. I eventually left but I have been in security ever since.

My recommendations for a security career are:

1. If you do not have experience in IT and want to go into the technical side of security; first get a job in IT. Having managed servers, desktops, etc. has only enhanced my security career. The only exception is if your goal is to be an auditor. This does not necessarily require a technical IT background.
2. Be indispensable and willing to do what others may not want to.
3. Take advantage of opportunities. The reality is that many times companies will not invest until something adverse happens. For example, after our server was defaced I was able to convince the company to have a pen test performed by a third party.

TIER 2—ADVANCED HELP DESK—HELP DESK SUPERVISOR

2.8

INTRODUCTION

> "Hello, IT. Have you tried turning it off and on again?"
>
> — **Roy Trenneman**

Advanced Help Desk, or Help Desk Supervisor in Tier 2 support, are those who have developed enough skills to address the problems that cannot be solved through a standard verbal script. After the ticket has been submitted, and the first level of support has attempted to gather as much material as possible about an issue they cannot fix, it will often be escalated to the second level of support engineers. These engineers are capable of working outside of a script to address problems that come up.

Even if they are not able to solve the problem themselves, Advanced Help Desk are able to work with end users to isolate where the problem is occurring. They can take a problem like "the Internet is not working" and turn it into "DNS can't properly resolve external domain names." They may not be able to fix the DNS infrastructure, but they provide the Systems Engineers with a clearly defined problem to address.

This position requires an intermediate level of technical understanding and skills. More importantly, it requires the ability to think critically under pressure. The pressure will vary, depending on the requester. If the chief executive officer (CEO) is contacting you, the pressure is higher. Think of this as training for your security career; clear thinking and comfort under pressure is critical when dealing with security situations.

In many organizations, the Help Desk Supervisor will have the technical responsibilities associated with this role, as well as management responsibilities for those individuals who are working on a given shift. The Help Desk Supervisor would then report to a Help Desk Manager that is responsible for all levels of shifts for that help desk.

HOW TO BREAK IN

People in this role often advanced from an entry-level help desk position. To get into this type of position, you must demonstrate three keys skills: solid general technical skills, excellent customer service skills, and solid problem-solving skills. Working as a help desk technician can give you many of these skills, but you may find that you need to develop your technical skills beyond what is required to at Tier 1. If you have spent time working as the go-to person for problems within your office, even though your main job was in other areas, you may have been working as an Advanced Help Desk Technician, even though you did not realize it. You may also be on your way to being a Wild Card.

For those people who have spent time as a Patch Manager or Security Coordinator, there may be a desire to move into a more people-focused role, or gain experience in a wider range of technologies.

HOW TO IMPROVE YOUR SKILLS

When working as an Advanced Help Desk Technician, you will find that you are exposed to a wide range of technologies. Lots of things break—different things at different times. As you work to isolate the problem, you will be learning more about networking, servers, workstations, and the Internet. The key is to learn as much as you can about the problems that you find. Talk to the engineers who address the problem and confirm that your diagnosis of the problem was correct. Learn about other ways you could have gone about diagnosing the problem. Were there other tools you could have used? Were there other questions that you should have asked? If you can manage to watch an engineer address the problem, that opportunity would be great, but it rarely presents itself.

The other key component to be alert to while in this role is how people interact with the help desk, and what they are willing to entrust you with. Most companies have strict policies against sharing passwords, yet people often volunteer them (always say no). Many of today's pen tests include a social engineering component. Take the time to learn how people interact with you, and think about how you could exploit it (only in the name of good!) as part of a security test. With solid people skills, you could become part of a pen test team that includes a social engineering component.

RECOGNIZING WHEN YOU'RE STUCK

If it took you more than one or two years to get to this Tier 2 role, you're probably already stuck. If you quickly got to this role in months from Help Desk, but haven't gotten further since, you may also be stuck. As with many other roles, if you find yourself doing just the minimum in order to get by, then you are stuck. If the corporate culture doesn't allow you the time to expand your technical skill set, or you just don't feel the urge, it is time to start looking for other opportunities.

HOW TO GET OUT

This is the type of role where moving between companies is generally easy, due to the high turnover in the field. However, since you want to move into security fields, ideally you want to use your general technical skills as an entry point to get more high-value technical skills. Depending on your skills, you may be able to become the sole technical person for a small company—someplace where they need a person who will be comfortable working with end users, and at the same time manage all of the back end systems also known as the Wildcard described in Chapter 2.7.

CRITICAL WARNINGS

Positions that don't provide any training or growth opportunities will stagnate your career. Look for positions and opportunities where you are able improve your skills through exposure to other roles.

If an organization has a habit of sharing credentials, be wary. Usernames and passwords should be kept confidential and never shared.

Table 2.8 Role at a Glance—Advanced Help Desk—Help Desk Supervisor

Hours	Travel	Stress Level	Creativity	Flexibility	Stability
8/day	Low	Medium	Low	Low	Moderate
General job duties	Isolating problems Some break/fix responsibilities in some organizations Developing decision trees As those who call a help desk are generally having problems. There is the inherent stress associated with frustrated individuals.				
Learning	Most learning will be done from working with the various technical people that you work with as you develop decision trees. Some business process education will be part of this role as well.				
Advancement	Supervisory roles are one possible direction to move from this role. Moving to more technically focused roles such as Server Administration/Engineering roles or Network Administration/Engineering roles. While Server Administrator and Network Administrator roles may be more entry-level, others will be there that will help you advance your career.				

2.9 TIER 2—SECURITY FACILITATOR

INTRODUCTION

A Security Facilitator, also known as a Delivery Lead, Project Coordinator, or Project Manager, is responsible for ensuring that projects reach completion. Project management is a specialty in and of itself, with varying ranges of formality to the process. The larger the project, the greater the requirement to have formalized and agreed-upon processes for managing each stage. As the Security Facilitator, it is your responsibility to ensure that all of the appropriate steps are followed. Identify and, where possible, work with management to mitigate those risks. One of the most common risks that a Security Facilitator will face is dealing with resource allocation issues. Working to identify as soon as possible when there are either not enough people, or people with the right skills, and working with management to address these issues, is a significant part of a Security Facilitator's role.

One component of this that can be very frustrating is that a Security Facilitator will often be tasked with managing a project and ensuring it reaches completion, but not be given the authority to ensure that the appropriate people or funds are assigned to the project. This will frustrate some, but for those with negotiation and communication skills, this can be an excellent fit.

While the general tasks associated with project management are common across all projects, the exact mechanism for doing so will vary. For example, all projects must identify the requirements that, upon completion, indicate that the project is done. The methodology for gathering those requirements will vary based on the framework in use for that specific project.

One of the bigger challenges associated with security projects is that what may appear to be a simple technology implementation may often impact many or all areas of the organization. This potential impact will require working with a wide range of people with a wide range of technical abilities. Being able to communicate with this wide range of individuals will be one of the key success factors for someone in this role.

What may be apparent at this point is that this is not primarily a technical role. You will not be responsible for doing any of the actual implementation yourself, though you may be asked to help in some cases. If you are someone who requires daily working with technology at a deep level on a daily basis, this role is not for you. This role focuses more on organization and communication. That said, there is still a need to be able to understand, at least at a high level, the underlying technology. Doing so will help as you gather people to help you, and helps to ensure that you ask for the right people.

HOW TO BREAK IN

This is the type of role where each previous small success will lead to the next bigger role. Open the door to larger projects by managing a smaller project for which you and a co-worker are responsible, demonstrate the ability to report accurate status reports to management, and keep the project both on time and under budget. Your role can be either as the technical expert or the business expert, but demonstrating the ability to understand an area that is not your specialty will be a key for future advancement.

Consider an example where you, as the technical expert, have been asked to work with someone in procurement who needs to set up a new application, and make the appropriate infrastructure changes to get a new application work with one of your company's suppliers. You will need to understand what the application needs to run, if it requires special network access, if other people may be using the application in the future, and the ramifications of the changes to the infrastructure this will require. You will work with the appropriate people, using your change process to get the solution.

This is a simplistic example, but the path to larger roles start with learning smaller roles, and demonstrating your ability to succeed.

For larger projects, and in some organizations, various project management certifications may be necessary to reach certain levels. Some certifications only require coursework and passing a test (such as a Certified Scrum Master), while others require a certain number of hours of work experience in the role.

HOW TO IMPROVE YOUR SKILLS

The most growth is going to be had by being involved in projects that are in as wide a range of fields as possible. If, for example, you have managed a mobile device management implementation, a new firewall rollout, and a new two-factor authentication subsystem, your breadth of experience will set you apart from others in the field.

RECOGNIZING WHEN YOU'RE STUCK

If the projects you are managing are getting smaller, have a lower visibility within the company, or have trouble getting the resources necessary to complete them, you are stuck. If your projects focus on maintaining legacy applications rather than implementing new technologies or mission critical tasks, then you are also starting to stagnate in this role. Those tasks are fine as you are starting in the role, but you want to move into projects involving newer technology as you advance.

HOW TO GET OUT

If you want to change organizations, there will be opportunities, as this role (as of this writing) is in moderately high demand. If you wish to change roles, a lateral move to Business Analyst, Patch Management, or Vulnerability Management will often be a logical step, as many of the underlying skills are similar. For more dramatic changes, a move to Risk Assessment or Security Assessment may be feasible, depending on your skill set.

Table 2.9 Role at a Glance—Security Facilitator

Hours	Travel	Stress Level	Creativity	Flexibility	Stability
8–10 hours/day	Low	Low	Moderate	High	High
General job duties	The job duties for a security facilitator will vary widely with what you are helping to facilitate. Generally, there will be a lot of reading and a lot of pulling together different documents, emails, and specification lists to make sure that everything is getting done as it should.				
Learning	This is a very learning-focused job as you will largely be doing work to help people who have less time than you. This means that, while they can guide you somewhat, you will have to do a lot of learning on your own.				
Advancement	Security Facilitators tend to move on to being assessors or project managers.				

TIER 2—SECURITY FACILITATOR—STORY

2.9.1

JIMMY VO

My story begins at age 10, where I received my first computer. In that day, it was a top-of-the-line Dell, with a blazing 333 MHz with 64MiB of RAM running Windows 98. I ended up spending a lot of time in front of the computer, mostly waiting for an AOL dial-in number that wasn't busy. Since then, I was fascinated by computers, taking them apart, making webpages, playing games and various geek activities. I didn't do anything remarkable like many other information security professionals did when they were younger like write crazy applications or break into something they weren't supposed to. Being in front of a computer was a hobby. Fast-forward to my high school years where I excelled (compared to the other students) in the programming classes. Believe it or not, I took two programming classes in high school. BASIC and visual basic, nothing crazy.

It was a natural that I wanted to work with technology. I applied to colleges and was accepted to Montclair State University to study Information Technology. At MSU, I had my first tech job, working the help desk where I help people with their connectivity and email problems. I transferred colleges and finally graduated from The Richard Stockton College of NJ after 5.5 years with my Computer Science degree. I recall finishing up my last semester, with little experience, and thinking the job hunt would be easy. Boy was I wrong.

I learned many lessons during my college days that I wish I would have known sooner. I wish I would have been more involved, networked more, and spent more time working jobs that added relevant experience. I luckily landed my first full time job as the Systems Analyst at a small company. It was at this time I really focused on self-improvement. I participated in Toastmasters and spent a lot of time building my professional network, focusing on my online presence (Twitter) and getting all of the knowledge I could. I also decided to pursue my master's in Computer Information Systems with a Security focus at Boston University. I occasionally applied for security jobs during my time at this organization; however, I was unexperienced and not hirable (even with a master's degree, take note).

I was a systems analyst for a couple of years until I approached my boss and came up with a plan to transition into a more security-based role. With a lot of convincing and a solid plan I was able to focus a bit on security planning. Now I was getting my hands on various domains of security, such as policy writing, bit of risk management, security ops, vendor management, etc. Being the only security guy and extremely inexperienced, I identified that I wasn't growing as a security professional. I needed to be around a smart team of experienced guys to mentor and help me grow.

When I decided to hit the job market, I did it in a different way than searching job boards. I reached out to my professional network and Twitter followers. I was able to land multiple interviews with organizations without having to deal with the application process because of Twitter. After months of interviewing, I was picked up by a consulting firm. All. Because. Of. Twitter. Let that sink in.

The Cliff Notes version of my long-winded story: be passionate, invest in yourself, meet people, hustle—and good things will happen.

TIER 2—POLICY ADMINISTRATOR

INTRODUCTION

Policies are the core of any organization's security infrastructure. Clearly defined policies provide guidance to those that are responsible for implementing security controls across the company.

While the above statement may appear simple, the management of those policies takes significant effort, especially in larger organizations. The process of gathering the policies, ensuring that they are all recorded properly per the organization's standards, reviewed periodically, and implemented properly can become a full-time responsibility. Some organizations, rather than have dedicated individuals who only focus on this role, will blend the responsibilities in with other roles, but the tasks are still necessary.

The Policy Administrator is not responsible for setting policy. Management and subject matter experts with expertise in the appropriate regulations are commonly responsible for setting the policy. Only people in certain roles being allowed access to a certain module within the enterprise resource planning (ERP) system, no visiting of certain types of websites, or only people within certain roles being allowed to view logs on the server are all parts of security policies.

All of these policies would be documented, and provided to the appropriate technical administrator (such as Network Administrator or System Administrator) for implementation. Depending on the organizational structure, the person responsible for collecting the policies might be responsible for the implementation as well but in other organizations this would be a conflict of interest.

Documentation of the implementation of the policy is necessary, and usually done through some type of change management system.

Finally, in well-run organizations, policies will be reviewed periodically for continued appropriateness. As the business changes, it is important to ensure that the group that has access to a system is still appropriate given the current organizational structure.

HOW TO BREAK IN

The method for breaking into Policy Administration is going to depend on the target organization's structure. If the organization is structured so that individuals have more vertical responsibilities, technical skills are going to be required. In this example, an individual would be responsible for gathering and implementing all policies around Active Directory. This type of role requires a combination of business and technical skill sets that would be necessary to demonstrate that you either possess or are capable of learning quickly. For this type of role, experience as a Systems Administrator, Network Administrator, or similar technical roles may be required.

If an organization is more skill-focused, working with business process owners and being able to work with technical people will be key. This role is going to be more focused on documenting and collecting, across a wide range of technologies, and leaving the implementation to the technical experts. Being able to work with the technical experts, to be able to ensure that the desired policies are possible for a given infrastructure, is important. For that kind of organization, Auditor, Risk Assessment, Security Assessment, or similar roles are potential previous experience.

HOW TO IMPROVE YOUR SKILLS

This role provides ample opportunity to grow in a variety of directions. By working with business process owners, you will develop an understanding of business needs and drivers. Understanding this is a key success factor in moving on to positions with more responsibility.

Whether you are responsible for implementing solutions, or working with those who implement solutions, your technical skills should improve as you go through the processes. Working to ensure that you are using the best method for the platform that you are on, or working to streamline the implementation, are important skills for future advancement.

RECOGNIZING WHEN YOU'RE STUCK

This role can turn into exclusively a bureaucratic paper-pusher role, where you gather and document. While this can be a useful stage in your career, especially if you are new to learning about business processes, if you find that you are no longer learning about the business then you have probably maximized your growth potential within this role and it is time to start investigating other roles.

HOW TO GET OUT

The policy administrator has business, documentation, and audit skills. Auditor would be a potential move, especially for an individual who has demonstrated the ability to audit an existing policy set to ensure it is appropriate for the current business model. Risk Assessment may be possible if you have developed your technical skills to understand the underlying technologies. Strong business and documentation skills with the front line experience in security may make others roles available such as a Tier 2 Trainer-Educator.

Table 2.a Role at a Glance—Policy Administrator

Hours	Travel	Stress Level	Creativity	Flexibility	Stability
8/day	Low	Low	Low	Low	Moderate
General job duties	Working with business process owners to identify the appropriate permissions for various roles. Ensuring that policies are implemented appropriately. This position is usually based out of the location where it is most needed, and all work with other offices can be done remotely. This position is rarely dealing with crisis level issues. If an individual is determined to have permissions that they should not have, then well documented histories should protect the policy administrator. If, however, policy decisions are not well documented, then stress levels can be higher. Creativity and flexibility are limited due the need to be guided by the business.				
Learning	Moderate early in the role, decreasing over time. When first in this role, you will have the opportunity to learn about many business processes. As time goes on, the learning will decrease.				
Advancement	Taking the time to learn about a range of business processes provides the opportunity to move into other roles where technology and business process intersect.				

2.b TIER 2—TRAINER-EDUCATOR

INTRODUCTION

At Tier 1, the Trainer-Educator generally is mostly limited to using materials developed by others—some centralized organization produces a standard set of documentation that you work from. At the more advanced Tier 2 Trainer-Educator level, you are responsible for creating your training materials for you and others. For example, education providers that focus on training professionals in one-week boot camps would use these materials for their training sessions. Some individuals work as consultants for training companies whose clients do not want to bring full-time personnel in house, but still have regular needs for trainers.

In some cases, an advanced trainer who has been hired to provide some level of customized training will be brought in for a training company. The contractor would take the standard core materials that the training company uses, and adjust them to meet the requirements of the client. These trainers must be able to work independently with very little guidance beyond, "The client wants you to focus on....."

Advanced Trainer-Educators need to have combined subject matter expertise and teaching ability. They must be able to go outside of the training materials when asked, and be able to adjust to a wide range of students in the class simultaneously.

HOW TO BREAK IN

Some form of training experience will be required. If you have worked as a trainer where you worked exclusively from others' materials, that can help provide the foundation, but a demonstrated ability to develop training materials is necessary. Such examples might include adjusting course materials for a course that you were teaching at the local community college, creating course work at a company where you work, or coming up with materials to teach a technical subject at a local community center.

Similarly, in order to develop these materials, a comprehensive understanding of the material that you will be teaching is required. Depending on the subject matter, this knowledge could be gained from hands-on experience or through coursework. When developing new materials, you will often find there are small gaps in your knowledge, where you did not fully understand why you were doing what you were doing. As you prepare to teach the material, the why becomes critical, as you will be called upon to display that knowledge frequently while teaching.

In order to teach certain subjects, it will often be expected that you have certifications in the field. This is especially true when you are teaching courses targeting preparation for a specific credential. It will generally be required that you have that credential in order for you to be hired to teach that material.

HOW TO IMPROVE YOUR SKILLS

When teaching in a technical field, it is critical that you maintain a current knowledge set. Whether it is in security, networking, or server management, the new material is something that you must keep up with in order to maintain your marketability within a given market.

Similarly, it is valuable to increase the breadth of courses that you can teach. If you can teach security and networking, you will be more employable than a trainer who only can teach one of those subjects. When working for an organization as a trainer, you will often have access to the training material for other courses for free or significantly reduced costs. Take advantage of that to improve your skills in other areas.

RECOGNIZING WHEN YOU'RE STUCK

If you keep teaching the same material without updating, you need to evaluate whether teaching continues to be an appropriate role for you. If you find that the classes that you are teaching have gone from being cutting-edge classes to being legacy technologies, you are in danger of becoming marginalized and not employable.

HOW TO GET OUT

If you have maintained a solid technical understanding of the material, you can often move into the roles that you are training others to become. Be forewarned, though, that if you have spent an extensive time teaching, it may be harder to break back into technical roles, as some may question whether you have lost the ability to Do. That will be less of a hurdle if you can demonstrate that you have developed materials, such as labs, that revolve around Doing.

Table 2.b Role at a Glance—Trainer-Educator

Hours	Travel	Stress Level	Creativity	Flexibility	Stability
8/day	High	Low–Moderate	Moderate	Varies	Low
General job duties	Presenting coursework, developing coursework If you teach boot camps, long days where 12 hours would exist. Travel may be high, due to going to different locations to do the training. Travel will be less frequent if you are in a major metropolitan area. Stress will vary based on the classes. Also, if there is a spike in stress, it is more likely to be short lived, just the duration of the class. Stability is low since in economic downturns, training is often the first to go, so demand for trainers is much more tied to economic cycles. Depending on the organization and training environment, you will have varying degrees of latitude in what you create for training material. Your flexibility will vary greatly based on whether you are an independent or working for an organization.				
Learning	It needs to be plentiful, either through the organization, or working independently to ensure that you are familiar with the current trends and technologies.				
Advancement	Not much. There may be opportunities to manage trainers, but there will not be many of those opportunities. Sometimes training classes can lead to consulting in other areas, but that varies dramatically based on the material and the trainer.				

2.c TIER 2—QUALITY ASSURANCE

INTRODUCTION

> "There are two ways to write error-free programs; only the third one works."
>
> — **Alan Perlis**

It is important to clarify the difference between Quality Assurance and Quality Control. As a Tier 1 Software Tester, you are doing quality control. You are making sure that the resulting product (software) has the functionality expected of it. Quality Assurance is making sure you are using proper processes to create that product. In some cases, positions that are advertised as Quality Assurance positions are actually Quality Control positions.

That said, as software development matures, the need for true Quality Assurance engineers is becoming more common. Many organizations need to ensure that their development is done to ISO-9000 standards or at certain levels of the SEI Capability Maturity Model (CMM). Fully describing those standards is outside the scope of this book, but they are ways of approaching software development so that the product produced meets the various system and functionality requirements. This involves ensuring requirements are documented, being able to demonstrate that all of the requirements are met, and having clearly defined processes for addressing issues that are discovered. Some standards also require the lessons learned while doing the development be used to improve the processes for subsequent development.

You will find that different organizations have very different levels of process associated with their software development. Organizations with poor processes will give software testers an approximate idea of what the software is supposed to do, based on very loose engineering requirements, and ask them to test the software. In this case, no quality assurance is being done. When an organization is managing an end-to-end requirements management system, where requirements are traced to test plans that are traced to test results, a true Quality Assurance system is in place.

There are other process models (such as Six Sigma or US Department of Defense standards) that can be used in association with software development as well. Which ones are in use in your organization will depend on the business culture and the regulating body to which your business reports (US EPA, US FDA, US Department of Defense, or others).

Understanding the software development processes is a key component to securing your organization. All too often, security is an afterthought in development, leaving systems vulnerable to attack. If you go into a role as a Chief Information Security Officer or similar role, you will have responsibility for ensuring that software developed internally is secure. Understanding the processes that support secure development is extremely valuable.

HOW TO BREAK IN

This position is one that can be advanced to from a Quality Tester position. While working as a tester, understand all of the various components associated with the system that your company is using. There are many common facets to all of the systems (requirements management, documentation of the various stages in the process), and understanding those will be critical for advancement within the field.

After you have learned the general concepts associated with a standardized software development process, lower-level Quality Assurance positions will be available to you. For upper-level positions, understanding of one or more of the standards that organizations must meet is required.

If you are a Systems Administrator, become the administrator for the systems that are responsible for supporting the processes at your company. This will give you the opportunity to learn about the standards from an implementation perspective, improving your marketability.

No matter what your role, if Quality Assurance is your goal, try to get involved in any team that is responsible for improving process. This will give you the opportunity to understand both the business drivers and the standards.

HOW TO IMPROVE YOUR SKILLS

The best way to improve your skills is through your day-to-day tasks. Be involved in the process of developing processes and systems.

RECOGNIZING WHEN YOU'RE STUCK

If you find yourself simply approving changes in processes that others are making, and not being a driver for change yourself, you are stuck. The key to growth is to be part of driving the changes that an organization implements. Have you created or improved processes? Are you making difference in the quality in the organization? Is quality at least not going down? If not, despite your best efforts, the problem may not be you, but the organization.

HOW TO GET OUT

If you are stuck because the organization does not give you the opportunity to be part of the changes, moving to a different company but in the same role is a logical step. If you find that you are not interested in the tasks any more, moving to Auditor is a logical step. Other roles may be feasible as well, depending upon the skills you have developed along the way.

Table 2.c Role at a Glance—Quality Assurance

Hours	Travel	Stress Level	Creativity	Flexibility	Stability
8/day	Low	Moderate	Low	Low	High
General job duties	Developing processes in order to meet standards. Ensuring that current processes meet with external standards. Changing processes as business needs change. Optimizing processes based upon lessons learned from other projects. There will be stresses in ensuring that the business processes are holding to the standards. One of the common stresses in this role is understanding how to enforce a standard when the business unit responsible for the process is unwilling or unable to work to the standard, but it is generally a stable position. There is little creativity or flexibility in this role due to the external forces that drive this role.				
Learning	There is a significant opportunity to learn about business process within this role. Additional opportunities to learn from peers and auditors that you work with are available.				
Advancement	Lateral to Auditor. Management opportunities may present themselves as well.				

TIER 2—SUBJECT MATTER EXPERT

2.d

INTRODUCTION

An information technology subject matter expert (SME), pronounced either as "ess em ee" or "smee," goes beyond the subject matter specialist. The SME may be the best in the company, and possibly the best in the field, or even in the top 20 in a software engineering organization. But an SME might just be someone who has some specialized knowledge that no one else has on the team. The particular meaning depends upon the organization and organizational culture.

The SME is the person that everyone in the organization turns to when there is an issue in that subject. They are the final person to work with. If you are the SME, and you do not have the answer, you will be expected to be able to do the research necessary to come up with the answer. For very specialized subjects, it may be part of one's overall job responsibilities.

HOW TO BREAK IN

Find the existing SMEs in any subject in the organization and learn from them, and refer other people to them. If you eventually learn enough in a subject, you may become an SME if either of you leaves the organization. There may be no master to learn from directly, but there might still be a mentor or master within or without the organization to learn from. For example, if a consultant comes in to work with a system, learn as much as you can from this person. If an organization has no SME position, that's an opportunity for *you* to become that SME, officially or not. If someone asks a question in a particular area, volunteer to find the answer. Do the deep research, find an expert if you can, go beyond just that question, and provide the answer and be able to answer the next question before it's even asked.

Some organizations have a formal or semiformal role of SME, or may be willing to create one; others may merely have a culture in which people know who the best are in any particular area.

An SME role might come about by accident; by simply spending the time as a normal part of a full-time job, someone may discover themselves to be considered the expert. However, by consciously choosing a particular area of focus, the prospective SME can accomplish the goal faster, in a distinctively useful area. Information technology is sufficiently broad that there are few SMEs in any organization. By choosing an area that no one else in the organization knows or knows well, a prospective SME can quickly become the expert. One example of this would be the management of a newly released product. By definition, there is no one who understands that tool. By taking ownership and responsibility for that product, you can quickly become the SME in the organization. To be recognized as an SME outside your organization will probably take more time, but as it's now part of your job, you can devote work time to benefit your organization and yourself.

It takes thousands of hours to become an expert. However, to be considered an expert in the local area can merely be knowing more than anyone else available.

HOW TO IMPROVE YOUR SKILLS

Growth can be upward (enhancing skills in your specific area) or outward (expanding your area of expertise). As the SME, growing upward will require independent, self-guided research. For gaining breadth, take advantage of the projects that you are working on with others. As an SME, you will frequently be part of larger teams; take advantage of that to expand your skill set.

RECOGNIZING WHEN YOU'RE STUCK

If you do not enjoy the tasks you are responsible for, and you likely won't learn to go any deeper, especially if the organization doesn't want you to, then you are stuck. It's time to move on.

HOW TO GET OUT

Being stuck as an SME may not be a bad thing, and can be a suitable end-point for a career. However, transitioning from being an SME can be difficult, as they tend to be highly valued in their area and may not have sufficient qualifications to get into another area and be as well-regarded, or as well-paid.

One way to get out is to develop additional skills needed to document and train others to do it. Another way is to work yourself out of a job by establishing automated systems and processes.

Some organizations may require an SME who has been within the organization a long time to move laterally, so others can gain knowledge in that area. Additionally, there may be opportunity for promotions where aspects of their experience can be applied in new ways.

Table 2.d Role at a Glance—Subject Matter Expert

Hours	Travel	Stress Level	Creativity	Flexibility	Stability
8+ hours/day	Varies	Moderate–High	Moderate	Moderate	High
General job duties	Project and program management (planning, scheduling, budgeting) Research. Mentoring. Writing whitepapers, documentation. Reviewing others' work. Stress can be lower because the job is well understood and well managed, but stress can be high due to high expectations. Can be very stable because no one else can do the job. The travel varies. In companies with many locations, there may be a high amount of travel due to being the only person who can do the job. There is only moderate creativity and flexibility. As the expert in your area, you are allowed significant freedoms with that area. However, being able to branch out can be challenging.				
Learning	The SME can be, by definition, limited in learning as there may be little more to learn from others. Although, few areas so small and so well known that there is truly nothing more to learn.				
Advancement	An SME may be the highest level available in an organization for that particular subject area. Some organizations have special non-managerial career paths for technical staff. This can include addition to titles such as: Senior, Principal, Chief, or "Vice President of". These can sometimes be paths to broader knowledge, not unlike a post-graduate education, but consider it on the job training.				

TIER 2—SUBJECT MATTER EXPERT— STORY

2.d.1

MICHAEL HUBER

I mentor in the SANS program in the more traditional sense informally and formally in the local community in NC. I am informally assisting three new professionals in entering the InfoSec field from their current positions.

So my recommendations are based on my path that I took as well as learning from the mistakes I made earlier in my career to help others in not hitting the same pitfalls.

My path into information security started while I was still in college in 01990 when I started working on removing viruses from Windows machines as well as bugs from the UNIX world. In my first ten years I dedicated myself to understanding both Windows and *nix worlds in all their complexity and to ensure that I became a subject matter expert in those areas. My focus was to understand down to the bits and bytes how and why these operating systems functioned to better protect them. I then moved on and in my next ten years I focused on understanding the non-technical portions of the information security profession. I still keep my hand in the technical arena with a home lab but my day job is one that is focused on risk mitigation and I have certifications in both the Information Security and Risk fields. I have added teaching and mentoring in the last ten years and giving back to the community.

My recommendation to someone starting out is to become the SME for your technical love (Windows, *nix, Macintosh, mobile, cloud) and understand how it functions down to the machine level, and then branch out from there. Keep focused on business processes and risk mitigation throughout your career. Good resources are SANS (301, 401, 501) when you start out, get CISSP and CRISC once you have three to five years under your belt of hands-on in the field while continuing to grow your skills through the many other classes and certifications that SANS, ISACA, (ISC)[2], and the European Council have available, depending on what part of the profession you love. Love what you do and you will go far.

CHAPTER

2.e — TIER 2—LATERAL: PHYSICAL SECURITY

INTRODUCTION—HOW THIS APPLIES

Traditionally, physical security and information security were completely isolated roles with no interaction. As the tools used for physical security increasingly involve a technological component, and the assets protected by information systems increase in value, the segregation has blurred, and increasingly the departments have become integrated.

In the 01960s, nearly all security was physical. While there were some electronic systems, and they may have been protected with passwords, the primary control was the location of the terminals, where the wires were accessible from, and the simple fact that electronics were essentially non-portable. As computers increased in processing power for their unit size, connectivity increased, and more assets were stored electronically, the need for information security increased. Simultaneously, those responsible for physical security began to use tools that were connected and computer-based.

Today information security specialists must consider physical security (how exactly will the server room be secured), and physical security specialists must ensure that their information systems are protected (how will the physical access control system network and servers be secured). Will the server room be secured with the physical access control system? Could a network vulnerability compromise the server room physical security which could then compromise the physical access control system which then compromises everything else in a cascade failure?

The key to remember is that in all cases, the goal is to reduce risk. The quality and types of locks used for a room are going to be dependent upon the value of the items that they are protecting. The evaluation process used to determine what controls are necessary on that room are essentially the same as the process for determining what technical controls will be put in place to protect a server.

Physical security is enough a part of information security that $(ISC)^2$ includes a whole domain on physical security as part of the CISSP exam. Similarly ASIS certification considers information security to be a part of information security and includes a section information security in its exam.

WHAT SKILLS THIS GIVES YOU

Physical security and information security both rely on the same processes for risk assessment: identifying the threats, understanding the vulnerabilities, and putting controls in place to bring the level of risk to the point that the organization is comfortable with it. Though the details may differ, the processes are similar enough that they can be transferable between the two areas.

Similarly, many penetration tests now include a physical access component. Are the pen testers able to gain access to the building when they should not have been? Doing so will often give them additional access to information assets, and so physical access tests are included when an all-encompassing

130

pen test is run. Being familiar with the underlying physical security processes, procedures, and tools will increase the value of the pen tests that you run.

WHAT SKILLS YOU MIGHT STILL NEED

The move into physical security from information security will require you to become familiar with the tools and terminology used in that field. Understanding such things as the concepts behind crime prevention through environmental design, what features make locks pick-resistant, and how to determine wall and door fire ratings requires understanding of new terms and concepts, and new definitions of old terms.

The move from physical to information security is similar. ASIS International physical security certifications, Associated Locksmiths of America (ALOA) certifications, or locksmithing apprenticeship and experience all will give you a solid grounding. Information security people can learn them in similar ways from physical security people, or from other information security people who learned physical security the hard way.

HOW TO FRAME YOUR SKILLS

For those interested in making the transition, you will need to focus on the areas where the two areas of security overlap: risk assessment. Demonstrating your ability to perform your skills, and apply them to the areas of information security that overlap with physical security will provide you with some common ground for discussion. Despite that, this type of transition will not be easy, as you will be competing against those who come from a background specializing in physical security.

DIFFERENCES BETWEEN WHERE YOU ARE AND INFORMATION SECURITY

CULTURE

Traditionally, the physical security specialist often came from a military or police background, because those professions provided training and experience that could be transferred to the private sector. The rigid structure found in those environments is very different from the freewheeling, independent environments that many information security professionals are used to. But as information security becomes a fundamental component of business, it will become more formalized, while those working in physical security are beginning to see the value in out-of-the-box thinking that is more traditionally seen in information security. There will be an increasing convergence between physical security and information security, as they become sub-specialties of a future holistic full-security discipline. A move in this direction is already apparent in companies that have a single converged security department, and is further demonstrated by the fact that the (ISC)^2 CBK contains physical security and ASIS has an information security domain.

TERMINOLOGY

Risk, threat, vulnerability, and other terms used for risk assessments will have different nuances based on the background that you come from. That really should not be a surprise, as you will find that even within information security, different standards organizations have different definitions. You will need to become familiar with the specific definitions for those you will be working with, to ensure that you are working from the same vocabulary.

2.f TIER 2—LATERAL: MILITARY

INTRODUCTION—HOW THIS APPLIES

The military includes such a wide range of skills that there is no way to cover them all here. However, as the military does provide an entry to information security for some, it is worth discussing.

Military service involves a wide range of roles. From the foot soldier that so many associate with the military to the quartermaster to the cook—all require their own sets of skills. As of the time of this writing, one of the biggest concerns within the military was that there were not enough information security experts to meet demand. Because of this, you may find your entry into information security through military service.

Keep in mind that the roles available to you within the military will be dependent upon your existing skills and what skills and roles are needed by that particular military organization. Being able to demonstrate technology skills (either through a degree or certification) will make it more likely that you will be able to convince your recruiter to slot you to one of those specialized roles. But there are no certainties, and recruiters may make unrealistic promises that cannot be kept.

Each branch of the military has its own roles. You can investigate to get more specific details not only about what roles are available, but what is required to get into that role. A quick Internet search of the branch you are interested in along with "information technology" in the search will get you to the various options available.

WHAT SKILLS THIS GIVES YOU

Beyond the specific skills you gain for the role you enter, you will learn discipline and teamwork. You will rely on others, just as others will rely on you to achieve a common goal—but one you will often quite deliberately not fully know or understand, but are able to work toward because of military discipline.

Many employing organizations view former military service favorably because of these skills and experience, and some have special programs for military veterans and current military people.

WHAT SKILLS YOU MIGHT STILL NEED

What options are available to you in the military will depend upon what skills you bring when enlisting. Civilian life and corporate culture are very different from the military. For example, some civilian organizations have specific uniforms and formal requirements, but most do not and it will be awkward to wear a three- piece suit when everyone else is wearing jeans and t-shirts.

More importantly, you will need to develop a feel for when processes need to be followed and when an ad-hoc approach is warranted. Civilian jobs will have less structure and more personal responsibility and flexibility. This is, however, a sword that cuts both ways. The same structure that restricts you, also protects you, and as that structure lessens in the corporate world, you will be exposing yourself to more risk as well as greater responsibility.

HOW TO FRAME YOUR SKILLS

There are multiple ways to enter the military. For young adults and students, a high school military academy or reserve officer training corps during college may provide opportunities. Which path you choose will determine how to best present yourself. This is a broad topic and outside the scope of this book.

DIFFERENCES BETWEEN WHERE YOU ARE AND INFORMATION SECURITY
CULTURE

The military's rigid structure and information security's renegade image are definitely at odds. However, as information security becomes a more integrated part of business, the need for professionals who are comfortable working within the system has continually increased. While former military may or may not be comfortable at the anarchy seen at security conventions such as DEF CON, they certainly are finding civilian employment.

TERMINOLOGY

The military frequently has its own set of terms that civilians may or may not be familiar with. If you move to civilian information security you will need to understand how military jargon maps to civilian terms. Some civilian information security terms came from the military, like "perimeter," and "defense in depth," but others aren't quite as common yet, and might be misunderstood or have poor connotations such as "kill-chain" or "exclusion zone."

2.g TIER 2—LATERAL: LAW ENFORCEMENT

INTRODUCTION—HOW THIS APPLIES

Like other broad fields, Law Enforcement encompasses a wide range of skills and abilities. While your local police officer is probably your image of Law Enforcement, there are many roles beyond, especially in larger organizations. This breadth of potential roles expands even further if you include federal law enforcement agencies.

The most obvious (and first) overlap between information security and law enforcement is in the area of computer forensics. The Incident Responder role will need to have some level of computer forensics skills, and larger teams often have a dedicated forensics person. That said, as information security expands, so do the opportunities within law enforcement. The US FBI now has a wide range of career opportunities in information security as does the US Department of Homeland Security. The US Secret Service will form Electronic Crimes Task Forces, which include establishing partnerships with a wide range of organizations. See the Appendix for links to these and other US government resources.

This breadth of opportunity within law enforcement provides entry points for those individuals who are comfortable working in a highly structured and regulated environment.

WHAT SKILLS THIS GIVES YOU

For those roles that are not information security-related, concepts in physical security will be at least part of your duties. Law enforcement skills and experience include formal process and procedures, crisis management, psychology, human nature, and de-escalation, and the justice system, all of which can be valuable in a holistic view of information security.

WHAT SKILLS YOU MIGHT STILL NEED

The most likely gap in your skills will be in your technical skills. This gap can be filled through formal or independent study.

HOW TO FRAME YOUR SKILLS

For those in law enforcement hoping to move into information security, the easiest path often will be within your organization or to a similar organization. If, through some form of study or certification program, you can demonstrate an aptitude for learning computer technical skills, lateral opportunities within your organization are likely the simplest road to information security. Take advantage of the fact that you are already established within the organization.

DIFFERENCES BETWEEN WHERE YOU ARE AND INFORMATION SECURITY CULTURE

The cultural differences between law enforcement and the information security world has changed over time. While conferences such as DEF CON used to be primarily aimed at individuals, with an occasional law enforcement individual, they now are seen as important educational opportunities for information security professionals from all backgrounds.

There will still be distrust in some circles regarding those coming from a law enforcement background, but that should not limit one's career opportunities.

TERMINOLOGY

The biggest challenge will be ensuring that a common set of definitions is used, especially in the area of risk assessment and risk management, as those terms vary.

CHAPTER

2.g.1 TIER 2—LATERAL: LAW ENFORCEMENT— STORY

JOSHUA MARPET

Although all information security stories are unique, Joshua's is unusual. Although Joshua has a background in information technology, he was also a cop, a horse show announcer, a blacksmith, a certified horse dentist (still is), a bouncer on New Orleans' Bourbon Street during the Super Bowl and Mardi Gras, and waiter. To the best of his knowledge, he was the only Jewish jail guard in the United States Deep South. Joshua also has a BA in psychology.

His work in information technology was as a sysadmin, forensics, pen testing, and infosec entrepreneur. As he says, "If it's a job, I've done it;" and in those jobs, he says, "There's always got to be someone I can learn from."

He has had several turning points in his career, but the one that got him into information security was when he was working as a system administrator when his co-worker accidentally shut down one of the largest payroll systems in the US. The co-worker just didn't expect the shutdown command to work for non-privileged users. That was the moment Joshua decided to go into information security.

Joshua was in the dot com boom and bust of the late 01990s and early 02000s, and made the mistake of accepting stock options instead of actual pay. So he took his stock options and ended up as a Louisiana cop during Hurricane Katrina in 02005, and learned the hard way how to be prepared for disaster recovery in the devastating damage and floods. He stayed behind, but evacuated his girlfriend and children to New Jersey along with his mother.

Weeks later, he was able to tell his family that he and the house had survived the hurricane and they could come back to Louisiana. But his family had already settled down in New Jersey and wanted to stay. Even then, in the aftermath of Hurricane Katrina as he tried to leave and get to New Jersey, he had beat up someone to keep his truck (he had an ASP baton, they didn't, he won).

He did get to New Jersey and was reunited with his family. But he couldn't be a cop in New Jersey—he was too old at age 33—so he got back into computers, system administration, and various jobs.

Since then, he's learned digital forensics and pen testing, spoken at 30 to 40 conferences including Black Hat and DEF CON, and does security advisory services.

He got fired for doing a DEF CON presentation about shooting a camera from a flare launcher, that was later seen by someone at his employer, but he only found out the reason a year later. That firing prompted him to start his own company, and he's glad he did. He founded Guarded Risk. He says, "That exit story got me to a new origin story."

In the past year, he's been doing startups but this time he's getting paid by "taking stock options in addition to this thing called money."

136

He has a client list and is making money. His business is building and growing: "you can see the growth that's real magic."

Some advice from Joshua:

"It's a few different things that make a difference in infosec, who you know, what you know, and who knows what you know."

On being an entrepreneur: "You'd better have a lot of money squirreled away or be prepared to be poor."

He recommends having friends, helping people, and volunteering. He's on staff at several information security conferences where he's known as the "infosec megaphone" and the "infosec therapist."

2.h TIER 2—LATERAL: LEGAL— LAWYERS

INTRODUCTION—HOW THIS APPLIES

Information security and the legal professions used to have no overlap, well except when a lawyer defended or prosecuted an information security criminal case. Today, with the number of laws guiding the use of data, federal requirements for minimum levels of protection for a wide range of data types, and business agreements with third-party suppliers (such as cloud providers), information security is becoming an area of focus in the legal field.

The regulation of information security does not mean that lawyers are starting to become educated in the information security field. However, each side is becoming more aware of the issues the other faces, and the two fields are more likely to be working together. For example, when setting up an arrangement with a cloud provider, the legal team may work with an information security professional to determine what types of auditing and reporting would be necessary to meet certain standards the company must abide by.

The regulation of the financial industry has also led to greater interaction between legal and information security teams. Determining how to meet requirements for traceability, information isolation, and compliance will often require cooperation between both skill sets.

WHAT SKILLS THIS GIVES YOU

Being a lawyer will help you understand the drivers behind certain information security positions. The ability to evaluate and interpret the regulations surrounding the data a company manages is a key skill at the upper levels of information security. Because of this, lawyers are more likely to move to management or upper management positions such as chief information security officer (CISO) or chief privacy officer (CPO). In fact, the demands of the CPO position often make someone with a legal background an excellent fit.

WHAT SKILLS YOU MIGHT STILL NEED

Because of the way that the legal field and information security overlap, the fit is either going to be very good (such as the Chief Privacy Officer example mentioned above), or very poor (for example, as a pen tester) where strong technical skills are required. Thus, transitions from Lawyer to information security are generally constrained to those positions that focus more on dealing with regulatory compliance and other legal-focused drivers.

To move from information security into the legal field, exact requirements will vary from state to state. In most cases, passing a bar exam is required, but that is not true in all cases. That discussion is left for other texts. The legal field isn't just about lawyers and law degrees and passing the bar exam, considerable work in the legal field is done by paralegals and legal secretaries. Law firms also often directly employ non-legal staff for specialized knowledge such as technology, forensics, and investigators.

HOW TO FRAME YOUR SKILLS

While it is understood that those who are capable of filling a CISO- or CPO-level position are unlikely to use this book for career guidance, the process for moving into a new position is going to be similar to the general process all job hunters go through: find an organization that needs skills and demonstrate how your skills are a good fit for their needs. In the case of CPO, this would include demonstrating an understanding of the regulations the organization is held to, and how the applicant can help the organization achieve compliance with those regulations through their past work experience.

DIFFERENCES BETWEEN WHERE YOU ARE AND INFORMATION SECURITY
CULTURE

Law and information security both must deal with an ever-changing landscape. However, the process for change within the legal profession is much more methodical and event-driven. New laws and regulations generally come into being as a reaction to events that have occurred in the past, and when a new law comes into place, it may take years for the full impact of the law to be felt or even understood. The cycle of a new law coming into place, issues being found, and new laws being enacted can be a process that extends over years, or even decades.

In contrast, the action and reaction between a new exploitation technique and new security feature will often have a life cycle time of weeks or months. Though this life cycle time is increasing as infrastructures become more ingrained (and there are examples such as Internet Border Gateway Protocol (BGP) security that are taking decades to fix), response times are more often likely to be rapid, especially if your organization is at risk.

A similar split occurs when dealing with active attacks. If you are involved in a lawsuit, you can appeal deadlines, ask a judge to impose rules upon your adversary or avoid rules from the adversary, and have months to evaluate your course of action.

When dealing with an active security incident, there is no such arbiter, no such flexibility of time. The attacking entity will do whatever they can, without any external restrictions beyond the technology. In contrast, you may be limited in that you are bound by legal actions. For example, if a botnet is attacking you with a distributed denial-of-service attack, there is no law that allows you to disable the attacking computers. You may be able to work with Internet service providers (ISP) to limit activity, but you cannot directly counterattack.

TERMINOLOGY

As always, when two drastically different areas are working together, it is important to ensure that the vocabulary in use is the same. Regulations frequently define the vocabulary in use, and the information security professional must ensure that they are using the appropriate terms for the environment in which they are working.

2.i TIER 2—LATERAL: SALES

INTRODUCTION—HOW THIS APPLIES

The business world runs on sales. Most jobs are classified as "overhead" or cost center which costs money or "revenue generating" or profit center which makes money. Most information security roles outside of consulting firms are viewed as overhead. Sales, however, brings in the money—the lifeblood of all organizations. While a move from sales to an information security position will be challenging (because of the technical skills required), the move from information security to sales does have some paths available, should that be the direction you wish to go.

Sales is not for introverts. If you thrive working head-down in your cubicle, focusing on the technical task at hand, then the daily introduction to new people with a wide range of agendas will be challenging, even stressful, for you. You need to be prepared, and comfortable with, walking into situations where the people on the other side of the table may be merely curious, potential allies, or outright antagonistic, and not knowing which when you sit down.

If you thrive on the challenge of "hooking" the client, and turning a "maybe" into a big sale, Sales is a path to consider.

For technical people, the path to sales will generally depend upon the size of the organization you are in. If you are in a smaller organization, sales may be one of your duties, simply because the company does not have anyone who is dedicated to sales. If you naturally become the leader at the sales meetings, that may end up becoming your full-time responsibility.

There are many sales teams that are made up of a combination of sales only (those specializing in the person-to-person interactions) and sales engineers (those specializing in providing demonstrations, answering technical questions, and describing architecturally how the product or service would be a good fit for the organization). As a technical person interested in moving into sales, the sales engineering role will provide you an opportunity to learn about sales in general and, if you display an aptitude for sales, an opportunity for moving into a sales-only role. One warning, though: good sales engineers are hard to find. If you are very good in that role, the company you are working for may not be willing to have you move out of the technical role.

WHAT SKILLS THIS GIVES YOU

Sales is all about people skills. Your ability to understand what others want and match that with what your company can provide is the core of sales. You must possess a combination of communication and negotiation skills to be successful. While these are skills that are useful in any role, they are required for sales.

WHAT SKILLS YOU MIGHT STILL NEED

For any given product or service, you will need to understand the specific market. Why are people interested in this type of product? What drives people to purchase your product rather than a competitor's? What product features are going to get you in the door, and which are going to close the sale? Understanding the value of these questions, and the answers to them, is going to aid your success in the field.

HOW TO FRAME YOUR SKILLS

Demonstrate your abilities in the working with others. If you have spent time doing some type of customer service role (e.g., help desk), emphasize your ability to work with a wide range of individuals, identify their specific skill sets, and provide them solutions to their problems. The same pattern is used with sales, except you may first need to convince the potential client that they have a need.

Additional relevant skills could be displayed in your ability to work with sales representatives. If you have experience on the client side of the table working with sales representatives, use that to demonstrate your abilities in sales. If you are an experienced negotiator working with vendors, that gives you insight into what drives those individuals, allowing you to focus on their specific needs.

DIFFERENCES BETWEEN WHERE YOU ARE AND INFORMATION SECURITY
CULTURE

Technical skills are all about building the thing. Sales is all about building the relationship. This creates a different dynamic in how you work to solve the problem. Depending on the environment, sales can be much more antagonistic with others that you are working with to reach the end goal. When battling a technical problem, generally everyone you are working with will have the same goal. In sales, that is rarely the case.

In sales you will find that your peers are not necessarily your allies. In many environments, managers explicitly pit sales representatives against each other in an effort to drive the overall top line. As such, there is frequently an underlying wariness associated with helping your peers (or receiving help). If you are not comfortable working in a cutthroat environment such as this, you will either need to be very choosy in the company you work for, or this may not be the field for you.

TERMINOLOGY

Be prepared to learn a new language. You'll likely be comfortable with technical product terms, the language of business will become more important to you. A simplistic example is the concept of return on investment (ROI). Many business decisions to purchase will be based on the need to have an ROI above a certain point; be prepared to ask to demonstrate how this product will provide a return to the company making the purchase.

That is a basic example, and the business language around your product will vary. Working as a Sales Engineer, or having been responsible for making these purchases, will often provide insight into the language of sales in your industry.

2.j TIER 2—LATERAL: PROJECT MANAGEMENT

INTRODUCTION—HOW THIS APPLIES

Project Management: the art and science of herding cats. While that may not be the formal definition, if that is your role, it will feel that way at some point. This role is similar to that of Security Facilitator, with the difference being one of degrees. A Security Facilitator will generally be responsible for monitoring a few (3–5) people, while a Project Manager has responsibility for projects that could potentially include hundreds of people. In those cases where a project spans such a large number of people, there will frequently be multiple tiers of project management, rolling up to a top-level manager.

These large-scale projects span large numbers of disciplines and will invariably impact the organization, either positively or negatively. Because of the scope and impact, these people may report to C-level executives within the organization. They also will have more authority to draw in resources from within the organization.

WHAT SKILLS THIS GIVES YOU

The organizational and project tracking skills required to manage large projects are valuable for managerial roles such as CISO. The people skills, sometimes referred to as soft skills, used for project management are relevant to any career path, though they are used more in managerial and lead roles.

WHAT SKILLS YOU MIGHT STILL NEED

The most likely gap will be in security-specific knowledge. While project managers will be good at understanding and coordinating a project, the underlying business process and technical expertise is left to others. Often, project managers who work closely with those with operational knowledge will develop some skills in those areas, but rarely enough to move into those areas. Rather, this provides them with a greater understanding of what those people do when it comes to managing people in those areas.

HOW TO FRAME YOUR SKILLS

When moving into managerial roles, the people and project management skills that you have developed will be the most useful in demonstrating your ability to take on these other roles.

DIFFERENCES BETWEEN WHERE YOU ARE AND INFORMATION SECURITY
CULTURE

When moving from project management to information security, the cultural differences will vary dramatically, depending on the roles or organization you move into. The managerial roles at large organizations will have little variance from your current role, but at a smaller, more technology-focused organization, the lack of formal process could be jarring.

TERMINOLOGY

Project Management has its own terms and definitions that are used for describing the state of a task and the project as a whole. As this vocabulary has essentially no overlap with information security terminology, the task is to learn new terms, rather than understanding the difference in how the same terms are used.

2.k TIER 2—LATERAL: NON-IT ENGINEERING—ARCHITECTURE—SCIENCE

INTRODUCTION—HOW THIS APPLIES

STEM—science, technology, engineering, and math—is a general term for areas of education and jobs that are critical for overall technological advancement of a society. This covers such a broad range of fields that it is impossible to describe the details associated with the various fields here. However, there are some common characteristics that can be discussed.

These fields all require some level of degree in order to enter them. A bachelor's degree will be necessary to function at the Do level—implementing solutions, and using their knowledge as part of a team. For leadership roles, a master's degree is often required. To be in charge of any form of research, a PhD will generally be required. This need for a degree is in stark contrast to information security. Though formal education is becoming more available for information security professionals, it is entirely possible to have a complete career without ever attending an accredited university.

Many security professionals in the industry over 15 years originally came from science backgrounds. In many cases, after getting their degree, they did not enter the workforce as a scientist, but rather had some level of computer background that they developed on the side, possibly while in college. For those with only a bachelor's degree, the job opportunities in computers were much more plentiful than those in their major, so they went into information technology roles. From there, they progressed to information security roles.

If you are interested in seeing an early move from sciences into information security, take a look at *The Cuckoo's Egg* by Clifford Stoll. It is a classic and entertaining book on information technology infrastructure and security in the 01980s. While the technology has advanced significantly since then, the underlying processes involved have not changed much: Find anomalies, be creative, investigate until they can be explained. Although most astronomers don't expose Cold War spy rings, Clifford Stoll did.

WHAT SKILLS THIS GIVES YOU

The domain-specific knowledge found in science and engineering will rarely be applicable to information security. In contrast, the general skills—problem solving, detailed record keeping, plan development and the like—are all very appropriate for information security.

In many cases these roles will include computer skills such as writing code or basic computer administration. These can be a foundation for computer security.

WHAT SKILLS YOU MIGHT STILL NEED

For those moving into information security, the role you are interested in moving into, and what you are moving from, will dictate what skills you need. Auditor-type roles may be easier to move into if you have experience doing scientific or engineering audits. Your familiarity with those processes will reduce the amount of information security-specific skills you need to develop. If you are moving from chemistry to pen testing, the path will take longer, as you will need to develop many information security-specific skills.

For those moving out of information security, a degree in the field that you wish to move into will probably be required. In fact, this author has no examples of a degree not being required, but I hesitate to say always, as there may be some exception out there I am not aware of.

HOW TO FRAME YOUR SKILLS

Moving into information security will require you to demonstrate a minimum level of technical ability to do the required tasks. Additionally, you will need to demonstrate the ability to learn and develop rapidly within your new field. Give examples of your technical skills: the program you wrote to collect data from a sensor, the RAID array you managed to store the data, or any other examples of information technology-related tasks that you have successfully dealt with in your career.

DIFFERENCES BETWEEN WHERE YOU ARE AND INFORMATION SECURITY
CULTURE

The most likely difference you will encounter will be the degree of uncertainty that information security sees as compared to science fields. While engineering and sciences all have uncertainty, it is generally treated as a variable to be included in the analysis, and used to calculate the margin of error you must work within. Conversely, in information security you sometimes have to accept that complete unknowns exist and work as best as possible to contain them, never having complete control over the variables.

Information security best practices may call for certain policies and procedures, but if those are not feasible for a given corporate culture, you will often have to accept that the business is going to accept that risk, and not implement them. This lack of control can be uncomfortable; you will need to determine if it is comfortable for you.

TERMINOLOGY

Every discipline has its terminology and communication styles. Most engineering and scientific disciplines have had decades, if not centuries, to work to build this common language. In information security, the language is less standardized because it's so immature, and much more dynamic, to meet the still changing needs of the field. In a mature field like chemistry, an atom with two protons is always helium, and has the international standard notation of $_2$He. In information security, neither concepts nor terms are standardized. The plan for keeping an organization running could be a Business Continuity Plan (BCP) which is common in business, a Continuance of Operations Plan (COOP), common in government, or a Disaster Recovery Plan (DRP) as a general plan for disasters. Risks, threats, and other terms will have different definitions, and you will need to be able to adjust based on your audience.

2.1 TIER 2—LATERAL: ACCOUNTING

INTRODUCTION—HOW THIS APPLIES

Accountants manage the money. Whether it is the going in, the going out, or the movement within the organization, accountants are responsible for ensuring that the paths are completely traceable and appropriately assigned. Your level within the organization will determine the scope of this authority. For example, an entry-level position may only be responsible for a single process, such as dealing with the accounts payable for a single group or department. As you rise within the company, the scope of your responsibility will grow as you manage those doing the day-to-day work.

Being in accounting, with any level of authority, will require being a certified public accountant (CPA). The exact requirements vary by state, and are beyond the scope of this book.

In many organizations, accounting and information technology are closely aligned. The CIO and CISO may report to the CFO. Also, since the financial information systems are among those that need the highest security within an organization, it is common for those who work in information security to work closely with at least some of those who work in finance.

One of the main reasons for this close relationship is the audit and regulatory requirements the financial division is required to deal with. For public companies, regulations such as the US federal Sarbanes-Oxley law (SOX) include information security components to ensure that financial information of the company is appropriately protected. There may be other standards, such as the Payment Card Industry Data Security Standards (PCI-DSS), that overlap between the financial and information security groups, creating the need for a close working relationship between the two areas. Even smaller companies with no regulatory requirements will have financial audits that will frequently include an information security component.

WHAT SKILLS THIS GIVES YOU

The attention to detail, understanding of the documentation, and audit experience associated with Accounting is very appropriate for information security. Depending upon your target role, Accounting can thus have some clear paths to information security. Those preparing for financial audits may find themselves involved with information security components of those audits. From there, they add the information security-focused audits such as PCI-DSS to their repertoire, and thus become information security auditors.

Similarly, at the higher levels, the move from finance into roles such as CISO or CPO is often appropriate, and requires more understanding of general processes and company needs than an understanding of the specific day-to-day tasks.

WHAT SKILLS YOU MIGHT STILL NEED

While the transitions mentioned above, focused on process and procedure, can have relatively seamless transitions, moves to more technical roles will require developing appropriate skills. These skills will generally not be attainable as part of your regular job duties, so you will have to develop them on your own based on your specific goals.

HOW TO FRAME YOUR SKILLS

As you can see from the previous discussion, your path will dictate how to frame your skills. Moving between closely aligned fields will require the ability to work within an information security framework rather than a financial one. Demonstrate an understanding of the frameworks in general, and any specific information security knowledge you may have.

DIFFERENCES BETWEEN WHERE YOU ARE AND INFORMATION SECURITY

CULTURE

Making the lateral move from Accounting to Audit, CISO, or CPO will generally not have much difference in the culture between where you are and the new role. However, the type of people that will be working with you or for you will change somewhat. In accounting, there generally is little appreciation for someone who comes up with their own accounting method, and implements it. The accounting field is based on standards. An accounting manager needs no particular creativity, except when someone is trying to commit a crime.

In contrast, creative information security professionals can be some of the most valuable, as their problem-solving abilities can help find issues that would not have been found using standard practices. Similarly, the enthusiasm that many information security professionals have regarding the security process may be unfamiliar to those in accounting, who are less likely to feel passion for a specific accounting method. Being able to work with them is important for those who move into information security management.

TERMINOLOGY

Fortunately there are fewer cases of the same vocabulary used for different purposes as there are between information security and other fields. Because of that, it is more a case of learning the information security vocabulary, rather than the differences between the two fields.

2.m TIER 2—LATERAL: BUSINESS ANALYST

INTRODUCTION—HOW THIS APPLIES

Whenever a project begins, there are general high-level guidelines put in place by the management. "Roll out a new ERP System by the end of next year." "Have the new phone system in place by the end of the next quarter." Those high-level goals, while enough to get funding for resources, do not provide detailed requirements for what people need to be working on. The Business Analyst is responsible for taking those high-level requirements and, through discussions with various business process owners, generating a detailed set of requirements that the technical team can use to guide its implementation.

Identifying exactly what a business wants and needs takes work. Existing business processes may be used as models, but are often poorly documented or defined. An engineer cannot implement a task such as: "Joe fills out a form." It is the Business Analyst's job to identify what information is collected by the form, and if there are prerequisite activities that need to take place. Could the contents of the form change based on different circumstances? Finally—and this is the component that often is the biggest challenge—why is this information being collected? Sometimes the reasons can be clearly identified. Sometimes the answer is "Well, that's my job," at which point the impacts of that process on other areas need to be determined.

Whenever new processes are implemented, there is a drive to improve upon the current system. This then drives the question of what would be an improvement. If there are five people in a room, there will likely be at least seven different suggestions to improve the process presented. Yes, some people will have multiple ideas. The business analyst will be responsible for working with the business to produce a single model, and from there creating a set of requirements for the technical team to work from.

This generation of technical requirements means that a good business analyst will need to be able to translate from business to technical and back again. The more the business analyst can understand about the technical side, the greater the likelihood that the requirements generated will be things that can actually be implemented.

WHAT SKILLS THIS GIVES YOU

In many ways, a security professional functions as a business analyst. Security professionals need to be able to understand the business drivers behind their technical implementations, so they are not mitigating risks that the business does not care about, or leaving risks unaddressed that the business needs to address. The ability to work with the business leaders to understand the business drivers behind a project is an important skill for advanced security professionals.

WHAT SKILLS YOU MIGHT STILL NEED

Successful business analysts who want to get into information security will probably need to improve their background. Consider the security ramifications of what you have already worked on. For example, ERP systems almost always have security issues. If your ERP vendor doesn't understand security, there may not be much to find, so instead dig into the system components: the database, application, operating system. Look at vulnerabilities that directly affect a system that you already understand. For higher level learning, the broad but shallow (ISC)^2 CISSP is a start, not necessarily as a certification, but as a framework for learning.

MOVING FROM BUSINESS ANALYSIS TO A SECURITY FIELD

Security professionals, especially those who work in the risk mitigation areas such as Risk Assessment, Security Assessment, and Vulnerability Management, need to have a deeper understanding of the underlying technical issues than most Business Analysts have.

MOVING FROM SECURITY TO BUSINESS ANALYSIS

While security professionals often have an understanding of business processes, their ability to model business processes and identify all of the key components associated with a business process often needs improvement. Security processes are only touched upon at the high level, and deeply at the technical level, and the middle area is not focused upon as much.

HOW TO FRAME YOUR SKILLS

For those business analysts looking to move into security, focusing on your ability to understand both business and technical issues is extremely valuable in the security field. Furthermore, the ability to demonstrate the ability to learn technical skills is important for many security positions, and having examples of where you have done this in the past will be important for those wishing to transition to those areas.

DIFFERENCES BETWEEN WHERE YOU ARE AND INFORMATION SECURITY
CULTURE

Security roles exist across a wide range of corporate cultures. Both maverick security personnel and military-style precision-based security engineers can find their place, thrive, and excel. Business analysis culture tends more towards the well-defined process and procedure end of that spectrum, so finding a security position will require either being willing to limit where you look, or be willing to expand the cultural environments in which you are comfortable working.

TERMINOLOGY

It's necessary to understand the security field's many specific terms and concepts related to the analysis of risk. The process of analyzing threats, vulnerabilities, and exposures, while similar to dealing with business processes, involves enough outside actors that there will be some necessary adjustment.

TIER 3—TEACH

WHY TEACHING MATTERS

By now, you have learned things and done things. After a while, though, you get burnt out or, as author Ursula K. Le Guin once put it, "done with doing." In business, this may manifest as feeling a general lack of direction. When you are learning, your teacher gives you direction. When you are doing, you should have goals. However, once you achieve your goals, where do you go next? Teaching helps answer this question.

By teaching others, you may find yourself learning better than ever before. Your students will ask new questions you never considered which include new ways to be wrong and to learn, but also new ways to be right. As they learn, you'll also learn and see new ways for you to learn your material. Most importantly, working with someone else as you explore a field will lead you to explore nooks and crannies that you otherwise would have overlooked.

To complete your learning process, you must teach someone else what you know.

Teaching can serve as a business force multiplier. In physics, a force multiplier, such as a lever or wedge, increases the amount of force you can place on an object. In military terms, a force multiplier makes a military force more effective. For example, a fleet of drone craft can simplify reconnaissance to where a handful of analysts can do the work of hundreds. Information security can also use force multipliers. We must improve the effectiveness of both our tools and our people. By teaching others how to do security, you learn your tools better, and find new tools and ways to combine them so they are greater than the sum of their parts. By teaching others how to learn security, you increase the number of people on your side. By teaching effective techniques, you all spend less time, and become force multipliers yourselves.

To oversimplify the complex attack/defense landscape, there are attackers and defenders. If you are reading this book, you may be most interested in defense. This is a difficult path to choose, as attackers tend to be better funded for their goals and less restricted by laws and ethics. When you choose defense, you must accomplish your tasks with fewer resources, as the attackers focus on multiplying their forces with constantly improving tools. If you choose a mentorship path, as you teach more and more people, the number of people on defense begins to overwhelm the attackers. While it's true that a small number of people with quickly improving tools will win over those who move less quickly, a large number of people with a diverse set of slowly improving tools will win over faster attackers, as it takes a lot more human-centered analysis to attack such a wide group of defenses.

These concepts can be generalized into the Observe, Orient, Decide, Act (OODA) loop, which was originally developed for training fighter aircraft pilots—which, incidentally, are both primarily defensive and also creative. For example, observation includes the first knowledge of a vulnerability such as through a security advisory, patch release, or incident. Orient is understanding the consequences of an advisory, getting prepared for patch deployment, or responding to an incident. Decide is taking the output of observation and orientation and making a decision; not all advisories are applicable, not all patches should be applied, and not all incidents will have consequences. Act follows through on the decision, and must also be done to completion if the decision was correct at all. A shorter, faster, tighter OODA loop allows for faster response, more frequent correction, and better results. An OODA loop that runs inside of your adversaries' own OODA loop will mean your response occurs before your adversaries even know their attack didn't work as expected.

Research your environment and your industry, know what threats your organization faces both in terms of technology, your competition, and your customers' expectations.

SHORT-TERM TEACHING

There are at least as many different ways to teach people as there are people. However, many of them break down into short- and long-term teaching. With short-term teaching, you are likely working with one or more people on specific projects. This can be as short as an evening tutorial or as long as a few months helping people learn well enough to transition from Learning to Doing. You will be helping people learn either online or offline. These modes are very different, because only with offline teaching will you be physically in front of your student(s) and able to tell more immediately when they're failing to understand. Online teaching and learning are more difficult.

ONLINE TEACHING

Teaching online comes in several flavors. You can have a formal relationship with your students or, as is far more common, a highly informal one. Formal online teaching will be much like the offline teaching described below. You will define a syllabus, set a schedule, and run through the process with one or more students. The biggest difference between online and offline learning is that online learning requires you check in more often.

Checking in is critical in all modes of teaching, but it's even more important when working online. If you can't directly interact with your students, you will only know how well they're doing when they fail (or pass) a quiz. Quizzes and tests exist both for you to gauge how well your students are doing and how well you are teaching them. When teaching online, even formally, it is vital to get frequent feedback from your students as to their understanding. This can be done formally, by tests and quizzes, but it should also be done during the process of teaching, as you ask "do you understand?" and "does that make sense?" Ask people to explain things back to you or, as often works the best, have them implement something that illustrates some small piece of what you are trying to teach, such as in class laboratory exercises.

Teaching less formally online is vastly different. In this mode, you may be finding someone on Twitter with an immediate problem, someone on IRC that needs a bit of advice, or a long-term friend on a mailing list that needs help with direction in life. What makes each of these scenarios different is that you won't have any sort of prep time or structure. Instead, what you get and must notice are teachable moments.

A teachable moment is a question or statement that indicates a student is both in need of assistance and open to new ideas. It may take some time to notice teachable moments, and as you practice you'll make mistakes and anger people. It takes time to get good at this sort of teaching, but it doesn't have to require emotional involvement. If you get hurt every time someone misunderstands or demonstrates their unwillingness to learn, you'll never build the experience needed to get truly good at teaching and, therefore, will never experience the rewards of doing it well. Take advantage of the physical distance to provide emotional distance as needed.

You may have an opportunity to do one-to-many teaching in an online mode. Other than classes, which are addressed in greater detail in the next section, the Internet provides opportunities for you to teach via forums, mailing lists, webinars, and videos. Forums and mailing lists are text-based communication, so when engaging in these, realize that you're not just teaching for now, but also the future. Online media survives for a long time, and it is not uncommon to receive feedback on items you wrote and forgot about years ago. Take the time to write up your thoughts; proof your work and check it for spelling and grammar. Then do a fact check and test and take a short rest break and then do a final review before sending. Just taking one extra hour between writing and hitting the Send button can be the difference between creating a throwaway post and creating knowledge that will stand the test of time.

The same logic applies to multimedia pieces like webinars and online videos. Both require preparation. Webinars and videos often start with rough scripts. Webinars often take these scripts and turn them into presentations. Videos take the scripts, flesh them out, and become recordings. In both cases, it is sadly common to create the concept, perform the script, and be done. However you can do much better with some practice. Following the old programmer's adage of "build one to throw away," if you run a practice webinar or do one video recording, you can assess your performance and find ways to improve it. Few performances are perfect the first time; one rule of thumb states that it takes ten performances to start to become comfortable with that particular material.

Let us be clear. There is little in the working world that is less pleasant than watching your own performance while picking it apart and identifying where you did terribly, except perhaps watching someone else do it. Many people start this process and quit after one try. However, those that push all the way through will gain experience quickly, as each cycle will result in more change. You don't want to practice so much that your performance becomes robotic (a common failing of the approach of making a word-for-word script). However, a bit of formal structure will make your message much easier to understand and will make your teaching much more effective.

A more formal teaching plan will give more of these benefits in a shorter amount of time. However, formal teaching opportunities can be rare. To fill in the gaps, to gain experience more quickly, and to experiment, actively seek out teachable moments. As with everything else, the less time you waste, the faster you'll move forward. The more time you put into teaching, the better you make the world and the more you accelerate defensive capabilities.

OFFLINE TEACHING

As noted earlier, offline teaching has the primary benefit of being able to see, in real time, how you are affecting your students. Maybe you're just sitting down with someone at a conference, one-on-one, discussing your thoughts. Perhaps you're leading a discussion in a user group setting. You could be giving a live presentation to a room full of beginners, your co-workers, or even business owners.

You can choose to be formal or informal. However, since you'll be right in front of your student(s), you'll get immediate feedback from them. It should be immediately obvious when you say something that is confusing or, worse, factually incorrect. This both raises the stakes and allows you to improve significantly faster, as constant feedback results in faster learning cycles for you. It's okay to make mistakes—this is how to learn.

As you go through this process, remember what works and what doesn't, taking notes if necessary. Record yourself, if you can, and ask your students if you can record them. Your worst errors will likely stick in your mind and prevent you from making them again. Highly successful communication methods are harder to remember. If you're lucky, phrasings that resonate particularly well will stick with you and be available for future discussions. If you're like most people, though, they won't.

However, even if you can't record yourself or remember specific elements that work or fail, you can still maximize your success by pre-thinking what and how you want to teach. Odds are that, while you have a lot to teach, the material falls into specific areas into which you've given a great deal of thought. If that's the case, you can think about the type of people you are likely to teach and come up with metaphors that can help them to understand.

This book lacks the room for a full course on metaphor mapping. See the Appendix for several books on the topic or chapter 8 of *Job Reconnaissance* by Josh More. The nutshell version is to think about who you need to teach and what their lives are like. By choosing metaphors that match with their experiences, you will decrease their difficulty in learning. You will understand them better, they will perceive you as being more like them, and—as a bonus—you will look a whole lot smarter. If you're teaching a room full of college students, it would be a fairly safe bet to assume that they have much greater familiarity with modern technology and culture than a similar room full of senior citizens. Some college age students respond well to metaphors that reference video games, and may not need explanations of how the Internet works. In contrast, senior citizens may need help with some technical concepts, but having personally lived through several periods of war, economic depression, and political and social change, will likely find relevance in topics framed as organized attacks and the importance of defending the helpless.

This is just one example of metaphor mapping, based on generational differences. You can find similar metaphor divergence along lines of class, nationality, ethnicity, sex, race, and gender. The more you think about your audience's responses to different concepts framed in different ways, the more you build up your own metaphor "library." With a collection of metaphors that you know will work or fail depending on your audience, you can build toward a more targeted ad hoc method of teaching. This can give the appearance of having a very informal structure, to which people respond to quite well, while still having the formal underpinning that helps to maximize success.

LONG-TERM TEACHING

Long-term teaching is exactly like short-term teaching, except that you have a lot more chances to fail. Since one teaching session builds on the next, and mentorship and community involvement don't follow set curricula, there is ample opportunity for one misstep early in the process to build upon others, until the entire process falls down in a massive cascade of failure.

If that seems a bit daunting, it should. Long-term teaching is the best way to amplify your thoughts through many people. *This means that if you're wrong, and give bad advice, this mistake will be amplified through the community, and could last for years...even decades. Be careful.*

However, that's not to say that you shouldn't try. It is very difficult and extremely rare for any person to hold the same position—and be correct—their entire life. It's far more common for people to realize that they've been wrong and try to correct. It is, of course, difficult to correct your failure without losing face, which keeps people locked into dubious positions for far too long. For example, both Bill Gates and Steve Jobs were often wrong, even publicly, but when they realized it they both corrected it, admitting their mistakes by changing products and company direction. To truly maximize the benefits of teaching as a force multiplier, you must maximize the time you spend on effective methods and avoid the dead ends that result from people retrenching and defending their positions. Recognize and admit when you're wrong and teach others to do the same.

Admit your failures as quickly as possible, and take feedback so you can correct yourself when you're wrong. This is, of course, incredibly difficult to do. When you start teaching, you must not stop the Learn or Do phases. When you stop learning from others and testing your ideas, you lose effectiveness as a teacher.

MENTORING

By this point in your career, you should have good time management. It's unlikely that you'll be a master at it—this book, for example, is being delivered years late (sorry, Syngress). However, it is quite likely that you will have had enough time management failures in your life to recognize them in others.

This ability puts you in a position of helping others learn not just the intended material but also how to learn more effectively. This means you must be comfortable putting them in a position to fail faster, fail smaller, and, hopefully, gain confidence. When you see your people wasting their time, try to point it out to them. More than just reminding them of deadlines or playing boss, try to serve as a true mentor. To be an effective mentor, your students must trust you. This will only happen when they believe they can make mistakes without upsetting you, that you'll do all that's reasonable to help them fix their mistakes, and that you truly care about them as people. Mentorship is an extremely rare and difficult skill. Many people in so-called mentoring programs fail to be good mentors, mostly because they were never mentored in mentoring. Break the vicious cycle and make a virtuous cycle. Be the best mentor you can be, if it's not good enough, stop.

Thus, when you see people veer off task, try first to understand why. Do they not understand? Do you not understand? Are they avoiding hard work? Are they chasing a shortcut that you know isn't there? Once you understand them, work on getting them to understand you. Walk them through your own learning processes. Walk them through the learning processes that you've seen others go through. Initial sessions will feel painfully slow because you aren't teaching your topic yet; you're teaching trust and also learning to trust them. Build trust, so you're both comfortable making mistakes in front of one another. Start by admitting your mistakes as you make them and freely admit ignorance. Talk about past mistakes, major and minor as you feel comfortable, so your students will be both comfortable with you and comfortable with themselves about admitting their own mistakes.

As you go through this process, let them question you; it wasn't that long ago that you were Learning. Encourage them to question you, both by asking them, but also when they do ask a question. Don't only say encouraging words like "That's a good question." Also briefly answer the question, and if they want to know more, say more. If your body language skills are poor and you can't tell without asking them, admit that, and ask them directly. Be careful of both the content of answers, but also style and manner. If you habitually answer questions in ways that aren't useful or bother them, your students will habitually stop asking questions and then they will Learn less or might stop Learning. If their questions lead you in a direction you've not yet explored, admit your ignorance, and explore it together. This closes the loop between Learning and Teaching; and once the loop is closed, the faster you can cycle through the Learn/Do/Teach cycle. The faster you cycle, the faster your entire community can learn and, eventually, begin teaching on their own.

This is the force multiplier: There is no end to your journey, because there is no end to learning, doing, and teaching. Instead, as an entire community pulls together, it learns together and begins working together, and begins to out compete slower communities. Review the teaching roles that are common in the industry, and think about more than what you can get out of it. Think about what you can give back to your community and how you can make us all better.

TIER 3—PEN TEST LEAD

3.1

INTRODUCTION

Penetration testing was discussed earlier, and as there is no need to reiterate what has already been said, this section will focus specifically on the leadership role. The lead on a pen test team is both a contributor and manager. In addition to using your skills to help assess systems, you will have to prioritize the work of others and be front and center if something goes wrong during the test.

In some ways, it's just like being a regular penetration tester. You have to understand systems and networks, stay on top of the latest attacks, vulnerabilities, and tools, run tools, analyze output, and write understandable reports. However, in this role you become the face of the team to the client. You will be the one they contact to scope the test, to report oddities, and to question the report. You will have to mediate disputes between your own team members and help to foster understanding between the client and your team.

In short, the jump from penetration tester to penetration testing lead is much like the jump from one who does system or network administration to one who manages a team of those people. You will need technical skill so your people respect you, business knowledge so your clients respect you, and soft skills so both will understand you and you will understand them, and so everyone will understand and do what is needed.

HOW TO BREAK IN

Breaking in to this role requires that you be able to demonstrate both technical and business skills. This can often happen as you are testing and eliminating false positives. The better you get at identifying what systems exist on the network, how they support the business, and how to better protect them, the more easily you will be able to explain this to others. You may find yourself taking a more public role, meeting with clients and giving presentations.

You can also break in at a technical level if you show aptitude for learning the business skills. Often, the most technical person on a penetration testing team winds up as the lead because they can quickly identify and resolve aspects of the test that are blocking others on the team. This is a useful skill, but without external communication skills, the team will only have half a leader. If you are in such a role and want to eventually convert this role into another, you should focus on your business and soft skills.

COMMON PATHS

The most common path, by far, is promotion from within. One penetration tester who is better/faster/calmer than others on the team will often rise to become a leader. The best way to do this is to work with your manager to identify where you lack skills, and develop them as best you can. You may need to transfer between teams or companies to make the final move as with any management position.

However, if you have shown decent technical skill in other roles, such as security assessment or vulnerability management, and have a high level of skill in communicating with non-technical people, as well as a decent business understanding, you may find opportunities to jump over the basic penetration testing role and go straight into the lead.

HOW TO IMPROVE SKILLS—YOURS AND OTHERS

This is a management role, so improving the skills of others is an important component to the work. This involves first understanding where they are strong and where they are weak. Then, you need to identify which areas of weakness actually matter to the team. For example, if you have a tester who is great at networking but completely lost when it comes to HTTP-based attacks, it only matters if you don't have someone else on the team to cover that area of work.

Outside of the technical, learning to manage personality conflicts and helping people to better communicate their desires and frustrations with their teammates will go a long way to helping them grow.

This is very interesting work if you like working with people. If you don't much like people, it's probably not the job for you. Network with your peers. There aren't a lot of people doing penetration testing, and the attackers are better at working together than we are. To keep up, you have to share your cool tricks in hopes of getting some back in turn. Be prepared to argue about scope. Many people artificially reduce scope to make it easier to pass. As a lead, it is your job to tell them when the scope is no longer sufficient to provide legitimate business value.

Finally, you must always keep in mind that their most likely avenue for personal growth may be to take over your job. On one hand, you don't want to stifle your team, but on the other, you don't want to lose your job. Managing this issue can be quite challenging. However, one thing you may wish to consider is to designate a different team member as a "test lead" for a single penetration test so they get to experience running a team and decide whether or not they want that responsibility. If you can let your competitors leave for jobs like yours, with your blessing, and keep those who realize they don't like that sort of work, you can wind up in a very stable job with a team of people who trust you implicitly because you gave them a chance when they wanted it.

RECOGNIZING WHEN YOU'RE STUCK

You can get stuck as a penetration testing lead in several ways. You can get stuck within a company that has no role above "lead" in your area. You can get stuck with a bad team. You can get stuck with bad clients.

If your company leaves you no advancement opportunities, your best bet is to try to find another job elsewhere. You can take a penetration testing lead job at another company, but your skills may also translate into doing auditing, architect work, or as a more general manager for information security or IT.

If you find yourself stuck with a bad team and you want to keep working there, you either have to start shifting those people out or change their attitudes. This can be done by firing them, giving them unpleasant tasks in the hopes they leave, or finding and addressing their concerns. The former is the easier, but more expensive method as you have to put up with getting a lower quality of work for what the organization is paying on top of having to pay for severance and unemployment insurance. The latter is difficult, and can also be quite expensive, both in time and money. A lot of leaders just choose to suffer through. The middle path, trying to force people out by giving them unpleasant work can work, but can also create a team based on bullying and punishment and the ill effects may last well after the bad people have left. Before you select any of these options, think critically about how bad the work will be if you choose to tolerate the situation, and see if you can justify it.

Finally, if you get stuck with bad clients, you have to educate your sales team (if you're selling the service) or the business unit managers (if you're performing testing internally). Most commonly, people react poorly to penetration testing because they think of the testing team as the enemy. If you approach them from a position of asking for help instead of telling them what to do, their attitudes may well change.

ROLE AT A GLANCE—PENETRATION TESTING LEAD

Table 3.1 Role at a Glance—Penetration Testing Lead

Hours	Travel	Stress Level	Creativity	Flexibility	Stability
8–10 hours/day	Low to Moderate	Moderate	Moderate	High	High
General job duties	As with the Pen Tester role has most of the same tasks of performing scans, identifying vulnerabilities, performing social engineering and generating post-test reports. But common tasks are more likely to be delegated to Pen Testers, while the experienced Penetration Testing Lead works with and presents to management and may do more advanced tasks such as create new exploits, research, and presenting at conferences. Mentorship and teaching are part of being a team lead.				
Learning	There is a fair amount of learning in this role, but there will be some rote. A lot of tests will involve similar setup and reconnaissance activities. You will have to stay on top of changes in the industry, but as a leader, you must also trust your people to stay on top of their areas. There may be less technical learning in this role than as a regular penetration tester. However, it would be wise to replace that lost learning with a focus on practicing soft skills and learning business theories.				
Advancement	There are often no direct advancement opportunities for a penetration testing lead. You may choose to move laterally into Security Management or an advanced level of assessment or auditing.				

3.2 TIER 3—SECURITY ARCHITECT

INTRODUCTION

"If builders built buildings the way programmers wrote programs, then the first woodpecker that came along would destroy civilization."

— **Gerald Weinberg**

The Security Architect role is broad and may have other names, such as Lead Engineer, Senior Engineer, Chief Systems Programmer, or Computer Scientist. In some companies, "Architect" is simply a more senior engineer or systems analyst.

Architecture is about the details at a high level. To use the building architect metaphor, architects don't individually place the bricks and mortar; instead, they need to communicate to the bricklayers exactly what bricks to use, how to place them, what, how much, and where the mortar goes, how it is faced. If they don't communicate this information, they need to understand exactly what the bricklayers will do by default. The goal is to achieve an end result that is not just pleasing, but will also work and stand the test of time.

Architects may have a mix of technical, managerial, and political duties. Although all roles typically have at least some political aspects, the architect role often negotiates with technical and non-technical peers, both inside and outside of information security. An architect may be a trusted advisor to non-technical staff.

Security Architects research, specify, design, and document security architectures. They may also be directly involved with implementation, quality assurance, testing, and user acceptance. To do this, Security Architects usually work closely with information technology architects, engineers, management, users, and vendors.

Security architects have to see the big picture: not just how the system can work, should work, and will work, but also how it will interact with all of the other existing and future systems that haven't even been conceived of yet. The ideal security architect is beyond Subject Matter Expert, and expert in all things. Most security architects must specialize or rely upon others with subject matter expertise. Either path requires superior communications skills and ability to work with a team.

Some information technology organizations use the "architect" role as a top-level technical but non-managerial position. Other organizations use "architect" as the highest purely technical position, with the highest technical and managerial position being a C-level position such as CIO, or CISO, who may also be the senior information security architect, in duties if not title. However, C-level positions tend to be much more managerial and political in nature and may not be deeply technical. They may heavily rely upon technical architects, engineers, and subject matter experts.

In most organizations, the architect position is a full-time job, but not necessarily full-time information security. Particularly large organizations will have teams of architects, and perhaps teams of dedicated security architects. In very well-developed security organizations, there will be teams of specialist security architects who work closely with other specialist architects and specialist engineers for particular security controls in operating systems, software engineering, networking, and databases.

The information security architect is usually directly involved in the requirements, specifications, design, architecture, and high-level implementation of information security systems.

HOW TO BREAK IN

A senior engineer can break into security architecture through simple promotion within the same organization, or by joining another organization as an architect. However, architecture is different from engineering in that engineers solve a problem, but architects set and define the problem and how it could be solved. An engineer may solve the problem for the short term, but an architect solves the problem for the long term.

Smaller firms may have no architects, but that doesn't mean they don't need architecture. The senior engineer, who in small organizations is the sole engineer, must also be an architect if solutions are to last longer than the engineer's employment.

Software engineers often wonder if their solutions are still in use after they leave an organization, but software architects know that their solutions must still be in use; otherwise they've failed and the organization will have lost time and money creating a new solution.

HOW TO IMPROVE YOUR SKILLS

Communication skills for this role include lots of reading: very deep technical documents, high-level but still technical documents, business plans, HR policy, information security policy, and standards documents. So to improve yourself, you need to dedicate a certain amount of your time to just learning what others are doing.

Architects need strong and clear communications skills, and enough political savvy and social awareness to know when and what not to communicate. Social awareness and diversity training are particularly useful for architects because of the wide range of organizations where they will work.

Both formal and informal writing skills are critical. A poorly written informal email can cause immediate political issues and, if not caught, long-term technical issues, followed by more political issues. Architects may write both informal and formal short- and long-form documents. Some organizations require lengthy architectural documentation.

Speaking skills are important, both informally in small meetings, and also in formal settings such as all-hands organizational meetings with a set agenda, time limits, and presentation slides. Public speaking, and organizations such as Toastmasters and the affiliate Techmasters "Toastmasters for geeks" groups are one way to do all three of Learn/Do/Teach. See also the Boosting section of this book.

Different people learn and comprehend complex subjects in different ways. Although writing is critical, even poor diagraming, drawing, and presentation material skills can be useful. Good skills in this area will make you a better communicator, and being an artist will make you stand out.

RECOGNIZING WHEN YOU'RE STUCK

Architects who yearn to write code, wire up a server cluster, or break into systems may decide they would rather be a Senior Engineer in software development, systems administration, and penetration testing.

If an architect would prefer to be coordinating and planning than researching and designing, perhaps project management would be an appropriate career path.

HOW TO GET OUT

There are many paths for an architect to move on and still stay an architect. Security architects tend to be generalists, and could move into any of the other technical areas; however, there is plenty of room for specialization in larger organizations, or for the independent consultant or entrepreneur.

Some organizations provide a technical manager path for architects where they still do architecture but also are managing junior architects and engineers.

CRITICAL WARNINGS

Engineers with obsolete skills but are too senior to fire are sometimes promoted to architect. Even when this is not the case, an architect's hands-on skills can quickly become obsolete because engineers and technicians do that work. Some organizations require that for separation of duties architects do no hands-on work. Architects risk becoming irrelevant unless they keep up with and use current technology. If your organization can't or won't provide hands-on experience or training, then you'll need to do this on your own time. This may also be an opportunity to train for your next job beyond architect or into a specialization.

Table 3.2 Role at a Glance—Security Architect

Hours	Travel	Stress Level	Creativity	Flexibility	Stability
8+ hours/day	Moderate to High	Moderate to High	High	High	High
General job duties	Technical analysis, reading and sometimes summarizing papers, presentations, writing papers, preparing for presentations, advocacy, evangelism.				
Learning	High				
Advancement	Medium				

TIER 3—LEAD AUDITOR

3.3

INTRODUCTION

> "He who knows does not speak; he who speaks does not know."
>
> **— Laozi**

The Lead Auditor is a bridge between technical and non-technical, between management and non-management. Lead Auditor is a full-time position and will usually be a formal or informal leader of a dedicated audit team. As with the Auditor position described in Tier 2, there are internal and external Lead Auditors. The role of "Lead" varies considerably. In some organizations, Lead is a formal management title and role at the start of the management track, and may have formal direct reports. In other organizations, Lead is not formally part of management, but is a promotion to a more senior position. Still other organizations use Lead as an informal title that isn't technically a promotion and has no recognition outside of the immediate management. The Lead position may even be totally informal and merely be by consensus or simple seniority.

The Lead Auditor may have the authority to decide what is being audited against or, if this is determined elsewhere, to what detail and depth the auditing is done. The Lead Auditor may also be the primary author, editor, and approver of the final audit report.

HOW TO BREAK IN

Becoming a Lead Auditor can range from as simple as just hanging around long enough to gain seniority, or it may require substantial investment in time and effort to get into the management track. A Lead may even simply be the only person in that role. However, a fully-functioning Lead Auditor needs good communications, management, and technical skills. Auditors do not need coding skills, but if they are auditing a development environment, they do need to know enough to recognize bad environments and poor excuses. A skilled and experienced auditor in a large organization with decentralized auditing may be able to transfer into a Lead Auditor position in another part of the organization, or get a new job as Lead Auditor in another organization. Certifications may be useful, or even mandatory (official or not), so find out what certifications the Lead Auditors you know have. Propose certification study groups to gauge interest. If there is no interest from your peers or management, perhaps that certification isn't useful in that organization, but it may be useful elsewhere.

HOW TO IMPROVE YOUR SKILLS

Auditors who have information technology backgrounds may be missing the communications skills and knowledge needed by a Lead Auditor. Other roles that include writing can be a good background, such Trainer-Educator. See also the Boosting Author chapter. If you aren't completely familiar with your particular industry's auditing requirements, learn them. Prepare for jobs in other industries by learning those industries' auditing requirements as well. Although not always a requirement, ISO 27000 is a common knowledge base.

Auditors from outside of information technology, such as in accounting, finance, and business, can grow through technical Learn/Do/Teach by studying or transferring into information technology roles, but not usually the lowest Tier 1 roles such as Help Desk and Log Reviewer. The Security Assessment and Risk Assessment roles are particularly well-suited for study or transfer before the Lead Auditor role. Some Lead Auditor roles require highly industry-specific training and qualifications, such as the Payment Card Industry—Data Security Standards (PCI-DSS QSA) which is common in financial services and retail. Although not always expected, some Lead Auditors may need to personally present audit reports, so public speaking may be useful, also present in Trainer-Educator, and in Boosting—Speaker.

RECOGNIZING WHEN YOU'RE STUCK

Auditing is a crucial part of any organization's success. If your organization doesn't learn from and improve with your best auditing practices, even as the Lead Auditor, it's time to leave. Becoming a jaded, cynical Lead Auditor isn't going to help the organization and it's not going to help your career; get out before that happens.

HOW TO GET OUT

A successful Lead Auditor will have strong communications and management skills, and at least some technical skills. The Security Assessment and Risk Assessment roles can be good lateral moves. A particularly technically proficient Lead Auditor may be able to move into Vulnerability Management, and possibly Pen Testing.

Table 3.3 Role at a Glance—Lead Auditor

Hours	Travel	Stress Level	Creativity	Flexibility	Stability
8–10 hours/day after hours	Varies	Moderate	Low	Low	High
General job duties	Review standards, set specific requirements. Manage/supervise other auditors. Write reports, present summaries. Run Audits As with consultants in general, may have high load and travel. As with auditors in general, auditors can be exposed to the stress of those being audited.				
Learning	Many opportunities especially for external auditors or internal auditors in large organizations.				
Advancement	Can be a step towards full management positions in infosec and elsewhere.				

TIER 3—LEAD SECURITY-RISK ASSESSOR

INTRODUCTION

The Lead Security-Risk Assessor role is that of management of the combination of Security Assessment and Risk Assessment. It may actually be two separate roles or, in smaller organizations, a single role that has separate or combined security and risk assessment components. This role also is the interface between technical skills of the risk assessors and those whose systems and environments are being assessed. See the separate Tier 2 chapters of Risk Assessment and Security Assessment for specific details.

Both as a lead and as a bridge between roles, communications skills are very important. Technical skills are also very important, both to properly understand the technicalities of the security as it exists, and how to assess the component risks of the larger problem. Although these may appear to be very similar, or even identical, tasks, understanding this difference is a critical aspect of understanding this role. Security weaknesses, vulnerabilities, threats, and attacks are different from, and can even have some independence from, the actual risk. For an extreme example, consider a weak, vulnerable system under attack. It may actually have very low risk, because the consequences of the system being compromised are very low. Also, you cannot view all compromises as the same. Some systems, such as honeynets, are designed to be compromised so the defenders can learn from what the attackers do. An assessor that cannot see the subtleties in how organizations use their systems is not useful to their clients.

Those who perform this role know where the bodies are buried, or at least who's most likely to be buried next. Their job is to keep it from happening.

HOW TO BREAK IN

The Lead Security-Risk Assessor may be a peer or possibly more senior position from Security Architect, Lead Auditor, and Pen Test Lead. Each can be a leading step. Technical, management, and communications skills are all very important, but most especially critical is an understanding of the organization and the industry of which it is a part. At this level, unlike most others, comparisons and contrasts with competitors are likely to be important. The particular risk of an occurrence may be less important than risk comparison—the likelihood it will happen first or more often to your organization than to your organization's competitors. Experience at a competing or very similar organization can be extremely useful.

HOW TO IMPROVE YOUR SKILLS

At this level, communications—publishing—and political boosting become particularly important. Writing just one published book or pamphlet, having even a semi-successful business, or being a well-known industry speaker, even if only locally, can be a huge difference. Evangelizing the right area inside or outside the organization brings knowledge, and others' awareness of that knowledge. Leadership community contributions provide political experience and social skills building.

RECOGNIZING WHEN YOU'RE STUCK

If you're not making a difference in the quality of information security in your organization at this level; if your recommendations aren't at least sometimes heeded; if your internal mentoring rightly leads people away from the organization, never to return; if you keep running into the same problems year after year—then it may be time for you to move on. Although information security has many recurring cycles, doing it in another organization and perhaps another industry may be the way to growth, or at least to avoid stagnation.

HOW TO GET OUT

The Lead Security-Risk Assessor position is a step into the management track; however, it can also lead to peer roles such as Lead Auditor, Security Architecture, or, for the more technically minded, Pen Testing Lead, Tiger Team, or going independent as a Security Consultant. Try any of the Boosting categories you haven't done yet, or pursue those you did well at and enjoyed.

Table 3.4 Role at a Glance—Lead Security-Risk Assessor

Hours	Travel	Stress Level	Creativity	Flexibility	Stability
8–10 hours/day after hours	Varies	High	High	Moderate	High
General job duties	Security, audit, and risk document writing, editing, reviewing. Executive presentations and summaries.				
Learning	As a process choke-point and information funnel, there is much to learn.				
Advancement	A step towards management track, or to parallel technical and non-technical roles.				

TIER 3—TIGER TEAM MEMBER—TIGER TEAM LEAD (RED TEAM)

3.5

INTRODUCTION

"Tiger Team," sometimes also known as a "Red Team," is a fancy name for the group of people who scramble into action. Typically, incident response teams are local to an organization and are both under-staffed and underfunded. This all changes when you get to the world of tiger teams. A tiger team can be run as a service to other companies or run within a single, typically large, company.

These teams will be activated during a particularly nasty incident and will often be sent into the line of fire. Working on a tiger team will often involve working more than 24 hours at a time for a week or two.

On the positive side, you will be working with the best people in the world as you dig into network and forensics dumps, set traps, isolate attackers, and work to figure not only what happened and prevent it from happening again, but also (in some cases) how to retaliate. The work will be constantly new and challenging.

The negatives, however, are not inconsiderable. More than any other role, a tiger team works hard and long hours. Pulling an all-nighter is not just possible, but common. You may find yourself putting in a full week's worth of work in a mere two days, and then have to keep working. Much as emergency room and military doctors sleep for two hours at a time, you may find yourself working in this mode as you trace issues and work with your team to figure out what's going on. Stress will be extremely high, so if you don't handle it well, this may not be the best choice for you. However, if you thrive in stress-ful, challenging environments, there's little better.

HOW TO BREAK IN

These jobs usually open up when a new team is being developed or when an existing tiger team mem-ber has burned out and decided to go on to something else. Breaking into the role will require either being very convincing when creating a new team or being very aware of the status of teams you wish to join, so you can get on the hiring list when they replace roles or expand.

To identify potential groups with internal tiger teams and companies that focus on this sort of work, get involved in internal incident response groups. By helping the community, you become better known. Then, when opportunities arise, people will reach out to you.

As with security consulting, expect interesting and challenging work, but often, far too much of it. Being able to handle a constantly changing work environment is critical. This type of work is all crisis all the time. Develop the ability to identify which issues need to be handled immediately and which ones can wait. Learn the scientific method and to develop and test hypothesis very quickly.

Identifying and eliminating entire chains of thought can drastically reduce your levels of uncertainty. Readings in the hard sciences and scientific method can help you develop this skill. See the Appendix for references.

COMMON PATHS

You will not succeed as a tiger team member until you collect a lot of experience. You can go extremely deep into a specific field of study, such as penetration testing or incident response, or become a subject matter expert in something like networking or cryptography. Alternatively, you can try to become good, if not excellent, in multiple fields. The former approach makes you critical on the team when that phase of the investigation is ongoing, but it may become somewhat boring when your part is done. The latter approach may not allow you to contribute as much as others, but you will be able to contribute at a more modest level for a longer period of time during each incident.

RECOGNIZING WHEN YOU'RE STUCK

You'll never get stuck in this role. So long as attackers are given incentives to come up with new attacks (i.e., you have something worth taking), life will be a constant flow of new and interesting things to work on, either brought to you by clients, or found on your own as you do research. Instead, you may find yourself burning out.

A good tiger team will expect you to work hard when you're working, but also give you ample flex time to make up for it. Some groups require a minimum of 40 hours per week, and when you hit that number, if your specific skills are no longer required to contain the incident, you're off the rest of the week. This can result in some people working only two days per week, though three to four days per week is more common. Other organizations expect you to give your all for each week you work, but give you eight to twelve weeks of paid vacation to schedule your off hours. To avoid burning out, take advantage of your time off, and develop a non-computer and low-stress hobby, so your time off is actually relaxing.

If you find yourself burning out, ask first for a leave of absence. Typically, these sorts of jobs pay well enough that you should have sufficient savings to cover a month or two of unpaid vacation time. Rest, recover, and seriously consider whether you want to go back. If not, it shouldn't take long to leverage your tiger team experience into work as a consultant, manager, or security engineer.

WHEN OTHERS ARE STUCK

If you are mentoring or working with someone who is burning out in their role, advise them to do the same as if you were stuck yourself. They need a break, preferably a nice long one. Have them rest and take a bit of distance to really think things through. It takes about two weeks of not doing something to really start to get a sense of clarity. Make sure they take that time.

Table 3.5 Role at a Glance—Tiger Team Lead

Hours	Travel	Stress Level	Creativity	Flexibility	Stability
18–24 hours/day More time off	Considerable	High	High	Low	Low
General job duties	Nearly everything elsewhere, and more. Exceptions can include higher management, and long term planning such as architecture. Because of the secrecy of incident response even when there are other teams who would otherwise do some work, the Tiger Team may have to do it on their own, anyway.				
Learning	High—At the upper end of this role, you get to see a lot of interesting attacks and will spend a lot of time doing reverse engineering. However, in order to get to that point, you will likely have to go through a lot of "same old, same old" incidents. If you work with good people who only call the tiger team when absolutely needed, learning density will be extremely high. However, most people aren't quite so careful, so expect to see a lot of the same thing over and over again as you ramp up within this role. As this is a high-stress environment, you have to be sufficiently disciplined to cope with the immediate issue—contain the incident, prevent recurrence, and complete the documentation. Then, after everything is done, take the time to fill in your learning with true understanding. Consider duplicating the attack in a lab, writing up a public paper, or engaging in forensics against collected images. By closing the loop, you maximize the learning opportunities and increase your own effectiveness for future issues.				
Advancement	While tiger team members may advance to a leadership position, there are few advancement opportunities for a tiger team lead, as you're already at the top. That said, very few people can tolerate the extremely high stress levels of this role, and typically make a lateral move to security consultant, penetration testing lead, or security management after a few years. While this can be a very lucrative and engaging role for a long time, as your life's priorities change, you may find that you'd rather make less money in exchange for having reliable time off, weekends, and a better work/life balance.				

3.6 TIER 3—SECURITY CONSULTANT

INTRODUCTION

> "A consultant is someone who borrows your watch to tell you the time, and then keeps the watch."
>
> **— Carl Ally**

Being an independent security consultant is a very interesting job. Basically, your role is to be the smart person in the room. However, to be successful, you must know when to lead others as the smart person and when to guide other people, allowing them to be the smart ones in front of their co-workers. Knowing the difference will be the key to success and, sadly, is often learned from failure.

This role is one that many people want, as it is perceived as lucrative and consisting of only the "good parts" of working in security. Most security consultants don't get involved in the day-to-day operations of a business and are sheltered from politics. However, people who want to effect change but can't because of the political sheltering may get frustrated.

The hidden aspects of the job also involve endless negotiation over different ways to solve problems, continual reassessment, and project lengths in years rather than days or months. Also, if you're an independent consultant, you must line up new projects while you work on existing ones, bill your own time, and sometimes work on many emergencies at the same time. The stress level as a security consultant can be higher than that of any other information security role.

CONSULTING VERSUS CONTRACTING

It should be mentioned that many people with the title of "security consultant" are actually functioning as security contractors. There is nothing wrong with such work, but if you are not weighing different courses of actions and interacting with both the people doing the work and those making the decisions, you are not actually consulting. A contracting role will be like any of the other roles described within this book, except that you will technically be employed by a contracting company rather than the organization for whom you are doing the work. This can, in some ways, be even more lucrative than true consulting. What it lacks, however, is the strategic component that consulting involves.

DEPENDENCY

Most consulting functions in one of two modes. Either you are employed by someone or you are running your own business. The fundamental difference here is whether you are the one finding new clients. If you are responsible for both finding and servicing new clients, you will have a lot more freedom to do what you want, in exchange for having more stress. If you are given projects to work on, you can have more confidence that there will be work when your project ends, but you often trade the ability to work on what you want and accept a somewhat lower salary to gain this level of job security.

Typically, most consultants work for quite a while within an existing consultancy before starting their own practice.

NOTE

Clients and Customers

In consulting terms, a "client" is the organization or person for whom you are providing services. A "customer" is someone for whom you provide goods. Typically, as a consultant, you would work for clients, each of which would have customers. Some of them may have clients as well, but generally, if you are working in this role, you would never have a customer.

THE MONEY

We have not focused much on income in this book. That's because, although we like to get paid, we do this because we love information security. We're not in information security for the money, but we will do it for money. Frankly speaking, at the time of this writing, almost any job in security will pay better than most other information technology options for whatever level you happen to be at. An exception is made for this role. While salary surveys are unreliable to begin with, they are completely useless for consultants. Not only do regular contractors get lumped into this category, but so do business owners. One person may have a job title of "consultant" and be making USD $40,000 per year in 02015 doing contracted help desk work. Another may have the same title and oversee a team of 20 other consultants, as well as doing their own work, for a total take-home of over a million US dollars yearly.

If you are driven largely by a desire for income instead of quality of work or quality of life, you are unlikely to be successful in this role. To truly succeed as a consultant, you must both care for your client and be able to help them find the right solution—for them, not for you. Greedy consultants often drop out of the business because clients talk to one another and word will spread.

HOW TO BREAK IN

There is a saying in consulting: "Fake it 'til you make it." Distressingly, this is true. The only way to succeed at being a consultant is to be a consultant. You will need some experience to maximize your chances of "faking it," but at some point, you must be willing to step into an unfamiliar situation and confidently suggest solutions that you are not certain will work. Critical skills in this role involve not only being able to understand and simplify highly complex situations and environments, but also being able to rapidly understand when things are not going as well as they ought and being able to make on-the-fly corrections.

The most stringent requirement for a security consultant is to be able to project a sense of trustworthiness. The second most stringent requirement is being able to follow through. This means years of having, and losing, fights that you don't really need to be having. After all, until you've lost some fights, you can't really develop the intuition for which fights are and are not worth having.

Instead of the classic advice "pick your battles," the path to becoming a security consultant is "pick every battle." The security consultant is a mercenary, and mercenaries are hired to win wars. Only through fighting and losing battles will you get good enough to fight for your clients and develop the skills to fight and win wars. This will, obviously, result in some uncomfortable situations.

COMMON PATHS

Common paths toward becoming a security consultant involve having done work as a Penetration Tester, Security Assessor, or Risk Assessor and grown tired of providing only tactical guidance. However, before the jump can be made, you may need to develop your presentation skills and move from having discussions with the IT-level people to presenting to the CEO, CIO, and CFO—and, in some cases, the board of directors. To do this, you may also want to spend some time as a security facilitator, project manager, trainer, or other role that focuses more on the softer skills than on traditional heavy technology. Typically, you will need an equal blend of hard and soft skills to succeed in this role.

LESS COMMON PATHS

Though less common, people do sometimes become security consultants after working as a lead auditor or security architect. It is rare, but academics and entrepreneurs can also become highly successful security consultants, though often in a specialist role. Specialized security consulting, such as ISO 27000 compliance, PCI-DSS QSA, or developing and implementing sand-boxing or intelligent analytics can be extremely lucrative. However, you will constantly be fighting people offering to do the work for less money and, as the service becomes a commodity, you will likely lose such work altogether.

HOW TO IMPROVE SKILLS—YOURS AND OTHERS

Unlike other jobs, this role involves a constant stream of learning opportunities. Every problem you solve will be a chance to grow. Moreover, since you will be functioning strategically, you will have constant opportunity to teach others. Whether you are helping a company become PCI-DSS compliant that runs from the lowest to the highest levels, implementing a Security Operations Center (SOC), or just reviewing and redrafting its security policies, you will have to learn a lot about your project and then convert that knowledge into a form your clients can use.

You will be writing, presenting, talking, creating graphics, writing code, reviewing deep technical internals, and monitoring the industry as a whole. More than any other role in information security, consulting will involve something new every single day.

RECOGNIZING WHEN YOU'RE STUCK

> "A slow sort of country!" said the Queen. "Now, here, you see, it takes all the running you can do, to keep in the same place. If you want to get somewhere else, you must run at least twice as fast as that!"
>
> — the Red Queen

Unlike practically every other role in information security, you simply cannot get stuck as a security consultant. You can leave at any time, and you can change your practice whenever you like. In fact, to be successful, you must constantly reinvent yourself to keep pace with what the attackers are doing.

Instead, your risk is burnout. Change can come so quickly, and so much can rest on you, that you might not be able to take it. If you find yourself snapping at people, missing obvious issues and generally feeling tired all the time, it is time for a vacation. If you still feel that way when you get back, take another one. If, after that, you still can't handle the stress, it may be time to move into another role.

WHEN OTHERS ARE STUCK

In a teaching role, you must pay attention to the well-being of others. As a consultant, you may be working with a different team every day. This means you'll be in a good position to identify when people are experiencing stress and help address these issues. Commonly, you will work with operational people—keeping systems functional, helping to identify concerns, working through issues, and so on. However, you will report to management. This means that if the people you work with are experiencing personal problems, deserve a raise, need some help, need a break, or—in some cases—need to be fired, you can work with the organization to make these things happen.

Your loyalty must always be to the organization, even if you are working with friends. If it is in the best interest of the organization that someone you like, but who can't do the job, must be let go, that's what you must recommend. Similarly, if they're about to lose someone if they don't give them a raise, the organization's management needs to know that, even if the person would be likely to find better employment elsewhere. Communicate clearly and frequently to make your position understood by management, co-workers, and your friends.

RULES OF THUMB

- Extremely interesting and challenging work, but often, far too much of it.
- Resiliency is more important than being right. You will be wrong. You will fail. How you handle that situation will matter far more than the failure itself.
- Be sure to set aside enough time to stay on top of changes in the industry, so you can provide the best service and minimize the chances of being caught flat-footed by your clients.

Table 3.6 Role at a Glance—Security Consultant

Hours	Travel	Stress Level	Creativity	Flexibility	Stability
12–18 hours/day	Considerable	High	High	High	Moderate
Learning	Lots—more than any other role, there will be ample opportunities to learn. At times, this will be overwhelming. The trick will be managing the learning opportunities and balancing them against the work that must be done to get paid, the work that must be done to set up new jobs, and focusing enough on the boring stuff to make sure everything gets done properly. As you go through this process, be sure to increase all aspects of your learning, not just the stuff you like or you're best at. The two keys to being successful are: • Staying on top of changing technologies and environments, being the best you can. • Addressing your weakest areas to limit the amount of damage they cause.				
Advancement	There are no advancement opportunities for a security consultant. You're already at the top. You may choose to move laterally into Security Management or an advanced level of assessment or auditing. However, most people who find they can succeed as a consultant tend to stay in that role.				

3.7 TIER 3—SECURITY MANAGEMENT (CSO, CISO, CPO)

INTRODUCTION

> "Organizations Get the IT They Deserve."
>
> — **Phillip J. Windley**

Odds are that you've already worked for enough managers to have an idea what management involves, but your understanding is probably incomplete. Most people don't realize until they become a manager just how much involves doing what previously they consider work. As a manager, you are responsible for making sure the people under you are happy and, at the same time, that the people to whom you report are also happy. However, as a security manager, you also must make sure that all of the people your systems and processes protect are kept protected. As hard as it is to serve two sets of people, it's extremely difficult to serve all three of these masters simultaneously.

On top of that, at the C-level, you are responsible to the investors or owners of the organization and, in some cases, personally responsible for legal requirements, the violation of which could result in jail time.

Though these roles have different names, ranging from Information Security Manager to Chief Security Officer (CSO) and Chief Privacy Officer (CPO), they all involve a split understanding of security and basic management principles. However, this means that you may often find yourself torn between what's right for a company's bottom line and what's needed to protect the data you store. This role involves not just fighting the bad guys, but also fighting your own people as you argue for long-term investment over short-term return.

HOW TO BREAK IN

A good way to break into this job is to become a team lead from another job. Management responsibilities tend to aggregate with experience. Thus, it's common to find yourself running a small incident response team or penetration testing team and then gradually take over security responsibilities from the IT Director or CIO. As time goes by, you may find yourself promoted to CISO or even CSO. The process can take a very long time, but can be accelerated in environments with high turnover.

In many cases, the CISO/CSO/CPO is viewed by the rest of management as an unpleasant necessity; people tend to fall out of the jobs either because they try to do too much too quickly or they do too little and suffer from unexpected security issues, or get blamed for the security issues they tried to prevent but were stopped. In these environments, having the role is like having a target painted on your back. The jobs are easy to get, because no one really wants them, but they're also easy to get fired from. Thus, a typical avenue into the role is to get a job at a high-turnover organization and then, when your tenure comes to an end, find one in a more stable environment.

HOW TO IMPROVE SKILLS—YOURS AND OTHERS

This could be a job you stay in for the rest of your career if you are willing to constantly improve your management skills. Read many business books, current business literature and journals, and possibly take management classes. Some books and classes are bad, but you'll need to know about them because other managers may rely on them. You will also need to learn more about finance to make the proper arguments for or against a purchase. Being able to "talk the talk" will be required for you to be successful when negotiating with board members and your management team.

However, that is not enough on its own. Many technical people will not respect a manager who can't understand what they're talking about. You will have to maintain your skill level to a certain extent while also avoiding improvement opportunities that do not benefit your organization. Being able to win the respect of those you manage even when you lack the technical skills will require understanding a lot more about human psychology and behavior so you can remove roadblocks and ensure that they feel appreciated without them taking advantage of you in the process.

RECOGNIZING WHEN YOU'RE STUCK

You can get stuck as a manager when there are no further prospects for promotion. Some managers get burned out at this stage or start job-hopping. However, if you truly enjoy management, you may not want to move anywhere else. You can keep improving your people skills and have a greater challenge than anything technical for the rest of your life.

If you find yourself disliking your job, seriously explore the possibility that you might lack the skills to properly deal with your bosses or subordinates. If that's the case, and you're up to the challenge, you may find your job improving as you improve your own ability to understand and respond to those issues you face that involve people.

RULES OF THUMB

1. Non-technical but challenging work if you can make the transition.
2. Never stop reading. There are more business books than you can read in your lifetime and many of them have very useful information for this role. Ask people what books they found useful. Those books that aren't directly useful to you will help you better understand those who do find them useful, or think they are.
3. Get good at fighting. A weak manager gets nothing done. A strong manager who only tells others what to do is equally ineffective. Know when and how to fight and when to negotiate to get what you need.

Table 3.7 Role at a Glance—Security Management

Hours	Travel	Stress Level	Creativity	Flexibility	Stability
8–10 hours/day	Low	Moderate	Low—Technical High—People	Moderate	Moderate
Learning	Most of the learning in this role involves how to better work with people. If you're used to working with technology, this may be a very different form of learning than what you're used to. Expect to read a lot of business books and learn from attending management seminars. If this sounds boring to you, this may not be the right role for you.				
Advancement	There are often no direct advancement opportunities from here unless you want to go higher in terms of management. Many people like to just stay at this level forever.				

TIER 3—LATERAL: CPA

INTRODUCTION

What is Certified Public Accountant (CPA) doing in this list of information security roles?

It's a fair question. The answer is four simple letters—SSAE. The Statement on Standards for Attestation Engagements number 16, or SSAE-16, is a form of external audit that involves security and privacy analysis of a business. This is a more stringent form of the better-known SAS-70 reporting process. This is a standardized process for a company to be audited by an outside firm to produce a report for its customers. This is often done by commercial data centers and other hosting providers, but is becoming more common in general business-to-business service providers.

The catch? This work can only be done by CPAs.

HOW TO BREAK IN

You break in to work as a CPA by passing the CPA exam, after you meet the preliminary requirements. These vary by state, but in general, it can take a bit longer than a bachelor's degree. Odds are that if you're reading this book, you're really not that interested in transferring out of security into being a CPA.

HOW TO BREAK OUT

If you are already a CPA, however, you may find this an interesting opportunity to start moving into security work. Most of it will be on the auditing side of things, but it wouldn't be very hard to find a security or IT consulting firm that has a client who wants an inexpensive SSAE-16. You basically trade the cost of a full SSAE-16 engagement for one that covers your costs and allows you to learn. The more you do, the more experience you build, and you may find yourself moving towards less CPA-focused auditing and into compliance realms like PCI-DSS or US HIPAA. At that point, you are a basically an Auditor in the Doing phase of your career and the rest of this book applies just as it would to someone who started in information security.

DEALING WITH DIFFERENCES

You will experience many differences between information security and accounting work. In accounting, there is some uncertainty, but a lot of it can be resolved with some effort. In general, information security has a lot more uncertainty and many areas that simply cannot be fixed. You will have to become much more comfortable with uncertainty and grow to accept the fact that best practice doesn't always apply. This can be a difficult adjustment for people who like the relative certainty of numbers, but if you can make it, many more options will open up to you.

3.a TIER 3—LATERAL: GENERAL MANAGEMENT

INTRODUCTION

A general management job will consist of everything detailed in the Security Management job, except that you won't just be dealing with security. As with the security-focused role, there will be a lot of people- and business-based learning opportunities that stretch your understanding of psychology and economics. There will, however, be even less technical need than in the security-focused role. You will, instead, be largely focused on keeping people's performance metrics high and making sure that projects move properly toward completion.

HOW TO BREAK IN

If you wish to move out of security into general management, it should be relatively easy if you've already done some work as a security manager. If all you have is a lead position, you will likely need more experience before anyone would seriously consider you for a management position. As with any-one trying to move from a minority position to a majority one, you will have to be significantly better than the other candidates to overcome the perceived risk of hiring a non-manager for a manager role.

Focus on maximizing your learning, and demonstrating what you've learned by teaching other managers how to better manage. This can be done formally through some type of MBA program (various options exist) or informally through a program like the one outlined in the book *The Personal MBA*. The more you can understand about how both people and businesses work, the more successful you will become.

HOW TO BREAK OUT

If you find yourself in a general management job and wish to move into information security, your challenge will be greater. As you should know by this point in the book, information security is weird. Your managerial skills will be useful, but you will also need to be able to evaluate risk and identify when people are feeding you incomplete information or active misinformation to get you to agree to their view of things. Hanlon's razor is useful: Don't ascribe to malice that which can be attributed to stupidity, but don't rule out malice. Also consider causes like misinformation and ignorance.

To succeed, you will need to improve your overall technical and risk management skills. Though we have avoided recommending such solutions elsewhere in this book, the use of "boot camp" classes will go a long way to help. Some security for managers courses are available and focus on expanding your skills to a point where you can talk about real issues in ways that will be understandable to everyone on your team. Beware of out of date, mono-cultural, and outright wrong course material. For example, if you start using the terms "hacker" or "cyber" in ways that don't match your team's use of those terms, you risk making yourself appear to them as actually stupid, rather than merely misinformed or culturally tone-deaf.

It may also be wise to get hands-on technical experience. In the Resources section, you will see lists of self-study systems and websites, some of them in a game-based format. Start by playing some of the games to understand what attackers do and what defenders face. Showing that you can, at least in a small way, walk the walk will go a long way toward getting you into the meritocracy of information security. If you have some technical knowledge but also understand your technical limitations then you can greatly impress your team, most of whom will not expect any technical understanding from a manager. However, don't try to fake it, they may be able to immediately tell, and will not be impressed with lying, and even less so, if you fool them longer.

DEALING WITH DIFFERENCES

The biggest difference you will face between security management and general management is that security management is very methodical and process-driven until there's an incident, and then it's all about flexibility and thinking of different ways to address concerns. All of your regular business management skills will apply, and there will be little difference in terminology once you learn the basics. The challenge will be in helping your technical people understand the business drivers around cash flow and investment, and helping your non-technical people understand the technical risk of not taking action. Then, with every incident, you will need to readjust to the new reality and react appropriately.

3.b TIER 3—LATERAL: TECHNICAL ARCHITECT

INTRODUCTION

You're an Information Technology Architect. You're experienced, you're skilled, you're a Subject Matter Expert, you've been there and done that. You didn't just get the T-shirt, you got all the T-shirts and then you wrote the book. Information security is your next frontier, and you want to go where you haven't gone before.

You've got security awareness. You learned the hard way and learned from others' mistakes. You know that information security is different; that it's not just about getting things done, it's about making sure that *attackers* don't get *their* things done.

You get it. Now you're ready to break into information security and hit the ground running.

If you believe all that, then you're also going to need humility.

This book mostly assumes that if you're going into information security, you already know the basics or are going to learn it elsewhere. Except this chapter.

Information technology is hard. Just getting something to work at all takes time, thought, and energy. But once it's working it is almost certainly not secure.

Information security is even harder than information technology, because making it work *securely* requires the original effort just to make it work and then much more. Making it securely work consistently is even more work. And if it it's not consistently secure, then it's not secure. Information security often follows the Perverse Pareto Principle, the first 20% of the problem is solved with the first 80% of the work, the remaining 80% of the problem is solved using another 80% of the work, for 160% total work. The work required adds to more than 100%, because the amount of work was incorrectly estimated.

The best information security people fail constantly. Major corporations both deliver and use defective information security products. Experienced CISOs tend to be those who got fired because their previous organization got broken into, usually publicly. The best cryptologists in the world are routinely defeated during their own presentations, or worse, a few years later, when people are depending on the security of their products. There are few successes and many failures in information security. The worst failures can't be covered up; although most organizations still won't talk openly about either the cause or ramification of the failure. The best successes often don't talk about it, either, to avoid attracting unwanted attention.

Information security is so hard that nearly everyone fails and keeps failing. Success is often just failing less—sometimes it's failing less than others, or failing just less enough that there's still some reason to keep going.

There are many places to learn more about this. Bruce Schneier's essay "Inside the Twisted Mind of the Security Professional" is a place to start. See the Appendix: People for a URL.

Information security is still a young field in business, even younger than information technology. Most organizations still haven't figured out how important information security is and where it should go, if anywhere. Some organizations put information security in with technology, but because of conflict of interest issues, others put it in finance under the CFO, or audit and compliance, or in with corporate security (those people with the guards and guns). Some organizations completely outsource their information security.

If you can't find an information security mentor, look for other information security people who are willing to talk to you. Information security has the same specialties as information technology, and more. Finding information security people, books, organizations, and other resources for your technology will help, but don't get hung up there, either, because thinking security is as important as knowing security. As a prospective security architect, it helps to have some understanding of all of security, not just a narrow specialization.

If you don't think your specialty has information security requirements there, look more closely. Common security practice is usually barely adequate in any specialty and even state-of-the-art systems usually have information security problems.

Part of the problem of information security is that the other specialties don't know much about security, and don't even think about it. As you learn more, you'll probably also find information security for your specialty is also inadequate; it may work but run counter to normal practices, or it may be expensive or extremely difficult to use. This is, unfortunately, completely normal in information security.

That's the bad news.

The good news is you've already got a career of experience and knowledge that's valuable in information security. Your ability to think outside the information security box can make the difference. You know how to communicate with those in your specialty; you understand them because you are them, for now. You may find that, as you learn more about information security, that your co-workers and colleagues don't understand information security. You may also find that information security doesn't understand your specialty, either. But *you* can be the bridge of that gap between information technology and information security.

HOW TO BREAK IN

As an established technical architect, use your existing contacts to get an information security mentor. You may need to move through a few degrees of separation to find your mentor. Don't get too hung up on your contacts' or your mentor's information security job titles. Even in the same organization, the information security people may have very different or even oddly inappropriate titles. A senior architect outside information security may merely be a business analyst in information security. Many organizations still don't have CISOs, so the top information security job might be "Computer Scientist" or as junior-sounding as Assistant Vice President.

A Technical Architect interested in moving into information security can be an ideal candidate. However, the nature of information security is often more adversarial, and may be thought of as negative thinking. The wealth of experience and technical knowledge a Technical Architect brings to information security is extremely valuable, but making use of this also requires an information security mindset that can be difficult to understand. In large enough organizations, the Technical Architect can join an existing information security group and have a peer group of experienced security architects to learn from and share knowledge. It also requires some amount of humility and flexibility to learn just how ignorant they were about security and how insecure their architectures are.

If your current organization is big enough, there will be an information security group that you can start learning from and perhaps plan a lateral promotion into. Larger organizations will have training and education opportunities for you that may require nothing more than signing up and showing up. Organizations with good lateral mobility will make this easy. However, other organizations may make it difficult to make this move, either in general, or because of isolation within the information security group. If it's too difficult, then making such a move could even be politically limiting within the organization, so you may have to move to another organization entirely; make this your backup plan.

Small organizations won't have an information security group. This is bad because you won't have anyone to learn from internally, but *you* can create, officially or not, that information security group. It's better if you can get management buy-in, but if you don't, you just need to become your organization's information security subject matter expert. This is a lot of work, but if your organization is so small that it doesn't already have such a group, either it's doing really badly, or there will be less to learn.

If you want to become a generalist Security Architect (see that chapter) then use the entire rest of this book to start to learn about information security groups, and their roles and responsibilities. However, you can also focus on information security in your specialty—this book is just the beginning.

In some ways you'll be starting from scratch, and in some ways it will be worse, because you'll have to unlearn some things and yet have to retain those same things, because you'll need them to keep relating to your specialty.

HOW TO IMPROVE YOUR SKILLS

If you are going the generalist information security route, all the skills in this book and beyond are applicable. However, if you're going to focus on your current specialty, the approach is dependent upon that field. You'll probably find a lot in the information security field that pertains to your field, and possibly some within the field itself. There might be a security certification, or a concentration available. Having certifications tend to be less useful to those with experience, but the study materials may still be useful as long as they aren't focused solely on passing the exams.

CRITICAL WARNINGS

If your current organization or specialty doesn't have security awareness, you may run into opposition. If you are not politically or socially aware, you may inadvertently limit your opportunities, possibly resulting in you having to leave your organization or even your specialty. Even without these difficulties, you may find it difficult to continue to relate to your specialty and your field's colleagues.

If you're already a Technical Architect and going into Security Architecture, you'll see many similarities in architectural concepts. However, Information Technology and Information Security are different enough that what passes for Security Architecture is very different from Technical Architecture. Because information security is even less mature than information technology, you may find that security architecture is similarly immature in your organization, and even the field.

As a Security Architect, you might find that what you do is mostly ignored and considered irrelevant, or you might find that what you're really doing is security engineering because there are no information security engineers in the organization, only information technology operators who don't really know security. You might end up doing much more hands-on work than you are used to, or want to do.

TERMINOLOGY

There are confusing and subtle differences in terminology between information technology and information security. For example, "token" has a lot of meanings in general; some information security-specific meanings are even more confusing. Information security lacks many common definitions; an ongoing argument is the difference among a weakness, a defect, an error, or a vulnerability. What "random" means to most people, or in information technology, is different from information security, and different again in cryptography. Common words like "clear," "erase," "reset," "sanitize," "scrub," "wipe," and—less commonly—"zeroize" can be synonymous or each can have similar but precisely different meanings. The information security intent of the phrase "security through obscurity" can trip up even long-time information technology professionals.

3.c   TIER 3—LATERAL: ENTREPRENEUR

INTRODUCTION

Odds are that you know what an entrepreneur is. If you've been in the security field for a while, you know that entrepreneurs have partially formed ideas and make people do a lot of work, pull lots of late hours, and typically run in the wrong direction most of the time. If you're an entrepreneur coming from outside of the information security space, you know that entrepreneurs are brilliant innovators who are seldom understood in their time and have to constantly juggle funding concerns with vision and planning to hit the market just right at just the right time.

Clearly, there may be communication issues when trying to be an entrepreneur in the information security field.

Fundamentally, the field is ripe for innovation and companies come and go (or are acquired) with rapidity. There is ample room for an entrepreneur to make lots of money in information security—or lose it all. It is a high-risk, high-reward industry at present, which is ironic, since security should lower risks.

HOW TO BREAK IN

If you want to function as an entrepreneur in information security, you will either be an information security practitioner who wants to launch a company, or you are already an entrepreneur and want to move into a more lucrative field.

If you are the former, odds are that you understand a core problem and have a good solution in mind. You may need funding to create a proof-of-concept device or application. You may already have that and need help finding customers. You may just have a rough idea that you want to be your own boss and nothing beyond that. In all of these cases, the key is to find a partner. Most business ventures fail; the best way to keep that from happening to you is to get someone you trust to help you out. Some people work best with small "mastermind" groups, staying completely independent. Others work best by signing over a percentage of the business to someone else and trusting them to handle the business side of things while you focus on security or technology. Still others go through a fundraising process and get investors who function as a partner.

Conversely, if you are non-technical or not a security expert and wish to become an entrepreneur in the field, the critical element is similar. You are going to need help. The field is rife with people who have good ideas but little business sense. If you can't figure out who is trustworthy and who is not, you could lose your investment very quickly. It is often best to put together a small advisory team to help you assess the suggestions you get from potential partners or employees. The people to pick for this advisory team should have experience both in the technical side of things and on the business side. Current and former consultants are often good choices, as are current and former security managers.

However, each entrepreneurial journey is different, so there is little we can offer you here. Instead, you should read some of the many books out there about starting businesses. Read more than one book and find the books and paths that fit you. It would be wise to go through the basics, as described in the Tier 1—Learn section, and get some level of knowledge of the space before you jump in, but once you're there, success will largely be about your ability to choose good people.

3.c.1 TIER 3—LATERAL: ENTREPRENEUR— STORY

GREG SULLIVAN

Greg Sullivan was a double math/music major. His goal all along was to make enough money in computers to go back to making music for a living. In the 01980s and 01990s, he did business software.

> I remember our CTO for the company gave a talk to the whole company. He said, "Here's the deal with email, don't press send unless you are willing to stand on top of the building and shout the message with a megaphone. Once you press send you expose it to the Internet, where it's available to anyone with the means and the intent." That was a big eye-opener. I can remember where I was standing, I can remember where he was standing. I've never been able to let that go. I believed him.
>
> My biggest challenge has been convincing people to protect their data.

So Greg became an information technologist with a passion for security.

Part of his introduction to information security was the blatant willingness of kids with a sense of entitlement to not have to pay for content. He likens theft of copyrighted content to crashing into a convenience store and taking things off the shelf. He wanted to make a contribution to copy protection.

> The bad guys operate under business drivers and economic models like the rest of us do. If we don't drive up the cost of their business then we leave ourselves vulnerable. The only thing our adversaries are constrained by is their imagination because we digitize everything.

Sullivan created a company that grew from an apartment-based business developing custom software to businesses. A decade later, he restructured to embrace the Internet and help his clients leverage that new technology. His company grew to several hundred employees focused on the insurance, banking and securities industries, with operations in the U.S., Netherlands and the United Kingdom. He sold that company and looked for other opportunities.

Today, Greg is the CEO of Global Velocity, a data security startup that focuses on data management. It's smaller that his previous company, but it's growing. As an entrepreneur, Greg constantly deals with new resource constraints, but gets to solve brand new problems every day.

TIER 3—LATERAL: ACADEMIA 3.d

INTRODUCTION—HOW THIS APPLIES

> "Academic politics is the most vicious and bitter form of politics, because the stakes are so low."
> — **Wallace Stanley Sayre**

For this chapter, Academia refers to positions in accredited four-year colleges or universities. Positions at two-year technical colleges are closer to that described in the Trainer-Educator chapter. The two roles differ in both requirements and duties.

To start, let's set forth the various levels within academia. At the most basic level is an Instructor. This is someone who is usually hired for a very limited term to teach a single course, though sometimes more. This person will often be using someone else's curriculum, while adding small amounts from their own experience. This role is essentially the same as the Trainer-Educator. Because of its similarity to that role, and its distinction from the other levels, it will not be discussed here.

This brings us to a tenure track position within the college or university. These are full-time positions where individuals are part of some department. People with roles in information security are usually in the Computer Science Department, though other areas may be appropriate as well, depending upon the individual's skill set.

As a professor you will have responsibility for doing research and generally teaching one or more courses per semester, though some professors who have enough outside funding can exclusively do research. How academia prioritizes the two can be summed up with the phrase "publish or perish." Professors must publish some number of publications during their time as a professor, if not, they will not be able to continue in the field. Each scientific community has its own standards for publishing quantity and frequency. For those in tenure track-positions, but who have not achieved it, publishing is essential for receiving tenure. Unfortunately, this publishing expectation is often in conflict with both scientific rigor and their teaching responsibilities. Depending upon the expectations of the college, a professor may end up focusing on research at the expense of preparing for classes.

The challenge of not being able to spend time focusing on updating curriculum is much more drastic in information security than it is in other areas. As an extreme example if your Ancient Greek History curriculum is five years behind, some advances might be missed, but your students will walk out of your course with an otherwise complete and solid understanding of Ancient Greek History. If you are five years behind in your Information Security curriculum, your students will be at a severe disadvantage compared to those taught with up-to-date material. At least some, if not most of the material will be brand new in the past five years. The tools they know how to use may be no longer used anywhere else, the vulnerabilities they protect against may now be irrelevant, and new threats will be unknown to them.

To avoid teaching obsolete material you may even find it necessary to write your own course books, as cutting-edge information security researchers are nearly always too busy to create up-to-date teaching material.

Finally, in academia, there is an expectation of an advanced degree (generally a PhD) in the subject matter you are teaching. As a professional, degrees are helpful in some cases, but in other degrees may actually be viewed as negative due to a lack of hands-on experience within the field.

WHAT SKILLS THIS GIVES YOU

The benefits of teaching have been described in the Trainer-Educator role. For those with the research experience within computer science in general, and information security specifically, their knowledge of those areas can be significantly beyond anyone working professionally in the field, as their discoveries may not have real-world implications yet. Similarly, the skills necessary to do academic research are very similar to those for investigating security breaches or auditing: attention to detail, keeping of meticulous notes, problem solving, and understanding of security principles.

When doing security research in academia, you must be able to defend your research to people who have an in-depth understanding of security in general. Doing so develops your communications skills, both in analyzing the questions being asked of you, and being able to express your thoughts and results. Advanced research will be expected to extend the state of the art and of human knowledge in general.

WHAT SKILLS YOU MIGHT STILL NEED

The ability to handle unexpected and nonstandard situations may be challenging for those moving from academia to a corporate environment. While doing research in academia, you often need to break down an overarching theme into smaller, more manageable pieces, then take a single piece and focus exclusively on that challenge. Or there may a situation while doing research where you discover an interesting side branch that does not directly relate to your current research. In academia, you have the luxury of noting that on the side and then, if you have the time, coming back to that research component. In contrast, there are many times when dealing with security incidents you are not going to be able to ignore certain side paths in order to appropriately assess the situation. Being able to manage that growing challenge, either by yourself, or by bringing in additional resources, will be an important part of your corporate job.

HOW TO FRAME YOUR SKILLS

As an Academic, your research and communications skills will provide value within the corporate environment. Demonstrating an ability to solve problems and communicate solutions will be helpful in moving between the areas. If you can react quickly to changing situations, that will serve you well in moving into areas such as Incident Responder or Pen Tester.

DIFFERENCES BETWEEN WHERE YOU ARE AND INFORMATION SECURITY
CULTURE

Academia is often more focused on getting it right, as compared to the corporate environment of getting things done. Having a flaw in a research paper is entirely inappropriate, while having a less than idealized process may be perfectly acceptable. Being able to adjust to differences in expectations will be important for moves to or from the field. Additionally, while academia would like to view itself as pure meritocracy, the political components of working within the field can be challenging to those who were more used to focusing on the tasks of their job.

Information security often rewards rebellion and going off on your own more than academia will.

TERMINOLOGY

Academics tend to be more precise in their language use than most, forgoing slang terms that may be used as part of the common culture. That said, academic and corporate vocabularies are merging, as last year's hypothetical research paper has become this week's major security breach.

BOOSTING

4.0

INTRODUCTION

"Boosting" is what we call the process by which you can gain skills outside of your regular job. Boosting isn't required to land a good job in information security, but it can help a lot. The goal isn't to demonstrate why you are the *best* choice for an opening, it's to demonstrate why you are a *better* choice than your competition. If even one of your competitors has been spending time at home to improve their skills and you have not, they'll have the edge. And in this industry, an edge is all it takes.

Such edges include writing and getting published, software development and getting distributed, evangelist/advocate, original research, public speaking, community involvement, and volunteering at conferences and user groups.

As you consider whether or not to engage in boosting, consider two related factors.

First, there is the issue of work/life balance. Families demand your time. Any time spent on advancing your skills in your off hours will take time away from those you love. This can be done in short project-based runs, where you invest four weeks to build a skill and then move back for family time. Some do it full time, and the family knows that two hours each day (often, while they sleep) you are learning. Others don't do it at all. This is not a decision to be made lightly. Your decision may be to have less to offer at work than others. There's nothing wrong with this. You have to be who you are and what your family needs.

The second issue is burnout. Some people have no trouble working 80 hours a week—60 hours at their regular job and 20 hours on their own projects. For others, just the required work hours are difficult. Additionally, different people need different amounts of sleep. Eight hours of sleep per night is considered ideal by many. But some people need six hours or fewer while others need nine hours or more. Health and stress may affect your sleep requirements. Before you decide to pursue a boosting path, consider where your limits are and build a plan with that in mind. Don't lose sleep; it is a false economy, don't plan to catch up on sleep later, sleep when you need to, including naps. If you are already short of sleep, do not lose more sleep; instead, find other places to borrow time from. But don't skip on exercise. If you don't get some sort of exercise already, you probably should; not exercising is another false economy.

If your plan requires just one hour of your day, but your day has no time available, something has to give. Most people can give up an hour of television or other entertainment, but if your plan requires you to give up an hour of sleep or exercise, you shouldn't do it. Similarly, adding an hour sounds trivial, but if you're already physically and mentally exhausted at the end of each day, this one hour may push you over the edge into burnout. A day has only 24 hours, so an hour is slightly more than 4% of a day. Consider having 4% less money to put into perspective the loss of an hour a day.

Consider also that if just 4% of a day makes the difference then you have a 4% margin or less for error, change, or anything else. You are at the edge of burnout, just 4% more effort of anything may be disaster. If your manager doesn't see this, and doesn't appear to care when you bring it up, you've got another reason to get a new job. Examine what at work and home is pushing you to your physical, mental, and time limits. You may need to spend more time on other things, such as more or better sleep, rest, mediation, exercise, or diet. Talk to your physician, counselor, or trusted friend.

The phrase "quality time" is trite but is useful. Gain time by being mindful of time spent everywhere; budgeting time is even more important than budgeting money, as time can't be accumulated, nor is interest easily gained. Keep careful notes of where you spent your time so that at the end of the day you know what you did and how long it took. Use these metrics to find lost time and to plan better. Time can be gained from many places. You might find that every day you spend 5 minutes just looking for your wallet, phone, or keys. One way to gain that time back is to develop an every day carry (EDC) habit. You already have an EDC, unless you don't regularly wear clothing or anything else so if you're wasting time looking for anything every day, then you'll save time with a good EDC habit. Your EDC are the things you always need or have close at hand. Your EDC is a way to be organized and prepared, so that when time is unexpectedly available or unavailable, it is not wasted.

Typical EDCs include clothing, wallet, bag, or other containers that organize, hold, and keep everything else from being lost. Include in your everyday carry a book or other learning material as well as writing materials. If this seems like too much to carry, the phone, tablet, and other computing devices already part of your EDC may do it already.

Mobile devices that function as eBook readers or music players, connect to social media, and provide Internet access are common, but can be expensive both in initial purchase and ongoing use. In addition, such tools can be their own distraction; instead a special-purpose eBook reader or music player, despite being less functional, may pay dividends in time by being easier to use, cheaper, and in particular being less of a distraction.

Time spent traveling may be usefully spent thinking about ongoing problems or listening to audio-books, conference recordings, or podcasts. Recordings can be played faster without pitch distortion with the right software, allowing you to get even more learning out of limited time. Time spent waiting may be spent reading or participating in social media. Some types of exercise also allow these learning activities. Many menial but necessary tasks can be done just as well as listening and sometimes even reading.

TIME MANAGEMENT

Procrastination

"People commonly use the word "procrastination" to describe what they do on the Internet. It seems to me too mild to describe what's happening as merely not-doing-work. We don't call it procrastination when someone gets drunk instead of working." — Paul Graham, The Acceleration of Addictiveness

---

It used to be that being really productive required giving up television, but today that's not sufficient. Both smart phones and the Internet have many distractions, and are all the more so because they are truly useful. Don't allow your tools to be your undoing. Beware of "productivity porn" and even "EDC porn" in which researching and implementing new ways to be productive distracts, while allowing the delusion of being productive.

You may not know your limits without reaching them, perhaps many times. When you begin to feel overly stressed and you're not making the progress you need, take a week off and see if you feel better. If so, consider whether or not you're doing too much, and rework your plan to reevaluate your goals and process.

SEPARATE CYCLES

These options to boost your skills operate on a completely separate Learn/Do/Teach cycle. These cycles are unlikely to involve your employment, so they'll be smaller and faster. Learning in a group can be slow, and is highly dependent upon the group and the teacher if any. Faster learners will outpace the others and may grow dissatisfied and leave. However, group learning also is an opportunity to learn from others, especially the teacher. Organizations also provide additional structure to verify that when you're in a Doing phase, things are getting done properly. This is good from a verification perspective, but bad from a speed perspective. Finally, some organizations are actively hostile toward the Learning and Teaching phases. In their view, time spent learning or teaching is time spent not getting things done. Avoid these organizations unless you're a consultant and are willing to work under these conditions and charge them for their poor practices.

Thus, to maximize your effectiveness, think differently about your Learn/Do/Teach cycle speed at work and at home. You can often achieve more learning and a much faster pace on your own. However, you can also get misled much more easily. As you review your Boosting plan, be sure to double-check that you're not just learning but learning the right things.

EXPLORATIONS

Many times, you just don't know what you need to learn. This is particularly common before you get into your field of choice. If you're a penetration tester and want to become a team lead, odds are that you know where at least some of your faults are. However, if you're spending your day job doing workstation support and you really want to design firewalls, you may know some of the basics, but the gap between where you are and where you want to be is much wider, and wider gaps have many more hidden challenges.

Think of boosting as building bridges between the person you are and the person you want to be. In the physical world, bridging a broad valley is much more difficult than stepping over a small gap. As you build the bridge, you need anchor points and a plan and a straightforward path. Bigger and longer bridges across wider and deeper gaps will involve footings spread across the length of the bridge as well as exploration of the area below the bridge to discover unseen challenges. Some bridges may fail because the land where a footing went is sandy or marshy. Other footings fail because the land is too hard to drill into. Sometimes you'll move the bridge somewhere else. Sometimes you'll have to move many bridges.

The same is true for creating new paths for learning. Sometimes you just have to experiment so you can feel out the area in which you want to improve your learning. This can involve testing new operating systems, new tools, or visiting different user groups, and meeting new people. If you don't know precisely where you need to go, take a week or two and just explore. The time spent in this activity is far from lost. Instead, it will pay off many times in the time saved when you start working on real projects.

DISADVANTAGES OF BOOSTING

There are many advantages to boosting; however, it is not an always beneficial process. In addition to the potential waste of time if you misjudge the need for the skill you target, remember that the time you spent is time you cannot spend on other things. This may not mean much if the next pressing issue in your life is that you really want to get caught up on watching your DVD collection. However, if it means missing your child's winning goal in the hockey finals, giving up a chance to take on a leadership role in your church, or not being there when a dying parent needs you, then the cost is high.

Taking a less dramatic view, a narrow focus can disadvantage you by shrinking the diversity of your education. By focusing ever more narrowly on your career goals, you box yourself in. At the time this book is being written, there are many unemployed COBOL programmers; Java programmers may be next. This is a delicate trade-off to make, so approach it with the understanding that once you get where you want to be, shift your focus to improve your thinking and learning diversity. The more diversity you have, the better you will be able to see interesting patterns and also understand and communicate those patterns to others. Well-rounded security practitioners understand their field, but also have insights into other fields, both technical and not, such as current events, business, cooking, art, literature, economics, and history. These insights can prove critical in addressing a real-world attack.

Many of these paths involve doing public work. For many, this won't be a concern, but some people work within restrictive organizations, and being seen to publicly endorse a specific project, such as Ubuntu Linux, may have negative consequences. More often, organizations take a view of not caring what you do outside of work, so as long you don't get paid. Be sure to familiarize yourself with your employer's restrictions before you commit yourself to any of the ideas in this section.

Finally, there are some projects that are more likely to have negative repercussions than others. For example in open-source, both the OpenSSL cryptographic library and the Tor anonymization service provide a great deal of value to others. However, Tor is far more politicized. If you work for an organization dealing with sensitive data, such as a military organization, the discovery that you're working on what can be a data exfiltration tool could both harm your work and your Tor project effort much more than less politicized work.

Consider what others would think about your involvement in any particular project. If you think it is likely to work well for you, go for it. However, if there's some concern, you may wish to consult with your supervisor to get permission—in writing—first.

BOOSTING—AUTHOR (BLOGS, MAGAZINES, BOOKS)

4.1

INTRODUCTION—WHAT THIS IS

Writer. Author. Blogger. All have the same general goal: generating content, in some form, that someone else sees as valuable. The choice of medium (electronic or paper) will impact the format of that content, but keeping a focus on the content is where being an Author will improve your career prospects.

As a book author, you will be responsible for generating content to a quantity, quality, and format dictated by the publisher. If you are coauthoring a book, you must be able to collaborate with the other authors in order to ensure a cohesive book.

For those that are more independent-minded, you can create a blog. Keep in mind that even if you have developed a following, it will take work to maintain and generate traffic to your blog. That said, it is your blog. You can do with it as you please subject to your country's laws. You get full credit for the content generated. You also get the full blame for a lack of quality, or worse, should you plagiarize others' material, the legal issues.

For those who are more community minded, forums such as StackExchange provide a way to contribute to the community by addressing specific questions. You may be able to talk about the points and scores you have in interviews. Community involvement shows an interest and ability to help others, important characteristics for many organizations. While many may not consider this actual authorship, many of the advantages of authorship are present here. Your material is available. You can point prospective employers to the site and identify who you are, and they can evaluate your writing and knowledge.

For those interested in boosting their career through authorship, that is what it is all about: making your excellent knowledge available for others to appreciate.

WHY YOU MIGHT WANT TO DEVOTE TIME TO THIS

All authorship can be used to generate your brand. How much that will help you will vary based on the content and reputation of the items authored. Getting authorship for a book or article is generally viewed more highly, as it indicates that some external entity (the publisher) viewed your work as valuable. The simple fact that someone was willing to pay you for your efforts will raise the perception of value, for those who have not read the material.

For those who have read the material, the value is in the content. If your content does not display an understanding of the topic, is plagiarized, or is filled with errors, the authorship could potentially hurt your prospects. Do what you can to generate high-quality material.

HOW THIS MIGHT COST YOU

Writing is a high-paying career for only a very few individuals. Some individuals can generate a site with which they can support themselves (Brian Krebs is a classic example), but this takes significant experience, knowledge, and effort. If you want a high hourly rate for your writing time, you are going to have to spend a significant amount of time working to develop a following. Even putting forth that effort has no guarantee of success.

Those who have achieved some level of success at writing will then be introduced to the trials and tribulations of deadlines. Once someone starts paying you for your efforts, there is an expectation that the work will be produced by the agreed-upon time. Since writing is unlikely to be your regular job, this will take away from your personal time. Many times the deadlines are critical to the publisher, so failure to meet them may reduce your opportunities with them in the future.

Finally, if you plagiarize others' materials, you can permanently damage your personal brand. With the search abilities of the Internet, you can assume that if you do so, sooner or later someone will find you out.

HOW TO GET STARTED

There are books and articles aplenty on how to become an author; find one that works for you. Focus on material that you know. Generate quality content.

If you can find someone who is working on a book and you have an opportunity to coauthor with them, take full advantage of that opportunity. Opportunities such as that do not present themselves very often.

WHEN YOU MIGHT WANT TO STOP

Writing regularly is hard. Taking a blank slate, and producing valuable content takes a level of dedication that can be hard to maintain. The number of people who are working on a book is many orders of magnitude larger than those who have completed a book. If the time and effort necessary for you to generate the content is too high, then it is time to exit.

It is far better to stop generating content than to generate content that is of such low quality that others do not find value in it and you hurt your brand.

WHAT SKILLS THIS GIVES YOU

The ability to write well is a valuable skill by itself. Being able to clearly present concepts in written form is useful for any information security role, whether it be technologist, manager, or organizer.

Beyond the writing skills, doing the research necessary to produce material will be valuable as well. Not only will you develop your research skills, but you will be learning more details about an area that interests you.

WHAT SKILLS YOU MIGHT STILL NEED

One of the biggest challenges for those who want to become authors is understanding the time and effort involved in producing quality material. The process of generating the content will often involve multiple revisions, or at least multiple reviews as you go through the material.

BOOSTING—DEVELOPER (OPEN SOURCE)

4.2

INTRODUCTION—WHAT THIS IS

The job role of developer has already been discussed in the Developer chapter. However, for those who like to write code, or want to develop their coding skills, being a developer as part of an open-source project is a great way to build and maintain those skills.

Though you may be unfamiliar with what open source is, you probably use open-source software. The Linux kernel and Mozilla Firefox are two of the most widely used open-source software, while open source libraries such as Info-ZIP and OpenSSL are found in ubiquitous commercial software and hardware. This means that anyone is able to get a copy of the source code, and build or modify the code themselves. That said, there are frequently limitations put upon the changes that you make. Many open-source licenses require you to release your source code, should you wish to distribute anything based on their code. More information on open-source licenses and the idea of free software can be found at the Free Software Foundation's website.

There are literally thousands of active community open-source projects out there. And there are thousands of open-source projects that were started but are no longer being actively supported.

WHY YOU MIGHT WANT TO DEVOTE TIME TO THIS

Working on open-source software is a great way to develop your programming skills. If you are not already a professional developer, it provides an opportunity to learn about the development process. For those who are professional developers, it provides an opportunity to network and learn from a diverse peer group that you would not have access to otherwise.

For those in the security field, fixing security bugs is one of the best possible ways to understand the types of coding mistakes people make that lead to security vulnerabilities. By fixing bugs, you learn what attackers look for and you learn what their exploit code does to take advantage of the flaws in the system. This process will teach you multiple languages and multiple coding styles. If, in the future, you transition to penetration testing, you can take your skills and pivot to exploit development, writing the code to take advantage of the weaknesses your team finds.

Beyond the security-specific knowledge you may gain, working on projects you are interested in provides an opportunity to network with a wide range of people with similar interests. This may open doors to other career opportunities that you might not have otherwise.

Finally, providing enhancements to open-source projects is one way to truly demonstrate your skills to prospective employers. It is one more way to differentiate yourself from the other candidates.

HOW THIS MIGHT COST YOU

Working on open-source projects is guaranteed to cost you time: unpaid, no-glory time. If you are someone who enjoys the guts of code, that time may be time well spent, regardless of the outcome. There are relatively few paid open-source project jobs. They are usually commercial open source support companies but also a few funded open source organizations, and also large organizations that are heavily dependent upon open source. Some examples are the FSF, Google, Mozilla, and Red Hat. However, jobs that make some use of open-source are very common with few IT jobs not using open source somewhere. However, a few organizations still officially avoid and even ban open-source software to avoid perceived security open-source licensing issues.

Most open-source projects never catch on, get replaced by other projects, or fall apart due to bickering of the project team, just as most companies eventually go out of business. If this were to happen, there would be less value to your resume, but the experience you gain would be valuable no matter what happens to the project and no less than if your previous employers went out of business.

HOW TO GET STARTED

When working on an open-source project, there are three key pieces to consider: Project, Community, Technology.

First, are you interested in that project? If you love graphics programs, GIMP may be the perfect program for you, but if you couldn't care less about gray scale and transparency layers, it is unlikely to keep your attention. Focus on projects where you are excited about the finished project. That will help drive you to produce the highest quality code you can.

Second, is the community one you want to be part of? Every project has its own management style and community. Some projects are driven by a committee, while others have a single person who has final say with large numbers of people contributing to the code. Some projects are welcoming to inexperienced developers. Others have little patience for those who do not have a deep understanding of coding projects. If the community personality does not fit your personality, you are unlikely to be interested in staying engaged with the project.

Finally, there is technology. If you are interested in developing your PHP skills, working on the Linux kernel is not going to be a good project for you. Find a project that requires the skills you want to develop.

WHEN YOU MIGHT WANT TO STOP

Coding after hours can be draining. The idea of getting home from a long day at work staring at a computer, just to stare at another computer screen, may get to the point where it is no longer worthwhile. Sometimes the project's leadership or community may change to the point where it is no longer a group you are comfortable interacting with.

Stopping may mean leaving one project and moving on to another, or it may mean stopping doing development altogether.

WHAT SKILLS THIS GIVES YOU

At a minimum, your development skills will improve. Additionally, you may develop soft skills associated with working in a large diverse team. Potentially you will develop an understanding of security vulnerabilities within code.

WHAT SKILLS YOU MIGHT STILL NEED

Your development skills may or may not be to the level that are necessary for the project that you want in the role that you are interested in. Finding a role and project that matches your skill set may take some effort.

4.3 BOOSTING—DEVELOPER/ ENTREPRENEUR (CLOSED OR OPEN SOURCE)

INTRODUCTION—WHAT THIS IS

> "One percent inspiration, 99 percent perspiration."
>
> — **Thomas Edison**

You have the idea for the next Facebook, Google, Linux, or Flappy Bird. Well, maybe the next Flappy Bird. Time to start writing code. Writing in the morning. Writing in the evening. Writing in the lunch hour. You can be a devpreneur—a developer entrepreneur who creates a business with just software. However, as a booster, you have a day job, so make sure not to use business resources. Check your employer's policy on doing your own work on your own time with your own equipment. Most companies have rights to anything you do on their time on their equipment, but some claim anything you thought of while you were employed, and you do not want to do all of that work for their benefit or risk legal issues should there be any questions.

There are periods of time when there are massive spikes in Devpreneurs. In the 01980s, the platform was the personal computer. In the mid-01990s, it was the Internet accessed with personal computers. Later in the 02010s, it was smart phone, tablet, and mobile Internet applications. Each time, a new market was created by the emergence of a new, ubiquitous platform. After the initial surge, the market began to saturate, and finding opportunities became harder and harder, but they still exist. New platforms and technologies continue to be developed, such as smart watches, smart glasses, augmented reality, full speech control, and more.

If you have a passion for creating, this can be a chance to enjoy that and learn, with the potential for self-employment.

WHY YOU MIGHT WANT TO DEVOTE TIME TO THIS

Owning and running an independent company has great appeal for many. This drives many to work on creating their product. No matter what the outcome, the process is going to be educational. You will learn about development, market forces, and coding. Expect to learn about software vulnerabilities, the public relations and marketing response to those vulnerabilities, having to fix bugs, and generating interim releases.

Do not underestimate the value of going through this process. Whether a success or failure, there is much to be learned in starting your own company.

HOW THIS MIGHT COST YOU

The largest commodity this process will cost you is time. Depending on the development platform, there may be additional costs for hardware, server hosting, tool and developer registration fees, or even legal costs, depending on what you are developing. Standard costs for a business may also apply such as Internet domain name registration, email, web site, dedicated phone number, PO Box, and business cards, if you know anyone who still uses those, etc.

If you move to exclusively focusing on developing and selling your product, you will frequently have to rely on savings while the product ramps up. Additionally, if it does not succeed, moving back into the job market may be challenging.

HOW TO GET STARTED

You might think you should start by writing code. Actually, that may not be the best starting point. Investigate the market, determine if the concept has already been developed, and determine approximately how much effort it will take to produce the product you want. A common used software engineering concept is the minimum viable product (MVP), or rephrased "What is the simplest thing that could possibly work?"

If you have a truly viable product idea, and the ability, you may even be able to get funding and support from an incubator company in exchange for sharing future profits.

Often someone else has tried the idea before. Sometimes, it is part of a suite offered by a major player. You will have to decide if you can build it better, or if it is better to not attempt to enter the market.

WHAT SKILLS THIS GIVES YOU

You will start by developing your coding skills. After that, you will develop your marketing skills. After that you will develop your business skills.

That is, of course, an idealized progression. Most of your new skills will be developed as you build your product. Technical people often miss the importance of marketing. You should be marketing yourself and your product early in the process.

WHAT SKILLS YOU MIGHT STILL NEED

You'll need all of the skills above that you do not already have. If you are fortunate enough to have your business take off and grow, be prepared to move away from technology and into a more business-oriented role. A common strategy is to start the company with a partner who complements the other's skills, talents, and interests. For example if you don't want to go into the business side, then choose a partner who will. A classic example of this partner relationship is Steve Wozniak (software and hardware) who co-founded with Steve Jobs (marketing and business) what became Apple Inc.

4.4 BOOSTING—EVANGELIST (SECURITY, PRIVACY)

INTRODUCTION—WHAT THIS IS

Evangelism has been around for as long as people have been able to communicate. I would not be surprised if different groups had advocated for different means of starting fires. When someone feels passionate about a subject, they will work to bring others to it, either individually, when meeting with others, or in group settings. Technology evangelists have been around for generations. In some cases, they end up getting hired by the company they are passionate about such as Guy Kawasaki at Apple, Inc., and in others, they create an organization and a technology platform around their beliefs such as Richard Stallman at the Free Software Foundation (FSF).

In modern computing, evangelism has spread to include the computer security, privacy, and legal arenas. The platforms for evangelism have also changed as social media and the Internet have allowed individuals to have a much broader reach.

WHY YOU MIGHT WANT TO DEVOTE TIME TO THIS

If you want to change the world, or some small part of it, you will need to evangelize to get others who in turn get others to work toward the goal you are trying to achieve.

HOW THIS MIGHT COST YOU

If there is a need to evangelize for your point of view, that means there are others who disagree with you. After all, if everyone agreed, why bother taking the effort to espouse your point? You will thus need to be ready to defend your position against others. Is conflict something you are comfortable with? If not, then sleepless nights are potentially in your future. Also, because successful evangelism results in your cause being taken up by others, you may get caught in blowback from what others do. For example, you are evangelizing for privacy and some rogue group defaces a website to also evangelize for privacy, you could get branded as "one of those privacy nuts" even if you did not participate in the action.

Of course, if you do anything illegal as part of your advocacy, there may be legal challenges for you as well.

HOW TO GET STARTED

Evangelism is built around the platform that you have. If you have a LinkedIn or Facebook account use it to express your views. However, consider the medium for your message. For example, if you're a privacy evangelist, consider the irony of using anti-privacy platforms. Others may be able to speak at user group meetings or similar groups to express their views.

Be careful about doing evangelism at work. Depending on your work rules, what you are evangelizing for, and the laws applicable to your organization, evangelism can be grounds for discipline at work.

As with the Speaker boosting role, the more exposure you get, the more likely you are to get a larger platform. It's always necessary to work to expand your social circle.

WHEN YOU MIGHT WANT TO STOP

If what you are evangelizing for happens (or evangelizing against has happened yet), then victory is yours. Congratulations. However, before that happens, you may become drained by the combativeness of the situation, which will induce you to leave the subject. You may also change your views. New developments may change whether what you are advocating for is still necessary.

WHAT SKILLS THIS GIVES YOU

Written or verbal expression of your views is the core of evangelism. You will need to communicate in a clear and convincing manner. These skills are useful in many career tracks.

WHAT SKILLS YOU MIGHT STILL NEED

A thick skin, the ability to not let others' words affect you, will be important in this role. As you grow, you may need to develop your speaking skills.

CHAPTER

4.5 BOOSTING—RESEARCHER (SECURITY, VULNERABILITY, ETC.)

INTRODUCTION—WHAT THIS IS

"Research is what I'm doing when I don't know what I'm doing."

— Werner von Braun

To extend the boundaries of security, people investigate them. There are many areas, from reverse-engineering malware to identifying vulnerabilities in web browsers.

You get to name the bugs you find, unless it's so serious that others give it more popular names Heartbleed and Shell Shock. You know you have found a serious bug if it winds up being named, either by the community or the media. If this happens, you may find yourself working some lucrative consulting contracts. That said, those are rare situations, as most research results in little to no financial reward. Some bugs have financial bug bounties offered by the organization responsible for that vulnerable system (see the Appendix), but most don't. Most rewards are going to be in a sense of self-fulfillment, and potentially in speaking opportunities.

WHY YOU MIGHT WANT TO DEVOTE TIME TO THIS

Doing research is one of the single best ways to truly understand a topic. The knowledge and experience required to become a good security researcher will set you apart from nearly everyone in the industry.

It can be immensely rewarding. Finding a security vulnerability that no one else has reported is something to be proud of. If it's sufficiently novel, you could be asked to do talks on your research, increasing your personal brand.

HOW THIS MIGHT COST YOU

This will cost you time. Lots of time. And if you are not careful to stay within legal research, you could face the ultimate time loss: prison.

As long as you stay legal and do not plagiarize, the risks are essentially in time spent. If you learn anything, the time is not wasted.

204

HOW TO GET STARTED

Whatever the area you are planning to move into, you must find it interesting. Whether it is website vulnerabilities, software vulnerabilities, cryptography, malware, or some other area, the work is going to be hard, at times frustrating, and occasionally grueling.

> **WARNING**
>
> Identify what is legal to do in your jurisdiction. Attempting to break into websites is usually illegal. Make sure you understand any website's policy regarding security research. You must be careful to never violate others' privacy. Doing so may expose you to criminal liability. Similarly, many software licenses do not allow reverse-engineering. Make sure you understand ethical vulnerability disclosure guidelines. There are many different views on this, and you will have to decide what you are comfortable with. But, once again, whatever you do, ensure that you are within the laws of your jurisdiction.

In short, do not do *anything* until you understand what you can and cannot legally do.

The next step in the research will be to develop your background knowledge in the subject. Take a look at previous research. Many conferences publicly post presentations that have been given, such as DEF CON and Black Hat. You can get at cutting-edge research by looking at the more recent presentations, and develop a historical perspective by looking at older presentations.

Start small. Develop a lab with the equipment and tools where you can experiment safely and legally and consistently. Having dedicated space where you can keep your equipment and tools visible and available is a part of time management. But don't spend a week at the lab to save a day at the library, research both the historical and current industry literature. Reproduce others' work in your lab. Use the scientific method. This will give you an understanding of the process, tools, and skills. See the Appendix for references.

Start building from there, then move into unexplored areas.

WHEN YOU MIGHT WANT TO STOP

Making money as a security researcher is hard. While bug bounties are sometimes offered, very few individuals are able to make a living at it. If you are not making money at it, your motivation is going to be your interest in the subject matter. Once you lose interest and are no longer keeping up with the new advances, it is probably time to move on.

WHAT SKILLS THIS GIVES YOU

After spending significant time as a researcher, you will have a great understanding of that facet of security. Beyond that area, the overlap and extension into other areas can move you on the path to being an expert in this field.

WHAT SKILLS YOU MIGHT STILL NEED

Describing the skill gaps is not really feasible, given the range of possible security research. In almost all cases, a strong understanding of software development will be required, but what that means will vary from area to area.

4.6 BOOSTING—SPEAKER (LOCAL EVENTS, PODCASTS, WEBCASTS, ETC.)

INTRODUCTION—WHAT THIS IS

> "All the great speakers were bad speakers at first."
>
> — **Ralph Waldo Emerson**

Presenter. Speaker. Podcaster. All roles in which you are using your voice to transmit knowledge to someone else. With this booster, you have the opportunity to get out and share your hard-earned knowledge and experience with someone else, potentially with many others.

For those who prefer not to speak in front of people, at least to start, a recorded medium may be the best. Keep in mind that if you do well at podcasting, you will be asked to make live presentations. That additional exposure and opportunity to build your brand will be valuable, so think about doing so.

Whatever your medium, it will all be about the preparation. How much time you spend finding background material, and providing depth and breadth to your topic will impact the quality of your final product. Being able to provide a unique combination of fact, opinion, and speculation, making sure you identify which is which, will help make you an interesting speaker.

WHY YOU MIGHT WANT TO DEVOTE TIME TO THIS

Once you have presented well, additional opportunities to speak will often become available. Someone at a small conference saw you speak, and now they are looking for speakers at a large conference, and you come to mind. You can grow your brand and get additional opportunities this way. A good speaking engagement can provide new consulting or other career opportunities.

HOW THIS MIGHT COST YOU

Depending on your topic, and your format of choice, you could end up being branded in a certain category. If you are not comfortable being thought of as "the <x> person," where <x> is your topic of choice, speaking is probably not a good booster for you. Additionally, once you put yourself out there as a subject matter expert in a specific field, you are going to be scrutinized significantly. If you are not comfortable backing up your claims every time you present, speaking is probably not a good option.

HOW TO GET STARTED

As with all boosters, find a topic you are excited and passionate about. Speaking is all about presentation. It is easier to present well if you feel strongly about the subject. Learn proper citation techniques for the facts and information you use. Before you start understand how to give them appropriate credit.

Find small user groups. Smaller group meetings often have trouble finding speakers, and will be open to volunteer presenters. Do this as often as you can. This will help to build your brand, and potentially provide opportunities at larger engagements.

Put some speeches online. YouTube or other similar sites can provide additional exposure. They also provide a way for you to give an example of your work to those who might be interested in engaging you.

WHEN YOU MIGHT WANT TO STOP

As with any public figure, the more exposure you get, the greater the number of detractors you will have. If dealing with these detractors is no longer something you are willing to do, then lowering your profile by moving out of speaking may be the best option for you. If you are no longer able to find topics that interest you, it is often better to move to other areas, rather than lowering the overall quality of your speaking efforts.

WHAT SKILLS THIS GIVES YOU

Good speaking skills are valuable in any environment. Additionally, you will develop your networking skills, and potentially your debating skills as well.

WHAT SKILLS YOU MIGHT STILL NEED

You will often need to develop your skills in the area that you are talking about. For example, when you first start talking about malware, your reverse-engineering skills may need to be improved to allow you to understand more about the variants you find in the field.

4.7 COMMUNITY SUPPORT (DOCUMENTATION, BUG PRIORITIZATION, PROJECT MANAGEMENT)

INTRODUCTION—WHAT THIS IS

While we discussed previously the booster of Developer (Open Source), there are other ways to help the open-source community.

Documentation for open-source projects tends to need updates, tweaks, or additional sections written, and sometimes is poor quality or doesn't exist. If you are interested in learning deeply about a piece of open-source software, helping write documentation is one of the best ways to do so.

Testing of the code is also another way to develop skills with software. Being part of the development process by testing software is another way to help an open-source community while learning about software.

After you have established yourself within a development community, you can often contribute in other manners. Helping to reproduce and determine the severity of bugs, thus helping determine their priority, or even helping with coordinating of the project as a whole, may be an option.

WHY YOU MIGHT WANT TO DEVOTE TIME TO THIS

For those who want to help build open-source software, but are not development-focused, this can be an ideal way to be part of the community. It also provides a way to build your skills and experience with the development process.

HOW THIS MIGHT COST YOU

The primary cost will be time. Most open-source projects look upon anyone willing to put in the effort to try to help as a welcome addition. There are exceptions, so find a community that fits with your personality.

HOW TO GET STARTED

The first step is to find a project you are interested in. Without that core interest, it will be difficult for you to maintain focus. Once you have the project identified, investigate the community. Ensure that it will be a good fit for your personality.

Now that you have identified the project, you can start helping. Each project will have its own take on how to integrate volunteers into the system.

WHEN YOU MIGHT WANT TO STOP

Community support will be either energizing, as a result of seeing your efforts moving into a production system, or demotivating, because you struggle with the project's management chain, or you feel as if you have no support from others in the community. Some people are able to push through the latter, but you will need to determine your limit. Additionally, projects may split—fork, in open-source parlance. If that happens, you will need to determine which project to join, or decide if it is time to leave.

WHAT SKILLS THIS GIVES YOU

Working in these roles provides you with the opportunity to develop your skills in the area of your choice. You can become a better writer, tester, or project manager, depending on the role you take on. Additionally, you'll develop your communication soft skills working within a group, no matter how strong they were when you started.

WHAT SKILLS YOU MIGHT STILL NEED

As you develop a reputation for success within the community, you will likely find that you are asked to assist in areas outside your area of expertise. Be honest and acknowledge what you can and cannot do; if the group is still willing to have you work in that area, you now have the chance to build those skills. For example, if you come in as a tester, you may be asked to help with documentation. If that is not your strong point, you have the option to refuse, or you can take advantage of the opportunity to work on your skills in that area. As this is purely a volunteer organization, being willing to branch out and succeed in new areas will help you develop a reputation as someone who gets the job done.

4.8 CONFERENCE SUPPORT (FOUNDING, ATTENDING, VOLUNTEERING, RUNNING, LEADING)

INTRODUCTION—WHAT THIS IS

Conferences take significant effort. Even a small 80-person one day conference could take 100 to 150 hours of effort, depending on conference length, complexity, speakers, and facilities available to host the conference.

Conferences by local user groups or similar organizations often have trouble getting people to help. By volunteering or even taking a lead role, you help make these events happen.

Your role could be taking care of presenters, attendee enrollment, or food service and support. Those with more experience will tend toward leadership roles, such as managing a team of volunteers.

WHY YOU MIGHT WANT TO DEVOTE TIME TO THIS

Do you enjoy working with people? Do you like contributing to your local security community? Do you want to learn how to run conferences? If your answer is yes, then you just answered why you might want to devote time to this. For any conference, there will be stressful moments and scrambling leading up to and during the event, but the sense of accomplishment after it is done is a great feeling.

Doing this work will also provide you with an opportunity to network with others in the field, and perhaps have a chance to meet the presenters. However, remember that your job is so others can hear the presenters, not monopolize them for yourself.

HOW THIS MIGHT COST YOU

As with most volunteer efforts, the main cost will be time. There is the additional risk that if the conference ends up being viewed as run poorly, whether due to the errors of others or your own, it could taint people's views of your abilities.

HOW TO GET STARTED

Find a conference, especially one run by a small local user group or similar organization. They are the most likely to need, and be receptive to, those without experience helping them. From there you can expand your role in future conferences as you gain experience.

WHEN YOU MIGHT WANT TO STOP

You will take on one project, see it to the end, then continue on. Leaving a conference prematurely for any reason, so that others will need to cover for you, is a very effective way to taint your brand, not to mention just plain rude. Take some time after each one, and decide whether or not it is something that you are interested in doing again. Wait about a week after the conference to do your self-evaluation. Sooner, and the exhaustion from the conference may taint your view; later, and the event may not be fresh enough in your mind to evaluate completely.

WHAT SKILLS THIS GIVES YOU

Your organizational skills, project management, and people skills will all be improved by going through this process. Dealing with the various issues that come up will also help you with your crisis management skills, adjusting to situations on the fly—though hopefully everything that comes up is only an issue, not a crisis.

WHAT SKILLS YOU MIGHT STILL NEED

For those who have never worked in a conference, it can be overwhelming. There are multiple moving parts that come together at the last minute to make a whole experience for the attendees. Learning how to deal with those situations can be uncomfortable for some, since it can often feel as though you are out of control of the situation.

As you gain experience, you may find yourself founding or leading a user group or conference. The biggest skills you will need will focus on organization and communication. Try not to bite off more than you can chew and put a lot of effort into making sure that your support staff feels valued and that their work is worthwhile. It is all too common for a conference or user group to collapse when a handful of people who were carrying the weight get burned out and no one steps forward to keep things moving forward.

4.9 USER GROUP SUPPORT (FOUNDING, ATTENDING, VOLUNTEERING, RUNNING, LEADING)

INTRODUCTION

> "80 percent of life is showing up."
>
> — **Woody Allen**

Information security user groups vary a lot, but most are volunteer-run and semi-formal, and meet monthly at a fixed time and place to study some part of information technology. They can be exactly like other community groups, such as book clubs, knitting groups, motorcycle clubs, or local sporting activities. Some are more organized and formal and have strict meeting times, dress codes, membership fees, and requirements, while others are more informal and may be free to join and open to all.

To benefit from this boost doesn't require that these groups be information security-related, although it helps, as the skills you will gain – communication, marketing, presenting, etc., will all be applicable to the day job.

There are several roles that can be present in a user group. Common roles are: president, secretary, treasurer, membership, scheduler, facility liaison, and newsletter editor. However, the single most important thing in running a user group is having a time and a place to meet. Even a leader isn't needed as long as people know when and where to go. What people do at the meeting is important, but might not be structured. Some user groups are really just social clubs where people hang out and talk and—depending on the meeting location—eat or drink.

WHY YOU MIGHT WANT TO DEVOTE TIME TO THIS

As with conferences, a user group is an opportunity to work with people, contribute, and learn. However, unlike conferences, user groups tend to have shorter but more frequent meetings, carry lower expectations, cost less money (if any), and involve lower stress. Since they involve groups of people who have common interests, they are a great way to meet people and socially network, and may also provide opportunity to Learn, Do, and Teach. Some groups are very structured, and have recurring classes, sponsor industry training and certification, and even run their own conferences.

HOW THIS MIGHT COST YOU

The most important initial contribution you can make to a user group is simply to show up. Showing up, especially for a smaller group, may be both noticed and appreciated. Showing up consistently is even more important, especially if you wish to be a contributing member or an organizer. Your time commitments for a meeting might be as short as an hour, or might take several hours, including travel time to and from the meeting location.

Getting more involved with a user group usually takes additional administrative time outside of meetings, although some user groups are so informal and small that it's built into the existing meeting. Most groups have a small core of organizers who actually do most, if not all, of the work of running the group. Organizations are often thankful for any volunteers who will consistently show up or provide help at other times. The organizers may meet shortly before or after the regular user group meetings, which helps reduce travel time, but may also have separate special meetings at other locations, remote meetings over teleconference lines, or communicate through other electronic means.

HOW TO GET STARTED

If you can't find an information security group in your area, check the IT groups in your area, even if they aren't an information technology you know or have an interest in. They may have special interest groups (SIG) for information security. If no SIGs are available, attend the IT groups anyway for the networking, and Learn about that area; perhaps you'll find some other information security group you missed earlier. If, after asking around you still haven't found one, start a security SIG in an existing group. If they haven't already asked you to start one, you may not have asked around enough. If you can't find a group you can extend, start your own. There are existing resources, so you don't have to do all the work on your own. Several international information security organizations have provisions for local chapters, so you can be the one to start the local chapter. Some are extremely easy to start because the central information security organization is very informal; others might require more work.

WHEN YOU MIGHT WANT TO STOP

If you don't have time to show up to meetings, you're mostly stopped. However, it's critical to let people know you can't attend or make commitments if you're a contributing member, and especially if you are an organizer.

If you can no longer Learn, Do, or Teach, it may be time to move on. Note, however, that the social aspects of user groups are none of these things but still have their own benefit.

Bad politics in a user group is reason for people to leave and never return. If you're a new arrival to a group with troubled dynamics, it might be an opportunity to get involved. Beware, though—it can be especially bad for your brand to take sides and get entangled in such conflicts. The politics can be especially vicious in a user group since, as the truism goes, the fighting is never so fierce as when the stakes are so low.

If it's not fun or sociable for you, others may not find your contributions enjoyable, either. Although a very technically minded user group may be willing to acquire the learning, doing, and teaching you offer, even if it isn't particularly fun, most user groups won't. The social aspects of a user group are strong and should not be underestimated.

Some organizations have formal mechanisms to move old leaders out to make room for others, and others don't. Organizations often have a hard time recruiting and maintaining organizers. As with any job, paid or not, it's much better to move out on your own power than get fired from the group in a coup d'état.

If you want to move on and there is someone who could take your place, this is an opportunity to be a mentor and Teach, so that another may Learn, and the organization will move on and survive without you, which is better for both you and the user group.

WHAT SKILLS THIS GIVES YOU

User groups need ongoing and consistent organizational and social skills; otherwise, they die. The most important things are to show up, get other people to show up, and have everyone leave happy enough that they'll show up next time and maybe bring friends. Doing this may require other skills, such as finding good speakers, teachers, or interesting activities—or doing them yourself, using the other boosting skills of presenter. Some user groups will be interesting enough that they will be self-sustaining without special work, as long as they have a meeting time and place. But most won't be self-sustaining and will need at least some ongoing help. If you start a user group that lasts more than a year, you'll have accomplished something. But if your user group survives your leaving it, then you have *created* something.

User groups can have several expenses: meeting spaces, meeting equipment and storage, meeting food and beverages, newsletter printing and distribution, advertisement posters and cards, website, a library, or special equipment.

User groups with fund raising activities will also require budgeting, accounting, and auditing skills. If the user group has no funds, you won't learn those skills, but you will learn how to do something for almost nothing. User groups with formal nonprofit status have legal and tax record-keeping requirements that you will have to learn or delegate to someone who does.

WHAT SKILLS YOU MIGHT STILL NEED

Generally there aren't that many information security skills to be learned from *running* a user group, unless you make it a core part of what the user group does. A user group could teach almost anything, but it probably won't teach everything, so whatever the group doesn't have as part of its goal, you won't learn, except what you get from running the group itself. Not all user groups are about the technical skills; some are really just social clubs for like-minded people to hang out. What the user group wants and what it's even capable of are totally dependent upon the organizers' and members' time, interest, and resources. Make your user group what you will of it.

Be aware that running a user group is enough work that you may not have time to either learn or teach that much in the actual activities of the user group. It's entirely possible to be so busy that you'll only learn how to run a successful user group and not benefit at all from what the user group itself is teaching its members. However, the skills to run a successful user group are quite valuable, and you'll probably also gain valuable social network contacts.

CONCLUSION

> "If you want to build a ship, don't drum up people together to collect wood and don't assign them tasks and work, but rather teach them to long for the endless immensity of the sea."
>
> **— Antoine de Saint Exupery**

Congratulations on making it through the book! We hope this means you love information security as much as we do and perhaps you've found the book to be interesting if not useful.

In addition to Learn/Do/Teach two more big messages of this book are:

1. As a community, we only get better when we work together and share information. Information wants to be free, although the book is not free, please share the book's ideas with anyone interested.
2. There are many paths and careers that only make sense in hindsight. Be sure to experiment and take risks, as that's the only way to truly improve.

If you've read the book straight through from beginning to end, then you have reached the conclusion but not the end. You have Learning, Doing, and Teaching to do next.

If you didn't markup any pages, take notes, or plan your next steps, go back and do that now.

Really, go do that, now.

On the gripping hand, if you've read the book and Learned, Done, and Taught while you read it, that's great! You're already working on your information security career and may be looking forward to your next job. Keep Learning, Doing, and Teaching!

And if this book didn't work for you, please Teach us. We really do want to make this book better.

Information security is what we do, and we love doing it. Our hope is that you love it, too, and will keep loving it as part of your new career.

There are many paths into, through, and out of information security. We hope you'll share your journey with all of us in the community.

Though this is the end, this book is not about endings, but beginnings. We can't tell you what will make you happy, but I hope we've helped you figure out what will make you happier while on your journey.

Now go out and Learn for yourself, Do work, Teach others, and get your next job!

When you're done with this book, please lend or gift it to someone who would also love to break into information security.

APPENDIX

APPENDIX: INTRODUCTION

> "Cool URIs don't change."
>
> — **Sir Tim Berners-Lee, inventor of the World Wide Web**

All references were accurate and up to date at the time of submission. Which means if you are reading this right now in a paper book they are almost certainly out of date. If you're reading this in an ebook, there was a brief time before you started reading it when it wasn't out of date. URLs break, books go out of print, and new editions have new ISBNs. Organizations change names (or meanings), and sometimes go away. We hope at least some of these are cool enough to not change.

Use these resources names as search keywords but be careful of what search results you get because you're responsible for what you find and use.

SECURITY MODELS

ACI (CIA) triad — https://en.wikipedia.org/wiki/Information_security#Key_concepts
Parkerian Hexad — 01998, Donn B. Parker, https://en.wikipedia.org/wiki/Parkerian_hexad
(ISC)^2 Common Body of Knowledge (CBK) as of 02015-06 — https://www.isc2.org/cissp-domains/

JOB RESOURCES

In addition to the below, some organizations, national and local, have their own job postings. Some conferences have active job recruitment and job posting areas. See below Appendix: Communities.

Association of Information Technology Professionals (AITP) Career Center — http://jobs.aitp.org/
DAMA International, The Global Data Management Community, Careers
    http://dama-jobs.careerwebsite.com/
International Association for Cryptologic Research (IACR) — http://iacr.org/jobs/
US Government Clearance Jobs — https://www.clearancejobs.com/
US Department of Homeland Security— http://www.dhs.gov/join-dhs-cybersecurity
US FBI — http://www.fbijobs.gov/cybercareers/
US Secret Service — http://www.secretservice.gov/ectf_about.shtml
Y Combinator funded startup jobs — https://news.ycombinator.com/jobs

GENERAL BOOKS AND REFERENCES

NIST IR-7298 Rev. 2, Glossary of Key Information Security Terms
    http://nvlpubs.nist.gov/nistpubs/ir/2013/NIST.IR.7298r2.pdf

The Cuckoo's Egg by Cliff Stoll, 01989— ISBN:0-385-24946-2

The Security Principles of Saltzer and Schoeder — http://emergentchaos.com/the-security-principles-of-saltzer-and-schroeder see also Jerome Saltzer and Michael Schoeder "The Protection of Information in Computer Systems" http://www.cs.virginia.edu/~evans/cs551/saltzer/

The Personal MBA: A World-Class Business Education in a Single Volume — Kaufman, Josh, 02011 — ISBN:978-0-14-197109-4

TIME MANAGEMENT

The Long Now Foundation — http://longnow.org/ https://en.wikipedia.org/wiki/Long_Now_Foundation

Getting Things Done: The Art of Stress-Free Productivity by Allen — ISBN:0142000280

Personal Kanban: Mapping Work | Navigating Life by Benson and Barry — ISBN:1453802266

The 7 Habits of Highly Effective People by Covey — ISBN:0743269519

Pomodoro Technique — http://www.pomodorotechnique.com/ https://en.wikipedia.org/wiki/Pomodoro_Technique

Scrum and sprints — https://en.wikipedia.org/wiki/Scrum_(software_development) https://en.wikipedia.org/wiki/Scrum_%28software_development%29#Sprint

Paul Graham — The Acceleration of Addictiveness — http://paulgraham.com/addiction.html https://en.wikipedia.org/wiki/Minimum_viable_product

Simplest Thing That Could Possibly Work — http://c2.com/cgi/wiki?SimplestThingThatCouldPossiblyWork

Yak shaving — https://en.wiktionary.org/wiki/yak_shaving

The New York Times — Current History of the European War, 01915

STORY TELLING AND METAPHOR

I Is an Other: The Secret Life of Metaphor and How It Shapes the Way We See the World by Geary — ISBN:9780061710292

Images of Organization by Morgan — ISBN:1412939798

Made to Stick: Why Some Ideas Survive and Others Die by Heath and Heath —ISBN:1400064287

Master Metaphor List v2 by George Lakoff

Jane Espenson, and Alan Schwartz, 01991 — http://araw.mede.uic.edu/~alansz/metaphor/METAPHORLIST.pdf

Metaphors We Live By by Lakoff and Johnson — ISBN:0226468011

Pixar Story Rules by Emma Coats — http://twitter.com/lawnrocket http://filmmakeriq.com/2012/08/the-pixar-story-rules http://www.pixartouchbook.com/blog/2011/5/15/pixar-story-rules-one-version.html

Gripping hand — https://en.wikipedia.org/wiki/The_Gripping_Hand#Notes_and_references http://www.catb.org/jargon/html/O/on-the-gripping-hand.html

SCIENTIFIC METHOD

https://en.wikipedia.org/wiki/Scientific_method

https://en.wikipedia.org/wiki/List_of_fallacies

https://en.wikipedia.org/wiki/List_of_cognitive_biases

Richard Feynman — http://www.richardfeynman.com/ 01974 "Cargo Cult Science, Some remarks on science, pseudoscience, and learning how to not fool yourself. Caltech's 1974 commencement address." http://calteches.library.caltech.edu/51/02/CargoCult.pdf ; Engineering and Science 37 (7); Space Shuttle Challenger Disaster investigation, *What Do You Care What Other People Think?*, 01988, ISBN 0-393-02659-0, 02001 paperback: ISBN 0-393-32092-8;

Thomas Kuhn — *The Structure of Scientific Revolutions,* 01962 ISBN:9780226458113 https://en.wikipedia.org/wiki/The_Structure_of_Scientific_Revolutions

APPENDIX: COMMUNITIES

Association of Information Technology Professionals (AITP) — http://www.aitp.org/
DAMA International, Data Access Management Association (DAMA), The Global Data
    Management Community — http://www.dama.org/
Hackers for Charity — http://www.hackersforcharity.org/
FBI InfraGard — http://www.infragard.net/
Free Software Foundation — https://www.fsf.org/
Information Systems Security Association (ISSA) — https://issa.org/
Open Web Application Security Project (OWASP) — https://www.owasp.org/
Society of Hispanic Professional Engineers (SHPE) — http://www.shpe.org/

MAILING LISTS

The best mailing lists are private. The SANS Advisory Board is available to those who take and pass a
SANS course with a high enough score.

Full Disclosure and BugTraq RSS feeds, and more — http://seclists.org/
The Forum of Incident Response Teams (FIRST) private organization requires sponsorship and
    vetting that to join — http://www.first.org/
GPWN, SANS alumni only — https://lists.sans.org/mailman/listinfo/gpwn-list
PaulDotCom list — http://mail.pauldotcom.com/cgi-bin/mailman/listinfo/pauldotcom
SANS DFIR, job postings — https://lists.sans.org/mailman/listinfo/dfir
SANS @RISK — http://www.sans.org/newsletters/at-risk/
SANS Newsbites — http://www.sans.org/newsletters/newsbites/
SANS OUCH! — http://www.securingthehuman.org/resources/newsletters/ouch/

CONFERENCES AND COMMUNITIES

In addition to these, there are communities in some web sites and blogs, and national organizations often
have local chapters, if there isn't one, start it yourself, see the chapter "Boosting 4.9— User Groups".

Ada Initiative — http://adainitiative.org/
    http://geekfeminism.wikia.com/wiki/Feminist_and_women%27s_hackerspaces
AdaCamp — https://adacamp.org/
Black Hat, Las Vegas, NV USA, Europe, Asia — http://www.blackhat.com/
Security BSides, worldwide local volunteer run alternative information security conferences during
    other conferences, job recruitment — http://www.securitybsides.com/
CanSecWest, Vancouver, BC, Canada — http://www.cansecwest.com/
CarolinaCon, Raleigh, NC, USA — http://www.carolinacon.org/
Chaos Communications Congress, Hamburg, Germany — http://www.ccc.de/congress/
Chaos Communications Camp (CCC), Germany — https://events.ccc.de/camp/
DEF CON, Las Vegas, NV, USA — http://defcon.org/
    DEF CON Forums — https://forum.defcon.org/
    DEF CON Groups — https://defcongroups.org/
DerbyCon, Louisville, KY, USA — https://www.derbycon.com/

Hackers On Planet Earth (HOPE), New York, NY, USA — http://hope.net/

Hack-Tic events, Netherlands — http://www.hacktic.nl/ https://en.wikipedia.org/wiki/Hack-Tic

(ISC)^2 Twin Cites Chapter Information Security Events (MN & North America) — http://isc2tc.org/

MeetUp — search for "security", "infosec", "software", "development", "nerd", "geek", "hacker", security vendor and product names in your area http://www.meetup.com/

Notacon, Cleveland, OH, USA — http://www.notacon.org/

PhreakNIC, Nashville, TN, USA — http://phreaknic.info/

Reddit —
   https://www.reddit.com/r/HowToHack http://www.reddit.com/r/hacking/
   https://www.reddit.com/r/netsec https://www.reddit.com/r/security
   https://www.reddit.com/r/AskNetsec https://www.reddit.com/r/infosec
   https://www.reddit.com/r/malware https://www.reddit.com/r/pwned
   https://www.reddit.com/r/ReverseEngineering http://www.reddit.com/r/netsec/

ShmooCon Washington, DC, USA — https://www.shmoocon.org/

SkyDogCon — Nashville, TN, USA http://skydogcon.com/ http://skydogcon.blogspot.com/

StackExchange, Information Security — https://security.stackexchange.com/

ThotCon, Chicago, IL, USA — http://www.thotcon.org/

Toastmasters — http://www.toastmasters.org/ https://en.wikipedia.org/wiki/Toastmasters

ToorCon, San Diego, CA, USA — http://toorcon.org/

USENIX — Cyberlaw; HotBots; Workshop on Hot Topics in Security (HotSec); LISA; Symposium on Usable Privacy and Security (SOUPS); Usability, Psychology, and Security (UPSEC); Women in Advanced Computing Summit (WiAC); Workshop on Offensive Technologies (WOOT), USENIX Security Symposium, world wide, job recruitment — http://usenix.org/conference/

APPENDIX: SOFTWARE TOOLS

Amazon Web Services (AWS) Free Usage Tier — http://aws.amazon.com/free/
Duck Duck Go privacy oriented search engine — https://duckduckgo.com/
EFF HTTPS Everywhere and Privacy Badger for Mozilla Firefox — https://www.eff.org/
GnuPG, S/MIME and OpenPGP cryptography, encryption — http://www.gnupg.org/
LibreOffice — http://www.libreoffice.org/
Nessus— http://www.tenable.com/products/nessus
nginx web server — http://nginx.org/
nmap, network mapper and security scanner— http://nmap.org/
Mozilla Firefox with NoScript security add-on — https://www.mozilla.org/
OpenSSL cryptographic library — http://www.openssl.org/
Oracle VirtualBox — https://www.virtualbox.org/
PRISM Break privacy tools — https://prism-break.org/
Puppet, configuration management — https://puppetlabs.com/
SecTools.Org: Top 125 Network Security Tools — http://sectools.org/TOR, The Onion Router anonymity software and network — https://www.torproject.org/

Programming and Software Tools

Apache Tomcat, JBoss, ModSecurity — http://apache.org/
Burp Suite, web application Proxy, Spider, Scanner, Intruder, Repeater, Sequencer — https://portswigger.net/burp/
GNU Emacs "the extensible self-documenting text editor" — https://www.gnu.org/software/emacs
Fuzzers — http://crashme.codeplex.com/ http://pages.cs.wisc.edu/~bart/fuzz/ https://en.wikipedia.org/wiki/Fuzz_testing
SourceForge — http://sourceforge.net/
GitHub — https://github.com/
Microsoft
    Microsoft Developer Network (MSDN) — https://msdn.microsoft.com/
    PowerShell — http://microsoft.com/powershell
    CodePlex — https://www.codeplex.com/
Perl
    http://www.perl.org/
    Learning Perl by Randal L. Schwartz, brian d foy, Tom Phoenix — http://www.oreilly.com/ ISBN:978-1-4493-0358-7 (print) ISBN:978-1-4493-0458-4 (ebook)
    Programming Perl by Tom Christiansen, brian d foy, Larry Wall, Jon Orwant — http://www.oreilly.com/ ISBN:978-0-596-00492-7 (print) ISBN:978-1-4493-9890-3 (ebook)
    Mastering Regular Expressions by Jeffrey Friedl, O'Reilly Media — http://www.oreilly.com/ ISBN:0-596-52812-4
    Perl Best Practices by Damian Conway — http://www.oreilly.com/ ISBN:0-596-00173-8
    Advanced Perl — http://www.oreilly.com/
    Perl Mongers, community — http://www.pm.org/
    Perl Monks, communit — http://www.perlmonks.org/

Python
     https://www.python.org/
     Python the hard way — http://learnpythonthehardway.org/
     Python tools for penetration testers — http://dirk-loss.de/python-tools.htm
Ruby
     https://www.ruby-lang.org/
     http://learnrubythehardway.org/
Vim, Vi Improved — http://www.vim.org/

GNU/LINUX DISTRIBUTIONS

Debian — https://www.debian.org/
Kali Live distribution for digital forensics and penetration testing — https://www.kali.org/
Knoppix Live distribution for general use with hundreds of pre-installed software packages —
     http://www.knopper.net/knoppix/index-en.html
Security Onion, SIEM, intrusion detection, network security monitoring, and log management
     security tool system by Doug Burk — https://github.com/security-onion-solutions/security-onion
     contains Snort, Suricata, Bro, OSSEC, Sguil, Squert, Snorby, ELSA, Xplico, NetworkMiner, and
     many other security tools. http://securityonion.net/
Slackware — http://www.slackware.com/
The Amnesiac Incognito Live System (TAILS) privacy and anonymity — https://tails.boum.org/

APPENDIX: SELF STUDY

BugCrowd A comprehensive, up to date list of bug bounty and disclosure programs from across the web curated by the Bugcrowd researcher community. — https://bugcrowd.com/list-of-bug-bounty-programs/

Progressive Games

crackme — https://en.wikipedia.org/wiki/Crackme

code katas — https://en.wikipedia.org/wiki/Code_Kata

Matasano/Square Embedded Security Capture the Flag Challenge — https://microcorruption.com/

Starfighter CTF, programming competion instead of technical interviews or resumes — http://www.starfighters.io/ http://www.kalzumeus.com/2015/03/09/announcing-starfighter/

EnigmaGroup, wide range of excercizes — http://www.enigmagroup.org/

GameOver, insecure web applications — http://sourceforge.net/projects/null-gameover/

SecuraBit Gh0st PenLab, CTF — http://www.gh0st.net/

Google Gruyere, Web Application Exploits and Defenses, small, cheesy web application codelab — http://google-gruyere.appspot.com/

Hacker Challenge — http://www.dareyourmind.net/

Hacker Test, JavaScript, PHP, HTML — http://www.hackertest.net/

Hacking-Lab, CTF and mission style challenges for the European Cyber Security Challenge — https://www.hacking-lab.com/

Hack.me, vulnerable web applications, code samples and CMS's online — https://hack.me/ http://www.elearnsecurity.com/

HackThis, JavaScript, SQLi, Coding, Crypt, Captcha, Forensics, community — http://www.hackthis.co.uk/

Hack This Site, Programming, JavaScript, Forensics, Stego, Irc — https://www.hackthissite.org/

Hax.Tor, 02006 many levels deprecated, — http://hax.tor.hu/

hackxor, virtual machine image like WebGoat but with a plot — http://hackxor.sourceforge.net/cgi-bin/index.pl

OverTheWire, SSH shell access — http://www.overthewire.org/wargames/

p0wnlabs, free sample challenges forensics, password cracking, OpenVPN, Metasploitable, WebGoat, OWASPBWA, pay challenges — http://www.p0wnlabs.com/free

pwn0, VPN access — https://pwn0.com/home.php

Root Me, hundreds of challenges, virtual machines — http://www.root-me.org/?lang=en

Security Treasure Hunt, web vulnerability, forensics — http://www.securitytreasurehunt.com/

Smash The Stack, SSH shell access — http://www.smashthestack.org/

sqli-labs, a platform to learn SQLi — https://github.com/Audi-1/sqli-labs

TheBlackSheep and Erik, Programming, JavaScript, PHP, Java, Steganography, and Cryptography — http://www.bright-shadows.net/

ThisIsLegal, hacker wargames — http://thisislegal.com/

Try2Hack, — http://www.try2hack.nl/

WabLab, SQL, web application — http://www.wablab.com/hackme

VulnApp — http://www.nth-dimension.org.uk/blog.php?id=88

Network Targets

US NIST Computer Forensic Reference Data Sets (CFReDS) — http://www.cfreds.nist.gov/

Damn Vulnerable Linux, 02010 — http://sourceforge.net/projects/virtualhacking/files/os/dvl/

Handler Diaries, Digital Forensics and Incident Response — http://blog.handlerdiaries.com/

Kioptrix, virtual machine challenges — http://www.kioptrix.com/blog/test-page/

LAMPSecurity, vulnerable virtual machine images to teach linux,apache,php,mysql security —
   http://sourceforge.net/projects/lampsecurity/

Metasploitable, intentionally vulnerable Linux virtual machine —
   http://sourceforge.net/projects/virtualhacking/files/os/metasploitable/

Metasploitable2, intentionally vulnerable Linux virtual machine —
   http://sourceforge.net/projects/metasploitable/files/Metasploitable2/

GoatseLinux: It's Wide Open, 02009 — http://neutronstar.org/goatselinux.html

pWnOS — http://www.pwnos.com/

RebootUser Vulnix, vulnerable Linux host with configuration weaknesses rather than purposely
   vulnerable software versions. The goal; boot up, find the IP, hack away and obtain the trophy —
   http://www.rebootuser.com/?page_id=1041

UltimateLAMP, PHDays iBank CTF — http://www.amanhardikar.com/mindmaps/practice-links.html

Vulnserver, vulnerable Windows based threaded TCP server application —
   http://www.thegreycorner.com/2010/12/introducing-vulnserver.html

Web Targets

Metasploit Unleashed, free training from Hackers for Charity —
   http://www.offensive-security.com/metasploit-unleashed/Main_Page

Metasploitable, use with Metasploit Unleashed http://www.offensive-security.com/metasploit-
   unleashed/Metasploitable

Backtrack Tutorials — http://www.backtrack-linux.org/tutorials/

Hack This Site, Programming, JavaScript, Forensics, Stego, Irc — http://www.hackthissite.org/

BodgeIt Store, a vulnerable web application for those new to pen testing —
   https://github.com/psiinon/bodgeit

Butterfly Security, web application and PHP vulnerabilities and mitigation —
   http://sourceforge.net/projects/thebutterflytmp/

CryptOMG, common cryptographic flaws CTF — https://github.com/SpiderLabs/CryptOMG

Damn Vulnerable Web App (DVWA), PHP/MySQL — http://www.dvwa.co.uk/

Damn Vulnerable Web Services (DVWS) — http://dvws.professionallyevil.com/

Exploit KB Vulnerable Web App, SQLi, PHP, MySQL — http://exploit.co.il/projects/vuln-web-app/
   https://sourceforge.net/projects/exploitcoilvuln

Foundstone Hackme Bank, MS-Windows, 02006 —
   http://www.mcafee.com/us/downloads/free-tools/hacme-bank.aspx

Foundstone Hackme Books, MS-Windows, Java, 02006 —
   http://www.mcafee.com/us/downloads/free-tools/hacmebooks.aspx

Foundstone Hackme Casino, MS-Windows, 02006 —
   http://www.mcafee.com/us/downloads/free-tools/hacme-casino.aspx

Foundstone Hackme Shipping, MS-Windows, Adobe ColdFusion, MySQL, 02006 —
http://www.mcafee.com/us/downloads/free-tools/hacmeshipping.aspx
Foundstone Hackme Travel, MS-Windows client/server SQL —
http://www.mcafee.com/us/downloads/free-tools/hacmetravel.aspx
LAMPSecurity, vulnerable virtual machine images to teach linux,apache,php,mysql security —
http://sourceforge.net/projects/lampsecurity/
Magical Code Injection Rainbow (MCIR), SQLol, XMLmao, ShelLOL and XSSmh —
https://github.com/SpiderLabs/MCIR
Moth, VMware image with vulnerable Web Applications and scripts —
http://www.bonsai-sec.com/en/research/moth.php
NOWASP / Mutillidae 2, vulnerable web-application for Linux and Windows using LAMP, WAMP,
and XAMMP, pre-installed on SamuraiWTF, Rapid7 Metasploitable-2, and OWASP BWA —
http://sourceforge.net/projects/mutillidae/
http://www.irongeek.com/i.php?page=mutillidae/mutillidae-deliberately-vulnerable-php-owasp-top-10
OWASP Bricks, vulnerable web application built on PHP and MySQL exploitable using Mantra and
ZAP — http://sourceforge.net/projects/owaspbricks/
OWASP Broken Web Apps, vulnerable web applications on a Virtual Machine —
https://www.owasp.org/index.php/OWASP_Broken_Web_Applications_Project
OWASP Broken Web Applications Project (BWA), vulnerable web applications on VMware virtual
machine — http://code.google.com/p/owaspbwa/
OWASP Security Shepherd, web and mobile application security training platform —
https://www.owasp.org/index.php/OWASP_Security_Shepherd
OWASP SiteGenerator, dynamic websites based on XML files and predefined vulnerabilities —
https://www.owasp.org/index.php/Owasp_SiteGenerator
PuzzleMall, Java/JSP, Apache Derby, Temporal Session Race Conditions (TSRC) and Layer
Targeted AdoS, 02011 — http://code.google.com/p/puzzlemall/
SecuriBench, Java, SQL injection attacks, Cross-site scripting attacks, HTTP splitting attacks, Path
traversal attacks — http://suif.stanford.edu/~livshits/securibench/
SocketToMe, PHP, chat, a simple number guessing game and a few other hidden features —
http://digi.ninja/projects/sockettome.php
WackoPicko, part of OWASP BWA Project — https://github.com/adamdoupe/WackoPicko "Why
Johnny Can't Pentest: An Analysis of Black-box Web Vulnerability Scanners"
http://cs.ucsb.edu/%7Eadoupe/static/black-box-scanners-dimva2010.pdf
WebGoat.NET — https://github.com/jerryhoff/WebGoat.NET/
https://www.owasp.org/index.php/WebGoat_User_Guide_Table_of_Contents
WebSecurity Dojo, self-contained training environment for Web Application Security penetration
testing xubuntu 12.04 — http://sourceforge.net/projects/websecuritydojo/files/
http://dojo.mavensecurity.com/
OWASP Zed Attack Proxy - Web Application Vulnerability Examples (WAVE), for testing OWAP
ZAP — http://code.google.com/p/zaproxy/downloads/detail?name=zap-wave-0.1.zip
Hewlett-Packard Fortify WebInspect product demo Zero Bank — http://zero.webappsecurity.com/

APPENDIX: CERTIFICATIONS

ASIS Certified Protection Professional (CPP), Professional Certified Investigator (PCI), Physical Security Professional (PSP) — https://www.asisonline.org/

Cisco Certified Network Associate (CCNA) — https://learningnetwork.cisco.com/community/certifications/

CompTIA Security+ CE — http://certification.comptia.org/Training/testingcenters/examobjectives.aspx (registration required)

EC Council CEH — http://www.eccouncil.org/Certification/professional-series/ceh-course-outline

ISACA Certified in Risk and Information Systems Control (CRISC) — https://www.isaca.org/

$(ISC)^2$ CISSP — https://www.isc2.org/exam-outline/default.aspx (registration required)

JNCIA -Junos (Juniper Networks Certified Associate Junos) — http://www.juniper.net/us/en/training/certification/

Offensive Security OSCP — http://www.offensive-security.com/

SANS GIAC Certified Incident Handler (GCIH) — http://www.giac.org/certification/certified-incident-handler-gcih

US Department of Defense Approved 8570 Baseline — http://iase.disa.mil/iawip/Pages/index.aspx

---

APPENDIX: NEWS

Privacy Rights Clearinghouse — https://www.privacyrights.org/
CSO Online — http://csoonline.com/
Freedom to Tinker — https://freedom-to-tinker.com/
Cambridge University— https://www.lightbluetouchpaper.org/
Dark Reading — http://www.darkreading.com/
InfoWorld Security Channel — http://www.infoworld.com/category/security
BankInfoSecurity — http://www.bankinfosecurity.com/
Wired Threat Level — http://www.wired.com/category/security
The Risks Digest — https://catless.ncl.ac.uk/Risks/
Ycombinator Hacker News — https://news.ycombinator.com/

APPENDIX: PEOPLE

Douglas Adams — Hitchhiker's Guide to the Galaxy, http://douglasadams.com/

Carl Ally — 01965, http://www.barrypopik.com/index.php/new_york_city/entry/a_consultant_is_
someone_who_borrows_your_watch_to_tell_you_the_time_and_the/

Ross Anderson — http://www.ross-anderson.com/ *Security Engineering*
http://www.cl.cam.ac.uk/~rja14/book.htm

Programming Satan's Computer — http://www.cl.cam.ac.uk/~rja14/Papers/satan.pdf

Steve Bellovin — https://www.cs.columbia.edu/~smb/blog/

Richard Bejtlich — http://taosecurity.blogspot.com/
http://taosecurity.blogspot.com/search/label/bestbook

Tim Berners-Lee — http://www.w3.org/People/Berners-Lee/
https://en.wikipedia.org/wiki/Tim_Berners-Lee

Matt Blaze — https://twitter.com/mattblaze/ https://en.wikipedia.org/wiki/Matt_Blaze

Fredrick P. Brooks, Jr., The Mythical Man-Month, Essays on Software Engineering, 01975

George E. P. Box — https://en.wikipedia.org/wiki/George_E._P._Box

Albert Einstein — "On the Method of Theoretical Physics" *Philosophy of Science*, Vol. 1, No. 2
(April 01934), pp. 163–9, p. 165

Robert A. Heinlein, Time Enough for Love: the Lives of Lazarus Long, 01973

Mak Kolybabi — https://twitter.com/mogigoma http://mogigoma.com/

Alfred Korzybski "A Non-Aristotelian System and its Necessity for Rigour in Mathematics and
Physics", a paper presented before the American Mathematical Society at the New Orleans,
Louisiana, meeting of the American Association for the Advancement of Science, December 28,
1931. Reprinted in Science and Sanity, 1933, p. 747–61.
https://en.wikipedia.org/wiki/Alfred_Korzybski
https://en.wikipedia.org/wiki/Map-territory_relation

Ursula K. Le Guin — http://www.ursulakleguin.com/
https://en.wikipedia.org/wiki/Ursula_K._Le_Guin

Paul Graham, time management, The Acceleration of Addictiveness —
http://paulgraham.com/addiction.html

Jeremiah Grossman — http://www.whitehatsec.com/

Hanlon — https://en.wikipedia.org/wiki/Hanlon%27s_razor

C.A.R. Hoare, The Emporer's New Clothes —
https://en.wikiquote.org/wiki/Tony_Hoare#The_Emperor.27s_Old_Clothes

Juvenal — aka Decimus Iunius Iuvenalis c. 00055/00140

Dan Kaminsky — http://dankaminsky.com/

Guy Kawasaki — http://www.guykawasaki.com/

Brian Krebs on Security — http://www.krebsonsecurity.com/
http://krebsonsecurity.com/category/how-to-break-into-security/

Donald Knuth — http://cs.stanford.edu/~uno/ https://en.wikiquote.org/wiki/Donald_Knuth

Niccolo Machiavelli — Discourses on Livy, Book 1, Chapter XLVI

Josh More — http://www.starmind.org/ *Job Reconnaissance: Using Hacking Skills to Win the Job Hunt Game* by Josh More — Syngress ISBN-13:978-0124166011
http://www.starmind.org/2012/04/07/so-you-want-a-new-job-adapted-from-a-presentation/
http://www.starmind.org/2012/01/13/security-certification-23-learning/

Red Queen — Through the Looking-Glass by Lewis Carroll, 01871

Stephen Northcutt — http://www.sans.edu/about/governance/administrators#stephen-northcutt

Gunnar Peterson — http://1raindrop.typepad.com/

Terry Pratchett — https://en.wikiquote.org/wiki/Terry_Pratchett#Usenet

Thomas Ptacek — http://sockpuppet.org/ https://news.ycombinator.com/user?id=tptacek

PaulDotCom — Security Podcast http://pauldotcom.com/

Alan Perlis — "Epigrams on programming". ACM SIGPLAN Notices (New York, NY, USA: Association for Computing Machinery) 17 (9): 7–13. doi:10.1145/947955.1083808

Antoine de Saint Exupery — https://en.wikiquote.org/wiki/Antoine_de_Saint_Exupery

Bruce Schneier — https://www.schneier.com/ So You Want to Be a Security Expert by Bruce Schneier — http://www.schneier.com/blog/archives/2012/07/how_to_become_a_1.html
Inside the Twisted Mind of the Security Professional by Bruce Schneier — http://www.schneier.com/essay-210.html

Rick Smith — http://www.cryptosmith.com/

Gene Spafford — http://blog.spaf.us/

Richard Stallman — https://www.stallman.org/ https://en.wikipedia.org/wiki/Richard_Stallman

Cliff Stoll — "The Cuckoo's Egg: Tracking a Spy Through the Maze of Computer Espionage", 01989 ISBN:0-385-24946-2

Andrew S. Tanenbaum — *Computer Networks*, 4th ed., p. 91; http://www.cs.vu.nl/~ast; https://en.wikipedia.org/wiki/Andrew_S._Tanenbaum

Roy Trenneman — The IT Crowd, Channel 4 Television, UK
http://www.channel4.com/programmes/the-it-crowd

Jan L. A. van de Snepscheut — https://en.wikipedia.org/wiki/Jan_L._A._van_de_Snepscheut

Gerald Weinberg — http://www.geraldmweinberg.com/
https://en.wikiquote.org/wiki/Gerald_Weinberg

David Wheeler— https://en.wikipedia.org/wiki/David_Wheeler_%28computer_scientist%29
https://en.wikipedia.org/wiki/Fundamental_theorem_of_software_engineering

Phillip J. Windley, CIO of the state of Utah, USA 02001/02002 — http://phil.windley.org/
http://www.windley.com/archives/2005/05/organization_ge.shtml
http://www.cio.com.au/article/164604/just_desserts_/

Ira Winkler — https://twitter.com/irawinkler http://xcompanionguide.com/
http://www.securementem.com/about-us/

John Ziman — *Knowing Everything about Nothing: Specialization and Change in Scientific Careers,* 01987 ISBN:0-521-32385-1; https://en.wikipedia.org/wiki/John_Ziman

Subject Index

roles, 43, 64, 65
  develop applicable skills, limitations of, 65
  lateral movement to peer, 65
  writing skills, 65
Security facilitator, 90, **114**, 142
  certifications, 115
  challenges associated with security projects, 114
  improving skills, 115
  opportunities to change organizations, 115
  roles, 115
    stagnation in, 115
  story, 117
Security field, 184
Security Information and Event Management (SIEM) system, 37–39, 223
Security logs, 40
Security management, 174
  breaking in, aspects to, 174
  roles of, 176
  rules of thumb, 175
  skill improvement, 175
  stuck situation, recognizing factors, 175
Security management (CSO, CISO, CPO), **174**
Security models, 6, 217
Security news, 228
Security operations center (SOC), 37, 38, 81, 172
Security professionals, 155
  backgrounds, 144
Security researcher, 204
  knowledge and experience, 204
  and making money, 205
  skills, 205
  time to move on, 205
Security vulnerability, 43, 44, 204
Self-study, 34, 61
  network targets, 225
  progressive games, 224
  web targets, 225–226
Senior architect, 181
Senior Engineer, 160
Senior Incident Responder, 90
Server Administration, roles, 43
Sexism, 21
SGI IRIX, 78
SHPE. *See* Society of Hispanic Professional Engineers (SHPE)
SIEM system. *See* Security Information and Event Management (SIEM) system
SIG. *See* Special interest groups (SIG)
Six Sigma, 124
Skill boosting, 79
  defend against previous attacks, 79
  firewalls, 79
    attack and bypass policy, 79

    create and implement policy, 79
    migrate an advanced policy, 79
  learn basic IP routing, 79
  learn network protocols, 79
  troubleshoot and attack, 79
Skills, 2, 10, 50
  defending against laziness, 51
  improvement, 51, 164. *See also* Skill boosting
    learn from books, 56
    time management, 56
  new languages, 51
  ongoing analysis, 51
  programming, 52
SME. *See* Subject matter expert (SME)
SOC. *See* Security operations center (SOC)
Social engineers, 78–80
Social media, 20, 31, 196, 206
Social network contacts, 214
Social security numbers, 39
Society of Hispanic Professional Engineers (SHPE), 220
Software development, 49
Software engineers, 161
Software tools, 222
  programming, 222
Software vulnerabilities, 200, 205
SolarWinds Patch Manager, 42
SourceForge.net, 50
SOX. *See* Sarbanes-Oxley (SOX)
Spaghetti code, 52
Speaker, 206
  career opportunities, 206
  skills, 207
Speaking skills, 161
Special interest groups (SIG), 22, 213
Sports culture, 23
Sprint, 19, 77, 218
Sprinting, 77
SSAE. *See* Statement on standards for attestation engagements (SSAE)
StackExchange, 195
Stallman, Richard, 202
Statement on standards for attestation engagements (SSAE), 177
STEM. *See* Science, technology, engineering, and math (STEM)
Stoll, Clifford, 144, 217
Story telling and metaphor, 218
Stress, 71, 74, 212
Subject matter expert (SME), 40, 74, 76, 101, 119, 122, **127**, 160, 168, 180, 182, 206
  Coder-Developer SME, 76
  DBA specialists, 75
  finding area in organizationt, 75
  information security, 75

Congratulations on as thoroughly reading the book as we tried to be in writing it! You can use this space for planning your custom career path, writing your story, and for notes. — The Authors

ecosystem – at what point does its displacement of the finite natural ecosystem cost more in terms of lost life-support services than it is worth in terms of extra production? What is the optimal scale of the macro-economy relative to its enveloping ecosystem? This is certainly an economic question, one that will be examined in the following chapters.

A second confusion to avoid is to recognize clearly that, in countries where poverty predominates, growth is still required along with development. To overcome poverty it is all the more necessary to move to a steady state in wealthy countries, in order to free up resources and ecological space for the poor to grow into. Considerable sharing will be required to bring the poor up to a level of sufficiency that is assumed for a steady-state economy.

A third confusion to avoid from the beginning is the idea that a steady state is forever, that it implies 'sustainability' in the sense of a perpetual terrestrial existence for humankind, or 'ecological salvation', as some have claimed. The entropy law rules that out. The aim of a steady-state economy is sustainability in the sense of longevity with sufficiency. If some other disaster does not cause our extinction first, the entropy law guarantees that we will eventually burn out all our resource candles, even if we keep the flame in a steady state. We could opt, as we seem to be doing, for the 'Roman candle' strategy of burning it all up in a short fiery and extravagant blast. Either alternative is permitted by physical laws. The choice is a value judgment – sufficiency with longevity versus extravagance with impatience. Such ethical presuppositions (and implicit eschatology) will be considered, mainly in Part IV.

The essays in this book were written over a period of 40 years – from 1972 to the present. Certainly not everything I have written during that time is worth repeating, so I have selected only things that I think need repetition. This is often because they were ignored the first time, or because they consider issues that have become more important today. The other selection criterion is subject matter – economic growth, its ecological costs and limits, and the reasons why standard economics, in its obsession with economic growth, has failed to see that growth can be, and in some countries has become, *uneconomic*. Although covering a 40-year time span risks including some dated material, it has the redeeming benefit of revealing the development of arguments, concepts, and issues over time. Which facets of the limits to growth debate are no longer discussed, and which issues have become dominant? Of course this 40-year period of discussion is here viewed from the mind of a single participant. That is a limitation to be sure, but at least a unifying limitation that introduces some coherence into the collection that would be absent if the essays represented the diversity of a committee. Also, most of the book is recent. The nature of this coherence is elaborated in the introductory essay, 'Envisioning a successful steady-state economy'.

Part I consists of two articles from the early 1970s. They were published in standard economics journals, which at that time were a bit more open to discussion than today. The first sets forth basic concepts of steady-state economics as an alternative to the Keynesian–neoclassical growth synthesis, drawing on ideas from the classical economists. The second considers critically some initial objections raised against the idea of limits to growth by standard economists. The book *The Limits to Growth* sparked a lively debate beginning in 1972. Since my work was cited therein as a support, and because I thought that many of the criticisms of the book raised by standard economists were wrong, I naturally became involved in the debate. Although some references are dated, especially in Part I, the main issues remain relevant, as shown in Part III, where the debate is resumed currently. Both articles in Part I were written while I was in the Economics Department at Louisiana State University.

Part II presents some reflections from the 1980–90s. These two articles were written while I was at the World Bank. 'Towards an environmental macroeconomics' was also published in a standard economics journal, but in 1991 had to be placed in the journal's category labeled 'Speculations' because the fledgling field of environmental economics was claimed by microeconomics. The idea of an 'environmental macroeconomics' was at that time strange and therefore speculative. The piece on 'Growth, debt and the World Bank' was written later (2011) but draws on my experience at the World Bank during the late 1980s and early 1990s, and what I came to understand about that institution in retrospect.

Part III moves to the present. 'A further critique of growth economics' adds to and updates the critique in Part I, reviewing modern pro-growth positions and examining 11 fallacies currently and frequently committed in arguments for growth. It is one thing to criticize, but something else to suggest specific policies for 'Moving from a failed growth economy to a steady-state economy', as discussed in the next article. The articles in Part III were not acceptable to standard academic economics journals, so had to be published elsewhere, namely in *Ecological Economics*, a journal I had co-founded with Robert Costanza, Joan Martinez-Alier, and the late Ann-Marie Jansson in 1988, and in an edited collection on heterodox economics. Also included here is a speech to the American Meteorological Society on 'Climate policy: from "know how" to "do now"'. Climate change is presently the major symptom of uneconomic growth. Although much of the discussion has focused on finding alternatives to fossil fuels within the context of overall growth, it seems that more people are now recognizing growth itself as the main driver of climate change.

Part IV digs into the ethical dimensions of the growth debate, which were always just below the surface and are more influential than commonly realized. 'Incorporating values in a bottom-line ecological economy' was first given as a speech in the mid-1980s, and then revised in 2009. In 2014, the article 'Ethics in relation to economics, ecology and eschatology' was written for the *Oxford Handbook on Ethics and Economics*. I believe that particular *Oxford Handbook* was motivated by the visibly poor ethical standards exhibited by economists leading up to the financial crisis of 2008.

Part V changes the style of presentation. We move from article-length chapters to a number of editorial-style essays on currently topical issues related to the overall themes previously discussed. These were all written from 2010 to the present, and cover topics ranging from fractional reserve banking, to thermodynamics, to population, to globalization, to 'fracking', to philosophical materialism, and more – but always with a connection to the overriding issue of growth. These short essays were first presented in the blog, 'The Daly News', contained in the Center for the Advancement of the Steady State Economy (CASSE) website, and edited by Brian Czech and Rob Dietz.

Many thoughtful people have identified ecological destruction as one of the two biggest threats to humankind, even though not usually making the connection to growth as the underlying cause. The other threat is of course a war with nuclear, biological, or chemical weapons. This book deals only with the first threat – it does not discuss war. But there is an obvious connection. A growing economy will inevitably extend its footprint into the ecological space of other countries and into the remaining global commons. This is what 'globalization' is all about. It is painted as a peaceful and cooperative process. But in a world dominated by growth it is not likely to remain so, even falsely assuming that it has been so far. Consider the following dated but still relevant quote from growth proponent Harold E. Goeller ('An optimistic outlook for mineral resources', paper presented at Scarcity and Growth Conference, National Commission on Materials Policy, University of Minnesota, June, 1972):

> assuming reasonable management practices and adaptations, the remaining mineral resource base of the *Earth* is sufficient to maintain the *present state* of material affluence of the *United States*, and to share it to *some meaningful degree* with the *rest of the world*, for at least the *next hundred years*. (my italics)

In other words, if we move rapidly and efficiently to a steady state at 1972 levels, and draw on all the world's resources, and limit our sharing with the other 96 percent of the world to some 'meaningful degree', then our system could last for a hundred years. This was presented as an 'optimistic' outlook, and in so far as it assumes maintenance of the US economy in a steady state at 1972 resource throughput levels it certainly is optimistic. But the expectation that the United States will draw on the resource base of the entire earth to accomplish this, while limiting its sharing with the other 96 percent of the world's people to some 'meaningful' degree, while also writing off the future beyond 100 years, does not seem so optimistic. In fact, in 2014, with only 60 of the originally estimated 100 years left, it seems a recipe for conflict and wars for access to oil, water, agricultural land, and other resources, and for escalating ecological scarcity into military disaster. It is hard to imagine how a finite world of national economies all maximizing growth can manage to live in peace. Incentive to war is a major cost of growth that is not counted, and its reduction is an important argument in favor of a steady-state economy. Since such incentives to war are greater now than in 1972, and not discussed elsewhere in this book, this point should at least be emphasized in the Preface. Maybe steady-state economics will come to be seen as a part of the peace movement.

1. Introduction: envisioning a successful steady-state economy

How do you envision a successful economy without continuous growth?

It helps to consider a prior question: how do you envision a successful Planet Earth without continuous growth? That is easy to envision because it exists! The Earth as a whole does not grow in physical dimensions. Yet it changes qualitatively, it evolves and develops. Total matter on Earth cycles, but does not grow. Energy from the sun flows through the earth coming in as low-entropy radiant energy, and exiting as high-entropy heat. But the solar flow is not growing. Nearly all life is powered by this entropic throughput of solar energy. There is birth and death, production and depreciation. New things evolve; old things go extinct. There is continual change. But the Earth is not growing.

The economy is a subsystem of the Earth. Imagine that the economy grows to encompass the entire earth. Then the economy would have to conform to the behavior mode of the Earth. Namely, it could no longer grow, and would have to live on a constant solar flow, approximating a steady state – an exceedingly large steady state to be sure, well beyond optimal scale. The economy would have taken over the management of the entire ecosystem – every amoeba, every molecule, and every photon would be allocated according to human purposes and priced accordingly. All 'externalities' would be internalized, and nothing could any longer be external to the all-encompassing economy. The information and management problem would be astronomical – central planning raised to the thousandth power! Long before such total takeover, the human economy and the civilization it supports would have collapsed.

To arrive at a vision that promises success we must discard some dead-end dreams – especially the just-mentioned dream of internalizing all biospheric relationships into the monetary accounts of the economy. To keep the economy manageable we must limit its physical scale relative to the containing ecosystem. The way to do that is to leave a large part of the ecosphere alone, to limit our absorption of it into the economic subsystem – to keep a large part of the earth ecosystem *in natura* – as a source for low-entropy matter/energy inputs and as a sink for high-entropy waste, and as a provider of life-support services. *Laissez faire* takes on a new meaning – it is the ecosystem that must be left alone to manage itself and evolve by its own rules, while the economy is carefully constrained in aggregate scale to stay within the limits imposed by the ecosystem. Environmental sources and sinks necessarily must be used to support life and production, but the rate of use must remain within the regenerative and absorptive capacities of the ecosystem. The metabolic throughput from nature cannot keep growing. Limiting the physical throughput to sustainable levels will, by lowering supply, effectively internalize the external costs of excessive scale. Resulting higher resource prices will improve the microeconomic efficiency of allocation.

Every encroachment of the economy into the ecosystem is a physical transformation of ecosystem into economy. Growth means less habitat for other species, with loss both of their instrumental value to the ecosystem, and the intrinsic value of their own sentient life. Clearly, in addition to a maximum scale of the economy relative to the ecosystem, there is also an optimal scale (much smaller), beyond which growth becomes uneconomic in the literal sense that it increases environmental and social costs faster than production benefits. We fail to recognize the uneconomic nature of growth beyond this point because we measure only production benefits and fail to measure environmental and social costs. We ignore the fact that 'illth' is a negative joint product with wealth. Examples of illth are everywhere, even if usually unmeasured in national accounts, and include: climate change from excess carbon in the atmosphere, radioactive wastes and risks of nuclear power, biodiversity loss, depleted mines, deforestation, eroded topsoil, dry wells, rivers, and aquifers, sea-level rise, the dead zone in the Gulf of Mexico, gyres of plastic trash in the oceans, the ozone hole, exhausting and dangerous labor, and the unrepayable debt from trying to push growth in the symbolic financial sector beyond what is possible in the real sector.

Growth all the way to the very limit of carrying capacity has an unrecognized political cost as well. Excess capacity is a necessary condition for freedom and democracy. Living very close to the carrying capacity limit, as on a submarine or spaceship, requires very strict discipline. On submarines and spaceships we have a captain with absolute authority, not a democracy. If we want democracy, we should not grow up to the limit of carrying capacity – better to leave some slack – some margin of tolerance for the errors that freedom entails.

We need a nongrowing economy that strives to maintain itself in a steady state at something like the optimum scale. How to do that? Basically it is as simple (and difficult) as going on a diet. Cut the matter–energy throughput to a sustainable level by cap–auction–trade and/or ecological tax reform (taxing resource throughput – especially fossil fuels – rather than value added by labor and capital). We should cap or tax fossil fuels first. Then redistribute auction or eco-tax revenues by cutting income taxes for all, but first and mainly for the poor. A policy of quantitative limits on throughput (cap–auction–trade) raises resource prices and induces resource-saving technologies. The quantitative cap will also block the erosion of resource savings as induced efficiency makes resources effectively cheaper (the Jevons effect). In addition, the auction will raise much revenue and make it possible to tax value added (labor and capital) less, because in effect we will have shifted the tax base to resource throughput. Value added is a good, so we should stop taxing it. Depletion and pollution are bads, so we should tax them.

Along with a physical diet, we need a serious monetary diet for the obese financial sector, specifically movement away from fractional reserve banking toward a system of 100 percent reserve requirements. This would end the private banks' alchemical privilege to create money out of nothing and lend it at interest. Every dollar loaned would then be a dollar that someone previously saved, restoring the classical balance between abstinence and investment. This balance was abandoned by the Keynesian–neoclassical synthesis after the Great Depression because it was thought to be a drag on growth, the new panacea. But in the new era of uneconomic growth the classical discipline regains its relevance. Investors must choose only the best projects, thereby improving the quality of growth while limiting its quantity. This idea of 100 percent reserve requirements on demand deposits was championed by the early Chicago School in the 1930s, as well as by Irving Fisher of Yale, and probably first proposed in 1926 by Frederick Soddy, Nobel Prize-winning chemist and underground economist. Also, a small 'Tobin tax' on all financial trades would reduce speculative and destabilizing short-term trading (including algorithm-based computer trading on fraction of a second price differences) and raise significant revenue.

What about population growth? In my lifetime the world population has tripled, and the populations of other 'dissipative structures' (cars, houses, livestock, cell phones, and so on) have vastly more than tripled. Limiting the populations of artifacts by capping the metabolic throughput (food supply) that sustains them seems a good policy. However, limiting food supply to humans is nature's harsh limit, Malthus' positive check. There is also Malthus' preventive check (celibacy and late marriage), and the more palatable neo-Malthusian preventive check of contraception. Contraceptives should be made easily available for voluntary use every-where. More people are better than fewer, but not if all are alive at the same time. We should strive to maximize the cumulative number of people ever to live over time in a condition of sufficiency. That means no more people alive at the same time than could enjoy a per capita resource availability that is enough for a good (not luxurious) life, and sustainable for a long (not infinite) future. Exactly how many people at exactly what per capita standard would that be? We do not know, but we do know that it is not more people at a higher per capita consumption, and that is enough to get started in the right direction.

Even if we limit quantitative physical throughput (growth) it would still be possible to experience qualitative improvement (development), thanks to technological advance and to ethical improvement of our priorities. Some say that we should not limit growth itself, but only stop bad growth and encourage good growth. However, only if we limit total growth will we be forced to choose good growth over bad. And furthermore, we can also have too much 'good' growth, or as it is often called 'green growth'. There is a limit to how many trees we can plant as well as to how many cars we can make. Growth beyond optimal scale is uneconomic growth, and we should stop the folly of continuing it.

If you are an optimist regarding 'soft' technologies (for example, conservation, solar) please have the courage of your convictions and join in advocating these policies that will give incentive to the resource-saving technologies that you believe are within reach. You may be right – I hope you are. Let us find out. If you turn out to be wrong, there is really no downside, because it was still necessary to limit throughput and consequently the 'hard' resource-intensive technologies (for example, fossil fuel, nuclear) that are currently pushing uneconomic growth.

Our strategy so far has been to seek efficiency first in order to avoid frugality – to keep the throughput growing. But 'efficiency first' leads us to the Jevons paradox – we just consume more of the resources whose efficiency we have increased, thereby partially or even totally canceling the initial reduction in quantity of resource used. If we impose 'frugality first' (caps on basic resource throughput), then we will get 'efficiency second' as an induced adaptation to frugality, avoiding the Jevons paradox. Blocking the Jevons paradox is an advantage of the cap–auction–trade system over eco-taxes, although taxes have the advantage of being administratively simpler. Both will work.

Is this vision of a developing but nongrowing economy not more appealing and realistic than the deceptive dream of an economy based on continuous growth? Who, in the light of biophysical reality, can remain committed to the growth-forever vision? Apparently our decision-making elites can. They have figured out how to keep the dwindling extra benefits of growth for themselves, while 'sharing' the exploding extra costs with the poor, the future, and other species. The elite-owned media, the corporate-funded think tanks, and the kept economists of high academia, Wall Street, and the World Bank, all sing hymns to growth in perfect unison, deceiving average citizens, and perhaps themselves. Their commitment is not to maximize the cumulative number of people ever to live at a sufficient standard of consumption for a good life for all. Rather, it is to maximize the standard of resource consumption for a small minority of the present generation, and let the costs fall on the poor, the future, and other species.

Some of the elite do not realize the cost of their behavior and will change once they are made aware. Others, I suspect, are already quite aware and do not care. The former can be persuaded by argument; the latter require repentance and conversion – or revolution, as Marxists would argue. Probably this line of division in some way runs through each of us rather than only between us. Intellectual confusion is real and we need better understanding, but that is not the whole story. The elite may already understand that growth has become uneconomic. But they have adapted by learning how to keep the dwindling extra benefits of growth, while 'sharing' the rising extra costs.

Indeed why not, if we believe that Creation is just a purposeless happenstance, the random consequence of multiplying infinitesimal probabilities by an infinite number of trials, as taught by the reigning worldview of naturalism? I say Creation with a capital 'C' advisedly, certainly not in denial of the established facts of evolution, but rather in protest to the naturalistic metaphysics, widespread among the *intelligentsia*, that all is purposeless happenstance. It is hard to imagine, under such a vision, from where the elite, or anyone else, would get the inspiration to care for Creation, which of course naturalists would have to call by a different name, say, 'Randomdom'. Imagine calling on people to work hard and sacrifice to save 'Randomdom' – the blind result of atoms swirling in the void! Intellectual confusion is real, but the moral nihilism logically entailed by the naturalistic scientism uncritically accepted by so many, may be the bigger problem.

I am not able to solve this larger metaphysical and moral difficulty, least of all in a short article aimed only at explaining the idea of a steady-state economy. But it would be disingenuous to pretend that merely describing an idea will solve the problem that gave rise to it. So in closing I at least mention what seems to me the deeper issue, and note that we will consider it further in Part IV.

PART I

Early discussion of basic steady-state concepts

2. The economics of the steady state

> But if your theory is found to be against the second law of
> thermodynamics, I can give you no hope; there is nothing for it
> but to collapse in deepest humiliation.
>
> Sir Arthur Eddington

My title is somewhat pretentious since at present [1974] this 'new
economics' consists only of a definition of a steady-state economy, some
arguments for its necessity and desirability, and some disciplined speculations on its appropriate institutions and the problem of transition, each
of which will be briefly discussed below.

WHAT IS A STEADY-STATE ECONOMY?

A steady-state economy is defined by constant stocks of physical wealth
(artifacts) and a constant population, each maintained at some chosen,
desirable level by a low rate of throughput, in other words, by low birth
rates equal to low death rates and by low physical production rates equal
to low physical depreciation rates, so that longevity of people and
durability of physical stocks are high. The throughput flow, viewed as the
cost of maintaining the stocks, begins with the extraction (depletion) of
low-entropy resources at the input end, and terminates with an equal
quantity of high-entropy waste (pollution) at the output end. The throughput is the inevitable cost of maintaining the stocks of people and artifacts
and should be minimized subject to the maintenance of a chosen level of
stocks (Boulding, 1970).

The services (want-satisfaction) yielded by the stocks of artifacts (and
people) are the ultimate benefit of economic activity, and the throughput
is the ultimate cost. The stock of physical wealth is an accumulated flow
of throughput, and thus in the final analysis is a cost. Ultimate efficiency
is the ratio of service to throughput. But to yield a service, the throughput
flow must be first accumulated into stocks even if of short duration. It is
the existence of a table or a doctor at a point in time that yields services,
not their gradual depreciation nor the productive process by which they
are replaced. Stocks are intermediate magnitudes that yield services and

9

require throughput for maintenance and replacement. This may be expressed in the equation:

$$\underset{\text{Efficiency}}{\text{Ultimate}} = \underset{\text{Throughout}}{\overset{(1)}{\text{Service}}} = \underset{\text{Stock}}{\overset{(2)}{\text{Service}}} \times \underset{\text{Throughput}}{\overset{(3)}{\text{Stock}}}$$

Since by definition stocks are constant at a level corresponding to some concept of sufficiency or maturity, progress in the steady state consists in increasing ultimate efficiency (ratio 1) in two ways: by maintaining the stock with less throughput (increase ratio 3 or 'maintenance efficiency') and by getting more service per unit of time from the same stock (increase ratio 2 or 'service efficiency'). The laws of thermodynamics provide a theoretical limit to the improvement of maintenance efficiency. Whether there is any theoretical limit to increase in service efficiency resulting from the limits of the human stomach and nervous system is less clear, but in my opinion likely.

Over short periods of time, the throughput cost of maintaining the constant stock may decrease due to improvements in maintenance efficiency, but over the long run it must increase because as better grade (lower entropy) sources of raw materials are used up, it will be necessary to process ever larger amounts of materials using ever more energy and capital equipment to get the same quantity of needed mineral. Thus a steady-state economy, as here defined, does not imply constant throughput, much less static technology, nor does it imply eternal life for the economic system. It is simply a strategy for good stewardship, for maintaining our spaceship and permitting it to die of old age rather than from the cancer of growthmania. It is basically an extension of the demographers' model of a stationary population to include the populations of physical artifacts, and the fundamental idea is found in John Stuart Mill's discussion of the stationary state of classical economics.

The term 'economic growth' conventionally refers to an increase in the flow of 'real GNP (gross national product)', which is a value index of the physical flow of throughput. The (measurable) throughput is, in turn, an index of (unmeasurable) service only if ratios 2 and 3 (or their product) are constant or increasing. This may have been the case in the past, but for the future it is doubtful. As the growing throughput pushes against biophysical limits, it provokes a decline in service efficiency (more of the stock must be devoted to the defensive use of repairing life-support systems that formerly provided free services). Also, since our institutions are geared to a continually increasing throughput, we may willingly lower maintenance efficiency for the sake of permitting a larger throughput (for example, planned obsolescence and fashion). If someone wants to redefine 'economic growth' as an increase in nonmaterial services and then argue that it can and should grow forever, he is free to do so. But this hardly constitutes a refutation of the steady-state economy, which is defined in terms of measurable physical stocks, not unmeasurable psychic fluxes.

Nor are the levels at which the stocks of people and artifacts are maintained necessarily frozen for all eternity. As a result of technical and moral evolution it may become both possible and desirable to grow or to decline to a different level. But then growth or decline would be seen as a temporary transition from one steady state to another and not as the norm for a healthy economy. Technical and moral change would lead growth rather than being blindly pushed down the path of least resistance by the growth juggernaut.

At what point should growth in stocks and maximization of production flow give way to stock maintenance and the minimization of the production flow? There are a large number of steady-state levels of stocks to choose from, and such a choice is a difficult problem of ecology and ethics. But our inability to define the optimum level does not mean that we will not someday discover that we have grown beyond it. It is more important to learn to be stable at existing or nearby levels than to know in advance which level is optimal. Knowledge of the latter without the former merely allows us to recognize and wave goodbye to the optimum as we grow through it. Besides, the optimum may well be a broad plateau within which one place is as good as another as long as we do not go too near the edge.

The radical change implied by a steady state is evident from the foregoing, and from W.W. Rostow's characterization of our present economy of high mass consumption, to which all countries unrealistically aspire, as one 'in which compound interest becomes built, as it were, into our habits and institutions' (p. 7). This built-in exponential growth and its unfortunate consequences constitute the theme of the much-maligned little book, *The Limits to Growth*, by D.H. Meadows et al. (1972). Before discussing the radical departure of 'deinstitutionalizing' compound interest or at least uncoupling it from all physical dimensions, we must consider whether such a change is really necessary and/or desirable.

THE NECESSITY AND DESIRABILITY OF THE STEADY STATE

Our economy is a subsystem of the Earth, and the Earth is apparently a steady-state open system. The subsystem cannot grow beyond the frontiers of the total system and, if it is not to disrupt the functioning of the latter, must at some much earlier point conform to the steady-state mode. The technocratic project of redesigning the world (substituting technosphere for ecosphere) so as to allow for indefinite economic growth is a bit of hubris that has received the insufficiently pejorative label of 'growthmania'.

The conceptual roots of growthmania are to be found in the orthodox doctrines of 'relative scarcity' and 'absolute wants'. Relative (or 'Ricardian') scarcity refers to the scarcity of a particular resource relative to another resource or to a lower quality of the same resource. Absolute (or 'Malthusian') scarcity refers to the scarcity of all resources in general, relative to population and per capita consumption levels. The solution to relative scarcity is substitution. Absolute scarcity assumes that all economical substitutions are made so that the total burden of absolute scarcity is minimized but still exists and may still increase. Even an efficiently borne burden can become too heavy. Substitution is always of one form of low-entropy matter-energy for another. There is no substitute for low entropy itself, and low entropy is scarce, both in its terrestrial source (finite stocks of concentrated fossil fuels and minerals) and in its solar source (a fixed rate of inflow of solar energy) (see Georgescu-Roegen, 1971). Both the human economy and the nonhuman part of the biosphere depend on the same limited budget of low entropy and on the allocative pattern which that budget has evolved over millennia. The entropy of the human sector is reduced and kept low by the continual importation of low entropy from, and exportation of high entropy to, the nonhuman sector (Daly, 1968). If too much low entropy is diverted to economic growth in the human sector, or if too many evolutionary allocative patterns are disrupted in the process of diversion, then the complex life-support systems of the biosphere will begin to fail. Growth in population and per capita consumption result in increasing absolute scarcity, which is manifested in the increasing prevalence of 'external costs', in other words, the system becomes more generally sensitive to particular interferences as the web of general interdependence is stretched ever tighter by growth in the populations of people and artifacts and the resulting stress on the entropy budget.

Orthodox economic theory has assumed that all scarcity is relative: 'Nature imposes particular scarcities, not an inescapable general scarcity' (Barnett and Morse, 1963, p. 11). Therefore the answer to scarcity is always substitution, and since relative price changes induce substitution, the policy recommendation is 'internalization of externalities' usually via pollution taxes. The following statement is representative of orthodox complacency: 'the problem of environmental pollution is a simple matter of correcting a minor resource misallocation by means of pollution charges ...' (Beckerman, 1972, p. 327). But price rigging by itself is ineffective in coping with increasing absolute scarcity since its mode of operation is only to induce substitution. What substitute is there for resources in general, for low entropy? How is it possible to raise the relative price of all resources? Attempts to do so result in inflation rather than substitution.

A similar distinction between absolute and relative wants has also been obscured by orthodox economics. Following Keynes, we may define absolute wants as those we feel independent of the situation of our fellow human beings. Relative wants are those that we feel only if their satisfaction makes us feel superior to our fellows. The importance of this distinction is that only relative wants are infinite and that relative wants cannot be universally satisfied by growth because the relative satisfactions of the elite are canceled as growth raises the general level. This effect can be avoided, and often is, by allowing growth to increase inequality so that the relatively well off become relatively better off. But it is quite impossible for everyone to become better off relative to everyone else. In spite of this extremely important distinction, orthodox theory assumes that wants in general are insatiable and extends to all wants the dignity of absolute status, in other words, the satisfaction of relative and absolute wants is considered equally legitimate and equally capable of satisfaction in the aggregate by means of economic growth. The assumption of equal legitimacy is a value judgment (though it is treated by many economists as the avoidance of a value judgment), and the assumption of equal capability of satisfaction by growth is a logical error.

The implication of the dogmas of the relativity of all scarcity and the absoluteness of all wants is growthmania. If there is no absolute scarcity to limit the possibility of growth (infinite substitutability of relatively abundant for relatively scarce resources) and no merely relative wants to limit the desirability or efficacy of growth (wants in general are infinite and all wants are equally worthy and capable of satisfaction by growth), then 'growth forever and the more the better' is the logical consequence. It is also the *reductio ad absurdum* that exposes the growth orthodoxy as a rigorous exercise in wishful thinking, as a theory that is against the second law of thermodynamics as well as against common sense. It is simply a brute fact that there is such a thing as absolute scarcity and such a thing as relative wants. Furthermore, these latter categories eventually become dominant at the margin as growth continues. The implication of absolute scarcity and relative wants is the opposite of growthmania, namely, the steady state.

At this point the growthmaniacs usually make a burnt offering to the god of technology: surely economic growth can continue indefinitely because technology will continue to 'grow exponentially' as it has in the past. This elaborately misses the point. The alleged 'exponential growth' of technology is not directly measurable and is only inferred from the permissive role that it has played in making possible the measured exponential growth in the physical magnitudes of production, depletion and pollution (in other words, the throughput). Such technical progress is more a part of the problem than the solution. What must be appealed to is a qualitative change in the direction of technical progress, not a continuation of alleged quantitative trends. The institutions to be discussed in the next section seek to induce just such a change toward resource-saving technology and patterns of living, and to a greater reliance on solar energy and renewable resources. But we can be fairly certain that no new technology will abolish absolute scarcity because the laws of thermodynamics apply to all possible technologies. No one can be absolutely certain that we will not some day discover perpetual motion and how to create and destroy matter and energy. But the reasonable assumption for economists is that this is an unlikely prospect and that while technology will continue to pull rabbits out of hats, it will not pull an elephant out of a hat – much less an infinite series of ever larger elephants!

But the ideology of growth continues to transcend the ordinary logic of elementary economics. Growth is the basis of national power and prestige. Growth offers the prospect of prosperity for all with sacrifice by none. It is a substitute for redistribution. The present sins of poverty and injustice will be washed away in a future sea of abundance, vouchsafed by the amazing grace of compound interest. This evasion, common to both capitalism and communism, was never totally honest. It is now increasingly exposed as absurd.

SPECULATIONS ON THE STEADY STATE

The first design principle disciplining our speculations on institutions is to provide the necessary social control with a minimum sacrifice of personal freedom, to provide macro stability while allowing for micro variability, to combine the macro static with the micro dynamic. A second design principle, closely related to the first, is to maintain considerable slack between the actual environmental load and the maximum carrying capacity. The closer the actual approaches the maximum, the more rigorous, finely tuned, and micro-oriented our controls will have to be. We lack the knowledge and ability to assume detailed central control of the spaceship, even if such were desirable, so therefore we should leave it on 'automatic pilot' as it has been for eons. But the automatic pilot only works if the actual load is small relative to the maximum. A third design principle, important for making the transition, is to start from existing initial conditions rather than an imaginary 'clean slate', and a fourth is to build in the ability to tighten constraints gradually. Minimum faith is placed in our ability to plan a detailed blueprint for a new society. Maximum faith is placed in the basic regenerative powers of life and in the possibility of moral growth, once the root physical process of degeneration (unlimited growth) is arrested.

The kinds of institutions required follow directly from the definition. We need (1) an institution for stabilizing population, (2) an institution for stabilizing physical wealth and keeping throughput below ecological limits, and, less obviously but most importantly, (3) an institution limiting the degree of inequality in the distribution of the constant stocks among the constant population since growth can no longer be appealed to as the answer to poverty.

What specific institutions can perform these functions and are most in harmony with the general design principles discussed above? Elsewhere I have outlined a model and can here only briefly describe it (Daly, 1973a, 1974a). The model builds on the existing institutions of private property and the price system and is thus fundamentally conservative. But it extends these institutions to areas previously not included: control of aggregate births (marketable birth license plan as first proposed by Boulding, 1970) and control of aggregate depletion of basic resources (depletion quotas auctioned by the government). Extending the market, under the discipline of aggregate quotas, to these vital areas is necessary to deal with increasing absolute scarcity since, as argued above, price controls deal only with relative scarcity. Quantitative limits are set with reference to ecological and ethical criteria, and the price system is then allowed (by auction, exchange or gift), to allocate depletion quotas and birth quotas efficiently. The throughput is controlled at its input (depletion) end, rather than at its output (pollution) end, because physical control is easier at the point of lower entropy. Orthodox economics suggests price controls at the output end (pollution taxes), while steady-state economics suggests quantitative controls at the input end (depletion quotas).

With more vital areas of life officially subject to the discipline of the price system, it will become more urgent to establish the institutional preconditions of free and mutually beneficial exchange, namely, to limit the degree of inequality in the distribution of income and wealth and to limit the monopoly power of corporations. A distributist institution establishing a minimum income and a maximum income and wealth would go a long way toward achieving that end, while leaving room for differential reward and incentives within reasonable limits. There might be one set of limits for individuals, one for families, and one for corporations. Natural monopolies should be publicly owned and operated.

Birth quotas, depletion quotas, and distributive limits can all be varied continuously and applied with any degree of gradualism desired. Moreover, all three control points are price system parameters, and altering them does not interfere with the static allocative efficiency of the market. Externalities involving ecological, demographic, and distributive issues are 'externalized' by means of quotas rather than 'internalized' in rigged market prices. Yet the effect is much the same in that prices rise to reflect previously unaccounted dimensions of scarcity, and prices become a safer guide to market decisions. The net advantage of the quota scheme is that it limits aggregate throughput, whereas price controls merely alter throughput composition, providing a useful fine-tuning supplement to quotas, but not a substitute. The higher resource prices resulting from limited depletion would have the dynamic effect of inducing resource-saving technology and a shift to greater dependence on solar energy and renewable resources. The receipts of the depletion quota auction could help finance the minimum income. The marketable birth license plan would also have an equalizing effect on per capita income distribution.

Such institutional change is obviously not on the political agenda for 1974. Nor should it be since it is speculative, has not had the benefit of widespread professional criticism, and thus may contain terrible mistakes. But mistakes will not be discovered and better ideas will not be offered unless economists awake from the dogmatic slumber of growthmania induced by the soporific doctrines of relative scarcity and absolute wants and put the steady-state paradigm on the agenda for academic debate.

REFERENCES

Barnett, H.J. and C. Morse (1963), *Scarcity and Growth*, Baltimore, MD: Johns Hopkins University Press.

Beckerman, W. (1972), Economists, scientists, and environmental catastrophe, *Oxford Economic Papers*, Nov. 1972, **24**, 327.

Boulding, K.E. (1970), *Economics as a Science*, New York: McGraw-Hill.

Culbertson, J. (1971), *Economic Development: An Ecological Approach*, New York: Knopf.

Daly, H.E. (1968), On economics as a life science, *Journal of Political Economy*, May/June 1968, **76**, 392–406.

Daly, H.E. (1972), In defense of a steady-state economy, *American Journal of Agricultural Economics*, **54**, 945–54.

Daly, H.E., ed. (1973a), *Toward a Steady-state Economy*, San Francisco: W.H. Freeman.

Daly, H.E. (1973b), Long run environmental constraints and trade-offs between human and artifact populations, *International Population Conference, IUSSP*, Liege, **3**, 453–60.

Daly, H.E. (1974a), A model for a steady-state economy, in F.H. Bormann, W.R. Burch, and D.L. Meadows, eds., *Beyond Growth: Essays on Alternative Futures*, New Haven, CT: Yale University Press, pp. 127*ff*.

Daly, H.E. (1974b), Steady-state economics versus growthmania: a critique of the orthodox conceptions of growth, wants, scarcity, and efficiency, *Policy Science*, **5**, 149–67.

Editors (1972), A blueprint for survival, *The Ecologist*, **2**, 1–43.

Georgescu-Roegen, N. (1971), *The Entropy Law and the Economic Process*, Cambridge, MA: Harvard University Press.

Meadows, D.H., D.L. Meadows, J. Randers, and W.W. Behrens III (1972), *The Limits to Growth*, New York: Universe Books.

Meadows, D.H. and D.L. Meadows, eds. (1973), *Toward Global Equilibrium: Collected Papers*, Cambridge, MA: MIT Press.

Ophuls, W. (1973), *Prologue to a Political Theory of the Steady State*, (unpublished) Ph.D. dissertation in Political Science, Yale University.

Rostow, W.W. (1960), *The Stages of Economic Growth*, New York: Cambridge University Press.

'The No-Growth Society', *Daedalus*, American Academy of Arts and Sciences Proceedings, 102, Fall 1973.

3.   In defense of a steady-state economy

The case against continuous exponential growth in the physical co-ordinates of our economy has already been made (Mill, 1961; Mishan, 1967; Boulding, 1970; Daly, 1971, 1973; Georgescu-Roegen, 1971; Weisskopf, 1971; Barclay and Seclar, 1972; *The Ecologist*, 1972; Ehrlich et al., 1972; Meadows et al., 1972), but has not yet won majority acceptance. Rather than repeat the arguments establishing the necessity and desirability of a steady-state economy, I will confine myself to a critique of a number of counter-arguments and objections that have been raised against the steady-state view by those who remain committed to the orthodox growth paradigm.

What follows then is a kind of catechism of pro-growth fallacies, sophistries, casuistries, obfuscations, nonsequiturs, question-beggings, and misunderstandings, which, if properly refuted, should indirectly make the case for a steady-state economy.

CONFUSIONS AND OBFUSCATIONS ARISING FROM VAGUE DEFINITIONS AND THE SUBSTITUTION OF CONNOTATIONS FOR DENOTATIONS

These misunderstandings are too numerous to catalog and arise mainly from the unhappy term 'zero growth', which many people interpret as implying an end to all technical and moral progress, an absolute, relative, and eternal static freeze. The verb 'to grow' has become so over-laden with positive value connotations that we have forgotten its first literal dictionary denotation, 'to spring up and develop to maturity'. Thus, the very notion of growth includes some concept of maturity at which point physical accumulation gives way to a steady state. Thus, 'steady state' is a more descriptive term than 'zero growth', although both imply the essential cessation of gross physical accumulation. The steady-state economy is a physical concept. It is defined by constant stocks of people and physical wealth (artifacts) maintained at some chosen, desirable level by a low rate of throughput. The throughput flow begins with depletion (followed by production and consumption) and ends with an equal amount of waste effluent or pollution. The throughput is the maintenance cost of the stock and should be minimized for any given stock size, subject to some limits stemming from the legitimate need for novelty.[1] The psychic dimension of wealth, in other words, its want-satisfying capacity, may forever increase due to increasing knowledge and technical improvement. But the physical dimensions are limited. It is obvious that in a finite world nothing physical can grow forever. Yet, real GNP is a value index of quantity produced. It is overwhelmingly an index of physical throughput. Our current policy is to make this flow grow, although it is clearly more in the nature of a cost than a benefit. Benefits come from the services rendered by the stock of wealth. This service, or want-satisfaction, or psychic income, is unmeasurable, but it is clearly related to the stock, not the flow. The flow merely serves to maintain the stock and is a necessary cost. One cannot ride to town on the maintenance flow of the stock of automobiles but only in an existing automobile that is a current member of the stock. Nor, as Georgescu-Roegen (1971) points out, can one cross a river on the annual maintenance flow of a bridge. To maximize the throughput flow for its own sake is absurd. To maximize the inflow end of throughput for the sake of a larger stock is a limited process, and the limits are physical. The stock and its associated throughput are limited by space, by the mass of the earth, by heat release, and far more stringently by the intricate web of ecological relationships, which too large a throughput will rip to shreds. Moral and social limits, though less definable, are likely to be even more stringent. For example, the social problem of safeguarding plutonium from immoral uses and consequences is more likely to limit breeder reactor usage than is the physical constraint of thermal pollution. The steady state will be socially desirable long before it becomes an immediate physical necessity.

Unfortunately, economists long ago forgot about physical dimensions and concentrated their attention on value.[2] Value is measured in money. Money, as a unit of account, has no physical dimension. A sum on deposit at Chase Manhattan Bank can grow forever at 5 percent! Income and wealth are value concepts; they too are measured in money; why cannot they too grow forever at 5 percent? Money fetishism triumphs completely! The concrete reality being measured is reduced to identity with the abstract unit of measure. The physical dimensions of wealth are 'annihilated' by the Almighty Dollar! But, in fact, wealth always has a physical dimension. Even knowledge requires physical organisms with brains, calories to run the brain, and light for the transmission of information. Knowledge can increase the ability of the stock to satisfy wants, perhaps without limit. Knowledge can, within limits set by the second law of thermodynamics, reduce the flow throughput per unit of stock maintained.

Once we have attained a steady state at some level of population and wealth, we are not forever frozen at that level. As values and technology evolve we may find that a different level is both possible and desirable. But the growth (or decline) required to get to the new level is a temporary adjustment process, not a norm. Presently, the momentum of growth in population and capital pushes our technological and moral development. In the steady-state paradigm, technological and moral evolution would precede and lead growth instead of being pushed. Growth would always be seen as a temporary passage from one steady state to another, not as the norm of a 'healthy' economy.

CANNOT GET ENOUGH OF THAT WONDERFUL STUFF

The American people have been told by no less an authority than the President's Council of Economic Advisors that, 'If it is agreed that economic output is a good thing it follows by definition that there is not enough of it' (US President, 1971, p. 92). It is impossible to have too much of a good thing. If rain is a good thing, a torrential downpour is 'by definition' better! Has the learned council forgotten about diminishing marginal utility and increasing marginal costs? A charitable interpretation would be that 'economic' output means output for which marginal utility is greater than marginal cost. But it is clear from the context that what is meant is simply real GNP. But perhaps this amazing nonsequitur was just a slip of the pen. At another point in the same document (p. 88), the council admits that 'growth of GNP has its costs, and beyond some point they are not worth paying'. But instead of raising the obvious question – What determines the optimal point and how do we know when we have reached it? – the council relapses into nonsequitur and quickly closes this dangerous line of thinking with the following pontification: 'the existing propensities of the population and policies of the government constitute claims upon GNP itself that can only be satisfied by rapid economic growth'. Apparently, these 'existing propensities and policies' are beyond discussion. This is growthmania.

The theoretical answer to the avoided question is clear to any economist. Growth in GNP should cease when decreasing marginal benefits become equal to increasing marginal costs. But there is no statistical series that attempts to measure the cost of GNP. This is growthmania – literally not counting the costs of growth. But the situation is even worse.

We take the real costs of increasing GNP as measured by the defensive expenditures incurred to protect ourselves from the unwanted side effects of production and add these expenditures to GNP rather than subtract them. We count real costs as benefits. This is hyper-growthmania. Obviously, we should keep separate accounts of costs and benefits. But to do this would make it clear that, beyond some point, zero growth would be optimal, at least in the short run. Such an admission is inconvenient to the ideology of growth, which quite transcends the ordinary logic of elementary economics. More precisely, it is good growthmanship strategy to admit the theoretical existence of such a point way out in the future, but somehow it must always be thought of as far away. The ideological reasons for this are clear and have to do with the problem of distribution of output in an economy in which ownership of land and capital is highly concentrated and embodies labor-saving technology.

Full employment at a living wage requires high aggregate demand, which requires high net investment to offset the large savings made possible by concentrated income. High net investment signifies rapid growth.

THE HAIR OF THE DOG THAT BIT YOU

One of the most popular arguments against limiting growth is that we need more growth in order to be rich enough to afford the costs of cleaning up pollution and discovering new resources. Economist Neil Jacoby says, 'A rising GNP will enable the nation more easily to bear the costs of eliminating pollution' (Jacoby, 1970, p. 42).

Yale economist Henry Wallich makes a similar point:

> The environment will also be better taken care of if the economy grows. Nothing could cut more dangerously in to the resources that must be devoted to the Great Cleanup than an attempt to limit resources available for consumption. By ignoring the prohibitionist impulse and allowing everybody to have more, we shall also have more resources to do the environmental job. (Wallich, 1972, p. 62)

No one can deny that if we had more resources and were truly richer, all our economic problems would be more easily solved. The question is whether further growth in GNP will in fact make us richer. It may well make us poorer. How do we know that it will not, since we do not bother to measure the costs and even count many real costs as benefits? These critics simply assume that a rising per capita GNP is making us better off, when that is the very question at issue!

Even if marginal welfare benefits of GNP were presently greater than marginal welfare costs, we know that the curves will eventually cross as growth continues. Of course, the benefit curve could shift up and the cost curve shift down due to changes in tastes and technology, and the intersection would occur at a higher GNP. But even ignoring the possibility that the curves could also shift in the opposite directions, and assuming very unrealistically that the benefit curve will forever shift upwards and the cost curve downward, there is still the question of timing. Why must the curves always shift before we reach the intersection? Might not technical progress occasionally be delayed? Might we not find it optimal to cease growth temporarily while waiting for the curves to shift? Or must we go beyond the optimum, just to keep up the momentum of growth for the sake of avoiding unemployment? Once we have gone beyond the optimum and marginal costs exceed marginal benefits, growth will make us worse off. Will we then cease growing? On the contrary, our experience of diminished wellbeing will be blamed on the traditional heavy hand of product scarcity, and the only way the orthodox paradigm knows to deal with increased scarcity is to advocate increased growth – this will make us even less well off and will lead to the advocacy of still more growth! Sometimes one suspects that we are already on this 'other side of the looking glass' where images are inverted and the faster one runs the 'behinder' one gets.

Environmental degradation is an iatrogenic disease induced by the economic physicians who attempt to treat the basic sickness of unlimited wants by prescribing unlimited production. One does not cure a treatment-induced disease by increasing the treatment dosage! Yet, members of the hair-of-the-dog-that-bit-you school who reason that it is impossible to have too much of a good thing can hardly cope with such subtleties. If an overdose of medicine is making one sick, one needs an emetic, not more of the medicine. Physician, heal thyself … !

CONSISTENT INCONSISTENCIES AND AVOIDING THE MAIN ISSUE

Growthmen are forever claiming that neither they nor any other economist worth his salt has ever confused GNP with welfare. Consider, however, the following four statements from the same article (Nordhaus and Tobin, 1970):

1. 'Gross National Product is not a measure of economic welfare and its maximization is not a proper objective of economic policy. Economists all know that …'. (p. 6)
2. 'Although GNP and other national income aggregates are imperfect measures of welfare, the broad picture of secular progress which they convey remains after correction of their most obvious deficiencies'. (p. 25)
3. 'But for all its shortcomings, national output is about the only broadly-based index of economic welfare that has been constructed'. (p. 1, Appendix A)
4. 'there is no evidence to support the claim that welfare has grown less rapidly than NNP [net national product]. Rather NNP seems to underestimate the gain in welfare, chiefly because of the omission of leisure from consumption. Subject to the limitations of the estimates we conclude that the economic welfare of the average American has been growing at a rate which doubles every thirty years'. (p. 12)

It is asking too much of context and intervening qualification to reconcile statement (1) with statements (2), (3), and (4). Either GNP (or NNP) is an index of welfare, or it is not. The authors clearly believe that it is (in spite of the first statement). They offer many sensible adjustments to make GNP a better measure of welfare on the assumption that it is already an imperfect measure. But all of this avoids the fundamental objection that the GNP-flow is basically a cost. Wants are satisfied by the services of the stock of wealth. The annual production flow is the cost of maintaining the stock and, though necessary, should be minimized for any given stock level. If we want the stock to grow we must pay the added cost of a greater production flow (more depletion, more labor, and ultimately more pollution). Depletion, labor, and pollution are real costs that vary directly with the GNP throughput. If we must have some indices of welfare, why not take total stock per capita and the ratio of total stock to throughput flow? Welfare varies directly with the stock, inversely with the flow. Beyond some point the benefits of additions to the stock will not be worth the costs in terms of additional maintenance throughout.

Kenneth Boulding has for many years been making the point that GNP is really Gross National Cost and has never been taken seriously. If this way of looking at things is wrong, why does not some economist deal it a decisive refutation instead of avoiding it? Certainly it is not a minor issue.

The source of this flow-fetishism of orthodox economics is two-fold. First, it is a natural concomitant of early stages of ecological succession. Young ecosystems (and cowboy economies) tend to maximize production efficiency, in other words, the ratio of annual flow of biomass produced to the pre-existing biomass stock that produced it. Mature ecosystems (and spaceman economies) tend to maximize the inverse ratio of existing biomass stock to annual biomass flow. The latter ratio increases as maintenance efficiency increases. Economic theory is lagging behind ecological succession. The other reason for flow-fetishism is ideological. Concentrating on flows takes attention away from the very unequally distributed stock that is the real source of economic power. The income flow is unequally distributed also, but at least everyone gets some part of it, and marginal productivity theory makes it appear rather fair. Redistribution of income is liberal. Redistribution of wealth is radical. Politically, it is safer to keep income at the center of analysis. Not everyone owns a piece of the productive stock and there is no theory explaining wealth distribution.

Putting stocks at the center of analysis might raise impolite questions.

CROCODILE TEARS FROM LATTER-DAY MARIE ANTOINETTES

Economists and businessmen with no previous record of concern for the poor have now begun to attack steady-state advocates as upper-class birdwatchers, who, having gotten theirs, now want to kick the ladder down behind them and leave the poor forever on the ground floor. There may be such people and certainly they should be condemned. But most advocates of the steady state accept and proclaim the absolute necessity of radical redistribution of wealth as well as income. Indeed, many people who have long favored less inequality in the distribution of wealth on ethical and political grounds are only too happy to reach the same conclusion on ecological grounds. It is the orthodox growthmen who want to avoid the distribution issue. As Yale economist Henry C. Wallich (1972) so bluntly put it in defending growth, 'Growth is a substitute for equality of income. So long as there is growth there is hope, and that makes large income differentials tolerable'. We are addicted to growth because we are addicted to large inequalities in income and wealth. What about the poor? Let them eat growth! Better yet, let them feed on the hope of eating growth in the future!

We have been growing for some time and still have poverty. It should be obvious that what grows is the reinvested surplus, and the benefits of growth go to the owners of the surplus, who are not poor. Some of the growth dividends trickle down, but not much. The poor are given the sop of full employment – in other words, they are allowed to share fully in the economy's toil but not in its dividends – and unless we have enough growth to satisfy the dividend recipients even the booby prize of full employment is taken away.

On the issue of growth and poverty, Joan Robinson noted that,

> Not only subjective poverty is never overcome by growth, but absolute poverty is increased by it. Growth requires technical progress and technical progress alters the composition of the labor force, making more places for educated workers and fewer for uneducated, but opportunities to acquire qualifications are kept (with a few exceptions for exceptional talents) for those families who have them already. (1972, p. 7)

ADMITTING THE THIN EDGE OF A BIG WEDGE

'We know that population growth cannot continue forever' (Nordhaus and Tobin, 1970, p. 20). This apparently innocent commonplace is the thin edge of a wedge whose thick end is capable of cracking the growth orthodoxy in half. This results from the fact that in addition to the population of human bodies (endosomatic capital), we must also consider the population of extensions of the human body (exosomatic capital). Cars and bicycles extend our legs, buildings and clothes extend our skin, telephones extend our ears and voice, libraries and computers extend our brain, and so on. Both endosomatic and exosomatic capital are necessary for the maintenance and enjoyment of life. Both are physical open systems that maintain themselves in a kind of steady state by continually importing low-entropy matter-energy from the environment and exporting high-entropy matter-energy back to the environment. In other words, both populations require a physical throughput for short-run maintenance and long-run replacement of deaths by births. The two populations depend upon the environment in essentially the same way. The same biophysical constraints that limit the population of organisms apply with equal force to the population of extensions of organisms. If the first limitation is admitted, how can the second be denied?

MISPLACED CONCRETENESS AND TECHNOLOGICAL SALVATION

Technology is the rock upon which the growthmen built their church. Since rocks and foundations are concrete entities, it is natural that growthmen should begin to endow technology with a certain metaphorical concreteness, in other words, to begin speaking of it as a thing which grows in quantity. Then, it is but a short step to ask whether this 'thing' has grown exponentially like many other things and to consult the black art of econometrics and discover that indeed it has! Next, one can conceive of technology as a sort of antibody to the pollution and the depletion germs. Then, one concludes that depleting and polluting activities (production and consumption) can continue to grow exponentially because we have a problem-solving, anti-particle, technology, that can also grow exponentially!

Is the above an unfair caricature? Consider the following quote from a review of *The Limits to Growth* by two economists and a lawyer:

> While the team's world model hypothesizes exponential growth for industrial and agricultural needs, it places arbitrary, nonexponential, limits on the technical progress that might accommodate these needs ... It is true that exponential growth cannot go on forever if technology does not keep up and if that is the case we might save ourselves much misery by stopping before we reach the limits. But there is no particular criterion beyond myopia on which to base that speculation. Malthus was wrong; food capacity has kept up with population. While no one knows for certain, technical progress shows no signs of slowing down. The best econometric estimates suggest that it is indeed growing exponentially. (Passell et al., 1972)

These few sentences are very valuable in that they unite in one short space so many of the misconceptions of orthodox growthmen. Note that technology has become an exponentially growing quantity of some thing that solves problems but does not create any. Note the clear implication that exponential growth could go on forever if technology (that problem-solving anti-particle) can keep up. Can it in fact keep up? Consult the entrails of a nameless econometrician and, behold – it has in the past, so it probably will in the future. Most econometricians are more cautious in view of the fact that technical change cannot be directly measured but is merely the unexplained residual in their regressions after they have included as many measurable factors and dummy variables as they can think of. Sometimes the residual 'technology' component even includes the effect of increased raw material inputs! Note also the blind assertion that Malthus was wrong, when in fact his predictions have been painfully verified by the majority of mankind. But then majorities have never counted. Only the articulate, technically competent minority counts. But even for them Malthus was not really wrong, since this minority has heeded his advice and limited its reproduction.

A far more perceptive reviewer of *The Limits to Growth* has noted a similar confusion and lucidly comments on it in the following quote:

> Some critics of 'Limits' berate the authors for not including exponentially growing technical knowledge as a sixth constituent of the World Model. Such criticism elaborately misses the point. The other five constituents have real, physical referents that can be quantified: population can be counted, barrels of petroleum consumed can be enumerated and parts per million of abrasive chemicals in the smog of Los Angeles can be measured. Sheer 'knowledge' means nothing for the world system until it enters one of the other five constituents, and the tacit assumption that all technical knowledge necessarily enters as a good is unwarranted. Is the technical knowledge that performance of gasoline engines can be improved by adding tetraethyl lead to their fuel a 'good'? (Royall, 1970, p. 42)

In other words, the MIT projections of physical growth trends already include the effects of past technical 'progress' as these effects were registered in the five physical referents of the model. The tacit assumption is that the influence of technology on the physical world will in the future change in ways similar to the way it has changed in the past. One need not accept *The Limits to Growth* in its entirety, but it is clear that whether or not technology has 'grown exponentially' is largely irrelevant. The assumption of some critics that technical change is totally a part of the solution and no part of the problem is ridiculous on the face of it and totally demolished by the work of Barry Commoner (1971a). One need not accept Commoner's extreme emphasis on the importance of the problem-causing nature of post-World War II technology (with the consequent downplaying of the roles of population and affluence) in order to recognize that recent technical change is more a part of the problem than of the solution. The key question is: what kind of technology is part of the solution and what kind of institutional sieve will let pass the good kind while blocking the bad kind?

TWO-FACTOR MODELS WITH FREE RESOURCES AND FUNDS THAT ARE NEARLY PERFECT SUBSTITUTES FOR FLOWS

Economists routinely measure the productivity of the fund factors, labor, and capital (and Ricardian land). But the productivity of the flow factors, natural raw materials, and inanimate energy, are seldom even spoken of, much less calculated. This reflects a tacit presumption that they are not really scarce, that they are the free and inexhaustible gifts of nature. The only limit to the flow of product is assumed to be the capacity of the fund factors to process the inputs and turn them into products. Nordhaus and Tobin are specific on this point: 'The prevailing standard model of growth assumes that there are no limits on the feasibility of expanding the supplies of nonhuman agents of production. It is basically a two-factor model in which production depends only on labor and reproducible capital' (1970, p. 14).

How is this neglect of resource flows justified? According to Nordhaus and Tobin, 'the tacit justification has been that reproducible capital is a near perfect substitute for land and other exhaustible resources'. If factors are near perfect substitutes, then there is of course no point in considering them separate factors. From the point of view of economic analysis they are identical. But it is very odd to have such an identity between factors whose very dimensionality is different. Capital is a fund, material and energy resources are flows. The fund processes the flow and is the instrument for transforming the flow. The two are obviously complements in any given technology. But allowing for technological change does not alter the relationship. The usual reason for expanding or redesigning the capital fund is to process a larger, not a smaller flow of resources. New technology embodied in new capital may also permit one to process different materials, but this is the substitution of one resource flow for another, not the substitution of a capital fund for a resource flow.[3] After we deplete one resource we redesign our machines and set about depleting another. The assumption is that in the aggregate resources are infinite, that when one flow dries up there will always be another, and that technology will always find cheap ways to exploit the next resource. When the whales are gone, we will hunt dolphins, and so on till we are farming plankton. The ecologists tell us that it will not work, that there are other limits involved, and even if it would work, who wants it? But Professors Nordhaus and Tobin see little connection between economic growth and ecological catastrophe – 'As for the danger of global ecological catastrophe, there is probably very little that economics can say' (1970, p. 20). As long as economic growth models continue to assume away vast domains of material scarcity this is quite true and is simply another way of saying that current growth economics has uncoupled itself from the world and has become irrelevant. Worse, it has become a blind guide. But it need not remain so.

BUT RESOURCES ARE SUCH A SMALL PERCENTAGE OF GNP

Perhaps another 'justification' for ignoring resources is the small value component of GNP that they represent. In 1968 total minerals production represented 1.7 percent of GNP and total fossil fuels 2.0 percent (Goeller, 1972, p. 15).[4] Why is it that our price system imputes such a small share of total value produced to resources and such a large share (the remainder) to labor and capital? Does this vindicate the assumption that resources are ultimately not scarce? Or does it simply mean that they are underpriced? I believe the latter is the case, and that this underpricing results from the relative power of social classes that conditions the functioning of the market. Specifically, labor and capital are two powerful social classes, while resource owners for good reasons are not. Let us see how this rigs the market in favor of low resource prices.

In the short run we have a given technology and given amounts of the fund factors, labor, and capital. It takes time to change the capital stock and to change the size of the working-age population. Suppose it is desired to increase the incomes of both capital and labor in the short run. Since the incomes of capital and labor are tied to their respective productivities it becomes necessary to increase these productivities. Under short-run assumptions the only way to increase the productivities of both fund factors is to increase the flow factors of raw materials and power. As the flow of resource throughput is increased with a given fund of labor and capital, the productivity of the resource flow must, by the law of diminishing returns, decrease. All three productivities cannot increase in the short run. It is clear that the flow factor's productivity is the one most likely to be sacrificed, since in the short run it is the only one whose quantity can be increased. But furthermore, even in the longer run with all factors variable but no technical change, it is clear that resource productivity will also lose out. The tie between labor productivity and labor income, plus the monopoly power of labor unions, will keep labor productivity from being sacrificed. The tie between capital productivity and interest and profit, along with the monopoly power of large corporations, will keep capital productivity from being sacrificed. Capital and labor are the two social classes that produce and divide up the firm's product. They are in basic conflict but must live together. They minimize conflict by growth and by throwing the growth-induced burden of diminishing returns onto resource productivity. How do they get away with it? In earlier times it might not have worked; a strong landlord class would have had an interest in keeping resource prices from falling too low. But today we have no such class to exert countervailing upward pressure on resource prices. Although resource owners do exist and they do prefer higher to lower prices, other things equal, it remains true that no social class is as effective in promoting resource productivity as the capitalists and laborers are in promoting the productivities of their respective factors.

Suppose we allow for technological change in the long run. Now it is possible for all three productivities to increase. But how likely is it? Given the desire to increase incomes of labor and capital, it seems innovations that increase these two productivities will have first priority, while those that mainly increase resource productivity will not be stimulated. Given low prices for resources it will not matter much to entrepreneurs what happens to resource productivity. And surely it is easier to invent a new technology that increases the productivity of two factors than to invent one that increases all three productivities.

Should we, by a kind of reverse land reform, reinstate a landlord class? Landlord rent is unearned income, and we find income based on ownership of that which no one produced to be ethically distasteful. No one loves a landlord. Adam Smith tells us that landlords love to reap where they have never sown, and not many lament the historical demise of the landowning aristocracy. But not all the long-run consequences of this demise are favorable. Rent may be an illegitimate source of income, but it is a totally legitimate and necessary price, without which efficient allocation of scarce resources would be impossible. Henry George said, let rent be charged but then tax it away. Socialists, after trying to get along without the price, say charge some rent but pay it to the government, who is now the landlord. In the United States neither of these things has happened. The largest resource owner, the government, has followed a give-away and low-price policy, both on resources it owns and on those whose price it regulates (for example, natural gas). It has done this to favor certain capitalists, to promote growth, and to ease the labor–capital conflict and win votes in both camps.

Also imports of resources from underdeveloped countries, which have not yet learned how to use them, have naturally been cheap because of the low short-run opportunity cost to the exporting country. This is now changing, but in the past it has been a factor in keeping resource prices low. Some resources are owned by capitalists, but they are likely to be much more interested in maximizing growth and minimizing conflict through low resource prices than in making profits on sales of resources. In fact, the capitalist's ownership of resources will generally be for the purpose of lowering the cost price of those resources to himself as capitalist, in order to increase the returns to capital. Capital is the dynamic, controlling factor. It is not for nothing that our economic system is called 'capitalism' rather than 'resource-ism'.

Let us consider briefly two similar analyses of resource productivity.

Karl Marx had the following to say regarding the effect of capitalist production on soil productivity:

> Capitalist production [...] disturbs the circulation of matter between man and the soil, in other words, prevents the return to the soil of its elements consumed by man in the form of food and clothing; it therefore violates conditions necessary to the lasting fertility of the soil [...] Moreover, all progress in capitalistic agriculture is a progress in the art, not only of robbing the laborer, but of robbing the soil; all progress in increasing the fertility of the soil for a given time is a progress toward ruining the lasting sources of that fertility. The more a country starts its development on the foundation of modern industry, like the United States, for example, the more rapid is the process of destruction! Capitalist production, therefore, develops technology, and the combining together of various processes into a social whole, only by sapping the original sources of all wealth – soil and the laborer. (Marx, 1967, pp. 505–6)

Marx sees capitalists exploiting the soil as well as the laborer. Our analysis sees capital and labor maintaining an uneasy alliance by shifting the exploitation to the soil and other natural resources. It follows that if some institution were to play the role of the landlord class and raise resource prices, the labor–capital conflict would again become severe; hence the radical implications of the ecological crisis and hence the need for some distributist institution.

A more recent analysis of resource productivity, in the case of electric power, was made by Barry Commoner (1971b). He found the productivity of electric power to be falling in all individual industries considered and falling even more in the total economy as power-intensive industries displaced other industries in relative importance. His empirical findings suggest to him an,

> apparently unavoidable dilemma created by an effort to reduce overall power demanded by industrial production: either total production is curtailed, or power productivity is elevated; but if the latter course is taken, labor productivity must be reduced.[5] Thus, whichever course is taken, the effort to

reduce power demand would appear to clash head on with one or both of the two factors that are widely regarded as essential to the stability of the United States economic system – increased production and increased labor productivity.

These considerations raise the possibility, which it is to be hoped economists will investigate, that continued exponential increase in power consumption is not an accidental concomitant of industrial growth, but is rather a functional necessity for the continued operation of the United States economic system, as it is presently organized. If this should prove to be true, then the ultimate social choice signified by the power crisis becomes very stark. One course is to continue the present exponential growth in the supply of electric power, and risk our future on the ability to contain the huge mass of resultant chemical, radioactive, and thermal pollution. The other is to slow down the rate of power consumption, and accept as a necessary consequence that the economic system must be changed. (Commoner, 1971b, p. 31)

The social class relative power hypothesis presented as an explanation of low resource prices and productivities might be considered as a theoretical complement to Commoner's empirically based generalizations and conjectures. Social conflict is minimized in the short run by low productivity of the entire throughput, which is a consequence of high productivity (and incomes) for labor and capital. If one opts to avoid the risk of containing large masses of material, chemical, thermal, and radioactive pollution, not to mention aesthetic, moral, and social costs, one must limit growth in throughput. What is the most efficient and least painful way to limit throughput?[6]

PRESENT VALUE AND POSITIVE FEEDBACK

It is sometimes argued that the market automatically provides for conservation by offering high profits to far-sighted spectators who buy up materials and resell them later at a higher price. There are at least two things wrong with this argument. First, exponentially growing extraction leads to 'unexpectedly' sudden exhaustion. If the doubling time of the cumulative total amount extracted is in the order of 30 years, as it apparently is for many resources, then we would go from a condition of one-half depleted to totally depleted in the final 30-year period. Most resource owners probably find that surprising. For linear trends the past is a good guide to the future. For exponential growth, the past is a deceptive guide to the future. The second problem is that the future profit must be discounted to its present value. The investor has the alternative in an expanding economy of depleting now and investing the short-term profits in another line that will earn the expected 'going rate' which will be close to the growth rate of the economy. The discount rate he applies to future profit is the same as the rate at which he would expect his reinvested short-term profits to grow. This expected rate is determined largely by the current rate and by recent changes in the current rate. The result is that high and increasing current growth rates, based on high and increasing current depletion rates, lead to high and increasing discount rates applied to future values. The latter in turn leads to a low incentive to conserve, which feeds back to high current depletion and growth rates, high discount rates, and so on. Present value calculations thus have an element of positive feedback that is destabilizing from the point of view of conservation. 'Financial prudence' usually advises one to deplete now and invest his short-term earnings in depleting some other resource, and so on. The presumption again is infinite resources. There will always be more material and energy resources available to feed the march of compound interest with its consequent discounting of future values and disincentive to conservation.[7]

YOUTH CULTURE AND ITS FEAR OF GERONTOCRACY

A stationary population is a part of a steady-state economy. Assuming present mortality rates, the attainment of a stationary population would imply an increase in the average age of the population from the current 27 to about 37 years. This raises fears of social senility, excessive conservatism, loss of adaptability and dynamism, and so on. This hardly seems a reasonable fear, even for devotees of the 'Pepsi generation'. One need only compare Sweden, with one of the oldest age structures, to, say, Brazil with one of the youngest. It would certainly be stretching things a bit to say that old Sweden is a reactionary, non-innovative gerontocracy, while young Brazil is a progressive, innovative country run by young people. One might just as well argue that Brazil values youth less than Sweden because its infant mortality rates are higher, and therefore Sweden is more youth-oriented than Brazil. Such arguments are *simpliste* at best.

FRUSTRATED PYRAMID CLIMBERS

The stationary population 'pyramid' would be shaped more like a house (rectangular up to about age 50, where the roof begins and rapidly tapers to a peak). But the structure of authority in hierarchical organizations remains a pyramid. Thus, there would in the future be less of a congruence between advancing age and advancing position. More people would grow older at lower levels of authority, and many ambitions would be frustrated.

The observation is a highly interesting one, and no doubt has important sociological implications. But they are not all negative by any means. More individuals will learn to seek personal fulfillment outside of hierarchical organizations. Within such organizations fewer people will be automatically promoted to their level of incompetence, thus thwarting the so far relentless working of the Peter Principle. Perhaps giant bureaucracies will even begin to dissolve and life will reorganize on a more human scale.

PASCAL'S WAGER REVISITED

The growthmania position rests on the hypothesis that technical change can become entirely problem-solving and not at all problem-creating and can continually perform successively more impressive encores as resources are depleted. There is sufficient evidence to make reasonable people quite doubtful about this hypothesis. Yet, it cannot be definitely disproved. There is a certain amount of faith involved, and faith is risky. Let us then take a completely agnostic position and apply the logic of Pascal's Wager and statistical decision theory. We can err in two ways: we can accept the omnipotent technology hypothesis and then discover that it is false, or we can reject it and later discover that it is true. Which error do we most wish to avoid? If we accept the false hypothesis, the result will be catastrophic. If we reject the true hypothesis, we will forego marginal satisfactions and will have to learn to share, which, though difficult, might well be good for us. If we later discover that the hypothesis is true we could always resume growth. Thus, even in the agnostic case it would seem prudent to reject the omnipotent technology hypothesis, along with its corollary that reproducible capital is a near perfect substitute for resources.

NOTES

1. The lower the throughput the longer lived is the stock of wealth. Conceivably, commodities could last too long, though that hardly seems to be an immediate danger.
2. Fortunately, this is less true for agricultural economists, who have always kept at least one foot in the real biophysical world.

3. Nordhaus and Tobin (1970) state that the 'tacit assumption of environmentalists is that no substitutes are available for natural resources'. They consider this an extreme position, but what substitute is there for natural resources? They offer 'reproducible capital', but in addition to requiring natural resources for its very reproduction, capital funds are clearly complements to resource flows, not substitutes. The fact that one resource flow may substitute for another, if the capital fund is redesigned to allow it, is no basis for saying that the generic factor of capital is a substitute for the generic factor of natural resource!

4. The 'optimistic' conclusion of this paper is that 'assuming reasonable management practices and adaptations, the remaining mineral resource base of the earth is sufficient to maintain the present state of material affluence of the United States, and to share it to some meaningful degree with the rest of the world, for at least the next hundred years' (Goeller, 1972, p. 1; my italics). In other words, if we move rapidly and efficiently to a steady state at present levels, and draw on all the world's resources, and limit our sharing with the rest of the world to some 'meaningful degree', our system could continue for the next hundred years! Such 'optimism' makes pessimism redundant.

5. This is apparently an empirical generalization by Commoner, based on an observed inverse relationship between power productivity and labor productivity during the period 1946–68 (see Commoner, 1971b, Fig. 31).

6. Elsewhere I have argued for a system of depletion quotas auctioned by the government as the basic institution, with effluent taxes as a fine-tuning supplement. See Daly (1973).

7. This tacit assumption sometimes becomes explicit, as in the following quotation from Samuel H. Ordway, president of a great oil company:

    > the fact seems to be that the first [resource] storehouse in which man found himself was only one of a series. As he used up what was piled in that first room, he found he could fashion a key to open a door into a much larger room. And as he used up the contents of this larger room, he discovered there was another room beyond, larger still. The room in which we stand at the middle of the twentieth century is so vast that its walls are beyond sight. Yet it is probably still quite near the beginning of the whole series of storehouses. It is not inconceivable that the entire globe – earth, ocean and air – represents raw material for mankind to utilize with more and more ingenuity and skill. (1953, p. 28)

    The above is also the assumption of orthodox growth economics. Even if this vision were correct, one should add that eventually we must live in the same rooms we work in. Living in intimate contact with garbage and noxious wastes is a by-product of growth. But then, optimists will argue that there is another infinite series of ever larger garbage dumps! The whole conceptual basis of the growth faith is equivalent to a generalization of the chain-letter swindle. There will always be five new resources for every depleted resource. The current beneficiaries of the swindle, those at the beginning of the chain, try hard to keep up the illusion among those doubters out at the end who are beginning to wonder if there are really sufficient people or resources in the world for the game to continue very much longer.

REFERENCES

Barclay, P. and D. Seclar (1972), *Economic Growth and Environmental Decay: The Solution Becomes the Problem*, New York: Harcourt, Brace, and Jovanovich, Inc.

Boulding, K.E. (1970), *Economics as a Science*, New York: McGraw-Hill.

Commoner, B. (1971a), *The Closing Circle*, New York: Alfred A. Knopf.

Commoner, B. (1971b), Power consumption and human welfare, paper presented at the American Association for the Advancement of Science Convention, Philadelphia, December 1971.

Daly, H.E. (1971), Toward a stationary-state economy, in J. Harte and R. Socolow, eds., *Patient Earth*, New York: Holt, Rinehart, and Winston, pp. 226–44.

Daly, H.E., ed. (1973), *Toward a Steady-state Economy*, San Francisco, CA: W.H. Freeman Co.

Daly, H.E. (1977), *Steady-state Economics*, San Francisco, CA: W.H. Freeman Co.

Editors (1972), A blueprint for survival, *The Ecologist*, **2**(1), 1–43.

Ehrlich, P.R., A.H. Ehrlich, and J. Holdren (1972), *Population/Resources/Environment*, San Francisco, CA: W.H. Freeman Co.

Georgescu-Roegen, N. (1971), *The Entropy Law and the Economic Process*, Cambridge, MA: Harvard University Press.

Goeller, H.E. (1972), An optimistic outlook for mineral resources, paper presented at *Scarcity and Growth* conference, National Commission on Materials Policy, University of Minnesota, June 1972, mimeo.

Jacoby, N. (1970), The environmental crisis, *Center Magazine*, **III**(6), 37–48.

Marx, K. (1967), *Capital*, Vol. I, New York: International Publishers, pp. 505–6.

Meadows, D.H., D.L. Meadows, J. Randers, and W.W. Behrens III (1972), *The Limits to Growth*, New York: Universe Books.

Mill, J.S. (1961), Of stationary state, Book IV in *Principles of Political Economy*, New York: August Kelley, Reprints of Economic Classics.

Mishan, E.H. (1967), *The Costs of Economic Growth*, New York: Frederick A. Praeger Co.

Nordhaus, W. and J. Tobin (1970), Is growth obsolete? National Bureau of Economic Research, Colloquium, San Francisco, December 10, 1970, mimeo.

Ordway, S.H. (1953), *Resources and the American Dream*, New York: Ronald Press.

Passell, P., M. Roberts, and L. Ross (1972), Review of Limits to Growth, *New York Times Book Review*, April 2, p. 12.

President, United States (1971), *Economic Report of the President*, Washington DC: US Government Printing Office.

Robinson, J. (1972), The second crisis of economic theory, *American Economic Review*, **62**, 1–10.

Royall, N. N., Jr. (1970), Review of *Limits to Growth*, *Kansas City Times*, April 28, p. 42.

Wallich, H. (1972), Zero Growth, *Newsweek*, **79**, 62.

Weisskopf, W.A. (1971), *Alienation and Economics*, New York: E.P. Dutton and Co., Inc.

PART II

Later extensions into standard economics

4. Towards an environmental macroeconomics

INTRODUCTION

Environmental economics, as it is taught in universities and practiced in government agencies and development banks, is overwhelmingly micro-economics. The theoretical focus is on prices, and the big issue is how to internalize external environmental costs so as to arrive at prices that reflect full social marginal opportunity costs. Once prices are right the environmental problem is 'solved' – there is no macroeconomic dimension. There are, of course, very good reasons for environmental economics to be closely tied to microeconomics, and it is not my intention to argue against that connection. Rather I want to ask if there is not a neglected connection between the environment and macroeconomics.

A search through the indexes of three leading textbooks in macroeconomics (Barro, 1987; Dornbusch and Fischer, 1987; Hall and Taylor, 1988) reveals no entries under any of the following subjects: environment, natural resources, pollution, depletion. Is it really the case, as prominent textbook writers seem to think, that macroeconomics has nothing to do with the environment? What historically has impeded the development of an environmental macroeconomics? If there is no such thing as environmental macroeconomics, should there be? What might it look like?

The reason that environmental macroeconomics is an empty box[1] lies in what Thomas Kuhn calls a 'paradigm', and what Joseph Schumpeter more descriptively called a 'pre-analytic vision'. As Schumpeter emphasized, analysis has to start somewhere – there has to be something to analyse. That something is given by a pre-analytic cognitive act that Schumpeter called 'vision'. One might say that vision is what the 'right brain' supplies to the 'left brain' for analysis. Whatever is omitted from the pre-analytic vision cannot be recaptured by subsequent analysis. Schumpeter is worth quoting at length on this point:

> In practice we all start our own research from the work of our predecessors, that is, we hardly ever start from scratch. But suppose we did start from

scratch, what are the steps we should have to take? Obviously, in order to be able to posit to ourselves any problems at all, we should first have to visualize a distinct set of coherent phenomena as a worthwhile object of our analytic effort. In other words, analytic effort is of necessity preceded by a pre-analytic cognitive act that supplies the raw material for the analytic effort. In this book, this pre-analytic cognitive act will be called Vision. It is interesting to note that vision of this kind not only must precede historically the emergence of analytic effort in any field, but also may re-enter the history of every established science each time somebody teaches us to see things in a light of which the source is not to be found in the facts, methods, and results of the pre-existing state of the science. (Schumpeter, 1954, p. 41)

The vision of modern economics in general, and especially of macro-economics, is the familiar circular flow diagram. The macroeconomy is seen as an isolated system (in other words, no exchanges of matter or energy with its environment) in which exchange value circulates between firms and households in a closed loop. What is 'flowing in a circle' is variously referred to as production or consumption, but these have physical dimensions, and the circular flow does not refer to materials recycling, which in any case could not be a completely closed loop, and of course would require energy which cannot be recycled at all. What is truly flowing in a circle can only be abstract exchange value, exchange value abstracted from the physical dimensions of the goods and factors that are exchanged. Since an isolated system of abstract exchange value flowing in a circle has no dependence on an environment, there can be no problem of natural resource depletion, nor environmental pollution, nor any dependence of the macroeconomy on natural services, or indeed on anything at all outside itself (Georgescu-Roegen, 1971; Daly, 1985).

Since analysis cannot supply what the pre-analytic vision omits, it is only to be expected that macroeconomics texts would be silent on environment, natural resources, depletion, and pollution. It is as if the pre-analytic vision that biologists had of animals recognized only the circulatory system and abstracted completely from the digestive tract. A biology textbook's index would then contain no entry under 'assimila-tion' or 'liver'. The dependence of the animal on its environment would not be evident. It would appear as a perpetual motion machine.

Things are no better when we turn to the advanced chapters at the end of most macroeconomics texts, where the topic is growth theory. True to the pre-analytic vision the aggregate production function is written as $Y = f(K,L)$, in other words, output is a function of capital (K) and labor stocks (L). Resource flows (R) do not even enter! Neither is any waste output flow noted. And if occasionally R is stuck in the function along with K and L it makes little difference since the production function is almost always a multiplicative form, such as Cobb–Douglas, in which R can approach zero with Y constant if only we increase K or L in a compensatory fashion. Resources are seen as 'necessary' for production, but the amount required can be as little as one likes!

What is needed is not ever more refined analysis of a faulty vision, but a new vision. This does not mean that everything built on the old vision will necessarily have to be scrapped – but fundamental changes are likely when the pre-analytic vision is altered. The necessary change in vision is to picture the macroeconomy as an open subsystem of the finite natural ecosystem (environment) and not as an isolated circular flow of abstract exchange value, unconstrained by mass balance, entropy, and finitude. The circular flow of exchange value is a useful abstraction for some purposes. It highlights issues of aggregate demand, unemployment, and inflation that were of interest to Keynes in his analysis of the Great Depression. But it casts an impenetrable shadow on all physical relation-ships between the macroeconomy and the environment. For Keynes this shadow was not very important, but for us it is. Once the macroeconomy is viewed as an open subsystem, rather than an isolated system, then the issue of its relation to its parent system (the environment) cannot be avoided. And the most obvious question is how big should the subsystem be relative to the overall system?

THE MACROECONOMICS OF OPTIMAL SCALE

Just as the micro unit of the economy (firm or household) operates as part of a larger system (the aggregate or macroeconomy), so the aggregate economy is likewise a part of a larger system, the natural ecosystem. The macroeconomy is an open subsystem of the ecosystem and is totally dependent upon it, both as a source for inputs of low-entropy matter-energy and as a sink for outputs of high-entropy matter-energy. The physical exchanges crossing the boundary between system and subsystem constitute the subject matter of environmental macroeconomics. These flows are considered in terms of their scale or total volume relative to the ecosystem, not in terms of the price of one component of the total flow relative to another. Just as standard macro-economics focuses on the volume of transactions rather than the relative prices of different items traded, so environmental macroeconomics focuses on the volume of exchanges that cross the boundary between system and subsystem, rather than the pricing and allocation of each part of the total flow within the human economy, or even within the nonhuman part of the ecosystem.

The term 'scale' is shorthand for 'the physical scale or size of the human presence in the ecosystem, as measured by population times per capita resource use'. Optimal allocation of a given scale of resource flow within the economy is one thing (a microeconomic problem). Optimal scale of the whole economy relative to the ecosystem is an entirely different problem (a macro-macro problem). The micro allocation problem is analogous to allocating optimally a given amount of weight in a boat. But once the best relative location of weight has been determined, there is still the question of the absolute amount of weight the boat should carry, even when optimally allocated. This absolute optimal scale of load is recognized in the maritime institution of the Plimsoll line. When the watermark hits the Plimsoll line the boat is full, it has reached its safe carrying capacity. Of course if the weight is badly allocated the waterline will touch the Plimsoll mark sooner. But eventually as the absolute load is increased the watermark will reach the Plimsoll line even for a boat whose load is optimally allocated. Optimally loaded boats will still sink under too much weight – even though they may sink optimally! It should be clear that optimal allocation and optimal scale are quite distinct problems. The major task of environmental macroeconomics is to design an economic institution analogous to the Plimsoll mark – to keep the weight, the absolute scale, of the economy from sinking our biospheric ark.

The market of course functions only within the economic subsystem, where it does only one thing: it solves the allocation problem by providing the necessary information and incentive. It does that one thing very well, given certain well-known assumptions. What it does not do is to solve the problems of optimal scale or of optimal distribution. The market's inability to solve the problem of just distribution is widely recognized, but its similar inability to solve the problem of optimal or even sustainable scale is not as widely appreciated.[2]

An example of the confusion that can result from the non-recognition of the independence of the scale issue from the question of allocation is provided by the following dilemma (Pearce et al., 1989, p. 135). Which puts more pressure on the environment, a high or a low discount rate? The usual answer is that a high discount rate is worse for the environment because it speeds the rate of depletion of nonrenewable resources and shortens the turnover and fallow periods in the exploitation of renewables. It shifts the allocation of capital and labor toward projects that exploit natural resources more intensively. But it restricts the total number of projects undertaken. A low discount rate will permit more projects to be undertaken even while encouraging less intensive resource use for each project. The allocation effect of a high discount rate is to increase throughput, but the scale effect is to lower throughput. Which effect is stronger is hard to say, although one suspects that over the long run the scale effect will dominate. The resolution to the dilemma is to recognize that two independent policy goals require two independent policy instruments – we cannot serve both optimal scale and optimal allocation with the single policy instrument of the discount rate (Tinbergen, 1952). The discount rate should be allowed to solve the allocation problem, within the confines of a solution to the scale problem provided by a presently nonexistent policy instrument that we may for now call an 'economic Plimsoll line' that limits the scale of the throughput. Economists have recognized the independence of the goals of efficient allocation and just distribution and are in general agreement that it is better to let prices serve efficiency, and to serve equity with income redistribution policies. Proper scale is a third independent policy goal and requires a third policy instrument. This latter point has not yet been accepted by economists, but its logic is parallel to the logic underlying the separation of allocation and distribution.

Microeconomics has not discovered in the price system any built-in tendency to grow only up to the scale of aggregate resource use that is optimal (or even merely sustainable) in its demands on the biosphere. Optimal scale, like distributive justice, full employment, or price level stability, is a macroeconomic goal. And it is a goal that is likely to conflict with the other macroeconomic goals. The traditional solution to unemployment is growth in production, which means a larger scale. Frequently the solution to inflation is also thought to be growth in real output and a larger scale. And most of all the issue of distributive justice is 'finessed' by the claim that aggregate growth will do more for the poor than redistributive measures. Macroeconomic goals tend to conflict, and certainly optimal scale conflicts with any goal that requires further growth, once the optimum has been reached.

HOW BIG IS THE ECONOMY?

Probably the best index of the scale of the human economy as a part of the biosphere is the percentage of human appropriation of the total world product of photosynthesis. Net primary production (NPP) is the amount of solar energy captured in photosynthesis by primary producers, less the energy used in their own growth and reproduction. NPP is thus the basic food resource for everything on earth not capable of photosynthesis. Vitousek et al. (1986) calculate that 25 percent of potential global (terrestrial and aquatic) NPP is now appropriated by human beings. If only terrestrial NPP is considered, the fraction rises to 40 percent.[3] Taking the 25 percent figure for the entire world it is apparent that two more doublings of the human scale will give 100 percent. Since this would mean zero energy left for all nonhuman and nondomesticated species, and since humans cannot survive without the services of ecosystems, which are made up of other species, it is clear that two more doublings of the human scale is an ecological impossibility, although arithmetically possible. Furthermore, the terrestrial figure of 40 percent is probably more relevant since we are unlikely to increase our take from the oceans very much. Total appropriation of the terrestrial NPP is only a bit over one doubling time in the future. Perhaps it is theoretically possible to increase the Earth's total photosynthetic capacity somewhat, but the actual trend of past economic growth is decidedly in the opposite direction. If the above figures are approximately correct, then expansion of the world economy by a factor of four (two doublings) is not possible. Yet the Brundtland Commission calls for economic expansion by a factor of five to ten. And the greenhouse effect, ozone layer depletion, and acid rain all constitute evidence that we have already gone beyond a prudent Plimsoll line for the scale of the macroeconomy.

HOW BIG SHOULD THE ECONOMY BE?

Optimal scale of a single activity is not a strange concept to economists. Indeed microeconomics is about little else. An activity is identified, be it producing shoes or consuming ice cream. A cost function and a benefit function for the activity in question are defined. Good reasons are given for believing that marginal costs increase and marginal benefits decline as the scale of the activity grows. The message of microeconomics is to expand the scale of the activity in question up to the point where marginal costs equal marginal benefits, a condition that defines the optimal scale. All of microeconomics is an extended variation of this theme.

When we move to macroeconomics, however, we never again hear about optimal scale. There is apparently no optimal scale for the macroeconomy. There are no cost and benefit functions defined for growth in scale of the economy as a whole. It just does not matter how many people there are, or how much they each consume, as long as the proportions and relative prices are right! But if every micro activity has an optimal scale then why does not the aggregate of all micro activities have an optimal scale? If I am told in reply that the reason is that the constraint on any one activity is the fixity of all the others and that when all economic activities increase proportionally the restraints cancel out, then I will invite the economist to increase the scale of the carbon cycle and the hydrologic cycle in proportion to the growth of industry and agriculture. I will admit that if the ecosystem can grow indefinitely then so can the aggregate economy. But, until the surface of the earth begins to grow at a rate equal to the rate of interest, one should not take this answer too seriously. The indifference to scale of the macroeconomy is due to the pre-analytic vision of the economy as an isolated system – a view the inappropriateness of which has already been discussed.

Two concepts of optimal scale can be distinguished, both formalisms at this stage, but important for clarity.

1. *The anthropocentric optimum*. The rule is to expand scale, in other words, grow, to the point at which the marginal benefit to human beings of additional manmade physical capital is just equal to the marginal cost to human beings of sacrificed natural capital. All nonhuman species and their habitats are valued only instrumentally according to their capacity to satisfy human wants. Their intrinsic value (capacity to enjoy their own lives) is assumed to be zero.
2. *The biocentric optimum*. Other species and their habitats are preserved beyond the point of maximum instrumental convenience, out of recognition that other species have intrinsic value independent of their instrumental value to human beings. The biocentric optimal scale of the human niche would therefore be smaller than the anthropocentric optimum. The notion of sustainable development does not specify which concept of optimal scale to use. Sustainability is a necessary, but not sufficient condition for optimal scale and for the further elaboration of an environmental macroeconomics.

NOTES

1. The box is not entirely empty. Recent work on correcting national income accounts, along with applications of input–output models to environmental problems, should be noted.
2. This can be illustrated in terms of the familiar microeconomic tool of the Edgeworth box. Moving to the contract curve is an improvement in efficiency of allocation. Moving along the contract curve is a change in distribution, which may be deemed just or unjust on ethical grounds. The scale is represented by the dimensions of the box, which are taken as given. Consequently the issue of optimal scale of the box itself escapes the limits of the analytical tool. A microeconomic tool cannot be expected to answer a macroeconomic question. But so far macroeconomics has not

answered the question either – indeed, has not even asked it. The tacit answer to the implicit question seems to be that a bigger Edgeworth box is always better than a smaller one.

3. The definition of human appropriation underlying the figures quoted includes direct use by human beings (food, fuel, fiber, timber), plus the reduction from the potential due to degradation of ecosystems caused by humans. The latter reflects deforestation, desertification, paving over, and human conversion to less productive systems (such as agriculture).

REFERENCES

Barro, R.J. (1987), *Macroeconomics*, 2nd edn, New York: John Wiley and Sons.

Daly, H.E. (1985), The circular flow of exchange value and the linear throughput of matter-energy: a case of misplaced concreteness, *Review of Social Economy*, **43**(3), 279–97.

Dornbusch, R. and S. Fischer (1987), *Macroeconomics*, 4th edn, New York: McGraw-Hill.

Georgescu-Roegen, N. (1971), *The Entropy Law and the Economic Process*, Cambridge, MA: Harvard University Press.

Hall, R.E. and J.B. Taylor (1988), *Macroeconomics*, 2nd edn, New York: W.W. Norton.

Pearce, D., A. Markandya, and E.B. Barbier (1989), *Blueprint for a Green Economy*, London: Earthscan, Ltd., p. 135.

Schumpeter, J. (1954), *History of Economic Analysis*, New York: Oxford University Press, p. 41.

Tinbergen, J. (1952), *On the Theory of Economic Policy*, Amsterdam: North-Holland Press.

Vitousek, P.M., P.R. Ehrlich, A.H. Ehrlich, and P.A. Matson (1986), Human appropriation of the products of photosynthesis, *BioScience*, **34** (May), 368–73.

5. Growth, debt and the World Bank

When I was in graduate school in economics in the early 1960s we were taught that capital was the limiting factor in growth and development. Just inject capital into an economy and it would grow. As the economy grew, you could then re-invest the growth increment as new capital and make the economy grow exponentially. Social development would follow. Originally, to get things started, capital came from savings, from confiscation, or from foreign aid or investment, but later out of the national growth increment itself. Capital embodied technology, the source of its power. Capital was magic stuff, but scarce. It all seemed convincing at the time.[1]

Many years later (early 1990s) when I worked for the World Bank it was evident that capital was no longer the limiting factor. Trillions of dollars of capital was circling the globe looking for projects in which to become invested so it could grow. The World Bank understood that in practice, if not in theory, the limiting factor was what they called 'bankable projects' – concrete investments that could embody abstract financial capital and make its value grow at an acceptable rate, usually 10 percent per annum or more, doubling every seven years.

Since there were not enough bankable projects to absorb the available financial capital the World Bank decided to stimulate the creation of such projects with 'country development teams' set up in the borrowing countries, but with World Bank technical assistance. No doubt many such projects were useful, but it was still hard to grow at 10 percent without involuntarily displacing people, or running down natural capital and counting it as income, both of which were done on a grand scale.

And the loans had to be repaid. Of course they did get repaid, frequently not out of the earnings of the projects which were often disappointing, but out of the general tax revenues of the borrowing governments. Lending to sovereign governments with the ability to tax greatly increases the likelihood of being repaid – and perhaps encourages a bit of laxity in approving projects.

Where did all this excess financial capital come from? Not so much from savings (China excepted), but mainly from new money and easy credit generated by fractional reserve banking systems, amplified by increased leverage in the purchase of stocks, and recently by 'financial innovation' – in other words, the invention of complex 'assets' that are basically 'bets on debts' – on whether or not they will be repaid. The increased concentration of ownership of financial wealth also intensified the search for places to invest the owner's growing excess capital. The basic money supply underlying all this 'innovation' lost its last fictitious or at least tenuous contact with anything physical in 1971 with the abolition of gold convertibility for foreign officially held dollars. The US money supply (the world's reserve currency) is now fiat currency (non-interest-bearing government debt), plus demand deposits (interest-bearing debt issued by private banks). The latter is a large multiple of the former.

Most of this new money is borrowed into existence by people who think they can make it grow at a rate greater than the rate of interest. They use it to bid real resources away from existing uses (or idleness if there is unemployment) by offering a higher price. If the new uses are profitable then the temporary rise in prices is offset by new production – by growth. But increasing natural resource and environmental scarcity, along with a shortage of bankable projects, put the brakes on this growth, and resulted in too much financial capital trying to become incarnate in too few bankable projects, and led to low rates of return as 'not-so-bankable' projects were financed.

So the World Bank had to figure out why its projects yielded low returns. The answer just outlined was ideologically unacceptable because it suggested both ecological limits to real growth and a swelling of the financial sector – which now absorbs some 40 percent of total profit. Growth, after all, is the sanctified solution to all our problems and the apple cart would be totally upset without it.

A more acceptable answer soon became clear to World Bank economists – microeconomic projects could not be productive in macroeconomic circumstances of irrational and inefficient government policy. The solution was to restructure the macroeconomies by 'structural adjustment' – free trade, export-led growth, privatization, deregulation, balanced budgets, control of inflation, elimination of social subsidies, suspension of labor and environmental protection laws – the so-called Washington Consensus. This was frequently referred to as the elimination of 'distortions'. How to convince borrowing countries to make these painful 'structural adjustments' at the macro level to create the environment, free of 'distortions', in which World Bank-financed projects would be productive?

The answer was, conveniently, a new form of lending, structural adjustment loans, to encourage or bribe the policy reforms stipulated by the term 'structural adjustment'. An added reason for structural adjustment, or 'policy lending', was to move lots of dollars quickly to countries like Mexico to ease their balance of payments difficulty in repaying loans they had made from private US banks. Also, policy loans, now about half of World Bank lending, require no lengthy and expensive planning, construction, and supervision the way project loans do. The World Bank definition of efficiency became, it seemed, 'to move the maximum amount of money with the minimum of time, effort, and thought'.

Why, one might ask, would a country borrow money at interest to make policy changes that it could make on its own without any loans, if it thought the policies were good ones? Maybe they did not really favor the policies, and therefore needed a bribe to do what was 'in their own best interests'. Or maybe the goal of the current borrowing government was simply to get the new loan, splash the money around among friends and relatives, and leave the next government to pay it back with interest. Similar behavior in the United States is not unknown.

Such thoughts got little attention at the World Bank, which was spooked by the specter of an impending 'negative payments flow', that is, repayments of old loans plus interest greater than the volume of new loans. Would the World Bank eventually cease to be a creditor and disappear as unnecessary? A horrible thought for any bureaucracy! But the alternative to a negative payments flow for the World Bank is ever-increasing debt for the borrowing countries. Of course the World Bank did not claim to be in the business of increasing the debt of poor countries. Rather, as I was taught in the 1960s, it saw itself as fostering growth by injecting capital and increasing the debtor countries' capacity to absorb capital from outside. So what if the debt grew, as long as GDP was growing. The critical (and tacit) assumption was that the real sector could grow as fast as the financial sector – that physical wealth could grow as fast as monetary debt, and therefore the debt could be repaid. And as long as the old loans were being repaid on schedule then new loans could continue to be made.

The main goal of the World Bank is to make loans, to be a money pump. If financial capital were really the limiting factor then countries would line up with good 'bankable projects' and the World Bank would allocate capital to the best ones. But financial capital is superabundant and good projects are scarce, so the World Bank had to actively push the money. To speed up the pump they send country development teams out to invent projects; if the projects fail, then they invent structural adjustment loans to induce a more favorable macro context; if structural adjustment loans are treated as bribes by corrupt borrowing governments, the World Bank does not complain too much for fear of slowing the money pump and incurring a 'negative payments flow'.

If capital is no longer the limiting factor whose presence unleashes economic growth, then two big questions arise: (1) what is 'capital' anyway? and (2) has another factor become limiting?

WHAT IS 'CAPITAL'?

'Capital', said Nobel chemist and pioneer ecological economist Frederick Soddy,[2] 'merely means unearned income divided by the rate of interest and multiplied by 100' (1924, p. 27). He further explained that, 'Although it may comfort the lender to think that his wealth still exists somewhere in the form of "capital," it has been or is being used up by the borrower either in consumption or investment, and no more than food or fuel can it be used again later. Rather it has become debt, an indent on future revenues ...'. In other words capital in the financial sense is the perennial net revenue stream expected from the project it will finance, divided by the assumed rate of interest and multiplied by 100. Rather than magic growth-producing real stuff, it is a hypothetical calculation of the present value of a permanent lien on the future real production of the economy. The fact that the lien can be traded among individuals for real wealth in the present does not change the fact that it is still a lien against the future revenue of society – in a word it is a debt that the future must pay, no matter who owns it or how often it is traded as an asset in the present.[3]

Soddy believed that the ruling passion of our age is to convert wealth into debt in order to derive a permanent future income from it – to convert wealth that perishes into debt that endures, debt that does not rot or rust, costs nothing to maintain, and brings in perennial 'unearned income', as both Internal Revenue Service (IRS) accountants and Marxists accurately call it. No individual could amass the physical requirements sufficient for maintenance during old age, for like manna it would spoil if accumulated much beyond current need. Therefore one must convert one's non-storable current surplus into a lien on future revenue by letting others consume and invest one's surplus now in exchange for the right to share in the expected future revenue. But future real physical revenue simply cannot grow as fast as symbolic monetary debt! In Soddy's words: 'You cannot permanently pit an absurd human convention, such as the spontaneous increment of debt [compound interest], against the natural law of the spontaneous decrement of wealth [entropy]' (1924, p. 30).

In case that is a too abstract statement of a too general principle, Soddy gave a simple example. Minus two pigs (debt) is a mathematical quantity having no physical existence, and the population of negative pigs can grow without limit. Plus two pigs (wealth) is a physical quantity, and its growth is limited by the need to feed the pigs, dispose of their waste, find space for them, and so on. Both may grow at a given x percent for a while, but before long the population of negative pigs will greatly outnumber that of the positive pigs, because the population of positive pigs is limited by the physical constraints of a finite and entropic world. The value of a negative pig will fall to a small fraction of the value of a positive pig. Owners of negative pigs will be greatly disappointed and angered when they try to exchange them for positive pigs. In today's terms, instead of negative pigs, think 'unfunded pension liabilities' or 'sub-prime mortgages'.

Soddy went on to speculate about how historically we came to confuse wealth with debt:

> Because formerly ownership of land – which, with the sunshine that falls on it, provides a revenue of wealth – secured, in the form of rent, a share in the annual harvest without labor or service, upon which a cultured and leisured class could permanently establish itself, the age seems to have conceived the preposterous notion that money, which can buy land, must therefore itself have the same revenue producing power.[4]

The idea that future people can live off the interest of their mutual indebtedness is just another perpetual motion delusion. The exponentially growing indent of debt on future real revenue will, in a finite and entropic world, become greater than future producers are either willing or able to transfer to owners of the debt. Debt will be repudiated either by inflation, bankruptcy, or confiscation, likely leading to serious violence.

This prospect of violence especially bothered Soddy because, as the discoverer of the existence of isotopes, he had contributed substantially to the theory of atomic structure that made atomic energy feasible. He predicted in 1926 that the first fruit of this discovery would be a bomb of unprecedented power. He lived to see his prediction come true. Removing the economic causes of conflict therefore became for him a kind of redeeming priority.

HAS ANOTHER FACTOR BECOME LIMITING?

Capital used to be considered the limiting factor in economic growth. If capital is no longer the limiting factor then what, if anything, is? And what, besides the World Bank experience already discussed, makes me think that capital is not the limiting factor?

Consider. What limits the annual fish catch – fishing boats (capital) or remaining fish in the sea (natural resources)? Clearly the latter. What limits barrels crude oil extracted – drilling rigs and pumps, or remaining accessible deposits of petroleum – or capacity of the atmosphere to absorb the CO_2 from burning petroleum?[5] What limits production of cut timber – number of chain saws and lumber mills, or standing forests and their rate of growth? What limits irrigated agriculture – pumps and sprinklers, or aquifer recharge rates and river flow volumes? That should be enough to at least suggest that we live in a natural resource-constrained world, not a capital-constrained world.

Economic logic says to invest in and economize on the limiting factor. Economic logic has not changed; what has changed is the limiting factor. It is now natural resources, not capital, that we must economize on and invest in. Economists in general, and the World Bank in particular, have not recognized this fundamental shift in the pattern of scarcity. Soddy predicted the shift 50 years ago. He argued that mankind ultimately lives on current sunshine (captured with the aid of plants, soil and water) – temporarily supplemented by the release of trapped sunshine of Paleozoic summers that is being rapidly depleted to fuel what he called 'the flamboyant age'.

What has kept economists from recognizing Soddy's insight? In part a theoretical commitment to factor substitutability and a neglect of complementarity by today's neoclassical economists. In the absence of complementarity there can be no limiting factor – if capital and natural resources are substitutes in production then neither can be limiting – if one is in short supply you just substitute the other and continue producing. Since economists used to believe that capital was the limiting factor, they implicitly must have believed in complementarity between capital and natural resources back in the empty-world economy. But when resources became limiting in the new full-world economy, rather than recognizing the shift in the pattern of scarcity, they abandoned the whole idea of limiting factor by emphasizing substitutability to the exclusion of complementarity. The new reason for emphasizing capital over natural resources is the claim that capital is a near perfect substitute for resources.

Nordhaus and Tobin (1972) were quite explicit:

> The prevailing standard model of growth assumes that there are no limits on the feasibility of expanding the supplies of nonhuman agents of production. It is basically a two-factor model in which production depends only on labor and reproducible capital. Land and resources, the third member of the

classical triad, have generally been dropped [...] the tacit justification has
been that reproducible capital is a near perfect substitute for land and other
exhaustible resources.

The claim that capital is a near perfect substitute for natural resources is
absurd. For one thing substitution is reversible. If capital is a near perfect
substitute for resources, then resources are a near perfect substitute for
capital – so why then did we ever bother to accumulate capital in the first
place if nature already endowed us with a near perfect substitute?

It is not for nothing that our system is called 'capitalism' rather than
'natural resource-ism'. It is ideologically inconvenient for capitalism if
capital is no longer the limiting factor. But that inconvenience has been
met by claiming that capital is a good substitute for natural resources.
The animus of neoclassical economics is to deny any fundamental
dependence on nature – either nature is not scarce and capital is limiting;
or nature's scarcity does not matter because manmade capital is a near
perfect substitute for natural resources. In either case man is in control of
nature thanks to capital.

The absurdity of the claim that capital and natural resources are good
substitutes has been further demonstrated by Georgescu-Roegen (1971)
in his fund-flow theory of production. It recognizes that factors of
production are of two qualitatively different kinds: (1) resource flows that
are physically transformed into flows of product and waste; and (2)
capital and labor funds, the agents or instruments of transformation that
are not themselves physically embodied in the product. There are varying
degrees of substitution between different natural resource flows, and
between the funds of labor and capital. But the basic relation between
resource flow on the one hand, and capital (or labor) fund on the other, is
complementarity. Efficient cause (capital) does not substitute for material
cause (resources). You cannot bake the same cake with half the ingredients no matter if you double or triple the number of cooks and ovens.
Funds and flows are complements.

Further, capital, we have seen, is current surplus production exchanged
for a lien against future production – physically it is made from natural
resources. It is not easy to substitute away from natural resources when
the substitute is itself made from natural resources.[6]

If capital finances a project that embodies new technology that can
extract new resources from the Earth more rapidly than before, then the
debt (that used to be capital) can be paid off with interest, and with some
of the extra revenue left over as profit. But this requires an increased
entropic throughput of matter and energy, as well as increased labor – in
other words it requires physical growth of the economy – a lot more than

a mere injection of 'capital' into a hypothetical world of unlimited labor, and unlimited natural resources. Such growth in yesterday's empty-world economy was temporarily feasible – in today's full-world economy it is not. To be economic the benefit of physical growth today must overcome an ever larger opportunity cost of depleted resources, displaced eco-system services, displaced people, destroyed livelihoods, and ruined habitats of other species. The fact that these costs were often ignored did not make them go away.

It is now generally recognized, even by economists, that there is far too much debt worldwide, both public and private. The reason so much debt was incurred is that we have had absurdly unrealistic expectations about the efficacy of capital to produce the real growth needed to redeem the debt that is 'capital' by another name. In other words the debt that piled up in failed attempts to make wealth grow as fast as debt is evidence of the reality of limits to growth. But instead of being seen as such by the World Bank, it is taken as the main reason to attempt still more growth by issuing more debt.

The wishful thought leading to such unfounded expectations was the belief that by growth we would cure poverty without the need to share. As the poor got richer the rich could get still richer! Few expected that aggregate growth itself would become uneconomic, would begin to cost us more than it was worth at the margin, making us collectively poorer, not richer. But it did.[7] In spite of that, our economists, bankers, and politicians still have unrealistic expectations about growth. Like the losing gambler, they try to get even by betting double or nothing on more growth.

Could we not at least take a short time-out from growth roulette to reconsider the steady-state economy? After all the idea is deeply rooted in classical economics, as well as in physics and biology. Perpetual motion and infinite growth are not reasonable premises on which to base economic policy.

At some level many people surely know this. Why then do we keep growth as the top national priority? First, we are misled because our measure of growth, GDP, counts only 'economic activity' thereby conflating costs and benefits, rather than comparing them at the margin. Second, because even though the benefits of further growth are now less than the costs, our decision-making elites have figured out how to keep the benefits for themselves while 'sharing' the costs with the poor, the future, and other species. The elite-owned media, the corporate-funded think tanks, the kept economists of high academia, and the World Bank – all sing hymns to growth in perfect unison, and bamboozle average citizens.[8]

What is going to happen?

NOTES

1. These views were largely based on W. Arthur Lewis's 1954 classic 'Economic development with unlimited supplies of labor', which indeed was convincing at the time.
2. For an exposition of Soddy's economics and references, see Daly (1980).
3. It is worth noting that as the interest rate approaches zero, as at present, the calculation defining 'capital' approaches infinity. This would seem to indicate that capital is no longer scarce, so it can hardly continue to play its old theoretical role of limiting factor. Of course a zero interest rate is no longer a market price balancing time preference and productivity, but rather a policy variable aimed at inducing growth by giving banks free money. The trend toward uneconomic growth is surely boosted by a zero interest rate. Indeed, in real terms the interest rate is negative, which I suppose means that borrowers can make money if they will just invest in anything, even uneconomic projects, for the sake of maintaining monetary growth! The preferred investment seems to be to buy existing assets, which unfortunately generates no employment and tends to create a bubble.
4. According to Mason Gaffney (1994) it was just this 'preposterous notion' (blurring the distinction between producers and rentiers), that was the basis of the early American Neoclassical School's rejection of Henry George.
5. In some cases the depletion or source end of the entropic throughput is limiting, in others the pollution or sink end. But in either case it is the metabolic flow of natural resources through the economy that is limiting.
6. New technology embodied in the capital investment can sometimes be more efficient in the use of factors. This of course is the economists' big goal – efficiency. Usually they have meant efficiency of labor or capital, often achieved at the sacrifice of natural resource efficiency. But now there is increasing attention to resource efficiency. In a resource-constrained steady-state economy efficiency is an adaptation to imposed frugality in use of resources. But in a growth economy efficiency is considered an alternative to and an escape from frugality. In the latter case efficiency is undercut by the Jevons effect – what we can use more efficiently becomes cheaper, so we use more of it. A policy of 'frugality first' gives 'efficiency second' as a bonus, in a steady-state economy. The Jevons effect is blocked because resource use rates have been quantitatively limited. Although resource efficiency has improved (in other words, resource content per dollar of GDP has declined in some countries over some time periods), total matter-energy throughput has only increased. Scale increase has overcome efficiency improvement. This could not happen under the frugality-first sequence that begins with quantitative limits on the scale of resource throughput.
7. This of course is contested. But remember that growth becomes uneconomic when rising marginal costs of growth meet declining marginal benefits. The point at which growth becomes uneconomic is precisely the point at which the cumulative net benefits of past growth are maximized. Some people point to these large past net benefits as an argument for more growth, but surely economists of all people should not commit this fallacy!
8. For a review of the World Bank's recent reaffirmation of growth as usual, see Daly (2008).

REFERENCES

Daly, H.E. (1980), The economic thought of Frederick Soddy, *History of Political Economy*, **12**, 4.

Daly, H.E. (2008), Growth and development: critique of a credo, *Population and Development Review*, **34**(3), 511–18.

Gaffney, M. (with F. Harrison) (1994), *The Corruption of Economics*, London: Shepheard-Walwyn.

Georgescu-Roegen, N. (1971), *The Entropy Law and the Economic Process*, Cambridge, MA: Harvard University Press.

Lewis, W.A. (1954), Economic development with unlimited supplies of labor, *Manchester School of Economic and Social Studies*, **22**, 139–91.

Nordhaus, W. and J. Tobin (1972), Is growth obsolete? NBER, Economic Growth, New York: Columbia University Press.

Soddy, F. (1924), *Cartesian Economics: The Bearing of Physical Science upon State Stewardship*, London: Hendersons.

PART III

Recent revival of the growth debate and policies for a steady state

6. A further critique of growth economics

INTRODUCTION

Four years ago I wrote a critique of the 'Growth Report', a two-year study by the prestigious international Commission on Growth and Development (2008), published by the World Bank. Here I would like to reflect on the 'reaction' to my review – specifically that it was ignored! Many issues and many people are deservedly ignored. But should we ignore the question of whether growth still increases wealth faster than 'illth', as it did in the past empty world, or whether in the new full world it has begun to increase illth faster than wealth? Is growth still economic in the literal sense, or has it become uneconomic? This is the main question raised in my review. Surely it is not a trivial question, and my discomfort at seeing it roundly ignored transcends the mere personal pique that one feels at being brushed off. So I will begin with a few remarks on why I think my critical review failed to initiate a dialog with the authors of the Growth Report, and why I think that is indicative of a deeper failing within the economics profession. Following that I will consider the 11 fallacies and confusions that in my experience most frequently obstruct reasoning about growth.

THE GROWTH REPORT

The 'Growth Report' was done by a blue ribbon panel of 18 members from 16 countries, including two Nobel laureates in economics. It had many august sponsors, the main one being the World Bank. It can fairly be taken to represent the prevailing orthodox view on growth. My review was quite critical. I expected a debate, or at least a reply from the authors of the report. As indicated, they ignored it. Is this fact insignificant, or like Sherlock Holmes' dog that failed to bark in the night, might it be the clue to solving a mystery?

A few sympathetic former colleagues at the World Bank made sure that a copy of my review was sent to authors connected with the World

Bank, with the suggestion that a reply was in order. The editor of *Population and Development Review* renewed his offer to the authors to publish their reply, if they chose to make one. No reply. I realize, of course, that one could waste a lot of time replying to all critics. Some critics are morons. Forgive my immodesty, but for the time being I am assuming that I am not a moron.

Might there be other reasons for silence? Certainly the Commission did not lack intellectual firepower or financial backing for a reply. I think perhaps they made a political calculation of interest and advantage. What would be gained from their point of view by a reply? A blue ribbon panel of experts is presumed to be correct (especially if defending growth!), and a single critic is presumed to be wrong. Why risk upsetting that default presumption with a reply? The Report, after all, was a political manifesto (that is why it had so many coauthors and sponsors), a hymn to growth in the guise of an objective study. It had been widely and favorably reported by the establishment media and therefore had already achieved its goal – namely, to counter the emerging and threatening suspicion that the economic growth of the past empty-world era was morphing into uneconomic growth in the new full-world era. Scholarly debate about the correctness of the report, and the continued viability of growth as the supreme goal of all nations, were not on the agenda – it was very much off message. Probably the authors believed that the case for growth was so ironclad and obvious that any defense of it against criticism was unnecessary. But then, why did they bother to mount such a grand defense of growth in the first place?

I tell this story because it illustrates the unhappy state of public discourse on economic matters, and the lack of seriousness of many economists engaged in such discourse. *The Journal of Economic Perspectives*, for example, has a policy of not printing comments on articles they have published. Perhaps because they would get too many comments, exposing too much disagreement? Or so few comments because there is such a consensus among economists? Other economics journals do publish comments and replies, but it seems that this practice is less frequent than in the past. Why comment on someone else's work – there is not much academic credit in so doing. Correcting errors may be a necessary part of science, but since economics is not a science anyway, why waste time on it? Besides, you might make an enemy. Furthermore, consensus among experts is considered the hallmark of a mature science, so by prematurely declaring a consensus among 'all competent economists', and avoiding public debate on fundamental questions, economists preemptively lay claim to the status of a mature science.

The advantage of a reputation as a 'mature science' is that economists can profitably sell themselves as credibility-enhancing professional consultants to all sorts of interest groups. This was convincingly demonstrated in the documentary film, 'Inside Job', detailing the disgraceful behavior of some prominent economists leading up to the 2008 financial debacle.

Pointing to the silence of others when invited to reply to criticism, while a fair debating tactic, is a less than convincing argument against their position. One needs a more direct and specific critique. That was provided in my review (Daly, 2008), but limited to the specifics of the Growth Report, and will not be repeated here.

What I have called 'silence' could just be lack of a response to my particular review, invited by the editor of the journal in which it was published. Perhaps the authors of the Growth Report responded to other critics in other venues who might have raised the same or different issues. Also the Commission may have responded in their own subsequent publications. A wider review of the literature is in order.

There have been two further publications by the Growth Commission since their main Report in May of 2008. In 2009 they published *Post-Crisis Growth in Developing Countries*, which asked if the unforeseen financial crisis of September 2008 (four months after the publication of their Report) required any important changes in their conclusions. Understandably, the Commission was absorbed in considering massive 'critique' of growthmania coming from the real world. Academic criticisms could wait. The Commission's vision of growth as *summum bonum* remained undiminished, however, and was even reinforced by the crisis. Their next publication, *Equity and Growth in a Globalizing World* (2010), provided another opportunity to reply, but there was no direct reference, nor anything that might be construed as an indirect reply.

Google and Google Scholar searches of the Commission, the Report, and of the names of each of the Commission co-Chairmen (Danny Leipziger and Michael Spence) combined with my name, failed to turn up any replies. That did not surprise me as much as did the fact that a search for any reviews of the Report itself turned up only a few, and they were mainly just descriptive summaries. For example, *Amazon.com* urges prospective purchasers to 'be the first to review this book'. Help from a research librarian who surveyed other data bases failed to turn up critical reviews, replies, or rejoinders. The Commission was not overwhelmed with reviews, perhaps another reason, and an understandable one at that, for their belief that a reply was unnecessary. As lamented earlier, there is not much incentive to write reviews – especially critical ones. Alas, disagreements tend to remain unexpressed, doubtful claims un-debated, and errors uncorrected.

This unwillingness to engage in discussion, from both directions, leads me to reflect more broadly on the major fallacies of growth economics in the more general context of economic and environmental policy. In this larger context these fallacies also played a part in the 2012 US presidential election. The one thing the Democrats and Republicans agreed on is that economic growth is our number-one goal and is the basic solution to all problems. The idea that growth could conceivably cost more than it is worth at the margin, and therefore become uneconomic in the literal sense, was not considered, because if true, it would totally overturn the apple cart.[1] But, aside from political denial, why do many people (especially economists) not understand that continuous growth of the economy (measured either by real GDP or resource throughput) could in theory, and probably has in fact, become uneconomic? What is it that might confuse them? The remainder of this essay considers 11 confusions or fallacies that frequently serve as 'thought-stoppers' in discussions about growth.

ELEVEN CONFUSIONS ABOUT GROWTH

1. *One can nearly always find something whose growth would be both desirable and possible.* For example, we need more bicycles and can produce more bicycles. More bicycles mean growth. Therefore growth is both good and possible. QED.

However, this confuses aggregate growth with reallocation. Aggregate growth refers to growth in everything: bicycles, cars, houses, ships, cell phones, and so on. Aggregate growth is growth in scale of the economy, the size of real GDP, which is a value-based index of aggregate production and consequently of the total resource throughput required by that production. In the simplest case of aggregate growth everything produced goes up by the same percentage. Reallocation, by contrast, means that some things go up while others go down, the freed up resources from the latter are transferred to the former. The fact that reallocation remains possible and desirable does not mean that aggregate growth is possible and desirable. The fact that you can reallocate the weight in a boat more efficiently (and even redistribute it more equitably among passengers) does not mean that there is no Plimsoll line. Too much weight will sink a boat even if it is optimally allocated and justly distributed.

Reallocation of production away from more resource-intensive goods to less resource-intensive goods ('decoupling') is possible to some degree and often advocated, but is limited by two basic facts. First, the economy grows as an integrated whole, not as a loose aggregate of independently changeable sectors. A glance at the input–output table of an economy makes it clear that to increase output of any sector requires an increase in all the inputs to that sector from other sectors, and then a second round of increased inputs required by the first round of input increases, and so on. Second, in addition to this supply interdependence of sectors there are demand constraints – people are just not interested in information services unless they first have enough food and shelter. So trying to cut the resource-intensive food and shelter part of GDP to reallocate to less resource-intensive information services in the name of decoupling GDP from resources, will soon result in a shortage of food and shelter, and a glut of information services.

Aggregate growth was no problem back when the world was relatively empty. But now the world is full, and aggregate growth likely costs more than it is worth, even though more bicycles (and less of something else) might still be possible and desirable.

2. Another confusion is to argue *that since GDP is measured in value terms it is therefore not subject to physical limits.* This is another argument given for easy 'decoupling' of GDP from resource throughput. But growth refers to real GDP, which eliminates price level changes. Real GDP is a value-based index of aggregate quantitative change in real physical production. It is the best index we have of total resource throughput. The unit of measure of real GDP is not dollars, but rather 'dollar's worth'. A dollar's worth of gasoline is a physical quantity, currently about one-fourth of a gallon. The annual aggregate of all such dollar's worth amounts of all final commodities is real GDP, and even though not expressible in a simple physical unit, it remains a physical aggregate and subject to physical limits. The price level and nominal GDP might grow forever (inflation), but not real GDP, and the latter is the accepted measure of aggregate growth.

3. A more subtle confusion results from *looking at past totals rather than present margins.* Just look at the huge net benefits of past growth! How can anyone oppose growth when historically it has led to such enormous benefits? Well, there is a good reason: the net benefits of past growth reach a maximum precisely at the point where the rising marginal costs of growth equal the declining marginal benefits – that is to say, at precisely the point where further growth ceases to be economic and

becomes uneconomic! Before that point wealth grew faster than illth; beyond that point illth grows faster than wealth, making us poorer, not richer. No one is against being richer. No one denies that growth used to make us richer. The question is, does growth any longer make us richer, or is it now making us poorer? If aggregate growth now makes us poorer, then it can no longer be appealed to as 'necessary to end poverty'. Ending poverty requires sharing – redistribution rather than more uneconomic growth.

To understand the question requires that we recognize that real GDP has a cost, that illth is a negative joint product with wealth. Examples of illth are everywhere and include: nuclear wastes, climate change from excess carbon in the atmosphere, biodiversity loss, depleted mines, deforestation, eroded topsoil, dry wells and rivers, sea-level rise, the dead zone in the Gulf of Mexico, gyres of plastic trash in the oceans, the ozone hole, exhausting and dangerous labor, and the unrepayable debt from trying to push growth in the symbolic financial sector beyond what is possible in the real sector. Since no one buys these annually produced bads (that accumulate into illth) they have no market prices, and since their implicit negative shadow values are hard to estimate in a way comparable to positive market prices, they are usually ignored, or mentioned and quickly forgotten.

The logic of maximization embodied in equating rising marginal cost with declining marginal benefit requires a moment's thought for the average citizen to understand clearly, but surely it is familiar to anyone who has taken Econ 101.

4. *Even if it is theoretically possible that someday the marginal cost of growth will become greater than the marginal benefit, there is no empirical evidence that this has happened yet.* On the contrary, there is plenty of casual evidence for anyone who has not been anesthetized by the official party line of Madison Avenue and Wall Street. As for empirical evidence of the statistical type, there are two independent sources that give the same basic answer. First are the objective measures that separate GDP sub-accounts into costs and benefits and then subtract the costs from GDP to approximate net benefits of growth. The Index of Sustainable Economic Welfare (ISEW) and its later modifications into the Genuine Progress Indicator (GPI) both show that, for the United States and some other wealthy countries, GDP and GPI were positively correlated up until around 1980, after which GPI leveled off and GDP continued to rise. In other words, increasing throughput as measured by real GDP no longer increased welfare as measuredly GPI.

A similar disconnect is confirmed using the different measure of self-evaluated happiness. Self-reported happiness increases with per capita GDP up to a level of around $20 000 per annum, and then stops rising. The interpretation given is that while absolute real income is important for happiness up to a sufficiency, beyond that point happiness is overwhelmingly a function of the quality of relationships by which our very identity is constituted. Friendships, marriage and family, social stability, trust, fairness, and so on, not per capita GDP, are the overwhelming determinants of happiness at the present margin, especially in high-income countries. If we sacrifice friendships, social stability, family time, environmental services, and trust – for the sake of labor mobility, a second job, and quarterly financial returns, we often reduce happiness while increasing GDP.

Relative income gains may still increase individual happiness even when increases in absolute income no longer do, but aggregate growth is powerless to increase everyone's relative income because we cannot all be above average. Beyond some level of sufficiency, growth in GDP no longer increases either self-evaluated happiness or measured economic welfare, but it continues to increase costs of depletion, pollution, congestion, stress, and so on. Why is there such resistance to measuring the very magnitudes that could tell us if we have reached this point? A possible answer follows.

5. Many believe that *the way we measure GDP automatically makes its growth a trustworthy guide to economic policy*. To be counted in GDP, there must be a market transaction, and that implies a willing buyer and seller, neither of whom would have made the transaction if it did not make them better off in their own judgment. *Ergo*, growth in GDP must be good or it would not have happened. The problem here is that there are many third parties who are affected by many transactions, but did not agree to them. These external costs (or sometimes benefits) are not counted in GDP. Who are these third parties? The public in general, but more specifically the poor who lack the money to express their preferences in the market, future generations who of course cannot bid in present markets, and other species whose interests have no influence on markets at all.

In addition, GDP, the largest component of which is national income, counts consumption of natural capital as income. Counting capital consumption as income is the cardinal sin of accounting. Cut down the entire forest this year and sell it, and the entire amount is treated as this year's income. Pump all the petroleum and sell it, and add that to this year's income. But income in economics is by definition the maximum amount that a community can produce and consume this year, and still be able to produce and consume the same amount next year (Hicks, 1946). In other words income is the maximum consumption that still leaves intact the capacity to produce the same amount next year. Only the sustainable yield of forests, fisheries, croplands, and livestock herds is this year's income – the rest is capital needed to reproduce the same yield next year. Consuming capital means reduced production and consumption in the future. Income is by definition sustainable; capital consumption is not. The whole historical reason for income accounting is to avoid impoverishment by inadvertent consumption of capital. By contrast our national accounting tends to encourage capital consumption (at least consumption of natural capital), first by counting it in GDP, and then claiming that whatever increases GDP is good!

As already noted we fail to subtract negative by-products (external costs) from GDP on the grounds that they have no market price since obviously no one wants to buy bads. But people do buy anti-bads, and we count those expenditures. For example, the costs of pollution (a bad) are not subtracted, but the expenditures on pollution cleanup (an anti-bad) are added. This is asymmetric accounting – adding anti-bads without having subtracted the bads that made the anti-bads necessary in the first place. The more bads, the more anti-bads, and the greater is GDP – wheel spinning registered as forward motion.

There are other problems with GDP but these should be enough to refute the mistaken idea that if something is not a net benefit it would not have been counted in GDP, so therefore GDP growth must always be good.

6. *As natural resources become scarce we can substitute capital for resources and continue to grow.* Growth economists assume a high degree of substitutability between factors of production, including capital for resources (Daly, 2007). But if one considers a realistic analytic description of production, as given in Georgescu-Roegen's (1971) fund-flow model, one sees that factors are of two qualitatively different kinds: resource flows that are physically transformed into flows of product and waste; and capital and labor funds, the agents or instruments of trans-formation that are not themselves physically embodied in the product. There are varying degrees of substitution between different resource flows, and between the funds of labor and capital. But the basic relation between resource flow on the one hand, and capital (or labor) fund on the other, is complementarity. You cannot bake a 10-pound cake with only 1 pound of ingredients, no matter how many cooks and ovens you have. Efficient cause (capital) does not substitute for material cause

(resources). Material cause and efficient cause are related as complements, and the one in short supply is limiting. Complementarity makes
possible the existence of a limiting factor, which cannot exist under
substitutability. In yesterday's empty world the limiting factor was
capital; in today's full world remaining natural resources have become
limiting. This fundamental change in the pattern of scarcity has not been
incorporated into the thinking of growth economists. Nor have they paid
sufficient attention to the fact that capital is itself made and maintained
from, as well as powered by, natural resources. It is hard for a factor to
substitute for that from which it is made! And consider yet another
oversight. Substitution is reversible – if capital is a good substitute for
resources, then resources are a good substitute for capital. But then why,
historically, would we ever have accumulated capital in the first place, if
nature had already given us a good substitute? In sum, the claim that
capital is a good substitute for natural resources is absurd.

In reply to these criticisms growth economists point to modern
agriculture, which they consider the prime example of substitution of
capital for resources. But modern, mechanized agriculture has simply
substituted one set of resource flows for another, and one set of funds for
another. The old resource flows (soil, sunlight, rain, manure) were to a
significant degree replaced by new resource flows (chemical fertilizer,
fossil fuels, irrigation water), not by 'capital'! The old fund factors of
labor, draft animals, and hand tools were replaced by new fund factors of
tractors, harvesters, and so on. In other words new fund factors substituted for old fund factors, and new resource flows substituted for old
resource flows. Modern agriculture involved the substitution of capital
for labor (both funds), and the substitution of nonrenewable resources for
renewable resources (both flows). In energy terms it was largely the
substitution of fossil fuels for solar energy, a move with short-term
benefits and long-term costs. But there was no substitution of capital
funds for resource flows. The case of mechanization of agriculture does
not contradict the complementarity of fund and flow factors in production, nor the new role of resources as limiting factor.

*7. Knowledge is the ultimate resource and since knowledge growth is
infinite it can fuel economic growth without limit.* Like many, I am eager
for knowledge to substitute physical resources to the extent possible, and
consequently advocate severance taxes to make resources expensive, and
patent reform to make knowledge cheap. But if I am hungry, I want real
food on the plate, not the knowledge of a thousand recipes on the
Internet. Furthermore, the fact that knowledge is naturally depleting
while ignorance is naturally renewing makes me doubt that knowledge

can save the growth economy. Ignorance is renewable, mainly because ignorant babies continually replace learned elders. In addition, vast amounts of recorded knowledge are destroyed not only by death, but also by decay, fires, floods, bombs, and bookworms. Modern digital storage does not seem to be immune to the teeth of time, or to that new bookworm, the computer virus. To be effective in the world, knowledge must exist in someone's mind (not just in the library or on the Internet) – otherwise it is inert. And even when knowledge increases, it does not grow exponentially like money in the bank. Some old knowledge is disproved or canceled out by new knowledge, and some new knowledge is discovery of new biophysical or social limits to growth.

New knowledge must always be something of a surprise – if we could predict its content then we would know it already, and it would not really be new. Contrary to common expectation, new knowledge is not always a pleasant surprise for the growth economy – frequently it is bad news. For example, climate change from greenhouse gases was recently new knowledge, as was discovery of the ozone hole. How can one appeal to new knowledge as the panacea when the content of new knowledge must of necessity be a surprise? Of course we sometimes get lucky with new knowledge, but should we borrow against that uncertainty? Why not count the chickens after they hatch?

8. *Without growth we are condemned to unemployment.* The Full Employment Act of 1946 declared full employment to be a major goal of US policy. Economic growth was then seen as the means to attain the end of full employment. Today that relation has been inverted – economic growth has become the end, and if the means to attain that end – automation, off-shoring, excessive immigration – result in unemployment, well that is the price 'we' just have to pay for the supreme goal of growth. If we really want full employment we must reverse this inversion of ends and means. We can serve the goal of full employment by restricting automation, off-shoring, and easy immigration to periods of true domestic labor shortage as indicated by high and rising wages. In addition, full employment can also be served by reducing the length of the working day, week, or year, in exchange for more leisure, rather than more GDP.

Real wages have been falling for decades, yet our corporations, hungry for cheaper labor, keep bleating about a labor shortage. They mean a shortage of cheap labor in the service of growing profits. Actually a labor shortage in a capitalist economy with 80 percent of the population earning wages is not a bad thing. How else will wages and standard of living for that 80 percent increase? What the corporations really want is a surplus of labor, and falling wages. With surplus labor wages generally do not rise and therefore all the gains from productivity increase will go to profit, not wages. Hence the elitist support for automation, off-shoring, and lax enforcement of democratically enacted immigration laws.

9. *We live in a globalized economy and have no choice but to compete in the global growth race.* Globalization was a policy choice of our elites, not an inevitability. Free trade agreements had to be negotiated. Who negotiated and signed the treaties? Who has pushed for free capital mobility and signed onto the World Trade Organization (WTO)? Who wants to enforce US intellectual property rights worldwide with trade sanctions? The Bretton Woods system was a major achievement aimed at facilitating international trade after World War II. It fostered trade for mutual advantage among separate countries. Free capital mobility and global integration were not part of the deal. That came with the WTO and the effective abandonment by the World Bank and International Monetary Fund (IMF) of their Bretton Woods charter. Globalization is the engineered integration of many formerly relatively independent national economies into a single tightly bound global economy organized around absolute advantage, not comparative advantage (which assumes capital immobility internationally).

Once a country has adopted free trade and free capital mobility it has effectively been integrated into the global economy and is no longer free not to specialize and trade. Yet all of the theorems in economics about the gains from specialization and trade assume that trade is voluntary. How can trade be voluntary if countries are so specialized as to be no longer free not to trade? Countries can no longer account for social and environmental costs and internalize them in their prices unless all other countries do so, and to the same degree. To integrate the global omelet you must disintegrate the national eggs. While nations have many sins to atone for, they remain the main locus of community and policy-making authority. It will not do to disintegrate them in the name of abstract 'globalism', even though we certainly require some global federation of national communities. But when nations disintegrate there will be nothing left to federate in the interest of legitimately global purposes. 'Globalization' (national disintegration) was an actively pursued policy, not an inertial force of nature. It was done to increase the power and growth of transnational corporations by moving them out from under the authority of nation states and into a nonexistent 'global community'. It can be undone, as is currently being contemplated by some in the European Union, formerly heralded as the forerunner of more inclusive globalization.

10. *Space, the high frontier, frees us from the finitude of the earth, and opens unlimited resources for growth.* In a secular age where many have lost faith in the spiritual dimension of existence, and where the concept of 'man as creature' is eclipsed by that of 'man as creator', it is to be expected that science fiction might be called on to fill the apparently dead void of space with a happy population of the 'scientifically raptured'. The spiritual insights of centuries are replaced by technocratic projections of the 'Singularity' in which mankind attains the final goal of (random?) evolution and becomes a new and immortal species, thanks to the salvific power of exponential growth in information processing technology. Eternal silicon-based life awaits the new elect who can stay alive until the Singularity; oblivion for those who die too soon! And this comes from materialists who think that they have outgrown religion!

Of course, many technical space accomplishments are real and amazing. But how do they free us from the finitude of the earth and open up unlimited resources for growth? Space accomplishments have been extremely expensive in terms of terrestrial resources, and have yielded few extraterrestrial resources – mainly those useless moon rocks that incited thievery by a NASA intern. As for new services, space tourism has provided orbital joy rides to a few billionaires. On the truly positive side of the ledger we can list communications satellites, but they are oriented to earth, and while they provide valuable services, they do not bring in new resources. And apparently some orbits are getting crowded with satellite carcasses.

Robotic space exploration is a lot cheaper than manned space missions, and may (or may not) yield knowledge worth the investment to a society that has not yet provided basic necessities and elementary education for many. In such a world political willingness to finance the expensive curiosity of a scientific elite might be less, were it not for the heavy military connection (muted in the official NASA propaganda). Cuts in NASA's budget have led to the hyped reaction by the 'space community' in proclaiming a pseudo-religious technical quest to discover 'whether or not we are alone in the universe'. Another major goal is to find a planet suitable for colonization by earthlings. The latter is sometimes justified by the claim that since we are clearly destroying the earth we need a new home – to also destroy?

The numbers – astronomical distances and timescales – effectively rule out dreams of space colonization. But another consideration is equally daunting. If we are unable to limit population and production growth on earth, which is our natural and forgiving home, out of which we were created and with which we have evolved and adapted, then what makes us think we can live as aliens within the much tighter and unforgiving discipline of a space colony on a dead rock in a cold vacuum? There we would encounter limits to growth raised to the hundredth power.

11. *Without economic growth all progress is at an end.* On the contrary, without growth, now actually uneconomic growth if correctly measured, true progress finally will have a chance. As ecological economists have long argued, growth is quantitative physical increase in the matter–energy throughput, the metabolic maintenance flow of the economy beginning with depletion and ending with pollution. Development is qualitative improvement in the capacity of a given throughput to provide for the maintenance and enjoyment of life in community. Growth means larger jaws and a bigger digestive tract for more rapidly converting more resources into more waste, in the service of frequently destructive individual wants. Development means better digestion of a nongrowing throughput, and more worthy and satisfying goals to which our life energies could be devoted. Development without growth beyond the Earth's carrying capacity is true progress. The main ways to develop are through technical improvement in resource efficiency, and ethical improvement in our wants and priorities. Resource efficiency must be an adaptation to lower resource throughput. So far we have sought efficiency independently of limiting throughput and have consequently run into the Jevons paradox – better efficiency in using a resource tends to increase the total amount used. If we first limit throughput then we will get efficiency increase as a secondary adaptation; if we first seek efficiency increase we secondarily get the Jevons paradox. Limiting physical growth is necessary to force the path of progress onto development. Since physical growth has become uneconomic one might think that limiting it would not be so controversial! But of course most economists do not admit that growth is, or even could be, uneconomic. They seem determined to avoid discussion of arguments or evidence to the contrary.

CONCLUSION

If growth economists will make an effort to overcome these 11 fallacies, and break their guild's stonewalling silence, then maybe we can have a productive dialog about whether or not what used to be economic growth has now become uneconomic growth, and what to do about it. It was too much to hope that the issue of uneconomic growth would make it into the 2012 election, but maybe 2016, or 2020, … or sometime?

One can hope. But hope must embrace not just a better understanding regarding these confusions, but also, at a deeper level, more love and care for our fellow humans, and for all of Creation. I say Creation with a capital 'C' advisedly, and certainly not in denial of the facts of evolution. If our world and our lives are not in some sense a Creation, but just a purposeless happenstance – a random statistical fluke of multiplying infinitesimal probabilities by an infinite number of trials – then it is hard to see from where we will get the will and inspiration to care for it. Indeed, our decision-making elites may already tacitly understand that growth has become uneconomic. But apparently they have also figured out how to keep the dwindling extra benefits for themselves, while 'sharing' the exploding extra costs with the poor, the future, and other species. Why not, if it is all just a purposeless happenstance? The elite-owned media, the corporate-funded think tanks, the kept economists of high academia, and the World Bank – not to mention Gold Sacks and Wall Street – all sing hymns to growth in harmony with class interest and greed. The public is bamboozled by technical obfuscation, and by the false promise that, thanks to growth, they too will one day be rich. Intellectual confusion is real, but moral nihilism, abetted by naturalistic scientism, may be the bigger problem.

NOTE

1. For a cogent argument that ecological economics must be more willing to overturn apple carts, see Andersen and M'Gonigle (2012).

REFERENCES

Andersen, B. and M. M'Gonigle (2012), Does ecological economics have a future? Contradiction and reinvention in the age of climate change, *Ecological Economics*, **84**, 37–48.
Commission on Growth and Development (2008), *The Growth Report: Strategies for Sustained Growth and Inclusive Development*, Washington DC: The World Bank.
Commission on Growth and Development (2009), *Post-Crisis Growth in Developing Countries*, Washington DC: The World Bank.
Commission on Growth and Development (2010), *Equity and Growth in a Globalizing World*, Washington DC: The World Bank.
Daly, H.E. (2007), *Ecological Economics and Sustainable Development*, Cheltenham, UK and Northampton, MA, USA: Edward Elgar.
Daly, H.E. (2008), Growth and development: critique of a credo, *Population and Development Review*, **34**(3), 511–18.

Georgescu-Roegen, N. (1971), *The Entropy Law and the Economic Process*, Cambridge, MA: Harvard University Press.

Hicks, J.R. (1946), *Value and Capital: An Inquiry into Some Fundamental Principles of Economic Theory*, 2nd edn, Oxford: Clarendon Press.

7. Moving from a failed growth economy to a steady-state economy

> Systems, scientific and philosophical, come and go. Each method of limited understanding is at length exhausted. In its prime each system is a triumphant success; in its decay it is an obstructive nuisance.
>
> A. N. Whitehead

A steady-state economy is incompatible with continuous growth – either positive or negative growth. The goal of a steady state is to sustain a constant, sufficient stock of real wealth and people for a long time. A downward spiral of negative growth, a depression, is a failed growth economy, not a steady-state economy. Halting a downward spiral is necessary, but is not the same thing as resuming continuous positive growth. The growth economy now fails in two ways: (1) positive growth becomes uneconomic in our full-world economy; (2) negative growth, resulting from the bursting of financial bubbles inflated beyond physical limits, though temporarily necessary, soon becomes self-destructive. That leaves a nongrowing or steady-state economy as the only long-run alternative. The level of physical wealth that the biosphere can sustain in a steady state is almost certainly below the present level. The fact that recent efforts at growth have resulted mainly in bubbles is evidence that this is so. Nevertheless, current policies all aim for the full reestablishment of the growth economy. No one denies that our problems would be easier to solve if we were richer. That rich is better than poor is a definitional truism. The question is, does growth any longer make us richer, or is it now making us poorer?

I will spend a few more minutes cursing the darkness of growth, but will then try to light 10 little candles along the path to a steady state. Some advise me to forget the darkness and focus on the policy candles. But I find that without a dark background the light of my little candles is not visible in the false dawn projected by the economists, whose campaigning optimism never gives hope a chance to shine.

We have many problems (poverty, unemployment, environmental destruction, budget deficit, trade deficit, bailouts, bankruptcy, foreclosures, and so on), but apparently only one solution: economic growth, or as the pundits now like to say, 'to grow the economy' – as if it were a potted plant.

But let us stop right there and ask two questions that all students should put to their economics professors.

First, there is a deep theorem in mathematics that says when something grows it gets bigger! So, when the economy grows it too gets bigger. How big can the economy be, Professor? How big is it now? How big should it be? Have economists ever considered these questions? And most pointedly, what makes them think that growth (in other words, physical expansion of the economic subsystem into the finite containing biosphere), is not already increasing environmental and social costs faster than production benefits, thereby becoming uneconomic growth, making us poorer, not richer? After all, real GDP, the measure of 'economic' growth so-called, does not separate costs from benefits, but conflates them as 'economic' activity. How would we know when growth became uneconomic? Remedial and defensive activity becomes ever greater as we grow from an 'empty world' to a 'full world' (a world full of us and our stuff), characterized by congestion, interference, displacement, depletion, and pollution. The defensive expenditures induced by these negatives are all added to GDP, not subtracted. Be prepared, students, for some hand waving, throat clearing, and subject changing. But do not be bluffed.

We must recognize that many developing countries are still in the phase of truly economic growth – their marginal benefits of growth are still greater than their marginal costs. Yet the world as a whole is 'full'. Therefore the duty of limiting growth, and the policies discussed below, apply first to the richer countries where in fact growth has become uneconomic. The rich must free up ecological space for the poor to grow into, leading to a process of convergence to a common level of resource use that is sufficient for a good (not luxurious) life and sustainable for a long (not infinite) future. Some worry that slowing growth in rich countries will hurt poor countries by reducing their export markets. That just means that developing countries will have to shift from the export-led model back toward the import-substitution model, developing their own internal markets. Nor can rich countries continue to off-shore production and jobs in the face of their own high unemployment rates.

Second question: do you then, Professor, see growth as a continuing process, desirable in itself – or as a temporary process required to reach a sufficient level of wealth, that would thereafter be maintained more or less in a steady state? At least 99 percent of modern neoclassical economists hold the growth-forever view. We have to go back to John Stuart Mill and the earlier classical economists to find serious treatment of the idea of a nongrowing economy, the stationary state. What makes modern economists so sure that the classical economists were wrong? Just dropping history of economic thought from the curriculum is not a refutation!

Here are some reasons to think that the classical economists are right.

A long-run norm of continuous growth could make sense, only if one of the three following conditions were true:

1. the economy were not an open subsystem of a finite and non-growing biophysical system,
2. the economy were growing in a non-physical dimension, or
3. the laws of thermodynamics did not hold.

Let us consider each of these three logical alternatives. (If you can think of a fourth one let me know.)

1. Some economists in fact think of nature as the set of extractive subsectors of the economy (forests, fisheries, mines, wells, pastures, and even agriculture ...). The economy, not the ecosystem or biosphere, is seen as the whole; nature is a collection of parts. If the economy is the whole then it is not a part of any larger thing or system that might restrain its expansion. If some extractive natural subsector gets scarce we will just substitute other sectors for it and growth of the whole economy will continue, not into any restraining biospheric envelope, but into sidereal space presumably full of resource-bearing asteroids and friendly highly evolved aliens eager to teach us how to grow forever into their territory. Sources and sinks are considered infinite.

2. Some economists say that what is growing in economic growth is value, and value is not reducible to physical units. The latter is true of course, but that does not mean that value is independent of physics! After all, value is price times quantity, and quantity is always basically physical. Even services are always the service of something or somebody for some time period, and people who render services have to eat. The unit of measure of GDP is not dollars, but dollar's worth. A dollar's worth of gasoline is a physical amount, currently about a fourth of a gallon. The aggregation of the dollars' worth amounts of many different physical commodities (GDP) does not abolish the physicality of the measure even though the aggregate can no longer be expressed in physical units. True, $\$/q \times q = \$$. But the fact that q cancels out mathematically does not mean that the aggregate measure, 'dollars' worth', is just a pile of

dollars. GDP is a value-weighted index of real quantities. And it does not help to speak instead of 'value added' (by labor and capital) because we must ask, to what is the value added? And the answer is natural resources, low-entropy matter/energy – not fairy dust or frog's hair! Development (squeezing more welfare from the same throughput of resources) is a good thing. Growth (pushing more resources through a physically larger economy) is the problem. Limiting quantitative growth is the way to force qualitative development as the path of progress.

3. If resources could be created out of nothing, and wastes could be annihilated into nothing, then we could have an ever-growing resource throughput by which to fuel the continuous growth of the economy. But the first law of thermodynamics says NO. Or if we could just recycle the same matter and energy through the economy faster and faster we could keep growth going. The circular flow diagram of many economics principles texts unfortunately comes very close to affirming this. But the second law of thermodynamics says NO.

So – if we cannot grow our way out of all problems, then maybe we should reconsider the logic and virtues of nongrowth, the steady-state economy. Why this refusal by neoclassical economists both to face common sense, and to reconsider the ideas of the early classical economists?

I think the answer is distressingly simple. Without growth the only way to cure poverty is by sharing. But redistribution is anathema. Without growth to push the hoped for demographic transition, the only way to cure overpopulation is by population control. A second anathema. Without growth the only way to increase funds to invest in environmental repair is by reducing current consumption. Anathema number three. Three anathemas and you are out!

And without growth how will we build up arsenals to protect democracy (and remaining petroleum reserves)? How will we go to Mars and Saturn and 'conquer' space? Where can technical progress come from if not from unintended spin-offs from the military and from space research? Gnostic techno-fantasies of colonizing outer space, partially turning off the sun to make more thermal room for greenhouse gases in the atmosphere, and of abolishing disease and death itself, feed on the perpetual growth myth of no limits. Digital-brained tekkies, who have never heard of the problem of evil, see Heaven on Earth just around the corner – 'let us build a smarter planet', IBM modestly suggests. How about some smarter economists first? Without growth we must face the difficult religious task of finding a different god to worship. The communist growth god has already failed. Surely the capitalist growth god will not fail! Let us jump-start the GDP and the Dow-Jones! Let us build another Tower of Babel with obfuscating technical terms like sub-prime mortgage, derivative, securitized investment vehicle, collateralized debt obligation, credit default swap, 'toxic' assets, and so on.

Well, let us not do that. Let us ignore the anathemas and instead think about what policies would be required to move to a steady-state economy. They are a bit radical by present standards, but not insanely unrealistic as are the three alternatives for validating continuous growth, just discussed.

Let us look briefly at 10 specific policy proposals for moving from our unsustainable growth economy to a steady-state economy. A steady-state economy is one that develops qualitatively (by improvement in science, technology, and ethics) without growing quantitatively in physical dimensions; it lives on a diet – a constant metabolic flow of resources from depletion to pollution (the entropic throughput) maintained at a level that is within the assimilative and regenerative capacities of the ecosystem of which the economy is a subsystem.

The policies recommended are more sensible than the current policies of 'growth forever' – especially after growth has become uneconomic in the basic sense of costing more than it is worth at the margin. Ten is an arbitrary number – just a way to get specific. Although, the whole package fits together in the sense that some policies supplement and balance others, most of them could be adopted singly and gradually.

1. *Cap-auction-trade systems for basic resources*. Caps limit biophysical scale by quotas on depletion or pollution, whichever is more limiting. Auctioning the quotas captures scarcity rents for equitable redistribution. Trade allows efficient allocation to highest uses. This policy has the advantage of transparency. There is a limit to the amount and rate of depletion and pollution that the economy can be allowed to impose on the ecosystem. Caps are quotas, limits to the throughput of basic resources, especially fossil fuels. The quota usually should be applied at the input end because depletion is more spatially concentrated than pollution and hence easier to monitor. Also the higher price of basic resources will induce their more economical use at each upstream stage of production, as well as at the final stage of consumption. It may be that the effective limit in use of a resource comes from the pollution it causes rather than from depletion – no matter, we indirectly limit pollution by restricting depletion of the resource that ultimately is converted into wastes. Limiting barrels, tons, and cubic feet of carbon fuels extracted

per time period will limit tons of CO_2 emitted per time period. Only very toxic or spatially concentrated wastes require separate (and geographically specific) pollution quotas.

This scale limit serves the goal of biophysical sustainability. Ownership of the quotas is initially public – the government auctions them to the individuals and firms. The revenues go to the treasury and are used to replace regressive taxes, such as the payroll tax, and to reduce income tax on the lowest incomes. Once purchased at auction the quotas can be freely bought and sold by third parties, just as can the resources whose rate of depletion they limit. The trading allows efficient allocation; the auction serves just distribution, and the cap serves the goal of sustainable scale – three goals, three policy instruments. The same logic can be applied to limiting the off-take from renewable resources, such as fisheries and forests. With renewables the quota should be set to approximate sustainable yield. For non renewables, sustainable rates of absorption of resulting pollution, or of the development of renewable substitutes may provide a criterion.

2. *Ecological tax reform* – shift the tax base from value added (labor and capital) and on to 'that to which value is added', namely the entropic throughput of resources extracted from nature (depletion), and returned to nature (pollution). This internalizes external costs as well as raises revenue more equitably. It prices the scarce but previously unpriced contribution of nature. Value added is something we want to encourage, so stop taxing it. Depletion and pollution are things we want to discourage, so tax them. Ecological tax reform can be an alternative or a supplement to cap–auction–trade systems. Value added is simultaneously created and distributed in the very process of production. Therefore, economists argue that there is no 'pie' to be independently distributed according to ethical principles. As Kenneth Boulding put it, instead of a pie, there are only a lot of little 'tarts' consisting of the value added by different people or different countries, and blindly aggregated by statisticians into an abstract 'pie' that does not really exist as an undivided totality. If one wants to redistribute this imaginary 'pie' he should appeal to the generosity of those who baked larger tarts to share with those who baked smaller tarts, not to some invidious notion of equal participation in a fictitious common inheritance.

I have considerable sympathy with this view, as far as it goes. But it leaves out something very important.

In our one-eyed focus on value added we economists have neglected 'that to which value is added', namely the flow of resources and services from nature. 'Value added' by labor and capital has to be added to something, and the quality and quantity of that something is important. Now there is a real and important sense in which the original contribution of nature is indeed a 'pie', a pre-existing, undivided totality that we all share as an inheritance. It is not an aggregation of little tarts that we each baked ourselves. Rather it is the seed, soil, air, sunlight, and rain (not to mention the gene pools and suitable climate) from which the wheat and apples grew that we converted into tarts by our labor and capital. The claim for equal access to nature's gifts is not the invidious coveting of what our neighbor accumulated by her own labor and abstinence. The focus of our demands for income to redistribute to the poor, therefore, should be on the value of the contribution of nature, the original value of that to which further value is added by labor and capital. People generally resent seeing the value they added by their own labor and enterprise taxed away, although they accept it to some degree as necessary. But they do not resent seeing the value freely added by nature taxed away. Rather they resent seeing it accrue as unearned income (scarcity rents) to owners who added no value to what nature provided.

3. *Limit the range of inequality in income distribution* – a minimum income and a maximum income. Without aggregate growth poverty reduction requires redistribution. Complete equality is unfair; unlimited inequality is unfair. Seek fair limits to the range of inequality.

The civil service, the military, and the university manage with a range of inequality of a factor of 15 or 20. Corporate America has a range of 500 or more. Many industrial nations are below 25. Could we not limit the range to, say, 100, and see how it works? This might mean a minimum of 20 thousand dollars and a maximum of 2 million. Is that not more than enough to compensate real differences? People who have reached the limit could either work for nothing at the margin if they enjoy their work, or devote their extra time to hobbies or public service. The demand left unmet by those at the top will be filled by those who are below the maximum. A sense of community, necessary for democracy, is hard to maintain across the vast income differences current in the United States. Rich and poor separated by a factor of 500 seem to become almost different species, having few experiences or interests in common. The main justification for such differences has been that they stimulate growth, which will one day make everyone rich. This may have had superficial plausibility in an empty world, but in our full world it is a fairy tale. I have advocated a maximum income as well as a minimum income for a long time. The maximum part has been very unpopular, but thanks to the banksters and their bonuses it is now becoming more acceptable. And almost too obvious to mention, a substantial inheritance tax is needed to restrain accumulation of unearned wealth over generations.

4. *Free up the length of the working day, week, and year* – allow greater option for part-time or personal work. Full-time external employment for all is hard to provide without growth. Other industrial countries have much longer vacations and maternity leaves than the United States. For the classical economists the length of the working day was a key variable by which the worker (self-employed yeoman or artisan) balanced the marginal disutility of labor with the marginal utility of income and of leisure so as to maximize enjoyment of life. Under industrialism the length of the working day became a parameter rather than a variable (and for Karl Marx was the key determinant of the rate of exploitation). We need to make it more of a variable subject to choice by the worker. Milton Friedman wanted 'Freedom to Choose' – OK, here is an important choice most of us are not allowed to make! And we should stop biasing the labor–leisure choice by advertising to stimulate more consumption and more labor to pay for it. At a minimum advertising should no longer be treated as a tax-deductible ordinary expense of production. Is it really a good thing to subsidize the expenditure of billions of dollars to convince people to buy things they do not need, with money they do not have, to impress people they do not know?

5. *Re-regulate international commerce* – move away from free trade, free capital mobility, and globalization. Cap–auction–trade, ecological tax reform, and other national measures that internalize environmental costs will raise prices and put us at a competitive disadvantage in international trade with countries that do not internalize costs. We should adopt compensating tariffs to protect, not inefficient firms, but efficient national policies of cost internalization from standards-lowering competition with foreign firms that are not required to pay the social and environmental costs they inflict. This 'new protectionism' is very different from the 'old protectionism' that was designed to protect a truly inefficient domestic firm from a more efficient foreign firm. We cannot integrate with the global economy and at the same time have higher wages, environmental standards, and social safety nets than the rest of the world. Trade and capital mobility must be balanced and fair, not deregulated or 'free'. We should recognize the interdependence of separate national economies, but reject integration into a single global economy. The first rule of efficiency is 'count all the costs' – not 'free trade', which coupled with free capital mobility leads to a standards-lowering competition to count as few costs

as possible. Tariffs are also a good source of public revenue. This will run afoul of the WTO–WB–IMF, so …

6. *Downgrade the WTO–WB–IMF* to something like Keynes's original plan for a multilateral payments clearing union, charging penalty rates on surplus as well as deficit balances with the union – seek balance on current account, and thereby avoid large foreign debts and capital account transfers. For example, under Keynes's plan the United States would pay a penalty charge to the clearing union for its large deficit with the rest of the world, and China would also pay a similar penalty for its surplus. Both sides of the imbalance would be pressured to balance their current accounts by financial penalties, and if need be by exchange rate adjustments relative to the clearing account unit, called the 'bancor' by Keynes. The bancor would also serve as world reserve currency, a privilege that should not be enjoyed by any national currency, including the US dollar. Reserve currency status for the dollar is a benefit to the United States – rather like a truckload of free heroin is a benefit to an addict. The bancor would be like gold under the gold standard, only you would not have to dig it out of the ground.

The IMF preaches free trade based on comparative advantage, and has done so for a long time. More recently the WTO–WB–IMF have started preaching the gospel of globalization, which, in addition to free trade, means free capital mobility internationally. The classical comparative advantage argument, however, explicitly assumes international immobility of capital.[1] When confronted with this contradiction the IMF waves its hands, suggests that you might be a xenophobe, and changes the subject. The WTO–WB–IMF contradict themselves in service to the interests of transnational corporations and their policy of off-shoring production and falsely calling it 'free trade'. International capital mobility, coupled with free trade, allows corporations to escape from national regulation in the public interest, playing one nation off against another. Since there is no global government they are in effect uncontrolled. The nearest thing we have to a global government (WTO–WB–IMF) has shown no interest in regulating transnational capital for the common good.

7. *Move away from fractional reserve banking toward a system of 100 percent reserve requirements.* This would put control of the money supply and seigniorage (profit made by the issuer of fiat money) in the hands of the government rather than private banks, which would no longer be able to live the alchemist's dream by creating money out of nothing and lending it at interest. All quasi-bank financial institutions should be brought under this rule, regulated as commercial banks subject

to 100 percent reserve requirements. Banks would earn their profit by financial intermediation only, lending savers' money for them (charging a loan rate higher than the rate paid to savings or 'time-account' depositors) and charging for checking, safekeeping, and other services. With 100 percent reserves every dollar loaned to a borrower would be a dollar previously saved by a depositor (and not available to him during the period of the loan), thereby re-establishing the classical balance between abstinence and investment. With credit limited by saving (abstinence from consumption) there will be less lending and borrowing and it will be done more carefully – no more easy credit to finance the massive purchase of 'assets' that are nothing but bets on dodgy debts. To make up for the decline in bank-created, interest-bearing money, the government can pay some of its expenses by issuing more non-interest-bearing fiat money. However, it can only do this up to a strict limit imposed by inflation. If the government issues more money than the public voluntarily wants to hold, the public will trade it for goods, driving the price level up. As soon as the price index begins to rise the government must print less and tax more. Thus a policy of maintaining a constant price index would govern the internal value of the dollar. The external value of the dollar could be left to freely fluctuating exchange rates (or preferably to the rate against the bancor in Keynes's clearing union).

How would the 100 percent reserve system serve the steady-state economy?

First, as just mentioned it would restrict borrowing for new investment to existing savings, greatly reducing speculative growth ventures – for example the leveraging of stock purchases with huge amounts of borrowed money (created by banks *ex nihilo* rather than saved out of past earnings) would be severely limited. Down payment on houses would be much higher, and consumer credit would be greatly diminished. Credit cards would become debit cards. Growth economists will scream, but a steady-state economy does not aim to grow.

Second, the money supply no longer has to grow in order for people to pay back the principal plus the interest required by the loan responsible for the money's very existence in the first place. The repayment of old loans with interest continually threatens to diminish the money supply unless new loans compensate. With 100 percent reserves money becomes neutral with respect to growth rather than biasing the system toward growth by requiring more loans just to keep the money supply from shrinking.

Third, the financial sector will no longer be able to capture such a large share of the nation's profits (around 40 percent!), freeing some smart people for more productive, less parasitic, activity.

Fourth, the money supply would no longer expand during a boom, when banks like to loan lots of money, and contract during a recession, when banks try to collect outstanding debts, thereby reinforcing the cyclical tendency of the economy.

Fifth, with 100 percent reserves there is no danger of a run on the bank leading to failure, and the Federal Deposit Insurance Corporation (FDIC) could be abolished, along with its consequent moral hazard. The danger of cascading collapse of the whole credit pyramid due to the failure of one or two 'too big to fail' banks would be eliminated. Congress then could not be frightened into giving huge bailouts to some banks to avoid the 'contagion' of failure.

Sixth, the explicit policy of a constant price index would reduce fears of inflation and the resultant quest to accumulate more as protection against inflation.

Seventh, a regime of fluctuating exchange rates (or Keynes' clearing union) automatically balances international trade accounts, eliminating big surpluses and deficits. US consumption growth would be reduced without its deficit; Chinese production growth would be reduced without its surplus. By making balance of payments lending unnecessary, fluctuating exchange rates would greatly shrink the role of the IMF and its 'conditionalities'.

To dismiss such sound policies as 'extreme' in the face of the demonstrated fraudulence of our current financial system is quite absurd. The idea is not to nationalize banks, but to nationalize money, which is a natural public utility in the first place. The leading economists of the 1920s (Irving Fisher, Frank Knight) favored 100 percent reserves, along with Frederick Soddy, Nobel Laureate in Chemistry and underground economist. The fact that this idea is hardly discussed today is testimony to the power of vested interests over good ideas.

8. *Stop treating the scarce as if it were non-scarce, and the non-scarce as if it were scarce.* Enclose the remaining open access commons of rival natural capital (for example, atmosphere, electromagnetic spectrum, public lands) in public trusts, and price it by cap–auction–trade systems, or by taxes – while freeing from private enclosure and prices the non-rival commonwealth of knowledge and information. Knowledge, unlike the resource throughput, is not divided in the sharing, but multiplied. Once knowledge exists, the opportunity cost of sharing it is zero, and its allocative price should be zero. International development aid should more and more take the form of freely and actively shared knowledge, along with small grants, and less and less the form of large interest-bearing loans. Sharing knowledge costs little, does not create

unrepayable debts, and it increases the productivity of the truly rival and scarce factors of production. Of course, sharing false knowledge (a non-rival 'bad') is a danger, amply demonstrated by many growth-based 'structural adjustment' programs.[2] Existing real knowledge is the most important input to the production of new knowledge, and keeping it artificially scarce and expensive is perverse. Patent monopolies (aka 'intellectual property rights') should be given for fewer 'inventions', and for fewer years. Costs of production of new knowledge should, more and more, be publicly financed and then the knowledge freely shared. Knowledge is a cumulative social product and we have the discovery of the laws of thermodynamics, the double helix, the polio vaccine, and so on without patent monopolies and royalties.

9. *Stabilize population.* Work toward a balance in which births plus in-migrants equals deaths plus out-migrants. This is controversial and difficult, but as a start contraception should be made available for voluntary use everywhere. And while each nation can debate whether it should accept many or few immigrants, and who should get priority, such a debate is rendered moot if immigration laws are not enforced. We should support voluntary family planning, and enforcement of reasonable immigration laws, democratically enacted. A lot of the pro-natalist and open-borders rhetoric claims to be motivated by generosity. Perhaps it is, but in effect it turns out to be 'generosity' at the expense of the US working class and to the benefit of the employing class – an elitist cheap labor policy. The federal government, ever sensitive to the interests of the corporate employing class, has done an obligingly poor job of enforcing our immigration laws. Progressives have been slow to understand this. The environmental movement began with a focus on population, but has for some years now given in to 'political correctness' on this issue. Ironically, our tolerance for illegal immigration seems to have caused a compensatory tightening up on legal immigrants – longer waiting periods and more stringent requirements. In cost–benefit terms it is no doubt cheaper to 'enforce' our immigration laws against those who obey them than against those who break them – but quite unfair, and perceived as such by many legal immigrants and people attempting to immigrate legally. This is a very perverse selection process for new residents.

10. *Reform national accounts* – separate GDP into a cost account and a benefits account. Natural capital consumption and 'regrettably necessary defensive expenditures' belong in the cost account. Compare costs and benefits of a growing throughput at the margin, stop throughput growth when marginal costs equal marginal benefits. In addition to this objective

approach, recognize the importance of the subjective studies that show that, beyond a threshold, further GDP growth does not increase self-evaluated happiness. Beyond a level already reached in many countries GDP growth delivers no more happiness, but continues to generate depletion and pollution. At a minimum, we must not just assume that GDP growth is economic growth, but prove that it is not uneconomic growth.

CONCLUSIONS

The conceptual change in vision from the norm of a growth economy to that of a steady-state economy is radical, but the policies advocated are subject to gradual application. For example, 100 percent reserves can be approached gradually, the range of distributive inequality can be restricted gradually, caps can be adjusted gradually, and so on.

Also these measures are based on the impeccably conservative institutions of private property and decentralized market allocation. The policies advocated simply recognize that: (1) private property loses its legitimacy if too unequally distributed; (2) markets lose their legitimacy if prices do not tell the truth about opportunity costs; and (3) that the macroeconomy becomes an absurdity if its scale is required to grow beyond the biophysical limits of the earth. Well before reaching that radical biophysical limit we are encountering the orthodox economic limit in which extra costs of growth become greater than the extra benefits, ushering in the era of uneconomic growth, so far denied by the regnant growth paradigm, which seems intent on fulfilling the role of obstructive nuisance described in the epigraph by Whitehead.

NOTES

1. See Daly (1993).
2. See Daly (2008).

REFERENCES

Daly, H.E. (1993), The perils of free trade, *Scientific American*, **269**(5), 50–57.
Daly, H.E. (2008), Growth and development: critique of a credo, *Population and Development Review*, **34**(3), 511–18.

8. Climate policy: from 'know how' to 'do now'

The recent increase in attention to global warming is very welcome. Logically, it is part of the revived growth debate since climate change is the major symptom of uneconomic growth. However, the discussion of climate change usually fails to make the connection to growth. Most of the attention seems to be given to how to accommodate growth within the limits of the complex climate models and their predictions. Even that is welcome. However, it is useful to back up a bit and remember an observation by physicist John Wheeler, 'We make the world by the questions we ask'. What are the questions asked by the climate models, and what kind of world are they making, and what other questions might we ask that would make other worlds? Could we ask other questions that would make a more tractable world for policy?

The climate models ask whether CO_2 emissions will lead to atmospheric concentrations of 450–500 parts per million, and will that raise temperatures by 2 or 3° Celsius, by a certain date, and what will be the likely physical consequences in climate and geography, and in what sequence, and according to what probability distributions, and what will be the damages inflicted by such changes, as well as the costs of abating them, and what are the ratios of the present values of the damage costs compared to abatement expenditures at various discount rates, and which discount rate should we use, and how likely is it that new information learned while we are constructing the model, will invalidate the results? What kind of world is created by such questions? Perhaps a world of such enormous uncertainty and complexity as to paralyse policy. Scientists will disagree on the answers to every one of these empirical questions.

Could we ask a different question that creates a different world? Why not ask, can we systematically continue to emit increasing amounts of CO_2 and other greenhouse gases into the atmosphere without eventually provoking unacceptable climate changes? Scientists will overwhelmingly agree that the answer is no. The basic science, first principles, and directions of causality are very clear. Svante Arrhenius discovered the basics a century ago. Focusing on them creates a world of relative certainty, at least as to the thrust and direction of policy. True, the rates, sequences, and valuations are uncertain and subject to debate. But as long as we focus on measuring these inherently uncertain empirical consequences, rather than on the certain first principles that cause them, we will overwhelm the consensus to 'do something now' with ditherings about what we might someday consider doing if ever the evidence is sufficiently compelling. I am afraid that once the evidence is really compelling then our response will also be compelled, and policy choice will be irrelevant.

To make the point more simply, if you jump out of an airplane you need a crude parachute more than an accurate altimeter. And if you also take an altimeter with you, at least do not become so bemused in tracking your descent that you forget to pull the ripcord on your parachute. We should be thinking in terms of a parachute, however crude.

The next question we should ask is, What is it that is causing us to systematically emit ever more CO_2 into the atmosphere? It is the same thing that causes us to emit more and more of all kind of wastes into the biosphere, namely our irrational commitment to exponential growth forever on a finite planet subject to the laws of thermodynamics. If we overcome the growth idolatry we could then go on to ask an intelligent question like, 'How can we design and manage a steady-state economy, one that respects the limits of the biosphere?' Instead we ask a wrong-headed, growth-bound question, specifically: 'By how much will we have to increase energy efficiency, or carbon efficiency, in order to maintain customary growth rates in GDP?' Suppose we get an answer, say we need to double efficiency in 10 years and we actually do it. So what? We will then just do more of all the things that have become more efficient and therefore cheaper, and will then emit more wastes, including greenhouse gases – the famous rebound or Jevons effect. A policy of 'efficiency first' does not give us 'frugality second' – it makes frugality less necessary. In the nineteenth century words of William Stanley Jevons,

> It is wholly a confusion of ideas to suppose that the economical use of fuel is equivalent to a diminished consumption. The very contrary is the truth. (Jevons, 1866, p. 123)

And further,

> Now, if the quantity of coal used in a blast-furnace, for instance, be diminished in comparison with the yield, the profits of the trade will increase, new capital will be attracted, the price of pig-iron will fall, but the demand for

it increase; and eventually the greater number of furnaces will more than make up for the diminished consumption of each. (Jevons, 1866, pp. 124–5)

In modern words, if we increase miles per gallon we are likely to travel more miles because it is cheaper. Or suppose instead of driving more we save the money. What then do we do with it? Travel by airplane? Buy a second house? Invest in nuclear power or ethanol production? Better to pay it to our psychiatrist for the low-energy service of listening while we confess our sins. Yes, but does that not help him pay for his airplane trip or second house? Jevons has us by the tail – 'It is wholly a confusion of ideas to suppose that the economical use of fuel is equivalent to a diminished consumption. The very contrary is the truth'. Our energy policy is too much about 'efficient patterns of consumption' and not enough about 'sustainable aggregate levels of consumption'. It is wholly a confusion of ideas to suppose that an efficient pattern of energy consumption is equivalent to, or even leads to, a sustainable aggregate level of energy consumption.

But if we go for 'frugality first' (in other words, sustainable level first) as our direct policy variable (for example, a carbon tax, or a cap–auction–trade system) then we will get 'efficiency second' as an adaptation to more expensive carbon fuels. 'Frugality first gives efficiency second, not vice versa' should be the first design principle for energy and climate policy. Efficiency is an adaptation to scarcity that makes it less painful; it is not the abolition of scarcity, the so-called 'win–win' solution beloved by politicians.

The second thing wrong with our misleading question is its assumption that we need to maintain current growth rates in GDP. There is a lot of evidence that GDP growth at the current margin in the United States is in fact uneconomic growth – that is, growth that increases social and environmental costs faster than it increases production benefits, growth that accumulates 'illth' faster than it accumulates wealth. I know that there is still poverty in the world and that GDP growth in some countries is still economic – all the more reason to stop uneconomic growth and free up resources and ecological space for truly economic growth by the poor! That should be the second design principle.

You will not find the term 'uneconomic growth' in the index of any economics textbook. My word-processing program even underlines it in red warning me that I probably made a syntactical error! But it is not hard to see how the reality of uneconomic growth sneaks up on us. We have moved from a world relatively empty of us and our stuff, to a world relatively full of us, in just one lifetime. The world population has tripled in my lifetime and the populations of cars, houses, livestock, refrigerators, TVs, and so on, have increased by much more. As we transform natural capital into manmade capital the former becomes more scarce and the latter more abundant – an inversion of the traditional pattern of scarcity. This inversion is furthered by the fact that manmade capital is often private property while natural capital frequently is an open access commons.

In the empty world the limiting factor was manmade capital; in the full world it is remaining natural capital. For example, the annual fish catch used to be limited by the number of fishing boats; now it is limited by the remaining stocks of fish in the ocean and their capacity to reproduce. Barrels of petroleum extracted used to be limited by drilling rigs and pumps; now it is limited by remaining deposits in the ground, or alternatively by capacity of the atmosphere to absorb the products of its combustion. There seems to be a race between peak oil and global warming, between source and sink limits – but both are natural capital so for my point it does not matter which proves more limiting. Economic logic stays the same – it says invest in and economize on the limiting factor. But the identity of the limiting factor has changed, and we have not adapted. We continue to invest in manmade capital rather than in restoration of natural capital. This further depletes natural capital and eventually drives down the value of complementary manmade capital, a double loss!

The reason that mainstream economists do not see this is that they think manmade capital and natural capital are substitutes rather than complements. With substitutes you do not have a limiting factor, so they overlook the scarcity-augmenting fact of limitationality. I am not sure why they do this, but suspect that they prize substitution's mathematical tractability more than complementarity's conformity to the first law of thermodynamics. Furthermore, conformity to the first law is ideologically inconvenient because it slows down growth. Others may have a better explanation, but the fact remains that natural resource flows and capital funds are mistakenly treated as substitutes – when natural resources are included in the production function at all, which usually they are not!

In addition to this monumental error on the production or supply side, we have an equally monumental error on the utility or demand side – the failure to take seriously the fact that beyond a threshold of absolute income already passed in the United States, welfare or self-evaluated happiness becomes a function of relative income rather than absolute income. Since it is impossible to increase everyone's relative income, further absolute growth in GDP becomes a self-canceling arms race.

Enough of what is wrong. Can one offer a reasonable policy based only on first principles? Yes – one such policy is called ecological tax reform – a stiff severance tax on carbon, levied at the well head and mine mouth, accompanied by equalizing tariffs on carbon-intensive imports, and rebating the revenues by abolishing regressive taxes on low incomes. Such a policy would reduce total carbon use, give an incentive for developing less carbon-intensive technologies, and redistribute income progressively. Yes, but how do we know what is the optimal tax rate, and would it not be regressive, and is there really a 'double dividend', as some have claimed, and so on? Once again we make the world by the questions we ask. We need to raise public revenue somehow, so why not tax carbon extraction heavily and compensate by taxing income lightly, especially low incomes? More generally, tax the resource throughput (that to which value is added) and stop taxing value added. Whether you tax the throughput at the input or output end is a matter of convenience, although I generally prefer the input end because depletion is spatially more concentrated than pollution. Also higher input prices induce efficiency at all subsequent stages of the production process, and limiting depletion ultimately limits pollution, at least in a gross aggregate sense.

Tax bads (depletion and pollution), not goods (income). Does anyone imagine that we currently tax income at the optimal rate? Better first to tax the right thing and later worry about the 'optimal' rate of taxation, and so on. People do not like to see the value added by their own efforts taxed away, even though we accept it as necessary up to a point. But most people do not mind seeing resource scarcity rents, value that no one added, taxed away. And the most important public good served by the carbon tax would be climate stability, a benefit in which everyone shares. The revenue from the carbon severance tax could be rebated to the public by abolishing other taxes, especially regressive ones. And even though the incidence of the tax by itself is regressive with respect to income, that can be more than compensated by spending the revenues progressively. It also has the advantage that it is paid by all consumers, including the income tax evaders and avoiders.

Setting policy in accord with first principles allows us to act now without getting mired in endless delays caused by the uncertainties of complex empirical measurements and predictions. Of course, the uncertainties do not disappear. We will experience them as surprising consequences, both agreeable and disagreeable, necessitating mid-course correction to the policies enacted on the basis of first principles. Recognizing the need for mid-course corrections should be a third policy design principle. But at least we would have begun a process of moving in the right direction. To continue business as usual while debating the predictions of complex models in a world made even more uncertain by the questions we ask, is to fail to pull the ripcord. The empirical consequences of this last failure, unfortunately, are all too certain.

REFERENCE

Jevons, W.S. (1866); *The Coal Question*, London: Macmillan and Co.

PART IV

Ethical foundations of a steady-state economy

9. Incorporating values in a bottom-line ecological economy

> Beware of the man who works hard to learn something, learns it, and finds himself no wiser than before. He is full of murderous resentment of people who are ignorant without having come by their ignorance the hard way.
>
> Kurt Vonnegut

INTRODUCTION

Values are different from tastes. Tastes are personal and subjective. They belong to the private sphere of our life. Values, in contrast, are impersonal and objective. They belong to the public sphere. We all have a right to our own individual tastes, but not to our own individual values or our own individual facts. Of course, relativists will deny this, claiming that we all have the right to determine values for ourselves. Some postmodernists would even allow us to construct and deconstruct our own facts. Such license in choosing our own values and facts eliminates the basis for affirming the objective truth of anything, including relativism, and is therefore self-contradictory.

Ecological economics has inherited the same value presupposition from both of its parents, making it quite a strong legacy. This is the idea that individual selfishness and competitive struggle lead to the greater collective good. From economics, beginning with Adam Smith, comes the 'invisible hand'. From biology, via ecology, comes Darwin's natural selection of the best adapted individuals in the face of competition for the limited means of subsistence forced by Malthusian population pressure. In part, these are two factual insights into how the world works, rather than the affirmation of a value. Competition is a fact. But in both cases the lamentable fact is blessed by its valued consequences – market efficiency and evolutionary progress.

There are other traditions both in economics and biology that are contrary to the selfishness emphasis. Adam Smith himself wrote *The Theory of Moral Sentiments* emphasizing cooperation and community as the overall context in which competition could be trusted. In biology,

Kropotkin emphasized mutual aid as a factor in evolution. Nevertheless, in both disciplines the selfishness tradition has been quite dominant, and we should be aware in ecological economics that we have received a double dose of this inheritance, for better or worse.

What is meant by 'the bottom line'? What is a 'bottom-line society'? The term bottom line is commonly understood as 'profit', 'net worth', 'how much money you make' – the score that tells whether you won or lost. These are popular understandings of the term in economics. In neo-Darwinian biology, the bottom line is how many of your genes you forward on to the next generation. Or as some prefer, how many of your selfish genes got themselves replicated in the next generation by manipulating you.

I would like to imagine a perfect bottom line for a minute. Imagine a supercomputer programed with the ultimate goodness function. You could put into it data describing any state of the world, hypothetical or real, and it would give you back a number that measured how good that state of the world is. Should we enact a certain policy? Plug in the change. If the computer spits out a higher bottom line number, we make the change. If the bottom line goes down, we leave things as they are. Several people suggest different incompatible changes in the state of the world, all of which raise the bottom line. We choose the one that raises the bottom line the most. Each person can enter a change at his or her own initiative. This computer can also calculate the contribution that each individual makes to the total goodness of the world and is programed to write to him or her a monthly check in exact proportion to that contribution. It does not matter to the computer if your motivation is selfish or altruistic. The program rewards you according to how much your actions increase the general goodness index, the bottom line. Private selfishness leads to public good. In T.S. Eliot's words, 'The system is so perfect that no one needs to be good'. No one needs to be wise or well-informed either. All questions are quickly and correctly resolved by the supercomputer and the ultimate goodness function. The economy of information, thought, debate, and conscience searching is complete. Qualitative, dialectical, judgmental issues are given automatic, precise, numerical answers.

That is my fantasy of the ultimate bottom-line society. I describe it because I think that, while no one believes it exists, many of us see our existing imperfect system as an approximation to this 'perfect' system. The goodness index is profit, the goodness function program is a giant set of simultaneous equations describing supply and demand of all people for all commodities and factors. The competitive market is the computer that by systematic trial and error solves the giant set of simultaneous equations, giving a general equilibrium solution in which everyone is as well off as he or she can possibly be, by his or her own estimation, without causing someone else to be worse off.

Do we speak as if the competitive market were a reasonable approximation to the ultimate goodness function? Listen to former US Presidential Economics Advisor, Charles Schultze: 'Market-like arrangements ... reduce the need for compassion, patriotism, brotherly love, and cultural solidarity as motivating forces behind social improvement. Harnessing the 'base' motive of material self-interest to promote the common good is perhaps the most important social invention mankind has achieved' (quoted in Schwartz, 1987, p. 247).

Critics of economic orthodoxy, such as E.F. Schumacher (1973), lament the dominance of the market goodness function:

> In the current vocabulary of condemnation there are few words as final and conclusive as the word 'uneconomic'. If an activity has been branded as 'uneconomic', its right to existence is not merely questioned but energetically denied. Anything that is found to be an impediment to economic growth is a shameful thing, and if people cling to it, they are thought of as either saboteurs or fools. Call a thing immoral or ugly, soul-destroying or a degradation of man, a peril to the peace of the world or to the wellbeing of future generations; as long as you have not shown it to be 'uneconomic' you have not really questioned its right to exist, grow, and prosper. (p. 39)

A bottom-line society is one in which the word 'uneconomic' is a death sentence – the only legitimate death sentence. Assuming the perfect goodness of the algorithm that computes the bottom line, then it would indeed be a shameful thing to oppose its growth – if something really were immoral or ugly it would have a negative effect on the bottom line and no right to exist. But we all know that our bottom line is not a perfect goodness function, and many of us believe that the very concept of a perfect goodness function is a dangerous abstraction – 'a system so perfect that no one needs to be good', will cause goodness to atrophy, like a muscle that is never used. It is absurd to think that the social good can be defined independently of the nature of the motive force of our actions.

Yet our actual, imperfect bottom lines do tell us something important, and I suspect that as many mistakes result from paying too little attention to the bottom line as from paying too much.

Is our existing bottom line a good enough approximation to the ultimate goodness function to make it an indispensable practical guide for putting first things first? Or is it a very poor approximation that reduces unique values to an inappropriately low common denominator, namely, willingness to pay for satisfaction of personal tastes, and thereby distorts more than it informs? Or is it sometimes one, and sometimes the other, depending on context? Perhaps, like the Bible, the bottom line requires contextual, not literal interpretation.

In an attempt to deal with this question (I do not say answer it), I would like to consider the practical bottom line in three different contexts:

1. In its natural habitat, the profit sector of a market economy, the bottom line is considered as profit.
2. In its artificial habitat, the not-for-profit sector, where it exists, but in captivity, not allowed free range – the bottom line is considered as something other than profit. Profit is a constraint – but not what is maximized. The not-for-profit sector has to be disciplined by a budget – but that is not the same as seeking profit.
3. In the aggregate economy – the collective sum total of all enterprises, profit and nonprofit – GNP is considered as the grand *lineus bottomus bottomorum*, if classicists will allow such pig Latin.

THE PROFIT SECTOR

In the profit sector, an activity is economic if it yields an adequate near-term money profit to those who undertake the activity. Operationally and in accord with common usage this is what 'economic' means. But common usage has been very disrespectful of etymology and classical learning. Aristotle made a very important distinction between 'oikonomia' and 'chrematistics'. Chrematistics is a word that nowadays is most commonly found in unabridged dictionaries, where it is defined as the branch of political economy relating to the manipulation of property and wealth so as to maximize the short-term monetary exchange value to the owners. In contrast, oikonomia is the management of the property and wealth of the household so as to increase its use value for all members of the household over the long run. We may expand the scope of 'household' to include the larger community in which members are dependent on one another for their livelihood and cultural nurture. For oikonomia, the bottom line is use value, welfare, or enjoyment of life, and money (exchange value) is a tool. For chrematistics, the bottom line is money (exchange value) that is considered to be synonymous with welfare, or at least the best available measure.

Our word economic is a derivative from oikonomia, but its current meaning is often closer to chrematistics. Wall Street's activities are chrematistic, not economic. If that was ever in doubt, it should no longer be in 2009. The modern world is full of chrematists. Nor were they uncommon in the ancient world. The great philosopher Thales of Miletus was a part-time chrematist. According to Aristotle, Thales was reproached with his personal poverty as clear evidence that his philosophy was of no use: 'Thales, if you're so smart, how come you ain't rich?' To silence these morons of Miletus, Thales decided to get rich. By his knowledge of the stars, he was able to foresee an early bumper crop of olives. While it was still winter he leased all the olive presses in the area at a low price, and at harvest time made large monopoly profits. Afterward the wealthy Thales's lectures on the fundamental importance of water got a better hearing than when he was poor. I know that many professors would like to emulate Thales's pedagogical technique.

But neither Thales nor Aristotle took this little trick very seriously. After all, Thales planted no olive trees, built no olive presses, discovered no new uses for olive oil, and made no one but himself better off. In fact, he enriched himself at other people's expense. Thales enriched the world with his ideas vastly more than he bilked it with his olive press monopoly. But that is not true for most modern chrematists – the litigious lawyers, the tax-gimmicky accountants, the merger manipulators, hedge-fund operators, monopolists, and unproductive rent-seekers of all kinds. Our 'ultimate goodness program' seems to be writing out some awfully large checks to people whose contributions are very hard to see. Only when one's contribution is 'hard to see' can it be so wildly exaggerated. A lot of this exaggeration has been written down in the financial panic of 2008–2009. Unfortunately, market 'corrections' come also at the expense of people whose incomes were never exaggerated.

Oikonomia differs from chrematistics in three ways:

1. It takes a long-run rather than short-run view.
2. It considers costs and benefits to the whole community, not just to the parties to the transaction.
3. It focuses on concrete use value and the limited accumulation thereof, rather than on abstract exchange value and its stimulus toward unlimited accumulation. Unlimited accumulation is the goal of the chrematist and is evidence for Aristotle of the unnaturalness of the activity. True wealth is limited by the satisfaction of the concrete use it was designed for. There is such a thing as enough for oikonomia. For chrematistics, more is always better.

One reason that our bottom line of profit is an imperfect and sometimes perverse goodness index is that it reflects chrematistics as well as oikonomia. At this point, I can imagine an objection from some economists. Adam Smith's doctrine of the invisible hand of market competition carefully laid out the conditions for converting private chrematistics into social oikonomia. Those conditions are a competitive market, secure property rights, and no externalities. Economists admit that externalities can be important, but the basic role of the bottom line as a goodness index can be restored by adjusting prices to reflect all costs and all benefits. By internalizing externalities we can make the bottom line reflect costs to third parties, to future generations, to subhuman life, or whatever. Once externalities have been internalized in prices by appropriate taxes or subsidies, we can go back to keeping our eye on the bottom line, 'and economizing on compassion, patriotism, information, brotherly love'.

My colleagues have a point. I will give two hearty cheers for internalization of externalities, and withhold the third cheer only because it seems to me that the logic of internalization is not carried to its full conclusion. To see this, let us consider the specific case of internalizing the various external costs associated with the mining and use of coal.

First, consider black lung disease (pneumoconiosis). If the labor market were perfect and the miners had safe alternative employment and were perfectly mobile, and if they understood the risk of black lung, they would require a higher wage to be miners. In either case, the money costs to the coal company would increase to compensate for the real cost of black lung. That cost will be reflected in a higher price of coal and will ultimately be paid by the users of coal. The previously external cost is now internalized into the price of coal. But if there are few alternatives, little information, lack of mobility, the market wage will not count the cost of black lung. The real suffering and medical expense will fall on the worker and will not be compensated by the mine owners. The users of coal will not be paying the full cost of production of coal.

This cost could be internalized by legislation obliging the coal companies to pay the medical expenses of black lung disease contracted by its employees, plus a premium for suffering and reduced life expectancy. These costs, of course, are added to the price of coal.

At this point, the chrematist will squawk – 'Can we afford the higher price of coal?' he will ask. The higher price will hurt consumers, especially the poor. It will raise prices of all commodities whose production requires coal. Higher domestic prices hurt our exports and encourage imports, worsening our balance of payments and competitive position in the world market. Can we afford those costs?

The true economist has a ready answer for the chrematist – 'we are already paying the costs' – the costs are simply there and will not go away as long as we mine coal – the question is who pays them, and have they been minimized? The costs are the sacrifice of other good things required to dig coal out of the ground and burn it. If users of coal feel that at the margin coal is not worth the price that now reflects all costs (including the sacrifice of healthy lungs and the resources dedicated to their partial repair), and consequently coal sales fall – why that is exactly as it should be. Or do you want people to buy more coal even when the extra coal costs more than it is worth? In addition, once the coal companies are paying the cost, they have an incentive to reduce those costs, to take measures to make mining safer to the lungs. Such an incentive is lacking as long as taxpayers or miners' families foot the bill.

I am entirely on the side of the economist in this debate. It is regrettable that we have so many chrematists in business and politics who oppose the internalization of externalities because they cannot see beyond the gross bottom line. Internalizing externalities does not remove the bottom line, but recomputes it, substituting a net for a gross bottom line. Opposition to this sensible policy stems from the fact that the recalculated bottom line is less favorable to the mining company – in effect coal-mining companies lose a subsidy.

But once we win the battle for internalization of externalities, can we then go back to the invisible hand, dedicating ourselves to chrematistic personal enrichment secure in the knowledge that what is good for our recalculated bottom line is good for the world. Would the system again be sufficiently perfect that no one needs to be good?

Before jumping to that conclusion let us consider other more pervasive external costs arising from coal: acid rain and the greenhouse effect of CO_2. It still makes sense to internalize external costs but is now vastly more difficult. For one thing, these are global problems. British coal causes acid rain in Sweden. US coal causes acid rain in Canada. Furthermore, coal is not the only cause of acid rain or the greenhouse effect. What percentage of these problems is due to coal, what to other fuels, how much to synergistic reactions, how much to natural causes? The full physical consequences of the global CO_2 buildup are not predictable. Even less predictable are the costs. Furthermore, the external costs are largely in the future, and the benefits of coal use are mainly in the present. Chrematists tell us to discount the costs by virtue of their futurity, but this is a questionable practice at best, and the rate of discount is largely arbitrary. Any calculation of how much to increase the price of coal so as to internalize the external cost of acid rain and CO_2 will be based largely on arbitrary assumptions and guesses.

The logic, the principle, is still valid, but the scale of the problem overwhelms the tool – like dredging the Mississippi River with a teaspoon. We are better off setting quantitative limits and minimum safety standards based on ecological and ethical criteria. Then, let prices adapt to those physical constraints. That may be considered a kind of internalization strategy, if you wish, but based on controlling aggregate quantity rather than price. Economists are shy about controlling quantities – the implications are more radical than adjusting prices.

Finally, take an intermediate case – not as easy as black lung but not as intractable as acid rain and CO_2 – the case of toxic wastes. Suppose that 25 years ago all the external costs of toxic wastes had been foreseen and that the expenditure to avoid, cleanup, and reimburse victims had been included in the price of the chemicals whose manufacture generated those wastes. How many bottom lines in the chemical industry would have been converted from positive to negative by including all those costs? How large a reduction in the chemical industry would have resulted? Quite a large reduction I would bet. If you can contemplate such a reduction with equanimity, you are a true economist. If the thought causes you to panic, you are still a chrematist! And the thought that nationalization of the chemical industry would solve the problem can be laid to rest by a look at the equally large unaccounted cleanup costs accumulated by the nationalized production of plutonium for bombs.

To summarize, even in its natural habitat, the profit sector, the bottom line is misinterpreted by chrematists. True economists understand the shortcomings of the bottom line and seek to correct them by internalizing externalities. This is fine for specific, localized, small-scale externalities such as black lung disease, but a more radical approach is needed for pervasive externalities such as acid rain and the greenhouse effect. Also, there are many initiatives within the profit sector that seek to remedy its defects by other means. For example, we have the institutions of worker-owned or consumer-owned cooperatives, publicly regulated private corporations, fair trade initiatives, and so on. These are important hybrids still within the profit sector but will not be pursued here.

Let us now turn to the not-for-profit sector and ask if their bottom lines offer a better approximation to our hypothetical 'goodness index'.

THE NOT-FOR-PROFIT SECTOR

The not-for-profit sector includes government services, charity, public research and information organizations, the military, the university, and, in the limit, the socialist state, where nearly everything is in the not-for-profit sector. In between there are actual welfare states, and models of market socialism that rely on profit significantly, and the instructive experience of Cuban socialism. Not-for-profit organizations do have bottom lines other than profit – a goodness index that reflects their main purpose. They also have to live within budgets. One might expect that not-for-profit organizations encounter less perversity and bias in their goodness index than do profit-based organizations. A few examples will cast doubt on that supposition.

The director of a public tuberculosis (TB) hospital was, so the story is told, instructed to improve efficiency by following a plan of management by quantitative objectives. The director was instructed to define the hospital's objective, develop a measurable index of success in attaining that objective, and to evaluate all activities and personnel in terms of their measured contribution to that goal. A clearer expression of the bottom-line philosophy would be hard to find. Stating the goal was easy: restoring TB patients to health. A measurable index of success was more difficult, but not impossible. TB victims cough a lot. As they get better, they cough less. Little microphones were placed by each pillow to record the coughs of each patient. Soon the staff and even the patients realized the significance of those tiny microphones. The frequency of coughing fell dramatically as prescriptions of valium and codeine increased. Relaxed patients cough less. Patients who cough less must be getting healthier, right? Wrong. They were getting worse, precisely because they were not coughing and spitting out the congestion. The cough index was abandoned.

The US Navy reportedly experimented with 'number of teeth pulled per month' as an index of how well their dentists were doing their job, with predictably unfortunate results. Number of teeth saved would be a more reasonable index, but too easy to exaggerate. A still better index would be teeth pulled that should have been pulled plus teeth saved that should have been saved. But now our clear quantitative index disappears in a fog of qualitative judgment, and we are back to trusting the judgment and integrity of the dentist – the very thing the objective index was designed to avoid in its implicit quest for a system so perfect that no one need be good.

Like the dentist evaluated on number of teeth pulled, the university professor is evaluated by articles published. Miraculously, the number of publications has soared. Is it because professors now work harder and smarter? No doubt! But there are also some more creative adaptations, in other words, ways to serve the index directly while totally bypassing the reality that the index was supposed to reflect. One obvious adaptation is to write shorter papers, aiming at the MPU or minimal publishable unit. In this way, you get three short, unintelligible papers instead of one longer, integrated and easier-to-understand article. Also expanding the number of coauthors allows the same article to feed more professors, reminiscent of the miracle of the multiplication of the loaves and the fishes. New journals can be started in each sub-discipline, further fractionating the wholeness of knowledge. Since the advent of computers, number crunching has become cheaper relative to thinking, so another adaptation is to think less and crunch more – to correlate anything with everything and publish the results as an empirical test of whatever hypothesis seems to have been confirmed after the fact.

I am old enough to remember the time before publish or perish, and I confess that university professors probably did not work quite as hard then. But books and articles did get published. Since there was no big extrinsic reward for publication, the intrinsic reward was dominant. Articles and books got published because someone really wanted to say something. From the readers' point of view, that is a good filter and probably contributed greatly to the coherence, unity, and relevance of knowledge.

A similar social filter against ill-conceived contributions to mankind was suggested by the great Swiss economist Sismondi in the eighteenth century. Sismondi argued against granting patents to inventors on the grounds that this would give an incentive for inventions whose only purpose would be to enrich the inventor. By relying on intrinsic motiv- ation, we are more likely to get inventions that benefit mankind rather than just enrich the inventor. Likewise, an article published only because its author had something to say and took the pains to write it, is probably more worth reading than an article motivated mainly by the desire for promotion.

I will come back to university bottom lines in a minute, but first let us look briefly at the ultimate in not-for-profit organizations, the socialist state. It too has a bottom line, an ultimate goodness function – ultimately the new socialist man in the classless society. But that, according to Marxist materialist determinism, requires the material precondition of overwhelming abundance, which in turn requires rapid growth, which in turn requires meeting the quota in the five-year plan. That quota is expressed in physical units. If the socialist nail factory's quota is set in pounds, then it tends to produce too many heavy spikes and not enough finishing nails and tacks. If the quota is set in number of nails, we get too many tacks and not enough spikes. If the plan tries to specify the quantity of every size and quality of nail, then it is overwhelmed with detailed information requirements. Similar examples can be multiplied, and led the Soviets to experiment with profit as a bottom line in some sectors, because it seemed a better quantitative reflection of the quality of usefulness – as judged by the person with the most information, namely, the user who buys the item. Physical units provide too coarse a quantitative mesh for capturing quality – the quality of usefulness or of being wanted for whatever reason. Monetary exchange value is a far from perfect index of value, but at least it means that someone is willing to pay that amount for the item. That information should not be despised.

But the lure of a monetary index can also be treacherous if it leads a not-for-profit entity to get confused about its basic purpose. This can happen – even in university. What is the university's bottom line? On my diploma, it says that my alma mater was founded '*ad maiorem Dei gloriam,* in freedom for research to sober fearless pursuit of truth, beauty, righteousness, and to all high emprise consecrated'. Its purpose is not to serve existing preferences, but to inform and improve those preferences by pursuit of objective value. Note the absence of any reference to a winning football team, or to turning out an employable workforce. The latter is probably a likely by-product of having spent four years in sufficient sobriety to attain a diploma, but is not the university's bottom line.

The lure of the monetary bottom line is so strong that sometimes universities seem to think of themselves as profit-maximizing entities – as when Professor X is lauded for having brought in grant monies in excess of his salary – as if 'grants minus salary equals profit' and as if profit were the bottom line. Grant money is an index of success to the chrematist, but to the economist it has the fatal defect of measuring input rather than output. If the grant results in greater output of published research into truth, beauty and righteousness then its benefit is already counted in the publication or citation index, which, for all its faults, is at least an index of output. If no extra publications result from the grant, then we would hardly want to reward Professor X for having unproductively absorbed public funds. Actually, the input of grant dollars is a social cost and should be counted in the denominator, not the numerator, of the efficiency ratio. The proper measure is research output of Professor X per dollar invested in him. The fact that grant money customarily gets put in the numerator, and the fact that my suggestion to put it in the denominator would be considered totally outrageous, do not alter the self-evident logic on which the proposal is based. If you can view this suggestion with equanimity you are a true economist. If it induces panic, you are still a chrematist.

THE MACROECONOMY AND GNP AS BOTTOM LINE

A logical extension of these remarks on the profit and not-for-profit contexts is to consider the GDP as a collective bottom line for the macroeconomy. There are many problems with GDP accounting, as evident to any reader (though not to the authors) of the Report of the Growth Commission (The Growth Report, World Bank, 2008). GDP is what they believe should be growing, but instead of explaining the measure and differentiating its components, the Commission simply praises it:

> GDP is a familiar but remarkable statistic. It is an astonishing feat of statistical compression, reducing the restless endeavor and bewildering variety of a national economy into a single number, which can increase over time ... A growing GDP is evidence of a society getting its collective act together. (p. 17)

Well, it may also be evidence of a society depleting its life-sustaining natural capital and counting it as current income, of asymmetric entries that count defensive expenditure on anti-bads (for example, pollution cleanup) but fail to enter negatively the bads (for example, pollution) that made the anti-bads necessary, or of shifting household production into the monetary economy because both spouses are now breadwinners. Also, since GDP counts gross rather than net investment, it increases with the depreciation and replacement of existing manmade capital. Rather than try to deal with these issues in detail, I will just show how easy it is, even for very prominent economists, to grossly misuse this macro bottom line.

1.   Reporting on a National Academy of Science study on climate change and greenhouse adaptation, *Science* magazine quotes Yale economist William Nordhaus (1991) as saying the following: 'Agriculture, the part of the economy that is sensitive to climate change, accounts for just 3 percent of national output. That means there is no way to get a very large effect on the US economy'. (p. 1206)

2.   Oxford economist Wilfred Beckerman, in his small 1995 book, *Small is Stupid*, also tells us that greenhouse-gas-induced climate change is no worry because it affects only agriculture, and agriculture is only 3 percent of GNP. Beckerman elaborates, 'Even if net output of agriculture fell by 50 percent by the end of the next century this is only a 1.5 percent cut in GNP'. (p. 91)

3.   In the November/December 1997 issue of *Foreign Affairs*, former president of the American Economic Association (and subsequent 2005 Nobel Laureate in Economics), Thomas C. Schelling, elaborates a bit more:

In the developed world hardly any component of the national income is
affected by climate. Agriculture is practically the only sector of the economy
affected by climate and it contributes only a small percentage – 3 percent in
the United States – of national income. If agricultural productivity were
drastically reduced by climate change, the cost of living would rise by 1 or 2
percent, and at a time when per capita income will likely have doubled. (p. 9)

First, it is not true that agriculture is the only climate-sensitive sector of
the economy – just ask the insurance firms (and the citizens of New
Orleans after Katrina!). But that is not the error that most concerns me.
The error that concerns me here is to treat the importance of agriculture
as if it were measured by its percentage of GDP – its presumed
contribution to the macro bottom line. Surely, these distinguished economists know all about the law of diminishing marginal utility, consumer
surplus, and the fact that exchange value (price) reflects marginal use
value, not total use value. They know that GDP is measured in units of
exchange value. They surely know that other economists have long
referred to agriculture as primary production and understand the reason
for that designation. Presumably, they also know that the demand for
food in the aggregate is famously inelastic. With this in mind, it should
be evident that in the event of a climate-induced collapse of agriculture
the relative price of food would skyrocket and the percentage of GNP
going to agriculture, which is not a constant of nature, could rise from 3
percent to 90 percent. No doubt, adaptation would be possible, since in
the past agriculture did account for 90 percent of national product and we
(many fewer of us, consuming much less per capita) survived. Clearly,
the percentage of the GNP derived from agriculture is a measure of the
importance only of marginal (very small) changes in current agricultural
output – certainly not Beckerman's (1995) '50 percent fall', or Schelling's (1997) 'drastic reduction', or Nordhaus' (1991) unqualified 'no
way'. One way of looking at the error is therefore that it represents an
elementary failure to distinguish marginal from infra-marginal change.

Another dimension of the error is neglect of structural interdependence. These economists are surely familiar with Leontief's input–
output matrix showing the amount of input that each sector of the
economy requires from all other sectors in order to produce its output.
And each input used by each sector is itself an output of another sector
that also required inputs from nearly every other sector – likewise for the
inputs to those inputs, and so on. All these technical interdependencies of
production are abstracted from in GDP, which leaves out intermediate
production, counting only what goes to the final consumer. What happens

to the output of nonagricultural sectors when agricultural inputs to them are drastically reduced?

Yet another related dimension of the error is that it treats all parts of GDP as substitutable, not only on the margin, but also on the average and on the whole. If GDP declines by 3 percent due to disruption of agriculture that will presumably be no problem if GDP simultaneously increases by 3 percent due to growth in information services. A dollar's worth of anything is assumed to be indifferently substitutable for a dollar's worth of anything else. This is the same for a hundred billion dollars' worth. Although money is indeed fungible, real GDP is not. We measure GDP in monetary units, but GDP is certainly not money. A dollar is a piece of paper or a book-keeping entry; a dollar's worth of food is a physical quantity of something necessary to support life. The fungibility of dollars does not imply the fungibility of food and, say, information services. Unless we first have enough food, we just will not be interested in information services. If I am hungry, I want a meal, not a recipe, not even a lot of recipes. Maybe that is why economists traditionally have called agriculture 'primary' and services 'tertiary'.

True, agriculture accounts for only 3 percent of GDP, but it is precisely the specific 3 percent on which the other 97 percent is based! It is not an indifferently fungible 3 percent. The foundation of a building may be only 3 percent of its height, but that does not mean that we can subtract the foundation if only we add 3 percent to the flagpole on top of the building. Like a building, GDP has a structure – neither is just a pile of fungible stuff. In addition to technical interdependence, this structure reflects objective valuation by consumers, a kind of 'lexicographic ordering'. No amount of information services will substitute for food until food needs are met – just as the second letter of words is irrelevant to the alphabetical order of a dictionary unless the first letter is the same.

But it is still hard to understand how such distinguished economists could make such a mistake. In all three cases, the bad argument was part of a larger defense of economic growth. Maybe the undoubted conclusion lent credence to the faulty reasoning leading to it. Maybe it reflects the bias of both capitalist and communist economists against peasants and farmers. I do not know. But I am sure that the error cannot be attributed to ignorance or stupidity of these three economists – people whom I know and have reason to respect. If these economists were stupid, their error would be of little interest. It is precisely because of their legitimately high prestige that one suspects that the error is to be found in the presuppositions of the discipline of neoclassical economics, to which they all firmly adhere.

I do not think that it is too much of an oversimplification to locate the origins of this error in a diagram found in the first pages of every economics textbook. This diagram shows the economic process as an isolated circular flow between firms and households. Nothing enters and nothing exits. No natural resources are brought in from the environment, no wastes are expelled to the environment – no waste, no replenishment – a perpetual motion machine! Of course, the justification offered is that economics deals with scarcity. In an empty world, resources and waste absorption services are not scarce and can be abstracted from. But in a full world, they are scarce. Now some economists try to retrofit depletion and pollution into the isolated circular flow by *ad hoc* introduction of 'externalities', thereby 'saving the phenomena' after the manner of Ptolemaic epicycles.

This is useful as far as it goes. But in standard textbooks, there is still no 'Copernican' pre-analytic vision of the economy as an open subsystem of the containing ecosystem – the basic picture is one of abstract exchange value, GDP divorced from its physical dimensions, flowing around in a circle. An index unaffected by its physical dimensions, reflecting no internal structure, no social distribution, and from which nothing can be subtracted, makes for a treacherous bottom line. A bottom-line index for the goodness of the macroeconomy whose growth eventually will push the economy beyond the biophysical limits of the earth is an absurdity.

CONCLUSION

I would like to conclude by suggesting that these problems are largely a function of the increasing scale of the human economy relative to the natural environment, the ecosystem. This shift from the empty to the full-world economy is the basic reason underlying the increasing prevalence of external costs and the increasing percentage of defensive expenditures in GNP. The increase in human scale has been dramatic: world population has tripled in my lifetime, and the populations of livestock, cars, houses, refrigerators, and so on have vastly more than tripled. All these populations consist of dissipative structures that put a load on the environment for both short-term maintenance and long-term replacement. This explosion of the human scale has occurred on a finite planet and might therefore better be termed an 'implosion'. Explosion suggests things flying apart in all directions. Implosion suggests that things are being smashed together producing interference, congestion, collision, and displacement. These mutual interferences are what give rise to external costs and defensive expenditures. Congestion and displacement force choice – either/or replaces both/and, as the human scale pushes against the confining environment and then implodes back in on itself. This forces more and more choices, and choice requires clear values and operational expressions of those values in sensible bottom lines.

Citizens should not trust economists with these increasingly difficult choices. Neoclassical economists have an unfortunate tendency to reduce all value to the level of personal, individual taste, matters about which consensus is neither necessary nor desirable. It is good to avoid conflict whenever possible. But if there are true values by which certain individual preferences can themselves be judged good or bad, and if citizens know and hold those values, then it would be good if they asked more aggressive questions of chrematistic bottom liners. Without Socratic gadflies willing to bite and risk getting slapped, we may find, as Schumacher (1973) feared, that truth, beauty and righteousness have simply become 'uneconomic'.

Of course, if citizens themselves have no values that transcend personal preferences, if they too blush at any concept of objective value and reduce all value to personal taste, no matter how refined and cultivated, then we might as well leave it to the economists. If we must leave it to the economists, I hope that our economics departments will produce what J.M. Keynes (1936) called, 'a brave army of heretics ... who following their intuitions, prefer to see truth obscurely and imperfectly rather than to maintain error, reached indeed with clearness and consistency and by easy logic, but on hypotheses inappropriate to the facts' (p. 371).

Nowadays, error in economics must be maintained by complicated mathematics rather than easy logic. Personally, I do not see a brave army of heretics yet emerging from the economics departments across our nation. The curriculum is designed to spot potential heretics early and flunk them out. Renewal is more likely to come from outside challenges to the discipline. Is it reasonable to hope for help from the physical sciences and the humanities? Is it part of the role of each discipline to challenge other disciplines? In the name of truth, beauty, and righteousness, can scientists, humanists, and citizens ask economists if maybe the system is sufficiently imperfect that people really do need to be good? It would be folly to pretend that people are so good that any system will work, but is it not also folly to believe that the system can be so perfect that it will really transform private evil into public good? Maybe economics should return to its origins as a part of moral philosophy.

REFERENCES

Beckerman, W. (1995), *Small is stupid: Blowing the Whistle on the Greens*, London: Duckworth.

Commission on Growth and Development (2008), *The Growth Report: Strategies for Sustained Growth and Inclusive Development*, Washington DC: The World Bank.

Keynes, J.M. (1936), *The General Theory of Employment, Interest, and Money*, New York: Harcourt Brace.

Nordhaus, W. (1991), *Science*, p. 1206.

Schelling, T. (1997), The cost of combating global warming: facing the tradeoffs, *Foreign Affairs*, **76**, 8–14.

Schumacher, E.F. (1973), *Small is Beautiful*, New York: Harper & Row.

Schwartz, B. (1987), *The Battle for Human Nature*, New York: Norton.

10. Ethics in relation to economics, ecology and eschatology

THE PROBLEM OF ETHICS

Ethics is the ordering of multiple ends into a hierarchy with reference to some vision of the Ultimate End, however dimly we perceive it. The ultimate end is that which is intrinsically good and does not derive its goodness by being instrumental to some other good. All other goods are instrumental to it indirectly and in varying degrees. Ethics is the problem of putting first things first, higher values ahead of lower values, and then, of course, acting according to that ordering of values in specific circumstances (Daly and Townsend, 1993, pp. 17–24). The specific circumstances may be medical, economic, familial, and so on, but the problem of ethics is basically the same – ethics is singular – knowing what goes in first place, second place, and so on, putting it there, and acting accordingly, with enough knowledge of how the world works to avoid perverse unintended consequences. If we had a clear vision of the ultimate end the process could be top-down, but often it is only in the bottom-up process of struggling to rank competing ends in specific situations that we get an insight into what the ultimate end must be like for our consciences to approve the decisions.

We do not have a different ultimate end and hierarchy of purposes for each area of life. Economic ethics, environmental ethics, medical ethics, and so on, are not different ethics (plural) but the same singular ethics applied in different circumstances. Consider the problem of separating 'agricultural ethics' and 'medical ethics'. As Wendell Berry noted, agriculture is devoted to what we eat without considering its effect on our health, while medicine is devoted to our health without considering what we eat. A more coherent singular ethics would rank health high in the values hierarchy, and would judge both agricultural and medical practices accordingly. It would not have a different ultimate end and value hierarchy for agriculture and for medicine. Pluralizing ethics by differing professions leads to incoherence.

Another ethical incoherence comes from pluralizing the ultimate end, in the sense of positing many 'ultimate' ends of either equal or non-comparable worth. In an age of pluralism there is considerable resistance to the notion of an ultimate end – one often hears that one person's values are as good as another's, that there is no objective value, just subjective preferences, and so on. This is incoherence equivalent to a denial of ethics in any operational sense. In the limit it means that any alternative can be 'ethically' chosen simply by declaring it to be one of many 'ultimate' ends. It is more than a grammatical error to treat ultimate as plural, and since ultimate must be singular, ethics, the prioritizing of plural ends with reference to the ultimate, must also be singular, or at least strive to be singular.

ECONOMICS AND ETHICS

So let us accept that 'economic ethics' means common, singular ethics applied in economic circumstances of life. But even so, does it mean ethics applied by individuals in their actual economic behavior, or ethics applied to governing public economic policy, or the code of ethics of professional practitioners of the 'science' of economics? Let us consider the latter first.

Trying to develop a professional ethics for economists presents special problems in addition to the general one discussed above. It is difficult for a discipline that models human behavior on the assumption that atomistic self-interest is the fundamental motive (our approximation to the ultimate end?) to then claim that its practitioners, unlike the rest of the human race, are differently motivated in the service of some professional 'code of ethics' that presumably transcends self-interest. And the claim of 'value neutrality', itself a value, is completely unconvincing. The self-interest assumption is first applied by economists to individuals in the private sector, then via public choice theory to individuals in the public sector to 'demonstrate' that the public interest is nothing but the private interests of those who work in the public sector. By logical extension academics and economics professionals who study private and public decisions should also be viewed as advancing their own self-interests by their pretensions to objective study, in the same way that public officials advance their interests by pretensions about the public good. For economists to have a professional code of ethics different from self-interest is therefore in contradiction with the discipline's basic assumptions about human motivation. Just as corporations supposedly exist only to maximize shareholder value (or is it CEO bonuses?), so the economics profession exists to maximize benefits to economists. Any 'professional code of ethics' would be just another disguise by which to disarm those who would unmask the economists' pretensions. Instead of dealing with ethics in the service of the good, economists have attempted to design, in T.S. Eliot's words, 'a system so perfect that no one needs to be good'. Ethics would be unnecessary, as illustrated by Mandeville's 'Fable of the Bees' and Adam Smith's 'invisible hand'.

The documentary film *Inside Job* about the 2008 financial collapse not only demonstrated the lack of a code of ethics for economists, but left one doubting that the current discipline of economics is capable of anything transcending the self-interest of its own *homo economicus* assumption, logically internalized into the behavior of economists themselves. Many of the important economists interviewed seemed incapable of even recognizing the possibility of a conflict of interest between truthful analysis in the public interest and 'consulting' for the interested client who is paying the fees.

A personal experience reinforces this point from another direction and is worth recounting as an insight into the professional ethics of economists. The Growth Report (2008) was a two-year study done by the Commission on Growth and Development, a blue ribbon panel of 18 members from 16 countries, including two Nobel Laureates in Economics. It had many august sponsors, including mainly the World Bank, and can fairly be taken to represent the mainline consensus on economic growth, namely that it is our best approximation to the Ultimate End. The journal, *Population and Development Review*, asked me to review it. My review (Daly, 2008) was quite critical. I expected a debate, or at least a reply from the authors of the report, or chairmen of the Commission, whom the editor had quite properly invited to reply. They ignored it. Is this fact insignificant, or like Sherlock Holmes' dog that failed to bark in the night, might it be the clue to solving a mystery? Many issues and many people are deservedly ignored. But should economists ignore the question of whether growth still increases wealth faster than illth, as it did in the past empty world, or whether in the new full world it has begun to increase illth faster than wealth? Is growth still economic in the literal sense, or has it become uneconomic? This is the main question not asked in the Report, and consequently raised in my review. Surely it is not a trivial question, and my discomfort at seeing it twice ignored transcends the mere personal pique that one feels at being brushed off. The failure of my critical review to initiate a dialog with the authors of the Growth Report, is, I believe, indicative of a deeper ethical failing within the economics profession. Ethics involves reasoning together in search of truth.

I tell this story because it illustrates the poor state of public discourse on economic matters (Daly, 2013). There were very few reviews of the

Growth Report and no replies, rejoinders, and so on. Why comment on someone else's work – there is not much academic credit in so doing, and besides you might make an enemy. Correcting errors through open debate is a fundamental part of the ethics that science proclaims, but since economics has only tenuous claims to being a science, why waste time on it? In any case consensus among experts is considered the hallmark of a mature science, so by prematurely declaring a consensus among 'all competent economists', and avoiding public debate on fundamental issues, economists preemptively lay claim to the status of a mature science.

The advantage of a reputation as a 'mature science' is that economists can profitably sell themselves as credibility-enhancing professional consultants to all sorts of interest groups. This at least is a professional ethics for economists that is highly consistent with the ethic of self-interest postulated by economists for all other actors in the economy.

Economics is the problem of applying scarce means to attain as many ordered values as possible within physical limits, but with care not to waste resources by satisfying lower values to the neglect of higher values. Scarcity is imposed by our environment, which is finite, non-growing, and materially closed, though open to a fixed rate of flow of solar energy. It is also subject to the laws of thermodynamics. The big ethical–economic problem is to apply our limited ultimate means to serve a hierarchy of ends ordered with reference to the ultimate end. Our ultimate means are low-entropy matter-energy – that which is required to satisfy our wants, but which we cannot produce in net terms but only use up (Georgescu-Roegen, 1971). We have two fundamentally different sources of low entropy: the solar flow, and the terrestrial stock. They differ in their pattern of scarcity – the solar is flow-limited but stock-abundant; the terrestrial is stock-limited but temporarily flow-abundant. We can use up scarce terrestrial low entropy at a rate of our own choosing, in effect using tomorrow's fossil fuels today; but we must wait for tomorrow to receive tomorrow's energy from the sun. We cannot 'mine' the sun. This fact is forcing upon us specific ethical questions that are new, even though the balancing of interests and the distribution of resources between present and future generations are traditional issues of singular ethics, and of economics.

The ethical question of balancing the interests of the present and the future also arises in the economics of education. A massive transfer of knowledge each generation is an unavoidable necessity. This transfer is not automatic. It requires two ethical decisions. The old must decide what knowledge is worth their effort to teach, and the young must decide what is worth their effort to learn. Some knowledge passes both ethical filters and becomes the basis for guiding the future and for discovering new knowledge. Other knowledge fails to pass one or both filters and is lost. Just as the world is always only one failed harvest away from mass hunger, so it is always only one failed generational transfer of knowledge away from mass ignorance.

What do we know about these two generational knowledge filters? What do they let pass and what do they filter out? I really do not know the answer, but I have one speculation, taken from E.F. Schumacher's reflections on Thomas Aquinas and Rene Descartes. Aquinas said that even uncertain knowledge of the highest things is worth more than certain knowledge of the lowest things. Descartes believed otherwise, that only knowledge that had the certainty of geometry was worth retaining, and uncertain knowledge should be abandoned even if it pertained to higher things. These two filters have very different selection biases. In their extreme forms they represent opposite errors of judgment about what knowledge to keep and what to jettison.

Which error are we most likely to commit today? I believe we overemphasize Descartes and pay too little attention to Aquinas. I take Aquinas' 'higher things' to mean purposes, knowledge about right purposes. Lower things I take to refer to techniques – how to efficiently do something, assuming it should be done in the first place. We have overdeveloped our relatively certain knowledge of technique, and left underdeveloped our less certain, but more important, knowledge of right purpose. The old seem more interested in teaching technique than purpose, and the young obligingly seem more interested in learning technique than purpose. So we develop more and more power, subject to less and less purpose. To paraphrase physicist S. Weinberg, the more science makes the universe comprehensible and subject to our control, the more it also seems to render it pointless, and the less our control is guided by purpose.

ECOLOGY AND ETHICS

Let us consider another area – environmental ethics, or rather singular ethics related to environmental issues. Ecology and its parent discipline biology have in common with economics a fundamental commitment to self-interest. In economics self-interest via the invisible hand of competition is thought to lead to the common good. In biology the 'selfish gene' via natural selection in a competitive environment is thought to lead to evolution and improved adaptation to the environment. There are of course countercurrents – the Adam Smith of *The Theory of Moral*

Sentiments and Peter Kropotkin of *Mutual Aid: A Factor of Evolution*. But the mainline thrust favors selfishness rewarded by adaptation and reproductive success, the latter seeming to play the role of Ultimate End in biology. Ecology, and by extension the biology, chemistry, and physics underlying it, seems even more barren ground for ethics than economics.

If the world we inhabit is an improbable ephemeral happenstance, long in coming and fated finally to dissolve, as naturalism teaches, and we as a part of it likewise are ephemeral chance happenings, then ethics is a sham. Ethics requires purposes, ordering of wants and actions relative to an objective value, final causation, teleology and a perception of ultimate value – all the things that the reigning naturalism and materialism deny. The prevailing view is that all is determined by the ancient Epicurean vision of atoms moving in their determined pathways through the void, as reconstructed in modern scientific materialism. Anything that did not fit this theory was 'explained' by Epicurus as caused by the 'clinamen', an unaccountable 'swerve' in the otherwise predetermined movement of atoms. This vision leaves no room for an Ultimate End and a hierarchy of values in reference to which actions are freely chosen, as required by ethics. Perhaps the clinamen should be recognized as the original 'fudge factor'. Ethics is doubly ruled out – if all is determined, then purpose is an illusion; if good and evil were nonexistent then there would be no criterion by which to choose ethically, even if choice were possible. Even pleasure, the proclaimed Ultimate End of the Epicurean, would be determined so it would be idle to advocate what could not be otherwise.

The idea of objective value or an ultimate end scares us because we think, with some evidence, that it might lead to intolerance and persecution of those whose vision of ultimate value is different from ours. This is certainly a danger, but the larger danger is that in denying objective value we no longer have anything to appeal to in an effort to persuade. It is just my subjective preferences versus yours, and since there is by assumption no higher authority we have nothing to point to in order to persuade, nor accede to in being persuaded. There is no alternative but to fight, either with force or deceit. A commitment to the reality of objective value, including our ability to reason together about it – however dimly it is perceived – is necessary to avoid arbitrary rule by force.

Some materialist biologists teach that morality and free will are illusions, but beneficial ones with survival value, they say, and therefore selected by their presumed contribution to reproductive success to fit our environment – our randomly changing environment, to be clear. However, they do not go on to consider the consequences of our (their) seeing through the illusions. Can an illusion be effective once it is exposed as an illusion? I doubt it. The consequences of drinking this poison were

strikingly evident in the 1924 Leopold–Loeb trial of the two young
Nietzschean–Darwinist nihilists who decided to prove to themselves that
they were free from the illusion of objective morality by murdering a
young man. The only defense that their attorney, the famous Clarence
Darrow, could muster for saving the admittedly guilty pair from execu-
tion was that their actions were determined, that in the great chain of
strict causation 'something slipped' (or swerved, as 'explained' by the
clinamen?). But why 'slipped' if there is no objective norm to fall short
of? Darrow was himself a determinist, and in principle should have been,
and perhaps was, against any legal punishment, not just the death penalty,
since for a determinist there can be no such thing as guilt.

   A more basic reason why it is idle to speak of economic or environmental or medical or agricultural ethics is that the very foundation for
any ethics at all is denied by philosophical materialists who seem to be in
the ascendancy these days, at least in academia. If good and bad, better
and worse, are meaningless concepts, as they are in a naturalist–
materialist worldview, and if that worldview is dominant, then any
discussion of ethics has to presuppose the prior rejection of the materialist worldview. Richard Dawkins, E.O. Wilson, Daniel Dennett, Christo-
pher Hitchens, and most recently Alexander Rosenberg, have led the
materialist attack on theism. The issue for now is not their atheism per se,
but the worldview that leads them to it, namely philosophical materialism
that not only rules out God, but also undercuts any notion of purpose, let
alone an ultimate end, required by ethics. One may say that Chance or
Survival or Pleasure or Self-Interest is the 'Ultimate End'. But the
materialists have been unsuccessful in demonstrating any convincing
ethics based on such assumptions. Yet the materialists seem reluctant to
give up on ethics, Rosenberg excepted. As a philosophical materialist,
Rosenberg is admirably consistent in disavowing any meaningful distinction between ethical and unethical behavior. Yet even he resorts to
advocacy of 'nice nihilism' – apparently as opposed to 'nasty nihilism' –
whatever those cutesy terms could possibly mean.

   A quote from Leon Wieseltier's review of Rosenberg will illustrate the
point,

> 'Is there a god? *No.* What is the nature of reality? *What physics says it is.*
> What is the purpose of the universe? *There is none.* What is the meaning of
> life? *Ditto.* Why am I here? *Just dumb luck.* Is there a soul? Is it immortal?
> *Are you kidding?* Is there freewill? *Not a chance!* What is the difference
> between right and wrong, good and bad? *There is no moral difference
> between them.* Why should I be moral? *Because it makes you feel better than
> being immoral* … Does history have any meaning or purpose? *It's full of
> sound and fury, but signifies nothing*'. I take this cutting-edge wisdom from

the worst book of the year, a shallow and supercilious thing called *The Atheist's Guide to Reality: Enjoying Life Without Illusions*, by Alex Rosenberg, a philosopher of science at Duke University. The book is a catechism for people who believe they have emancipated themselves from catechisms. The faith that it dogmatically expounds is scientism. It is a fine example of how the religion of science can turn an intelligent man into a fool. (Wieseltier, 2011)

Unfortunately, scientism (scientific materialism as a worldview) has rotted the brains of many intelligent people, economists not excepted. They have carried the facile neo-Darwinist logic to the self-contradictory extent of explaining away explanation itself. Along the way they dispose of right and wrong and any notion of ethics. So it makes no sense to advocate any concept of ethics, much less any 'code of professional ethics for economists', without first having rescued ethics itself from domination by scientism and 'nice nihilism'.

A similar problem was recognized and discussed long ago by Alfred North Whitehead under the term 'lurking inconsistency'. He expressed it in the following passage that repays careful reading:

> A scientific realism, based on mechanism, is conjoined with an unwavering belief in the world of men and of the higher animals as being composed of self-determining organisms. This radical inconsistency at the basis of modern thought accounts for much that is half-hearted and wavering in our civilization … It enfeebles [thought], by reason of the inconsistency lurking in the background … For instance, the enterprises produced by the individualistic energy of the European peoples presuppose physical actions directed to final causes. But the science which is employed in their development is based on a philosophy which asserts that physical causation is supreme, and which disjoins the physical cause from the final end. It is not popular to dwell on the absolute contradiction here involved. (Whitehead, 1925, p. 76)

In other words, our scientific understanding of nature is based on mechanism, on material and efficient causation with no room for final cause, for teleology or purpose. Yet we ourselves, and higher animals in general, directly experience purpose, and, within limits, act in a self-determining manner. Were that not the case we would not concern ourselves with ethics. If we are part of nature then so is purpose; if purpose is not part of nature then neither, in at least one significant way, are we. Whitehead (1925, ibid.) also put the contradiction more succinctly: 'Scientists animated by the purpose of proving that they are purposeless constitute an interesting subject for study'. Biologist Charles Birch (1990), a keen student of Whitehead, has restated the lurking inconsistency in his insightful book *On Purpose*: '[Purpose] has become the central problem for contemporary thought because of the mismatch in modernism between how we think of ourselves and how we think and act in relation to the rest of the world'. Clearly, not all biologists are guilty of the lurking inconsistency.

The directly experienced reality of purpose or final cause must, in the view of materialism, be an 'epiphenomenon' – an illusion which itself was selected because of the reproductive advantage that it chanced to confer on those under its spell. It is odd that the illusion of purpose should be thought to confer a selective advantage while purpose itself is held to be non-causative – but that is the neo-Darwinist's problem. The policy implication of the materialist dogma that purpose is not causative is *laissez faire* beyond the most libertarian economist's wildest model. The only 'policy' consistent with this view is, 'let it happen as it will anyway'. Is it too much to ask the neo-Darwinist to speculate about the possibility that the survival value of neo-Darwinism itself has become negative for the species that really accepts it as a metaphysical world-view? Could this lurking inconsistency have lethal consequences?

Teleology has its limits, of course, and from the Enlightenment onward it is evident that materialism has constituted an enormously powerful research paradigm for biology. The temptation to elevate a successful research paradigm to the level of a metaphysical worldview is perhaps irresistible. But materialism too has its limits. To deny the reality of our most immediate and universal experience (that of purpose) because it does not fit the presuppositions of methodological materialism, is profoundly anti-empirical. To refuse to recognize the devastating logical and moral consequences that also result from the denial of purpose is anti-rational. To those of us who view science as a rational and empirical enterprise this is disturbing. That some others, already unembarrassed by the fact that their major intellectual purpose is to deny of the reality of purpose, should now want to concern themselves deeply with the relative valuation of accidental pieces of their purposeless world is incoherence compounded.

If purpose does not exist then it is hard to imagine how we could experience the lure of value. To have a purpose means to serve an end, and value is imputed to whatever furthers attainment of that end. Alternatively, if there is objective value then surely the attainment of value should become a shared purpose. Neo-Darwinist biologists and ecologists, who do not accept the reality of purpose, owe it to the rest of us to remain silent about valuation – and conservation as well.

Economists, unlike biologists, do not usually go to the extreme of denying the existence of purpose. They recognize purpose under the rubric of individual preferences and do not generally consider them to be illusory. However, preferences are thought to be purely subjective, so that one person's preferences are as good as another's. Unlike public facts, private preferences cannot be right or wrong – there is, by assumption, no objective standard of value by which preferences can be judged. Nevertheless, according to economists, preferences are the ultimate standard of value. Witness economists' attempts to value species by asking consumers how much they would be willing to pay to save a threatened species, or how much they would accept in compensation for the species' disappearance. The fact that the two methods of this 'contingent valuation' give different answers only adds comic relief to the underlying tragedy, which is the reduction of value to taste weighted by income.

Economics too suffers from Whitehead's lurking inconsistency, but not to the extent that biology does. Purpose has not been excluded, just reduced to the level of tastes. But even an unexamined and unworthy purpose, such as unconstrained aggregate satisfaction of uninstructed private tastes weighted by income – GDP growth forever – will dominate the absence of purpose. So, in the public policy forum, economists with their attenuated, subjective concept of purpose (which at least is thought to be causative) will dominate the neo-Darwinist ecologists who are still crippled by the self-inflicted purpose of proving that they are purposeless. Consequently GDP growth will continue to dominate conservation.

Whitehead's observation (1925, ibid.) that, 'it is not popular to dwell on the absolute contradiction here involved', is even truer today, 85 years later. This willful neglect has allowed the lurking inconsistency to metastasize into the marrow of modernity. The Enlightenment, with its rejection of teleology, certainly illuminated some hidden recesses of superstition in the so-called Dark Ages. But the angle of its cold light has also cast a deep shadow forward into the modern world, obscuring the reality of purpose. To conserve Creation we will first have to reclaim purpose from that darkness. I say Creation with a capital 'C' advisedly, and not in denial of the common facts of evolution. If our world and our lives are not in some sense a Creation, but just a purposeless happenstance – a random statistical fluke of multiplying infinitesimal probabilities by an infinite number of trials – then it is hard to see from where we will get the will and inspiration to care for it.

Indeed, our decision-making elites may already tacitly understand that growth has become uneconomic. But apparently they have also figured out how to keep the dwindling extra benefits for themselves, while 'sharing' the exploding extra costs with the poor, the future, and other species. Why not, if it is all just a purposeless happenstance? The elite-owned media, the corporate-funded think tanks, the kept economists of high academia, and the World Bank – not to mention Gold Sacks and

Wall Street – all sing hymns to growth in harmony with class interest and greed. The public is bamboozled by technical obfuscation, and by the false promise that, thanks to growth, they too will one day be rich. Intellectual confusion is real, but moral nihilism, abetted by naturalistic scientism, may be the bigger problem. Such nihilism is hard to counter without strong appeal to the idea of purpose, of telos, and without raising its cosmic implications. Hence we are led, perhaps kicking and screaming for some of us, to eschatology.

ESCHATOLOGY AND ETHICS

Eschatology is not the most popular field of theology. It deals with last things, the end of time and final purpose of Creation – not something of which we have any experience, so it is more an expression of hope than knowledge. Many Christian theologians believe that our hope, both individual and collective, ultimately lies in New Creation (Rom. 8; 1 Cor. 15), which will be God's act at the end of the present creation (Polkinghorne, 2003; Wright, 2008; Moltmann, 2012). New Creation is seen as the manifestation of God's love and faithfulness. Most religions have an eschatology of some sort, and my focus on Christianity stems from my own religious commitments, which many will not share, including some Christians. However, the philosophical problems here discussed in the Christian context do not disappear in other contexts. Also, there are very many Christians in the world who do share these beliefs as a reasoned hope, and their views merit consideration. One can hardly understand the history and present of the West without understanding Christian thought. Furthermore, the issues raised are rather general. For example, one thing that science and Christianity agree on is that the present creation will ultimately die. The model for thinking about forever (whether personally or cosmically) is death and resurrection – New Creation, not perpetuity for the present creation, which would be both a Christian heresy and a scientific perpetual motion machine. Perhaps the cosmology of a 'big crunch' followed by another big bang is to some extent an analogous secular eschatology of new creation. But New Creation in Christian theology will be a miracle, as was the first act of creation, or as the first fruit of the New Creation witnessed in the Resurrection. This doctrine is not emphasized from mainline Protestant pulpits today, perhaps from legitimate fear of identification with apocalyptic sects, left-behind rapture theology, and end-of-the-world fanaticism. But it remains foundational and biblical.

I will let the theologians sort out the conflicting eschatologies of different branches of Christianity, and of other religions (including the secular ones of Scientism, Marxism and Growthism), and for now simply ask a question: what does the Christian belief in New Creation just outlined have to do with how we act in the world – specifically with the current economic/ecological crisis?

In God's New Creation death, decay, finitude and evil will, it is expected, be overcome. In the present creation they remain very real, built into its fundamental structure. We think that by building a modern Tower of Babel of unending economic growth and progress, we will reach heaven on earth, or maybe in space, and at least as a species escape death, decay, time, and entropy within the present creation. Furthermore, the secular intelligentsia assures us that the present creation (the Cosmos) is all there is, was, or ever will be, and in any case it is no longer considered a miracle, but the product of 'Chance' – not Creation but 'Randomdom' without any purpose. We now think that we understand this random evolutionary process and can control it in our quest for heaven on earth via genetic engineering, space colonization, and economic growth. Of course, if we can control evolution it will no longer be random, inconveniently removing the principle on which our understanding of it was based. Scientists were always a bit embarrassed by so much appeal to chance, and would be pleased to offer an ethical criterion by which to choose our direction. But it is hard for them to appeal to a 'moral compass' while denying any 'magnetic north', any objective value that lures us toward itself. So let GDP growth and technology be a proxy for magnetic north, they say, since that is what all nations in fact put in first place. And GDP at least includes the goods of food, clothing, and shelter, which many still need – never mind the unsubtracted 'bads' and the mistakenly added 'anti-bads'.

This idolatrous tower has collapsed before, and is badly out of plumb now. The basic reason is that, as creatures, we share subjection to entropy, evil, and finitude with the rest of this creation of which we are a part. Contrary to the dictates of 'Randomdom', Christianity teaches that we are also made in God's image and charged with dominion and responsibility for this creation – but as mere creatures, and fallen ones at that, are not put in charge of constructing the New Creation. The current loss of faith in the New Creation has contradictory implications for economic and environmental policy. On the one hand, people (many scientists) argue that this creation is all there is, so we better not undermine the intense seriousness of caring for it by allowing ourselves to hope for another gift – a New Creation, after we have trashed this one. Be grateful for the temporary gift of life and enjoy it while it lasts, and be content with subsequent meaningless oblivion. On the other hand, we find it hard to be content. Without faith in the Creator, and the promise of ultimate renewal, we have no place to direct our gratitude, except dumb luck, and are irresistibly tempted to try to build a 'new creation' ourselves. That seems to mean a modern Tower of Babel and the economic growth that supports it. As IBM forthrightly puts it in their advertisements, 'let us build a smarter planet'. They do not say: 'let us make a smarter adaptation to the earth from which we were created, and with which we have evolved, and by which we are sustained'. We are urged to change the planet, not ourselves! Indeed, many advocate escaping the doomed planet by colonizing space. Such techno-fantasies may constitute a secular eschatology that substitutes for the religious ones – salvation is replaced by the 'singularity' and immortality as silicon-based information-bearing structures.

The net destructive consequence of the current scale and growth of the economy for the present creation that sustains it, is greatly downplayed, if not totally ignored. Death, decay, and entropy are permanent features in the present creation, and without faith in the New Creation, what final purpose is there beyond 'eat, drink, and copulate, for tomorrow we dissipate'? We may well improve the material and social conditions in which we carry out these activities, and make it last a bit longer, but it all finally still dissipates unless there will be a radical renewal of the basic nature of creation. And who can renew creation other than the Creator?

Our attempt to reach Heaven on Earth by economic growth has led to the wholesale physical transformation of the Earth into ourselves and our furniture – with ever less remaining for future generations and for other species. In my lifetime, world population has more than tripled, and the populations of livestock, cars, houses, toasters, cell phones, and so on, have vastly more than tripled. These are all 'dissipative structures', to use Prigogine's term, and they depend on environmental depletion and pollution for maintenance and replacement, much as human bodies do. The world has moved from empty to full – full of economy and empty of ecology. Remaining natural capital has now replaced manmade capital as the limiting factor in production. The fish catch is no longer limited by fishing boats, but by remaining fish and their habitats. Barrels of pumped crude oil are no longer limited by drilling and pumping capacity, but by remaining deposits, and perhaps more stringently by capacity of the atmosphere to absorb the CO_2 from burning the oil. But absorptive capacity is also natural capital. Sometimes sources are more limiting – sometimes sinks.

Yet the World Bank's Growth Report (2008) expects a four- to five-fold increase in the size of the world economy by 2050, and is eager to help this happen. They do not tell us by how much they expect the earth to grow by 2050! The social and environmental costs of the Tower of Babel are already growing faster than the production benefits, making us poorer not richer. Such uneconomic growth will not help the poor, yet we keep claiming otherwise. We hide the truth from ourselves by faulty accounting (treating natural capital consumption as income, adding rather than subtracting defensive expenditures), and by issuing mountains of debt, liens against the projected growth of real wealth that is unlikely ever to happen, but in which we put our faith. We misleadingly refer to these debts as 'assets', or with slightly less dishonesty as 'troubled assets' when they become devalued by the common-sense realization that growth cannot redeem them. And then we make bets on which debts will be repaid and which will not. Those bets, incredibly, are then counted as additional assets!

If this sounds apocalyptic – well, that is why we are talking about eschatology! I have omitted the usual litany of ecological disasters consequent upon growth not because they are unlikely, but just because they are well known. Why this destructive refusal to face reality? I think the answer is distressingly simple within the context of our present assumptions. Without growth the only way to cure poverty is by sharing. But redistribution is political anathema. Without growth to push the hoped for demographic transition, the only way to cure overpopulation is by population control – a second anathema. Without growth the only way to invest in environmental repair is by reducing current consumption – the third anathema. Three anathemas and you are out. Even if current policy manages to jump-start the growth economy for another round, we will soon enough have to move from a failed growth economy to a steady-state economy – from idolatrous efforts to build a substitute 'new creation' or 'smarter planet' – to humble stewardship and sharing of the present creation, with the poor, with future generations, and with other species, for as long as it lasts.

This stewardship of the present creation (caring for the poor, feeding the hungry, fallowing the land) would not be the New Creation, but a partial, hopeful anticipation of it reflected back into the present order. The consequence of the current lack of eschatological hope, the secular belief that this creation – nay, random happenstance – is all there is, or ever will be, is to get as much as you can while it and you last. Even our higher ethical impulse to love and care for others in the present creation is undercut by the ultimate futility of randomness, luring us toward its cold meaningless dissipation. Far from being an escape from present problems, eschatological hope for the New Creation is necessary to sustain both technological and political efforts to care for the gift of

God's present creation. The New Creation will be a mysterious transformation of the present creation, we are told – somewhat like a tree is
the transformation of a seed. Although the New Creation is God's act, not
ours, it is the hopeful context in which our seed-saving actions can have
ultimate meaning. Although emphasis in the New Creation theology is
sometimes on the discontinuity with the present, there is also recognition
of continuity – something from the old creation is transformed into the
new, perhaps the broken pieces of our best efforts. And without a hopeful
vision of the new, we are left with the losing game of transforming the
old by our own efforts, with nothing but lame technological Gnosticism
to confront the power of entropy, finitude, and evil. But as heirs to the
New Creation, we are empowered to a limited degree to also be its
proleptic agents, or maybe just its welcoming committee.

As stated several times, science and Christianity agree that the present
creation, like we ourselves, will die. Without eschatological hope in New
Creation we are left with, at best, an increase in longevity of the present
creation, the much-discussed, though ill-defined, goal of 'sustainability'.
Although that is a good thing, and I certainly advocate it, is it enough to
inspire the enormous counter-cultural effort required to bring about even
this restricted purpose? Christian belief in the *imago Dei* requires us to
responsibly exercise our limited dominion over creation as its steward.
But faith in the New Creation saves us from despair over our repeated
failures, as well as over the ultimate impossibility of preserving this
Creation in the very long run.

Most scientists will, of course, not be happy with talk about miracles,
with hope in the New Creation. Yet when faced with the ultimate heat
death of the universe, and the meaninglessness implicit (and increasingly
explicit) in their materialist cosmology, some scientists seem to flinch,
and look for optimism, if not hope, somewhere within their materialism.
They invent the hypothesis of infinitely many (unobservable) universes in
which life may outlive our universe. They were led to this extraordinary
idea to escape the implications of the extreme fine-tuning inherent in the
anthropic principle – which argues that for life to have come about by
chance in our single universe would require far too many just-so
coincidences. To preserve the idea of chance as the only credible cause,
and thereby escape any notion of Creator or Telos, they argue that
although these fine-tuning coincidences discovered by scientists are
indeed overwhelmingly improbable in a single universe, they would
surely happen if there were infinitely many universes. And of course our
universe is obviously the one in which the improbable events all
happened. If you do not believe that Shakespeare wrote Hamlet, you can

claim that infinitely many monkeys pecking away at infinitely many typewriters had to hit upon it someday.

Unfortunately the evidence for infinitely many universes, or monkeys for that matter, is lacking. Likewise, the only 'evidence' that could be offered to support hope for a future miracle would be the occurrence of a similar miracle in the past. That of course would be the Creation itself. Science rightly tries to account for this Creation, as far as reasonable, in its own materialist terms, and of course understandably rejects 'miracle' or God as an explanatory category. Whether fact-free postulation of infinitely many unobservable universes qualifies as a reasonable explanatory category, I will leave to the reader's judgment.

The working hypothesis of scientific materialism, however fruitful it has been, should not be confused with an Ultimate Metaphysics of Chance. Nor does adding Darwinian natural selection to Mendelian random mutation mitigate the dominance of chance, since the selecting criterion of environmental conditions (other organisms and geophysical surroundings) is also considered to be a random product of chance. Mutations provide random change in the genetic menu from which natural selection picks according to the survival odds determined by a randomly changing environment.

This Metaphysics of Chance precludes explanation of some basic facts that, however, will not be silent: first, that there is something rather than nothing; second, the just-right physical fine-tuning 'coincidences' implicit in the anthropic principle; third, the 'spontaneous generation' of first life from inanimate matter before evolution can get started; fourth, the accumulation of an incredible amount of specified information in the genome of all the irreducibly complex living creatures that evolved from the relatively simple information in the first living thing (presumably by random change – ignoring that randomness destroys rather than creates information); fifth, the emergence of self-consciousness and rational thought itself (if my thoughts are ultimately the product of randomness why believe any of them, including this one?); and sixth, the innate human perception of right and wrong, of good and bad, which would be meaningless in a purely material world. Chance surely plays an important role in our world, but explaining all these facts 'by chance' strains credulity at least as much as 'by miracle'.

CONCLUSION

We economists, and people in general, have a lot of serious rethinking to do about ethics, beginning with a critical review of the modern culture of scientism that emphasizes determinism and downplays purpose to such an extent that ethics disappears, and hope along with it. Scientism, Marxism and Growthism have by a large margin failed to deliver on their secular eschatologies of heaven on earth. A cosmic metaphysics of hope, for example the Christian theology of New Creation, conceives of ethics in the present creation as the lure of objective value from the future, drawing us already into anticipatory participation in New Creation. This view of course is in contradiction to the naturalism (philosophical materialism) of our time, but in harmony with the traditional spiritual wisdom of mankind. The former offers no basis for ethics; the latter still does.

REFERENCES

Birch, C. (1990), *On Purpose*, Kensington, NSW: New South Wales University Press, Ltd.

Commission on Growth and Development (2008), *The Growth Report: Strategies for Sustained Growth and Inclusive Development*, Washington DC: The World Bank.

Daly, H.E. (2008), Growth and development: critique of a credo, *Population and Development Review*, **34**(3), 511–18.

Daly, H.E. (2013), A further critique of growth economics, *Ecological Economics*, **88**, 20–24.

Daly, H.E. and K. Townsend, eds. (1993), *Valuing the Earth*, Cambridge, MA: MIT Press.

Georgescu-Roegen, N. (1971), *The Entropy Law and the Economic Process*, Cambridge, MA: Harvard University Press.

Moltmann, J. (2012), *Ethics of Hope*, Minneapolis, MN: Fortress Press.

Polkinghorne, J. (2003), *The God of Hope and the End of the World*, New Haven, CT: Yale University Press.

Whitehead, A. (1925), *Science and the Modern World*, New York: Macmillan.

Wieseltier, L. (2011), *Washington Diarist*: 'The Answers'. Review of *The Atheist's Guide to Reality: Enjoying Life Without Illusions*, by Alex Rosenberg, *New Republic*, December 14.

Wright, N.T. (2008), *Surprised by Hope*, New York: Harper Collins.

PART V

Short essays on current issues related to
growth versus steady state

A.

Meaning of growth

1. TWO MEANINGS OF 'ECONOMIC GROWTH'

The term 'economic growth' has two distinct meanings. Sometimes it refers to the growth of that thing we call the economy (the physical subsystem of our world made up of the stocks of population and wealth; and the flows of production and consumption). When the economy gets physically bigger we call that 'economic growth'. This is normal English usage. But the term has a second, very different meaning – if the growth of some thing or some activity causes benefits to increase faster than costs, we also call that 'economic growth' – that is to say, growth that is economic in the sense that it yields a net benefit or a profit. That too is accepted English usage.

Now, does 'economic growth' in the first sense imply 'economic growth' in the second sense? No, absolutely not! Economic growth in the first sense (an economy that gets physically bigger) is logically quite consistent with *uneconomic growth* in the second sense, namely growth that increases costs faster than benefits, thereby making us poorer. Nevertheless, we assume that a bigger economy must always make us richer. This is pure confusion.

That economists should contribute to this confusion is puzzling because all of *micro*economics is devoted to finding the optimal scale of a given activity – the point beyond which marginal costs exceed marginal benefits and further growth would be uneconomic. Marginal Revenue = Marginal Cost is even called the 'when to stop rule' for growth of a firm. Why does this simple logic of optimization disappear in *macro*economics? Why is the growth of the macroeconomy not subject to an analogous 'when to stop rule'?

We recognize that all microeconomic activities are parts of the larger macroeconomic system, and their growth causes displacement and sacrifice of other parts of the system. But the macroeconomy itself is thought to be the whole shebang, and when it expands, presumably into the void, it displaces nothing, and therefore incurs no opportunity cost. But this is false of course. The macroeconomy too is a part, a subsystem of the biosphere, a part of the Greater Economy of the natural ecosystem. Growth of the macroeconomy too imposes a rising opportunity cost that at some point will constrain its growth.

But some say that if our empirical measure of growth is GDP, based on voluntary buying and selling of final goods and services in free markets, then that guarantees that growth consists of goods, not bads. This is because people will voluntarily buy only goods. If they in fact do buy a bad then we have to redefine it as a good. True enough as far as it goes, which is not very far. The free market does not price bads, true – but nevertheless bads are inevitably produced as joint products along with goods. Since bads are unpriced, GDP accounting cannot subtract them – instead it registers the additional production of anti-bads, and counts them as goods. For example, we do not subtract the cost of pollution, but we do add the value of the pollution cleanup. This is asymmetric accounting. In addition we count the consumption of natural capital (depletion of mines, wells, aquifers, forests, fisheries, topsoil, and so on) as if it were income. Paradoxically, therefore, GDP, whatever else it may measure, is also the best statistical index we have of the aggregate of pollution, depletion, congestion, and loss of biodiversity. Economist Kenneth Boulding suggested, with tongue only a little bit in cheek, that we relabel it Gross Domestic Cost. At least we should put the costs and the benefits in separate accounts for comparison. Not surprisingly, economists and psychologists are now discovering that, beyond a sufficiency threshold, the positive correlation between GDP and self-evaluated happiness disappears.

In sum, economic growth in sense one can be, and in the United States has become, *uneconomic* growth in sense two. And it is sense two that matters.

2. WHAT IS A 'GREEN ECONOMY'?

A green economy is an economy that imitates green plants as far as possible. Plants use scarce terrestrial materials to capture abundant solar energy, and are careful to recycle the materials for reuse. Although humans are not able to photosynthesize, we can imitate the strategy of maximizing use of the sun while economizing on terrestrial minerals, fossil fuels, and ecological services. Ever since the industrial revolution our strategy has been the opposite. Fortunately, as economist Nicholas Georgescu-Roegen noted, we have not yet learned how to mine the sun and use up tomorrow's solar energy for today's growth. But we can mine the earth and use up tomorrow's fossil fuels, minerals, and waste absorption capacities today. We have eagerly done this to grow the economy, but have neglected the fact that the costs of doing so have surpassed the benefits – that is to say, growth has actually become uneconomic.

In spite of the fact that green plants have no brains, they have managed to avoid the error of becoming dependent on the less abundant source of available energy. A green economy must do likewise – seek to maximize use of the abundant flow of solar low entropy and economize on the scarce stock of terrestrial low entropy. Specifically, a green economy would invest scarce terrestrial minerals in things like windmills, photovoltaic cells, and plows (or seed drills) – not squander them on armaments, Cadillacs, and manned space stunts. A green economy can be sufficient, sustainable, and even wealthy, but it cannot be a growth-based economy. A green economy must seek to develop qualitatively without growing quantitatively – to get better without getting bigger.

There is another kind of green economy that seeks to be green after the manner of greenback dollars, rather than green plants. Green dollars, unlike green plants, cannot photosynthesize. But dollars can miraculously be created out of nothing and grow exponentially at compound interest in banks. However, Aristotle noted that this kind of growth is very suspect, because money has no reproductive organs. Unlike green plants, green money seeks to grow forever in the realm of abstract exchange value, even as we encounter limits to growth in the realm of the concrete use values for which money is supposed to be an honest token and symbol.

Recently we have grown, or rather 'swollen', by expanding the symbolic realm of finance. Debt is a mere number (like negative pigs) and can easily grow faster than the real wealth (positive pigs), by which it is expected to be redeemed. Wall Street has bought and sold an astronomical number of negative pigs-in-a-poke – they have 'sold bets on debts and called them assets', as Wendell Berry succinctly put it. We have recently experienced the failure of this fraudulent attempt to force expansion. Yet we have so far been unable to imagine any policy other than restarting the old growth economy for another round. After the next crisis we should try to avoid the Ponzi scheme of growth and build a steady-state economy – a green economy that is sustainable, just, and sufficient for a good life.

3. WEALTH, ILLTH AND NET WELFARE

Wellbeing should be counted in net terms – that is to say we should consider not only the accumulated stock of wealth but also that of 'illth': and not only the annual flow of goods but also that of 'bads'. The fact that we have to stretch English usage to find words like illth and bads with which to name the negative consequences of production that should be subtracted from the positive consequences, is indicative of our having ignored the realities for which these words are the necessary names. Bads and illth consist of things like nuclear wastes, the dead zone in the Gulf of Mexico, biodiversity loss, climate change from excess carbon in the atmosphere, depleted mines, eroded topsoil, dry wells, exhausting and dangerous labor, congestion, and so on.

We are indebted to John Ruskin for the word 'illth', and to an anonymous economist, perhaps Kenneth Boulding, for the word 'bads'. In the empty world of the past these concepts and the names for them were not needed because the economy was so small relative to the containing natural world that our production did not incur any significant opportunity cost of displaced nature. We now live in a full world, full of us and our stuff, and such costs must be counted and netted out against the benefits of growth. Otherwise we might end up with extra bads outweighing extra goods, and increases in illth greater than the increases in wealth. What used to be economic growth could become uneconomic growth – that is, growth in production for which marginal costs are greater than marginal benefits, growth that in reality makes us poorer, not richer. No one is against being richer. The question is, does growth any longer really make us richer, or has it started to make us poorer?

I suspect it is now making us poorer, at least in some high GDP countries, and we have not recognized it. Indeed, how could we when our national accounting measures only 'economic activity'. Activity is not separated into costs and benefits. Everything is added in GDP, nothing subtracted. The reason that bads and illth, inevitable joint products with goods and wealth, are not counted, even when no longer negligible in the full world, is that obviously no one wants to buy them, so there is no market for them, and hence no price by which to value them. But it is worse – these bads are real and people are very willing to buy the anti-bads that protect them from the bads. For example, pollution is an unpriced, uncounted bad, but pollution cleanup is an anti-bad, which is accounted as a good. Pollution cleanup has a price and we willingly pay it up to a point and add it to GDP – but without having subtracted the negative value of the pollution itself that made the cleanup necessary. Such asymmetric accounting hides more than it reveals.

In addition to asymmetric accounting of anti-bads, we count natural capital depletion as if it were income, further misleading ourselves. If we cut down all the trees this year, catch all the fish, burn all the oil and coal, and so on, then GDP counts all that as this year's income. But true income is defined as the maximum that a community can consume this year, and still produce and consume the same amount next year – maximum production while maintaining intact future capacity to produce (capital in the broadest sense). Nor is it only depletion of natural capital that is falsely counted as income – failure to maintain and replace depreciation of manmade capital, such as roads and bridges, has the same effect. Much of what we count in GDP is capital consumption and anti-bads.

As argued above, one reason that growth may be uneconomic is that we discover that its neglected costs are greater than we thought. Another reason is that we discover that the extra benefits of growth are less than we thought. This second reason has been emphasized in the studies of self-evaluated happiness, which show that beyond a threshold annual income of some $20–25 thousand, further growth does not increase happiness. Happiness, beyond this threshold, is overwhelmingly a func-tion of the quality of our relationships in community by which our very identity is constituted, rather than the quantity of goods consumed. A relative increase in one's income still yields extra individual happiness, but aggregate growth is powerless to increase everyone's relative income. Growth in pursuit of relative income is like an arms race in which one party's advance cancels that of the other. It is like everyone standing and craning his neck in a football stadium while having no better view than if everyone had remained comfortably seated.

As aggregate growth beyond sufficiency loses its power to increase welfare, it increases its power to produce illth. This is because to maintain the same rate of growth ever more matter and energy has to be mined and processed through the economy, resulting in more depletion, more waste, and requiring the use of ever more powerful and violent technologies to mine the ever leaner and less accessible deposits. Petroleum from an easily accessible well in East Texas costs less labor and capital to extract, and therefore directly adds less to GDP, than petroleum from an inaccessible well a mile under the Gulf of Mexico. The extra labor and capital spent to extract a barrel in the Gulf of Mexico is not a good or an addition to wealth – it is more like an anti-bad made necessary by the bad of depletion, the loss of a natural subsidy to the economy. In a full-employment economy the extra labor and capital going to petroleum extraction would be taken from other sectors, so aggregate real GDP would likely fall. But the petroleum sector would increase its contribution to GDP as nature's subsidy to it diminished. We would be tempted to regard it as more rather than less productive.

The next time some economist or politician tells you we must do everything we can to grow (in order to fight poverty, win wars, colonize space, cure cancer, whatever ...), remind him that when something grows it gets bigger! Ask him how big he thinks the economy is now, relative to the ecosphere, and how big he thinks it should be. And what makes him think that growth is still causing wealth to increase faster than illth? How does he know that we have not already entered the era of uneconomic growth? And if we have, then is not the solution to poverty to be found in sharing now, rather than in the empty promise of growth in the future? If you get a reasoned, coherent answer, please send it to me!

4.   LIMITS TO GROWTH – 40 MORE YEARS?

Forty years ago, when I read *The Limits to Growth*, I already believed that growth in total resource use (population times per capita resource use) would stop within the next 40 years. The modeling analysis of the Meadows' team was a strong confirmation of that common-sense belief based on first principles going back at least to Malthus and the classical economists.

Well it is now 40 years later and economic growth is still the number-one policy goal of practically all nations – that is undeniable. Growth economists say that the 'neo-Malthusians' were simply wrong, and that we will keep on growing. But I think economic growth has already ended in the sense that the growth that continues is now uneconomic – it costs more than it is worth at the margin and makes us poorer rather than richer. We still call it economic growth, or simply 'growth' in the confused belief that growth must always be economic. I contend that we, especially in rich countries, have reached the economic limit to growth but we do not know it, and desperately hide the fact by faulty national accounting, because growth is our idol and to stop worshiping it is anathema.

It is no refutation to ask if I would rather live in a cave and freeze in the dark than accept all the historical benefits of growth. Of course not. The total cumulative benefits of growth are in my view greater than the total cumulative costs, although some economic historians debate that. In any case, we cannot undo the past and should be grateful to those who paid the costs of creating the wealth we now enjoy. But, as any economist should know, it is the marginal (not total) costs and benefits that are relevant to determining when growth becomes uneconomic. Marginal benefits decline because we satisfy our most pressing wants first; marginal costs rise because we first use the most accessible resources and sacrifice the least vital ecosystem services as we grow (convert nature into artifacts). Are the marginal benefits of a third car worth the marginal costs of climate disruption and sea-level rise? Declining marginal benefits will equal rising marginal costs while net benefits are positive – in fact, precisely when cumulative net benefits of past growth are a maximum! No one is against being richer, at least up to some sufficient level of wealth. That rich is better than poor is a definitional truism. That growth always makes us richer is an elementary mistake even within the basic logic of standard economics.

As suggested above we do not really want to know when growth becomes uneconomic because then we should stop growing at that point – and we do not know how to run a steady-state economy, and are religiously committed to an ideology of 'no limits'. We want to believe that growth can 'cure poverty' without sharing, and without limiting the scale of the human niche in creation. To maintain this state of delusion we confuse two distinct meanings of the term 'economic growth'. Sometimes it refers to the growth of that thing we call the economy (the physical subsystem of our world made up of the stocks of population and wealth, and the flows of production and consumption). When the economy gets physically bigger we call that 'economic growth'. But the term also has a second, very different meaning – if the growth of anything causes benefits to increase faster than costs we also call that 'economic growth' – growth that is economic in the sense that it yields a net benefit or a profit. Now, does 'economic growth' in the first sense imply 'economic growth' in the second sense? No, absolutely not. The idea that a bigger economy must always make us richer is pure confusion.

That economists should contribute to this confusion is puzzling because all of microeconomics is devoted to finding the optimal scale of a given activity – the point beyond which marginal costs exceed marginal benefits and further growth would be uneconomic. Marginal Revenue = Marginal Cost is even called the 'when to stop rule' for growth of a firm. Why does this simple logic of optimization disappear in macroeconomics? Why is the growth of the macroeconomy not subject to an analogous 'when to stop rule'?

We recognize that all microeconomic activities are parts of the larger macroeconomic system, and their growth causes displacement and sacrifice of other parts of the system. But the macroeconomy itself is thought to be the whole shebang, and when it expands, presumably into the void, it displaces nothing, and therefore incurs no opportunity cost. But this is false of course. The macroeconomy too is a part, a subsystem of the biosphere, a part of the Greater Economy of the natural ecosystem. Growth of the macroeconomy too imposes a rising opportunity cost of reduced natural capital that at some point will constrain further growth.

But some say that if our empirical measure of growth is GDP, based on voluntary buying and selling of final goods and services in free markets, then that guarantees that growth always consists of goods, not 'bads'. This is because people will voluntarily buy only goods. If they in fact do buy a bad then we have to redefine it as a good! True enough as far as it goes, which is not very far. The free market does not price bads – but nevertheless bads are inevitably produced as joint products along with goods. Since bads are unpriced, GDP accounting cannot subtract them – instead it registers the additional production of anti-bads (which do have a price), and counts them as goods. For example, we do not subtract the cost of pollution as a bad, yet we add the value of pollution cleanup as a good. This is asymmetric accounting. In addition we count the consumption of natural capital (depletion of mines, wells, aquifers, forests, fisheries, topsoil, and so on) as if it were income rather than capital drawdown – a colossal accounting error. Paradoxically, therefore, GDP, whatever else it may measure, is also the best statistical index we have of the aggregate of pollution, depletion, congestion, and loss of biodiversity. Economist Kenneth Boulding suggested, with tongue only a little bit in cheek, that we relabel it 'Gross Domestic Cost'. At least we should put the costs and the benefits in separate accounts for comparison. Economists and psychologists are now discovering that, beyond a sufficiency threshold, the positive correlation between GDP and self-evaluated happiness disappears. This is not surprising because GDP was never meant as a measure of happiness or welfare – only of activity; some of which is joyful, some beneficial, some regrettably necessary, some remedial, some trivial, some harmful, and some stupid.

In sum, economic growth in sense one (scale) can be, and in the United States has become, uneconomic growth in sense two (net benefits). And it is sense two that matters most. I think *The Limits to Growth* in sense two have been reached in the last 40 years, but that we have willfully denied it, much to the harm of most of us, but to the benefit of an elite minority who keeps on pushing the growth ideology, because they have found ways to privatize the benefits of growth while socializing the even greater costs. The big question in my mind is, can denial, delusion, and obfuscation last another 40 years? And if we keep on denying the economic limit to growth how long do we have before crashing into the more discontinuous and catastrophic biophysical limits? I am hopeful that in the next 40 years we can finally recognize and adapt to the more forgiving economic limit. Adaptation will mean moving from growth to a steady-state economy, one almost certainly at a smaller scale than at present. By scale I mean physical size of the economy relative to the ecosystem, probably best measured by resource throughput. And, ironically, the best existing index we have of throughput is probably real GDP!

I must confess surprise that denial has endured for 40 years. I think to wake up will require something like repentance and conversion, to put it in religious terms. It is idle to 'predict' whether we will have the spiritual strength and rational clarity for such a conversion. Prediction of the direction of history is premised on a determinism that negates purpose and effort as independently causative. No one gets a prize for predicting his own behavior. Prediction of the behavior of others is problematic because they are so much like one's self. And if we are really determinists then it does not matter what we predict – even our predictions are determined. As a non-determinist, I hope and work for an end to growthmania within the next 40 years. That is my personal bet on the medium-run future. How confident am I that I will win that bet? About 30 percent, maybe. It is entirely conceivable that we will totally exhaust earth's resources and life-support systems in ruinously expensive attempts to grow forever: perhaps by military conquest of other nations' resources and of the remaining global commons; perhaps by attempted conquest of the 'high frontier' of space. Many think, just because we have managed a few manned space stunts at enormous expense, that the science fiction of colonization of sidereal space is technically, economically, politically, and ethically viable. And these are the same people who tell us that a steady-state economy on Earth is too difficult a task to ever accomplish.

5. KRUGMAN'S GROWTHISM

Paul Krugman often writes sensibly and cogently about economic policy. But like many economists, he can become incoherent on the subject of growth. Consider the following (*New York Times*, April 17, 2014):

> [...] let us talk for a minute about the overall relationship between economic growth and the environment.
>
> Other things equal, more G.D.P. tends to mean more pollution. What transformed China into the world's largest emitter of greenhouse gases? Explosive economic growth. But other things don't have to be equal. There's no necessary one-to-one relationship between growth and pollution.
>
> People on both the left and the right often fail to understand this point [...] On the left, you sometimes find environmentalists asserting that to save the planet we must give up on the idea of an *ever-growing economy*; on the right, you often find assertions that any attempt to limit pollution will have devastating impacts on growth [...] [Krugman says both are wrong] [...] But there's no reason we can't *become richer* while reducing our impact on the environment. [emphasis mine]

Krugman distances himself from 'leftist' environmentalists who say we must give up the idea of an ever-growing economy, and is himself apparently unwilling to give it up. But he thinks the 'right-wingers' are wrong to believe that protecting the environment will devastate growth. Krugman then advocates the more sensible goal of 'becoming richer', but fails to ask if growth in GDP is any longer really making us richer. He seems to equate, or at least fails to distinguish, 'growing GDP' from 'becoming richer'. Does he assume that because GDP growth did make us richer in yesterday's empty world it must still do so in today's full world? The usual but unjustified assumption of many economists is that a growing GDP increases measured wealth by more than it increases unmeasured 'illth' (a word coined by John Ruskin to designate the opposite of wealth).

To elaborate, illth is a joint product with wealth. At the current margin, it is likely that the GDP flow component of 'bads' adds to the stock of 'illth' faster than the GDP flow of goods adds to the stock of wealth. We fail to measure bads and illth because there is no demand for them, consequently no market and no price, so there is no easy measure of negative value. However, what is unmeasured does not for that reason become unreal. It continues to exist, and even grow. Since we do not measure illth, I cannot prove that growth is currently making us poorer, any more than Krugman can prove that it is making us richer. I am just pointing out that his GDP growthism assumes a proposition that, while true in the past, is very doubtful today in the United States.

To see why it is doubtful, just consider a catalog of negative joint products whose value should be measured under the rubric of illth: climate change from excess carbon in the atmosphere; radioactive wastes and risks of nuclear power plants; biodiversity loss; depleted mines; deforestation; eroded topsoil; dry wells, rivers and aquifers; the dead zone in the Gulf of Mexico; gyres of plastic trash in the oceans; the ozone hole; exhausting and dangerous labor; and the unrepayable debt from trying to push growth in the symbolic financial sector beyond what is possible in the real sector (not to mention military expenditures to maintain access to global resources).

These negative joint products of GDP growth go far beyond Krugman's minimal nondescript category of 'pollution'. Not only are these public bads unsubtracted, but the private anti-bads they make necessary are *added* to GDP! For example, the bad of eroded topsoil is not subtracted, but the anti-bad of fertilizer is added. The bad of Gulf and Arctic oil spills is not subtracted, but the anti-bad of cleanup is added. The natural capital depletion of mines, wells, forests, and fisheries is falsely accounted as income rather than capital drawdown.

Such asymmetric accounting alone is sufficient to refute growthism, but for good measure note that the growthists also neglect the most basic laws of economics, namely, the diminishing marginal benefit of income and increasing marginal cost of production. Why do they think these two curves will never intersect? Is Krugman just advocating temporary growth up to some level of optimality or sufficiency, or an *ever-growing* economy? If the latter, then either the surface of the earth must grow at a rate approximating the rate of interest, or real GDP must become 'angel GDP' with no physical dimension.

Krugman is correct that there is no necessary 'one-to-one relationship between growth and pollution'. But there certainly is a very strong positive correlation between real GDP growth and resource throughput (the entropic physical flow that begins with depletion and ends with pollution). Since when do economists dismiss significant correlations just because they are not 'one-to-one'?

Probably we could indeed become richer (increase net wealth) while reducing our impact on the environment, as Krugman hopes. But it will be by reducing *uneconomic* growth (in throughput and its close correlate, GDP) rather than by increasing it. I would be glad if this were what Krugman has in mind, but I doubt that it is.

In any case, it would be good if he would specify whether he thinks current growth in real GDP is still economic in the literal sense that its benefits exceed its costs at the margin. What specifically makes him think this is so? In other words, is GDP growth currently making us richer or poorer, and how do we know?

Since GDP is a conflation of both costly and beneficial activity, should we not separate the cost and benefit items into separate accounts and compare them at the margin, instead of adding them together? How do we know that growth in GDP is a sensible goal if we do not know if the associated benefits are growing more or less rapidly than the associated costs? Mainstream economists, including Krugman, need to free their thinking from dogmatic GDP growthism.

B.

Biophysical limits

6. THERMODYNAMIC ROOTS OF ECONOMICS

The first and second laws of thermodynamics should also be called the first and second laws of economics. Why? Because without them there would be no scarcity, and without scarcity, no economics. Consider the first law: if we could create useful energy and matter as we needed it, as well as destroy waste matter and energy as it got in our way, we would have superabundant sources and sinks, no depletion, no pollution, more of everything we want without having to find a place for stuff we do not want. The first law rules out this direct abolition of scarcity. But consider the second law: even without creation and destruction of matter-energy, we might indirectly abolish scarcity if only we could use the same matter-energy over and over again for the same purposes – perfect recycling. But the second law rules that out. And if one thinks that time is the ultimate scarce resource, well, the entropy law is time's irreversible arrow in the physical world. So it is that scarcity and economics have deep roots in the physical world, as well as deep psychic roots in our wants and desires.

Economists have paid much attention to the psychic roots of value (for example, diminishing marginal utility), but not so much to the physical roots. Generally they have assumed that the biophysical world is so large relative to its economic subsystem that the physical constraints (the laws of thermodynamics and ecological interdependence) are not binding. But they are always binding to some degree and become very limiting as the scale of the economy becomes large relative to the containing biophysical system. Therefore attention to thermodynamic constraints on the economy, indeed to the entropic nature of the economic process, is now critical – as emphasized by Nicholas Georgescu-Roegen in his magisterial *The Entropy Law and the Economic Process* (1971).

Why has his profound contribution been so roundly ignored for 40 years? Because as limits to economic growth become more binding, the economists who made their reputations by pushing economic growth as panacea become uncomfortable. Indeed, were basic growth limits recognized, very many very prestigious economists would be seen to have been very wrong about some very basic issues for a very long time. Important economists, like most people, resist being proved wrong. They even bolster their threatened prestige with such pretension as 'the Sveriges Riksbank Prize in Economic Sciences in Memory of Alfred Nobel' – which by journalistic contraction becomes, 'the Nobel Prize in Economics', infringing on the prestige of a real science, like physics. Yet it is only by ignoring the most basic laws of physics that growth economics has endured. Honoring the worthy contributions of economists should not require such flummery.

I once asked Georgescu-Roegen why the 'MIT–Harvard mafia' (his term) of growth economists never cited his book. He replied with a Romanian proverb to the effect that, 'in the house of the condemned one does not mention the executioner'.

7. DUALIST ECONOMICS

Frederick Soddy (1877–1956) discovered the existence of isotopes and was a major contributor to atomic theory, for which he received the Nobel Prize in Chemistry in 1921. He foresaw the development of an atomic bomb and was disturbed by the fact that society often used the contributions of science (for which he was partly responsible) for such destructive purposes. The reason for this was, in his view, faulty economics. So in the second half of his 80 years he set out to reform economics. He was the first person coherently to lay out the policy of 100 percent reserve banking, later taken up by the Chicago School economists and by Irving Fisher of Yale – and still an excellent idea. Soddy was considered an outsider and a 'monetary crank' by mainstream economists. Nevertheless, his views on money are sound and highly relevant to today's financial debacle (see 'Nationalize money, not banks', essay 24). Another neglected but increasingly relevant contribution is his philosophical vision of the place of economics in the larger intellectual map of the world.

For Soddy economics occupies the middle ground between matter and spirit, or as he put it, 'between the electron and the soul'.

> In each direction possibilities of further knowledge extend ad infinitum, but in each direction diametrically away from and not towards the problems of life. It is in this middle field that economics lies, unaffected whether by the ultimate philosophy of the electron or the soul, and concerned rather with the interaction, with the middle world of life of these two end worlds of physics and mind in their commonest everyday aspects, matter and energy on the one hand, obeying the laws of mathematical probability or chance as exhibited in the inanimate universe, and, on the other, with the guidance, direction and willing of these blind forces and processes to predetermined ends. (*Cartesian Economics*, p. 6)

Soddy did not mean that economists should neglect the two end worlds of electron and soul – much to the contrary he insisted that wealth must reflect the independent reality of both end worlds. What must be resisted is the 'obsessive monism' of either idealism or materialism. We must recognize the fundamental dualism of the material and the spiritual and resist attempts to reduce everything to one or the other.

Wealth has both a physical dimension, matter-energy subject to the laws of inanimate mechanism, especially the laws of thermodynamics, and a teleological dimension of usefulness, subject to the purposes imposed by mind and will. Soddy's concept of wealth reflects his fundamental dualism and is why his first lectures on economics were entitled *Cartesian Economics*, meaning in effect, 'Dualist Economics' (not, as might be imagined today, economics diagrammed in terms of Cartesian coordinates). The subtitle of *Cartesian Economics*, 'The bearing of physical science on state stewardship', better reflects his dualism in the contrast between 'physical science' and 'stewardship'.

Philosophically Rene Descartes accepted dualism as a brute fact even though the interaction of the two worlds of mind and matter, of soul and body, of *res cogitans* and *res extensa*, remained mysterious. Subsequent philosophers have in Soddy's view succumbed to monistic reductionism, either materialism or idealism, both of which encounter philosophical problems no less grave than dualism, as well as provoke greater offenses against both common sense and direct experience. It is fashionable to reject dualism nowadays by saying that humans are a 'psychosomatic unity' even while recognizing a 'polarity' within that unity. Nevertheless, the two poles of electron and soul are very far apart, and the line connecting them is, as Soddy argued, twice discontinuous. While we are surely in some important sense a 'unity', it would be good to recognize the legitimate claims of dualism by writing the word 'psycho–somatic' with a long double hyphen.

soul (purpose, ultimate end)

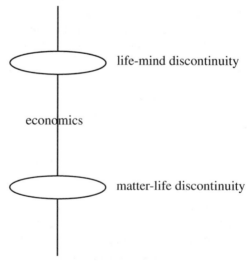

life-mind discontinuity

economics

matter-life discontinuity

electron (matter, energy, low entropy)

Figure B7.1   Soddy's dualist economics

Soddy's view can be represented by a vertical line connecting the electron (physical world, useful matter-energy, ultimate means) at the bottom, to the soul (will, purpose, ultimate end) at the top. In the middle is economics (efforts in ordinary life to use ultimate means to serve the ultimate end). Soddy did not draw such a diagram, but it is implicit in his writing. The vertical connecting line has two mysterious discontinuities that thwart monistic attempts to derive soul from electron, or electron from soul. The first discontinuity is between inanimate mechanism and life. The second discontinuity is between life and self-conscious mind (will, soul). Monists keep trying, and failing, to leap over both chasms. Dualists accept them as irreducible brute facts about the way the world is.

Dualists use the axiom of duality to interpret other phenomena instead of vainly pursuing the illusion of reductive monism. Nowadays the dominant monistic obsession is materialism, supported by the impressive successes of the physical sciences, and the lesser but still impressive extrapolations of Darwinist biologism. Idealism does not have so much support at present, although modern theoretical physics and cosmology seem to be converting electrons and elementary matter into mathematical equations and strange Platonic ideas that reside more in the minds of theoretical physicists than in the external world, thus perhaps bending the vertical line connecting mind and matter into something more like a circle. Also, a Whiteheadean interpretation of the world as consisting most fundamentally of 'occasions of experience' rather than substances, is a way to bridge dualism, but only with the help of widely separated and mysteriously combined 'polarities' of mentality and physicality posited or anticipated in each occasion of experience. While these are challenging and important philosophical developments, it remains true that materialism currently retains the upper hand and is claiming an ever-expanding monistic empire, including the middle ground of economics. In addition, physics' modern revival of idealism so far seems as morally vacuous as materialism – among the equations and Platonic ideas of modern physics one does not find ideas of justice or goodness, or even purpose, so the fact-value dimension of dualism remains.

As Soddy insisted, economics occupies the middle ground between these dualistic extremes. Economics in its everyday aspects remains largely 'unaffected whether by the ultimate philosophy of the electron or the soul', but this may be the big weakness of economics, the myopia that leads to its growth-forever vision. Each end world reflects unrecognized limits back toward the middle world – limits of possibility from below, and limits of desirability from above. Economics seems to assume that if it is possible it must be desirable, indeed practically mandatory.

Similarly, if it is desirable it must be possible. So everything possible is considered desirable, and everything desirable is considered possible. Ignoring the mutually limiting interaction of the two end worlds of possibility and desirability has led economists to assume a permissiveness to growth of the middle world of the economy that is proving to be false. For Soddy this is reflected concretely in the economy by our monetary conventions – fractional reserve banking, which allows alchemical creation of money as interest-bearing private debt: 'You cannot permanently pit an absurd human convention, such as the spontaneous increment of debt [compound interest], against the natural law of the spontaneous decrement of wealth [entropy]' (*Cartesian Economics*, p. 30).

Debt is confused with wealth. But unlike debt, wealth has a physical dimension that limits its growth. This reflects mainly a misunderstanding of the physical world and its limits on wealth. But Soddy also saw limits coming from the end world of the soul. 'Just as I am constrained to put a barrier between life and mechanism in the sense that there is no continuous chain of evolution from the atom to life, so I put a barrier between the assimilation and creation of knowledge' (*Cartesian Economics*, p. 28).

For Soddy the assimilation of knowledge was mere mimicry, and was discontinuous with the creation or discovery of new knowledge, which he saw as also involving a spiritual top-down influence from the soul, from the mysteriously self-conscious mind that could not be derived from mere animate life by a continuous chain of evolution. Soddy said little about the life–mind discontinuity relative to the matter–life discontinuity, but it was clearly part of his philosophy, and has come to the fore in modern philosophical debates about the 'hard problem of consciousness'.

To the mechanistic biologists, who were already around in his day, Soddy had the following barbed comment:

> I cannot conceive of inanimate mechanism, obeying the laws of probability, by any continued series of successive steps developing the powers of choice and reproduction any more than I can envisage any increase in the complexity of an engine resulting in the production of the 'engine-driver' and the power of its reproducing itself. I shall be told that this is a pontifical expression of personal opinion. Unfortunately, however, for this argument, inanimate mechanism happens to be my special study rather than that of the biologist. It is the invariable characteristic of all shallow and pretentious philosophy to seek the explanation of insoluble problems in some other field than that of which the philosopher has first hand acquaintance. (*Cartesian Economics*, p. 6)

To generalize a bit, monists, who deny the two discontinuities, seek to solve the insoluble problems that they thereby embrace by shallowly and pretentiously appealing to some other field than that of which they have first hand experience. This is a serious indictment – is it true? I will leave that question open, but will note on Soddy's behalf that regarding the matter–life discontinuity Francis Crick evidently thought it more likely that first life arrived from outer space (directed panspermia) than that it formed spontaneously from inanimate matter on earth, given the demonstration by Pasteur and Tyndall that 'spontaneous generation is not occurring on the earth nowadays'. And, as already mentioned, a number of philosophers and neuroscientists (including John Eccles and Karl Popper) have declared that the life-mind discontinuity presents 'the hard problem of consciousness', judged by many to be unbridgeable.

The relevance of Soddy's dualistic economics to steady-state economics is that there are two independent sets of limits to growth: the bottom-up biophysical, and the top-down ethical–economic. The biophysical limit says real GDP cannot grow indefinitely; the ethical–economic limit says that beyond some point GDP growth ceases to be worth what it displaces, although it may still be biophysically possible. Certainly Soddy did not speak the last word on dualism versus monism. Nevertheless, he was truly a pioneer in ecological economics, seen as the middle ground between the electron and the soul. Although no ecological economist has won the ersatz 'Swedish National Bank's Memorial Prize in Economics in Honor of Alfred Nobel', pioneer ecological economist, Frederick Soddy, has the distinction of having won a *real* Nobel Prize in Chemistry. That does not mean that he is right about dualist economics, but I think it earns him a serious hearing.

8.   A SMARTER PLANET?

'Let us build a smarter planet'. This is IBM's inspirational slogan, intoned as a benediction at the end of their 2010–14 advertisements. They do *not* say, 'Let us make a smarter adaptation to our planet earth, out of which we were created and by which we are sustained'. It is the planet that is insufficiently smart, not its evolutionary prize-winning, big-brained, star tenant.

What makes IBM think that the planet is dumb? Well, obviously the mentally challenged earth does not know how to keep on accommodating our continual economic growth, so we must redesign it with that remedial instruction in mind. For example, our growth requires fossil fuels, but when we burn a lot of them the resulting atmospheric CO_2 slows down the radiation of heat back to outer space, heating up the stupid planet and causing dumb climate change. It would be easier to radiate heat energy out and make more thermal room for necessary fossil fuel burning if only we had less solar energy coming in. So a smarter planet would have a higher albedo to reflect more of that troublesome incoming solar radiation. Blasting light-reflecting particles of sulfur into the stratosphere or troposphere should raise the planet's IQ a great deal.

This sophisticated planet-smartening pedagogy is known as geo-engineering. It will cheaply re-engineer the planet to allow BP to feed the sacred flame of economic growth by drilling deeper holes in more precarious places to pump more oil. That in turn will supply NASA with the resources to build more rockets, thereby to fulfill our cosmic destiny to escape this terminally dumb planet and build a really smart one from scratch in a better location. Scientists have long realized that geo-engineering and other retrofitting measures, while necessary to buy time for building up evacuation capacity, cannot be the final solution for a congenitally moronic planet. And if meanwhile an occasional oil spill reduces the photosynthetic capacity of life in the Gulf of Mexico – well, we have just seen that our silly planet already allows in too much solar energy, so if we reduce that inflow we will not have to trouble ourselves with converting it into food energy. Furthermore when NASA, BP, and IBM finish building our new smart planet, it will contain a new and smarter Gulf of Mexico.

To sum up, by serving only the interests of the growing economy, global corporations like IBM are providentially led, as if by an invisible hand, to also build a smarter planet! Of course, unlike Adam Smith, they do not really believe in any deistic providence with its invisible hand that converts private greed into public good. They know from modern science that random mutation plus natural selection explains everything, and that free will and purpose are illusions. But some of these illusions have survival value and must be persuasively advertised to secure support from the tax-paying masses (science is expensive) – at least until IBM, BP, and NASA have finished building a planet so smart that its inhabitants can safely be dumb.

9. GEO-ENGINEERING OR COSMIC PROTECTIONISM?

> We are capable of shutting off the sun and the stars because they do not pay a dividend.
>
> John Maynard Keynes (1933)

Frederic Bastiat's classic satire, 'Petition of the candlemakers against the sun', has been given new relevance. Written in 1845 in defense of free trade and against national protectionism in France, it can now be applied quite literally to the cosmic protectionists who want to protect the global fossil fuel-based growth economy against 'unfair' competition from sunlight – a free good.

The free flow of solar radiation that powers life on earth should be diminished, suggest some, including American Enterprise Institute's S. Thernstrom (*Washington Post*, 13 June 2009, p. A15), because it threatens the growth of our candle-making economy that requires filling the atmosphere with heat-trapping gases. The protectionist 'solution' of partially turning off the sun (by albedo-increasing particulate pollution of the atmosphere) will indeed make thermal room for more carbon-burning candles. Although this will likely increase GDP and employment, it is attended by the inconvenient fact that all life is pre-adapted by millions of years of evolution to the existing flow of solar energy. Reducing that flow cancels these adaptations wholesale – just as global warming cancels myriad existing adaptations to temperature. Artificially reducing our most basic and abundant source of low entropy (the solar flux) in order to more rapidly burn up our scarcer terrestrial source (fossil fuels), is contrary to the interests both of our species and of life in general. Add to that the fact that 'candles', and many other components of GDP, are at the margin increasingly unneeded and expensive, requiring aggressive advertising and Ponzi-style debt financing in order to be sold, and one must conclude that 'geo-engineering' the world for more candles and less sunlight is an even worse idea than credit default swaps.

Why then do some important and intelligent people advocate geo-engineering? As the lesser evil compared to absolutely catastrophic and imminent climate disaster, they say. If the American Enterprise Institute has now stopped offering scientists money to write papers disputing global warming, and in fact has come around to the view that climate change is bad, then why have they not advocated carbon taxes or cap–auction–trade limits? Because they think the technical geo-fix is cheap and will allow us to buy time and growth to better solve the problem in the future. One more double whiskey to help us get our courage up enough to really face our growth addiction! Probably we are irrevocably committed to serious climate change and will have to bear the costs, adapt, and hasten our transition to a steady-state economy at a sustainable (smaller) scale. Panicky protectionist interventions by arrogant geo-engineers to save growth for one more round will just make things worse.

At the earthly level, I am no free trader, and neither was Keynes, but 'shutting off the sun and the stars' to protect the fossil fuel economy is carrying protectionism to cosmic extremes. Reality has overtaken satire.

C.

Ethical and philosophical limits

10. PRESUPPOSITIONS OF POLICY

As you graduate I want to remind you of something you already know. Since you have not only chosen to study public policy, but have persevered to graduate with a Master's degree, you must already have rejected the perennial and pernicious philosophical doctrines of determinism and nihilism. That is what I want to remind you of.

Determinists believe that there is only one possible future, rigidly determined either by atoms in motion, selfish genes, dialectical materialism, toilet training, or the puppet strings of a predestining deity. If there is only one possible future state of the world then there are no options, nothing to choose from, and therefore no need for policy – or schools of public policy or Master's degrees in public policy. You should head straight to the unemployment office! You are necessarily non-determinists who must believe that there are at least a few possible alternative future states of the world, and that purposive policy can be causative in choosing among them.

Of course there are also many merely conceivable or imaginary futures that really can be ruled out as impossible – such as, for example, growing the economy forever on a finite planet that is subject to the laws of thermodynamics and ecological interdependence. Our commitment to the fantasy of unlimited growth as the foundation of all national policy should top the list of things to be reconsidered. But that is a story for another time. My point for today is that after eliminating all impossible futures we are still left with more than one possible future.

To choose from the remaining menu of possible futures we need a criterion of value by which to distinguish better from worse states of the world. Nihilists, or extreme relativists, deny the existence of any such criterion. For them it is all a matter of subjective individual preferences, suitably weighted by ability to pay, as modified by gender, race, and class interests. The nihilists say that there is no such thing as the common good or objective value, and that therefore we cannot distinguish better from worse future states. So even though real alternatives may exist, policy still would make no sense without an objective criterion of value, and some vision of the common good.

Without choice there can be no responsibility, so the determinists and nihilists are often undeservedly comfortable in their irresponsible irrelevance. 'Never knowing where they are going, they can never go astray'. As future policy makers, I am sure that you will have to confront some complacent determinists and nihilists, perhaps disguised as political pollsters, apocalyptic televangelists, cost–benefit analysts, bio-ethicists, evolutionary neuropsychologists, or growth economists. One way or another they will insist that there is no alternative, and even if there were, it would not matter. That such people should bother to argue publically about anything already involves them in a logical contradiction to which they are evidently blind. That makes rational dialog with them unpromising.

But, as I said earlier, this is something you must already know or you would not be here. I am just reminding you of it on your way out, like your mother telling you not to forget your umbrella.

11. *HOMO ECONOMICUS* VERSUS PERSON-IN-COMMUNITY

The problem with *Homo economicus* (the abstract picture of a human being on which economic theory is based) is that she is an atomistic individual connected to other people and things only by external relations. John Cobb and I (*For the Common Good*) proposed instead the concept of 'person-in-community' whose very identity is constituted by internal relations to others in the community. I can only define myself by reference to these relations in community. Who am I? I am son of ..., husband of ..., father of ..., friend of ..., citizen of ..., member of ..., and so on. Shorn of all these relations there is not much left of 'me'. I am defined by these relations, and therefore they are internal to my identity as a self-conscious, willing being, not just external connections between some abstract, atomistic, independent 'me' and other people, places, or things. Similarly, my relation to the environment is not just external, the economist's term 'externalities' notwithstanding. I am literally constituted by what I take in from the environment. My connection to air is not just external, it is an internal relation manifested in my lungs – I am an air-breather, just as I am the brother of ... This is an ontological statement about how the world is, how people are, not a wish about how they should be. The customary vision of *Homo economicus* is a wish about how people would have to be for neoclassical economics to work! *Homo economicus* is a misleading picture of people, consequently neoclassical economics is a misleading theory, and policy based on it has been badly misled.

The person-in-community understanding of who we are means that my welfare depends much more on the quality of all the relationships that define me than on my external relations to the commodities I buy or consume. And if advertisers convince me that my relation to certain commodities really is internal to and constitutive of my identity – I am a Marlboro man or a Lexus owner – then so much the worse for me. The idea that the welfare of a community or commonwealth can even be approximated by summing up the annual consumption-based marginal utilities of atomistic individuals related only externally through an exchange nexus is quite absurd.

Community is far more than an aggregation of individuals. Communities have boundaries that are both inclusive and exclusive. The relationships by which we are defined as persons-in-community are those with people and places we know, with whom we share some common history, language, and laws. They do not include all possible relations with all people all over the globe, except in a very abstract and tenuous way. World community should be viewed as a federation of national communities, a community of communities, not as an immediate community in which persons have direct membership. It sounds good to say that 'I am a citizen of the globe', but it is meaningless unless I am first defined by my more local relations in community.

Global community must be built up from below as the federated community of interdependent local and national communities. It cannot be some single, integrated, top-down, ahistorical, abstract global club. Free trade, free capital mobility, and free migration do not create a global community, they simply destroy national community. Globalization is just neoclassical atomistic individualism writ large. Such globalization destroys the local historical relations in community by which persons produce for and take care of each other, and from which we might step-by-step federate into a global community of communities following the principle of 'subsidiarity'. This is a rule that says problems should be dealt with at the most local community level capable of solving them. Climate change is irreducibly global, so let our fledgling institutions of world federation focus on that instead of trying to take over local markets for food, clothing, finance, and so on, by globalization, resulting in unnecessary dependence on transnational corporations and loss of local autonomy. Even if loosening global integration results in fewer commodities, which is questionable, it will increase welfare by allowing us to improve the quality of relationships in community that constitute our very identity.

12. THE LURKING INCONSISTENCY

Ecological economics of course has roots in ecology and biology as well
as in economics. Most of ecological economists' and steady-state economists' time has been well-spent correcting economics in the light of
biology and ecology. And there is still more to do in this direction.
However, we should be careful to avoid importing some deep metaphysical biases frequent in biology, along with its scientific truths.

According to biologists the existence of any species is an accident, and
its continued survival is always subject to cancellation by the all-
powerful process of random mutation and natural selection as it occurs
anywhere in the interdependent ecosystem. This blind process, over long
time periods, is held to explain not only the evolution of all living things
from a presumed common ancestor, but also, in some versions, the
'spontaneous generation' of the common ancestor itself from the 'primor-
dial chemical soup'. For human beings in particular, random mutation
and natural selection are thought to determine not only such characteristics as eye color and height, but also intelligence, consciousness, morality, and capacity for rational thought. Neo-Darwinism has been
extrapolated from a good explanation of many facts to the universal
explanation of everything.

Powerful though it certainly is, the neo-Darwinist theory cannot
explain consciousness and purpose. Even in the realm of materialism it
faces some serious glitches. I refer to the problem of how it happens that
many interdependent parts of a complex organ, each of which has no
independent survival value, can both occur and be retained until the
whole organ is assembled into a complete functioning unit, which only
then can contribute to survival and thus be selected. Also, there is the
anomaly of altruism. Kin selection does not explain Mother Teresa or
Oskar Schindler, and in any case is now disputed among biologists. But
let me leave all that for future debate. My point for now is that
biologists/ecologists who teach a materialist neo-Darwinist worldview to
sophomores on Monday, Wednesday, and Friday, and then devote their
Tuesdays, Thursdays and Saturdays to pleading with Congress and the
public to enact policies to save this or that endangered species are in the
tight grip of a serious inconsistency.

Naturally, the public asks the biologists what purpose would be served
by saving certain threatened species? Since many leading biologists, as
scientific materialists, claim not to believe in purpose (either in the sense
of cosmic *telos*, or mere individual preferences that are independently
causative in the physical world) this is not an easy question for them to

answer. They tell us about biodiversity, and ecosystem stability and resilience, and about a presumed instinct of biophilia that we (who systematically drive other species to extinction) are nevertheless alleged to posses, encoded in our genes. But the biologists cannot affirm any of these descriptive concepts as an abiding purpose, or an objective value, because doing so would contradict the fundamental assumption of their science. For example, biophilia could be appealed to as a virtue, a persuasive value rather than a wishfully imagined part of the deterministic genetic code. But that would be to admit purpose. Instead, biologists try to find some overlooked mechanistic cause that will make us do what we believe we ought to do, but cannot logically advocate without acknowledging the reality of purpose. Absent purpose and value, the biologists' appeals to Congress and the public for conservation are both logically lame and emotionally feeble.

Others have called attention to this problem in the past. The term 'lurking inconsistency', as well as its meaning, is taken from Alfred North Whitehead (*Science and the Modern World*, 1925, p. 76) who expressed it in the following passage that repays careful reading:

> A scientific realism, based on mechanism, is conjoined with an unwavering belief in the world of men and of the higher animals as being composed of self-determining organisms. This radical inconsistency at the basis of modern thought accounts for much that is half-hearted and wavering in our civilization [...] It enfeebles [thought], by reason of the inconsistency lurking in the background [...] For instance, the enterprises produced by the individualistic energy of the European peoples presuppose physical actions directed to final causes. But the science which is employed in their development is based on a philosophy which asserts that physical causation is supreme, and which disjoins the physical cause from the final end. It is not popular to dwell on the absolute contradiction here involved.

In other words, our scientific understanding of nature is based on mechanism, on material and efficient causation with no room for final cause, for teleology or purpose. Yet we ourselves, and higher animals in general, directly experience purpose, and, within limits, act in a self-determining manner. If we are part of nature then so is purpose; if purpose is not part of nature then neither, in at least one significant way, are we. Elsewhere Whitehead put the contradiction more pointedly: 'Scientists animated by the purpose of proving that they are purposeless constitute an interesting subject for study'. Biologist Charles Birch, a keen student of Whitehead, has restated the lurking inconsistency in his insightful book *On Purpose*: '[Purpose] has become the central problem for contemporary thought because of the mismatch in modernism between how we think of ourselves and how we think and act in relation to the rest of the world'. Clearly, not all biologists are guilty of the lurking inconsistency.

The directly experienced reality of purpose or final cause must, in the view of materialism, be an 'epiphenomenon' – an illusion which itself was selected because of the reproductive advantage that it chanced to confer on those under its spell. It is odd that the illusion of purpose should be thought to confer a selective advantage in the real biophysical world, while purpose itself is held to be a non-causative epiphenomenon – but that is the neo-Darwinist's problem, not mine. The policy implication of the materialist dogma that purpose is not causative is *laissez faire* beyond the most libertarian economist's wildest model. The only 'policy' consistent with this view is, 'let it happen as it will anyway'. Is it too much to ask the neo-Darwinist to speculate about the possibility that the survival value of neo-Darwinism itself has become negative for the species that really believes it as a metaphysical worldview? Does not this lurking inconsistency have lethal consequences for policy of any kind?

Teleology has its limits, of course, and from the Enlightenment onward it is evident that materialism has constituted an enormously powerful research paradigm for biology. The temptation to elevate a successful research paradigm to the level of a metaphysical worldview is perhaps irresistible. But materialism too has its limits. To deny the reality of our most immediately direct and universal experience (that of purpose) because it does not fit the presuppositions of methodological materialism, is profoundly anti-empirical. To then refuse to recognize the devastating logical and moral consequences that result from the denial of purpose is anti-rational. For those of us who consider science a rational and empirical enterprise, this is extremely troubling. That people already unembarrassed by the fact that their major intellectual purpose is to deny the reality of purpose should now want to concern themselves deeply with the relative valuation of accidental pieces of their purposeless world is incoherence compounded.

One cannot rescue neo-Darwinism from the domain of purposeless and randomness by pointing to the role of natural selection. Selection may sound purposeful, but in the accepted theory of natural selection chance dominates. Random mutation provides the menu from which natural selection 'chooses' by the criterion of the odds of surviving and reproducing in a randomly changing environment (consisting of randomly changing geophysical conditions, and other species that are also randomly evolving). It is a metaphysics of chance all the way down.

The relevance of the lurking inconsistency to conservation biology and steady-state economics should be evident – conservation and sustainable scale are, after all, purposes that are ruled out in a world governed only by chance.

If purpose does not exist then it is hard to imagine how we could experience the lure of value. To have a purpose means to serve an end, and value is imputed to whatever furthers attainment of that end. Alternatively, if there is objective value then surely the attainment of value should become a purpose. Neo-Darwinist biologists and ecologists, who deny the reality of purpose, owe it to the rest of us to remain silent about valuation – and conservation as well. If they simply cannot remain silent, then they must rethink their deterministic materialism. Distinguished philosopher Thomas Nagel (2012) has offered to help them in his recent book *Mind and Cosmos: Why the Materialist Neo-Darwinist Conception of Nature is Almost Certainly Wrong*. But his 'help' requires more recantation than the naturalists can bear, and, even though Nagel is a fellow atheist, he has been excommunicated from the Church of Neo-Darwinism for heresy.

Economists, unlike many biologists, do not usually go to the extreme of denying the existence of purpose. They recognize purpose in attenuated form under the rubric of individual preferences and do not generally consider them to be illusory. However, preferences are thought to be purely subjective, so that one person's preferences are as good as another's. Unlike public facts, private preferences cannot be right or wrong – there is, by assumption, no objective standard of value by which preferences can be judged. Nevertheless, according to economists, individual preferences are the ultimate standard of value. Witness economists' attempts to value species by asking consumers how much they would be willing to pay to save a threatened species, or how much they would accept in compensation for the species' disappearance. The fact that the two methods of this 'contingent valuation' give different answers only adds comic relief to the underlying tragedy, which is the reduction of value to taste weighted by income.

Economics too suffers from the lurking inconsistency, but not to the extent that biology does. Purpose has not been excluded, just reduced to the level of tastes. But even an unexamined and unworthy purpose, such as unconstrained aggregate satisfaction of uninstructed private tastes weighted by income – GDP growth forever – will dominate in the absence of purpose. So, in the public policy forum, economists with their attenuated, subjective concept of purpose (which at least is thought to be causative) will dominate the neo-Darwinist ecologists who are still crippled by the self-inflicted purpose of proving that they are purpose-less. Consequently GDP growth will continue to dominate conservation.

Whitehead's observation that, 'it is not popular to dwell on the absolute contradiction here involved', remains true 85 years later. This willful neglect has allowed the lurking inconsistency to metastasize into the marrow of modernity. The Enlightenment, with its rejection of teleology, certainly illuminated some hidden recesses of superstition in the so-called Dark Ages. But the angle of its cold light has also cast a deep shadow forward into the modern world, obscuring the reality of purpose. To conserve Creation we will first have to reclaim purpose from that darkness. I say Creation with a capital 'C' advisedly, and not in denial of the facts of evolution. Rather, if we think that our world, our lives, and our conscious, self-reflective thinking are just a random happenstance of matter in motion – a temporary statistical fluke of multiplying infinitesimal probabilities by an infinite number of trials – then it is hard to see why we should make any sacrifice to maintain the capacity of the earth to support life, or from where we would get the inspiration to do so. This is the lurking inconsistency's bottom-line consequence for conservation biology and steady-state economics. Our problem is not just faulty economics or biology; it is deep underlying metaphysical and philosophical contradiction.

13. RENEWABLE IGNORANCE

We are all born pig-ignorant. Upon having accumulated a lifetime of knowledge we all promptly die. Ignorant babies replace learned elders. Knowledge is a depleting resource; ignorance is renewable. Yes, libraries and data banks grow, but knowledge finally has to exist in the minds of living people to be effective and evolve – unread books, unseen videos, and unaccessed hard drives are inert. They are also subject to destruction by teeth of time: fire, flood, mildew and moth, as well as that modern bookworm, the computer virus.

Like Sisyphus, we push the rock up the hill only to have it roll back down again. Progress is not completely illusory. However, it is 3 steps up followed by 2.5 steps backward. Successive generations repeat earlier mistakes. They also invent new ones. Any solution to a given mistake is usually forgotten within two or three generations and we have to learn it again. But it is not all bad – after all, babies are delightful and happy while old people are grumpy – ignorance is bliss. Life consists of more than knowledge. Life expectancy has increased, so the old know more when they die, leaving the babies with still more to learn.

A massive transfer of knowledge each generation is an unavoidable necessity. This transfer is not automatic. It requires two decisions. The old must decide what knowledge is worth their effort to teach, and the young must decide what is worth their effort to learn. Some knowledge passes both filters and becomes the basis for guiding the future and for discovering new knowledge. Other knowledge fails to pass one or both filters and is lost. Just as the world is always only one failed harvest away from mass hunger, so it is always only one failed generational transfer away from mass ignorance.

What do we know about these two generational knowledge filters? What do they let pass and what do they filter out? I really do not know the answer, but I have one speculation, taken from E.F. Schumacher's reflections on Thomas Aquinas and Rene Descartes. Aquinas said that even uncertain knowledge of the highest things is worth more than certain knowledge of the lowest things. Descartes believed otherwise, that only knowledge that had the certainty of geometry was worth retaining, and uncertain knowledge should be abandoned even if it pertained to higher things. These two filters have very different selection biases. In their extreme forms they represent opposite errors of judgment about what knowledge to keep and what to jettison.

Which error are we most likely to commit today? I believe we overemphasize Descartes and pay too little attention to Aquinas. I take

Aquinas' 'higher things' to mean purposes, knowledge about right purposes. Lower things I take to refer to techniques – how to efficiently do something, assuming it should be done in the first place. We have overdeveloped our relatively certain knowledge of technique, and left underdeveloped our less certain but more important knowledge of right purpose. The old seem more interested in teaching technique than purpose, and the young obligingly seem more interested in learning technique than purpose. So we develop more and more power, subject to less and less purpose. As physicist S. Weinberg says, the more science makes the universe comprehensible and subject to our control, the more it also seems to render it pointless, and the less our control is guided by purpose.

These thoughts remind me of a public debate I participated in at Louisiana State University in the 1970s regarding the construction of the River Bend Nuclear Power Plant near Baton Rouge. I presented economic and safety reasons for believing that the plant should not be built, that there were cheaper and safer alternative sources of electricity, and so on. After my presentation a nuclear engineering consultant from MIT made his rebuttal on behalf of Gulf States Utilities. It consisted entirely of presenting a scale model of the reactor core and explaining how it worked. He never replied to any of my arguments or said a word about why the reactor should be built. But his exposition of technique easily won the public debate. Afterwards everyone crowded around his model pointing to this and that, asking how it worked. 'How to' questions of technique totally displaced 'what for' questions of purpose. Maybe I needed a scale model meltdown of a reactor core! Maybe I needed a course in public relations. I might as well have been whistling Dixie.

Also I am reminded of a conversation with a friend who was the film curator for the Library of Congress. He told me that digital recording techniques were now so advanced and cheap that the Library would soon be recording and preserving everything that appeared on TV, or YouTube, or the radio, or Twitter, and so on. Historians and scholars could then decide what was important and valuable. Librarians would avoid this difficult qualitative decision, and at the same time feel good about themselves for not imposing their value judgments on future historians. While I understand this point of view I cannot share it because it seems to me yet another example of 'how to' questions displacing 'what for' questions – a displacement likely to be continued by the 'value-free' future scholars for whose benefit this almost infinite attic of junk is to be saved.

Knowledge is offered as a panacea these days. Young people are urged to go deeply into debt to 'get a degree', and are assured that the growth economy will allow them to pay it back with interest and still come out ahead. Many have been disappointed, and more will be. As one who has spent over 40 years in universities I am doubtful about this exaltation of knowledge, even though in arguing for a steady-state economy, I have appealed to physical limits, not knowledge limits, leaving open the question of how much qualitative development could be supported within a biophysical steady state without quantitative growth. Also the 'knowledge limits' I have appealed to are themselves knowledge – knowledge of physical limits, mainly the laws of thermodynamics, rather than any inherent limits to knowledge itself.

Although I am eager for knowledge to substitute physical growth to the extent possible, the basic renewability of ignorance makes me doubt that knowledge can save the growth economy. Furthermore, knowledge, even when it increases, does not grow exponentially like money in the bank. Some old knowledge is disproved or canceled out by new knowledge, and some new knowledge is discovery of new biophysical or social limits to growth. New knowledge must always be something of a surprise – if we could predict its content then we would have to know it already and it would not really be new. Contrary to common expectation, new knowledge is not always a pleasant surprise for the growth economy – frequently it is bad news. For example, climate change from greenhouse gases was recently new knowledge, as was discovery of the ozone hole.

One thing I have learned about universities is that much of what is taught in them today is based on the labor theory of value – 'it was hard for me to learn this, so it must be worth teaching it to you'. This is a poor generational filter, and is even found in economics, which of all disciplines should know better! Also, much abandoned knowledge should have made the cut but did not. Indeed the whole field of history of economic thought has been cut from the curriculum to make room for more econometrics – the art of pretending to measure ephemeral and tenuous correlations among ill-defined variables in a world where the relationships to be measured change faster than the data for estimating them accumulates. The classical economists' concept of the stationary-state economy did not totally disappear, but almost.

Is just trying to save everything a solution? No. Do I have a solution? No. So I will stop here and simply ask that we all, young and old, pause, and calmly consider the proper balance between the 'what for' and the 'how to' questions as filters for the generational transfer of knowledge. Let us help the babies deal better with the perennial problem of renewable ignorance.

14. DEPLETION OF MORAL CAPITAL AS A LIMIT TO GROWTH

Fred Hirsh (*Social Limits to Growth*, Harvard University Press, 1976) argues that, 'Morality of the minimum order necessary for the functioning of a market system was assumed, nearly always implicitly, to be a kind of permanent free good, a natural resource of a non-depleting kind'.

Elaborating on the relation of Adam Smith's *Theory of Moral Sentiments* to his *Wealth of Nations*, Hirsh points out that, for Smith, men could safely be trusted not to harm the community in pursuing their own self-interest not only because of the invisible hand of competition, but also because of built-in restraints on individual behavior derived from shared morals, religion, custom, and education. The problem that Hirsh sees is that, '*continuation of the growth process itself rests on certain preconditions that its own success has jeopardized through its individualistic ethos. Economic growth undermines its social foundations*'.

The undermining of moral restraint has sources on both the demand and supply sides of the market for commodities. E.J. Mishan ('The growth of affluence and the decline of welfare' in H. Daly, ed., *Economics, Ecology, Ethics*, W.H. Freeman Co., San Francisco, 1980) has noted that 'a society in which "anything goes" is, *ipso facto*, a society in which anything sells'. A corollary is that self-restraint or abstinence in the interests of any higher claims than immediate gratification by consumption is bad for sales, therefore bad for production, employment, tax receipts and everything else. The growth economy cannot grow unless it can sell. The idea that something should not be bought because it is frivolous, degrading, tawdry, or immoral is subversive to the growth imperative. If demand is to be sufficient for continual growth then everything must sell, which requires that 'anything goes'.

On the supply side the success of science-based technology has fostered the pseudo-religion of 'scientism', in other words, the elevation of the deterministic, materialistic, mechanistic, and reductionistic research program of science to the status of an ultimate World View. Undeniably, the methodological approach of scientific materialism has led to great increases in our technological prowess. Its practical success argues for its promotion from working hypothesis or research program to World View. But a World View of scientific materialism leaves no room for purpose, for good and evil, for better and worse states of the world. It erodes morality in general and moral restraint in economic life in particular. As power has increased, purpose has shrunk.

The baleful consequence of this fragmenting of the moral order, which we are depleting just as surely as we are wrecking the ecological order, is, as Mishan points out, that, 'effective argument [about policy] becomes impossible if there is no longer a common set of ultimate values or beliefs to which appeal can be made in the endeavor to persuade others'. Just as all research in the physical sciences must dogmatically assume the existence of objective order in the physical world, so must research in the policy sciences dogmatically assume the existence of objective value in the moral world. Policy must be aimed at moving the world toward a better state of affairs or else it is senseless. If 'better' and 'worse' have no objective meaning, then policy can only be arbitrary and capricious. C.S. Lewis (*The Abolition of Man*, Macmillan, New York, 1965) forcefully stated this fundamental truth, 'A dogmatic belief in objective value is necessary to the very idea of a rule which is not tyranny or an obedience which is not slavery'.

Likewise, Mishan claims that 'a moral consensus that is to be enduring and effective is the product of a belief only in its divine origin'. In other words, an enduring ethic must be more than a social convention. It must have some objective, transcendental authority, regardless of whether one calls that authority 'God', or 'the Force', or whatever. All attempts to treat moral value as entirely a part of nature to be manipulated and programmed by psychology or genetics only ends in a logical circularity.

Moral value cannot be reduced to or explained as a mere result of genetic chance and natural selection, without at the same time losing its authority. Even if we knew how to remake moral values as human artifacts, we must still have a criterion for deciding which values should be emphasized and which stifled in the new order. But if that necessary criterion is itself an artifact of humanly manipulated mutation and selection, then it too is a candidate for being remade. There is nowhere to stand.

Once the false belief spreads (and it already has) that morality has no basis other than random chance and natural selection under impermanent environmental conditions, then it will have about as much authority and truth claim as the Easter Bunny. In sum, the attitudes of scientific materialism and cultural relativism actively undercut belief in a transcendental basis for objective value, which in turn undercuts moral consensus. Lacking that consensus there is no longer the 'morality of the minimum order necessary for the functioning of a market system' presupposed by Adam Smith and his followers.

D.

Real-world economics

15. NOT PRODUCTION, NOT CONSUMPTION, BUT TRANSFORMATION

Well-established words can be misleading. In economics 'production and consumption' are such common terms that it is easy to forget that they do not really mean what they literally say. Physically we do not produce anything; we just use energy to rearrange matter into a more useful form. Production really means transformation of what is already here. Likewise, consumption merely reflects the disarrangement of carefully structured materials by the wear and tear of use into a less useful form – another transformation, this time from useful product into worn out product and waste. Of course one might say that we are producing and consuming 'value' or 'utility', not really physical things. However, value is always added to something physical, namely resources, by labor and capital, which are also physical things ultimately made from the same low-entropy energy and materials that go into products. Nor does the service sector escape physical dimensions. Services are always rendered by some*thing* or some*body*. To abstract from physical dimensions and focus only on utility is to throw out the baby and keep the bathwater.

If we were to speak of a 'transformation function' rather than a production function then we would naturally have to specify what is being transformed, into what, by the agency of what? Natural resource flows are transformed into flows of goods (and wastes) by the fund agents of labor and capital. A transformation function must show both the agents of transformation (funds of labor and capital that are not themselves transformed into the product but are needed to effect the transformation), and the flow of resources that are indeed physically embodied in the flow of products, or waste. This distinction between fund and flow factors immediately reveals their complementary roles as efficient cause and material cause – any substitution between them is very limited. You cannot bake the same cake with half the flour, eggs, and so on, by doubling the number of cooks and the size of the oven. One natural resource can often substitute for another, and capital can often substitute for labor or vice versa, but more labor and capital can hardly substitute for a smaller resource flow, beyond the very limited extent of sweeping up and re-using process waste such as scraps, sawdust, and so on, which ought to have already been accounted for in specifying a technically efficient production function. In most textbooks the production function depicts output as a function of inputs, undifferentiated as to their fund or flow nature, and all considered fundamentally substitutable.

But if the usual production function does not distinguish fund agents of transformation from the flow of natural resources being transformed, then how does it envisage the process of converting factor inputs into product outputs? Usually by multiplying them together, as in the Cobb–Douglas and other multiplicative functions. What could be more natural linguistically than multiplying 'factors' to get a 'product'? But this is mathematics, not economics. There is absolutely nothing analogous to multiplication going on in what we customarily call production – there is only transformation. Try to multiply the resource flow by labor or capital to get product outflow and your 'production function' will have immediately run afoul of the law of conservation of mass. Perhaps to escape such incongruities most production functions contain only labor and capital, omitting resources entirely. We can now bake our cake with only the cook and her oven, no ingredients to be transformed at all! You can multiply cooks times ovens all you want and you still will not get a meal.

How did this nonsense come into economics? I suspect it represents a confusion between the production function as a theoretical analytical description of the physical process of transformation (a recipe), and production function as a mere statistical correlation between outputs and inputs. The latter is common in macroeconomics, the former in microeconomics, although that is not a hard and fast rule because the distinction between a theoretical description and a statistical correlation is often ignored in both areas. The statistical approach usually includes only labor and capital as factor inputs, and then discovers that these two factors 'explain' only 60 percent of the historical change in output, leaving a 40 percent residual to be explained by 'something else'. No problem, say the growth economists, that large residual is 'obviously' a measure of technological progress. However, the statistical residual is in fact a measure of everything that is not capital and labor – including specifically the quantity and quality of resources transformed. Increased resource use gets counted in the residual and attributed to technological progress. Then that same measure of technical progress is appealed to in order to demonstrate the unimportance of resources! If we thought in terms of a transformation function, rather than production *ex nihilo* it would be hard to make such an error.

The basic points just made were developed 40 years ago by Nicholas Georgescu-Roegen in his fund-flow critique of the neoclassical production function. Neoclassical growth economists have never answered his critique. Why bring it up again, and what is the relevance to steady-state economics? It is worth raising the issue again precisely because it has never been answered. What kind of a science is it that can get away with ignoring a fundamental critique for 40 years? It is relevant to steady-state economics because it views production as physical transformation subject to biophysical limits and the laws of thermodynamics. Also it shows that the force of resource scarcity is in the nature of a limiting factor, and not so easy to escape by substitution of capital for resources, as often claimed by neoclassical growth economists.

16.   WHAT IS THE LIMITING FACTOR?

In yesteryear's empty world capital was the limiting factor in economic growth. But we now live in a full world.

Consider: What limits the annual fish catch – fishing boats (capital) or remaining fish in the sea (natural resources)? Clearly the latter. What limits barrels of crude oil extracted – drilling rigs and pumps (capital), or remaining accessible deposits of petroleum – or capacity of the atmosphere to absorb the CO_2 from burning petroleum (both natural resources)? What limits production of cut timber – number of chain saws and lumber mills, or standing forests and their rate of growth? What limits irrigated agriculture – pumps and sprinklers, or aquifer recharge rates and river flow volumes? That should be enough to at least suggest that we live in a natural resource-constrained world, not a capital-constrained world.

Economic logic says to invest in and economize on the limiting factor. Economic logic has not changed; what has changed is the limiting factor. It is now natural resources, not capital, that we must economize on and invest in. Economists have not recognized this fundamental shift in the pattern of scarcity. Nobel Laureate in Chemistry and underground economist, Frederick Soddy, predicted the shift 80 years ago. He argued that mankind ultimately lives on current sunshine, captured with the aid of plants, soil, and water. This fundamental permanent basis for life is temporarily supplemented by the release of trapped sunshine of Paleozoic summers that is being rapidly depleted to fuel what he called 'the flamboyant age'. So addicted are we to this short-run subsidy that our technocrats advocate shutting out some of the incoming solar energy to make more thermal room for burning fossil fuels! These educated cretins are also busy chemically degrading the topsoil and polluting the water, while tinkering with the genetic basis of plants, all toward the purpose of maximizing short-run growth. As Wes Jackson says, agricultural plants now have genes selected by the Chicago Board of Trade, not by fitness to the ecosystem of surrounding organisms and geography.

What has kept economists from recognizing Soddy's insight? An animus against dependence on nature, and a devotion to dominance. This basic attitude has been served by a theoretical commitment to factor substitutability and a neglect of complementarity by today's neoclassical economists. In the absence of complementarity there can be no limiting factor – if capital and natural resources are substitutes in production then neither can be limiting – if one is in short supply you just substitute the other and continue producing. If they are complements both are necessary and the one in short supply is limiting.

Economists used to believe that capital was the limiting factor. Therefore they implicitly must have believed in complementarity between capital and natural resources back in the empty-world economy. But when resources became limiting in the new full-world economy, rather than recognizing the shift in the pattern of scarcity and the new limiting factor, they abandoned the whole idea of limiting factor by emphasizing substitutability to the exclusion of complementarity. The new reason for emphasizing capital over natural resources is the claim that capital is a near perfect substitute for resources.

William Nordhaus and James Tobin (1972) were quite explicit:

> The prevailing standard model of growth assumes that there are no limits on the feasibility of expanding the supplies of nonhuman agents of production. It is basically a two-factor model in which production depends only on labor and reproducible capital. Land and resources, the third member of the classical triad, have generally been dropped ... the tacit justification has been that reproducible capital is a near perfect substitute for land and other exhaustible resources.

The claim that capital is a near perfect substitute for natural resources is absurd. For one thing substitution is reversible. If capital is a near perfect substitute for resources, then resources are a near perfect substitute for capital – so why then did we ever bother to accumulate capital in the first place if nature already endowed us with a near perfect substitute?

It is not for nothing that our system is called 'capitalism' rather than 'natural resource-ism'. It is ideologically inconvenient for capitalism if capital is no longer the limiting factor. But that inconvenience has been met by claiming that capital is a good substitute for natural resources. Ever true to its basic animus of denying any fundamental dependence on nature, neoclassical economics saw only two alternatives – either nature is not scarce and capital is limiting, or nature's scarcity does not matter because manmade capital is a near perfect substitute for natural resources. In either case man is in control of nature, thanks to capital, and that is the main thing. Never mind that manmade capital is itself made from natural resources.

The absurdity of the claim that capital and natural resources are good substitutes has been further demonstrated by Georgescu-Roegen in his fund-flow theory of production. It recognizes that factors of production are of two qualitatively different kinds: (1) resource flows that are physically transformed into flows of product and waste; and (2) capital and labor funds, the agents or instruments of transformation that are not themselves physically embodied in the product. If one finds a machine screw or a piece of a worker's finger in one's can of soup, that is reason for a lawsuit, not confirmation of the metaphysical notion that capital and labor are somehow 'embodied' in the product!

There are varying degrees of substitution between different natural resource flows, and between the funds of labor and capital. But the basic relation between resource flow on the one hand, and capital (or labor) fund on the other, is complementarity. Efficient cause (capital) does not substitute for material cause (resources). You cannot bake the same cake with half the ingredients no matter if you double or triple the number of cooks and ovens. Funds and flows are complements.

Further, capital is current surplus production exchanged for a lien against future production – physically it is made from natural resources. It is not easy to substitute away from natural resources when the presumed substitute is itself made from natural resources.

It is now generally recognized, even by economists, that there is far too much debt worldwide, both public and private. The reason so much debt was incurred is that we have had absurdly unrealistic expectations about the efficacy of capital to produce the real growth needed to redeem the debt that is 'capital' by another name. In other words the debt that piled up in failed attempts to make wealth grow as fast as debt is evidence of the reality of limits to growth. But instead of being seen as such, it is taken as the main reason to attempt still more growth by issuing more debt, and by shifting bad debts from the balance sheet of private banks to that of the public treasury, in effect monetizing them.

The wishful thought leading to such unfounded growth expectations was the belief that by growth we would cure poverty without the need to share. As the poor got richer, the rich could get still richer! Few expected that aggregate growth itself would become *uneconomic*, would begin to cost us more than it was worth at the margin, making us collectively poorer, not richer. But it did. In spite of that, our economists, bankers, and politicians still have unrealistic expectations about growth. Like the losing gambler they try to get even by betting double or nothing on more growth.

Could we not take a short time-out from growth roulette to reconsider the steady-state economy? After all, the idea is deeply rooted in classical economics, as well as in physics and biology. Perpetual motion and infinite growth are not reasonable premises on which to base economic policy.

At some level many people surely know this. Why then do we keep growth as the top national priority? First, we are misled because our measure of growth, GDP, counts all 'economic activity' thereby conflating costs and benefits, rather than comparing them at the margin. Second, the cumulative net benefit of past growth is a maximum at precisely the point where further growth becomes uneconomic (where declining marginal benefit equals increasing marginal cost), and past experience ceases to be a good guide to the future in this respect. Third, because even though the benefits of further growth are now less than the costs, our decision-making elites have figured out how to keep the dwindling extra benefits for themselves, while 'sharing' the exploding extra costs with the poor, the future, and other species. The elite-owned media, the corporate-funded think tanks, the kept economists of high academia, and the World Bank – not to mention Gold Sacks and Wall Street – all sing hymns to growth in perfect unison, and bamboozle average citizens.

What is going to happen?

17. OPPORTUNITY COST OF GROWTH

Economics is about counting costs, and the cost to be counted is 'opportunity cost', arguably the most basic concept in economics. It is defined as the next best alternative to the one chosen, in other words, as the best of the sacrificed alternatives. You chose the best alternative, the opportunity cost is the second best, the alternative that you would choose if the best were unavailable. If there were no scarcity, choice would not be necessary, there would be no opportunity cost, and economics would not exist. More of everything means opportunity cost is zero, and is essentially the denial of economics. Yet 'more of everything' is the goal of so-called 'growth economics'. When the whole economy grows, the growth economists say that we get more of everything. Is there an opportunity cost to the growth of the whole macroeconomy? Not in the view of mainstream macroeconomists. In their view the economy is the Whole and nature (mines, wells, grasslands, fisheries, forests ...) are Parts of the economy. Used-up parts can be substituted by new parts; natural parts can be substituted by manmade parts; natural resources can be substituted by capital. The whole macroeconomy is not itself seen as a subsystem or part of a larger but finite ecosystem, into which the macroeconomy grows and encroaches. These economists imagine that the macroeconomy grows into the void, not into the constraining biophysical envelope of the ecosystem. Since macroeconomic growth is held to incur no opportunity cost (the displaced void is worthless!), one must conclude that 'growth economics' is really not economics – it is almost the negation of economics!

Almost – there is one remaining bit of scarcity. Growth economists recognize that we cannot have more of everything instantaneously. To get more of everything we must invest and wait. The opportunity cost of investment is forgone present consumption. But it is a temporary cost. Later we will have more of everything, and after that still more of everything, and so on. Is there no end to this? Not for the standard macroeconomists. In their view it might be possible to grow too fast, but never to get too big. That is, the opportunity cost of investment needed for rapid growth might be too high in terms of forgone present consumption. But that misallocation is temporary and will soon be washed away by growth itself that will give us more of everything in the future – more consumption and more investment. That is the growth economist's theory.

However, increasing takeover of the ecosystem is the necessary consequence of the physical growth of the macroeconomy. This displacement is really a transformation of ecosystem into economy in physical terms.

Trees are physically transformed into tables and chairs; soil, rain, and sunlight are physically transformed into crops and food and then into people; petroleum is physically transformed into motive force, plastics, and carbon dioxide. Thanks to the law of conservation of matter-energy, the more matter-energy appropriated by the economy, the less remains to build the structures and power the services of the ecosystem that sustains the economy. Thanks to the entropy law, the more dissipative structures (human bodies and artifacts) in the economy, the greater the rates of depletion and pollution of the remaining ecosystem required to maintain the growing populations of these structures against the eroding force of entropy. These are basic facts about how the world works. They could plausibly be ignored by economists only as long as the macroeconomy was tiny relative to the ecosystem, and the encroachment of the former into the latter did not constitute a noticeable opportunity cost. But now we live in a full world, no longer in an empty world – that is, in a finite ecosystem filled up largely by the economy. Remaining ecosystem services and natural capital are now scarce and their further reduction constitutes a significant opportunity cost of growth.

The new economic question is: are the extra benefits of physically transforming more of the ecosystem into the economy worth the extra opportunity cost of the ecosystem services lost in the transformation? Has the macroeconomy reached, or surpassed, its optimal physical scale relative to its containing and sustaining ecosystem? Is the economy now too big for the ecosystem from the point of view of maximum human welfare? Or from the point of view of all living species and the functioning of the biosphere as we know it? If these questions about the opportunity costs of growth sound too abstract, think of the following concrete examples: wholesale extinction of species, climate change, peak oil, water scarcity, topsoil loss, deforestation, risks from more powerful technologies, a huge military to maintain access to world resources, and an increase in the risk of wars over resources.

As the marginal costs of growth have increased, what has happened to the marginal benefits? Studies in the US and other countries show that, beyond a threshold of sufficiency, growth in real GDP does not increase happiness. In sum, growth has become uneconomic at the margin, making us poorer, not richer. Uneconomic growth leads to less available wealth to share with the poor, not more. And such growth in the US in recent years has been accompanied by increasing inequality in the distribution of income and wealth – that is, the marginal benefits of growth have gone overwhelmingly to the rich (third cars and second homes) while the marginal costs (polluted neighborhoods, unemployment and foreclosures) have gone mainly to the poor.

Surely economists have thought about such simple and basic questions as, can the economy be too big in its physical dimensions relative to the ecosystem? And, are the marginal costs of growth now larger than the marginal benefits? Surely economists have good answers to these obvious questions! Well, dear reader, I invite you to ask these questions to your favorite economics professor or pundit. If you get reasonable answers, please share them with me. If you get a lot of obfuscation, consider telling the economist to go to hell. Be open to learn – but also be prepared to show some disrespect when it is deserved!

18. SUSTAINING OUR COMMONWEALTH OF NATURE AND KNOWLEDGE

Let us start with this phrase: 'sustaining our commonwealth'. By sustaining, I do not mean preserving inviolate; I mean using, without using up. Using with maintenance and replenishment is an important idea in economics. It is the very basis of the concept of income, because income is the maximum that you can consume today and still be able to produce and consume the same amount tomorrow – that is, maximum consumption without depleting capital in the broad sense of future productive capacity. By commonwealth, I mean the wealth that no one has made, or the wealth that practically everyone has made. So it is either nature – nobody made it, we all inherited it – or knowledge – everybody contributed to making it, but everyone's contribution is small in relation to the total and depends on the contributions of others. In managing the commonwealth of nature, our big problem is that we tend to treat the truly scarce as if it were non-scarce. The opposite problem arises with the commonwealth of knowledge, in which we tend to treat what is truly not scarce as if it were.

Clarifying Scarcity

There are two sets of important distinctions about goods, and they make four cross-classifications (see figure below). Goods can be either rival or non-rival, and they can be either excludable or non-excludable. My shirt, for example, is a rival good because if I'm wearing it, you cannot wear it at the same time. The warmth of the sun is non-rival because I can enjoy the warmth of the sun, and everyone else can enjoy it at the same time. Rivalness is a physical property that precludes the simultaneous use of goods by more than one person. Goods are also excludable or non-excludable. That is not a physical concept, that is a legal concept, a question of property. For example, you could wear my shirt tomorrow if I let you, but that is up to me because it is my property. My shirt is both rival and excludable, and that is the case with most market goods. Meanwhile, the warmth of the sun is both non-rival and also non-excludable. We cannot buy and sell solar warmth; we cannot bottle it and charge for it. Goods that are rival and excludable are market goods. Goods that are non-rival and non-excludable are public goods. That leaves two other categories. Fish in the ocean are an example of goods that are rival and non-excludable. They are rival, because if I catch the fish, you cannot catch it. But they are also non-excludable, because I cannot stop you from fishing in the open seas. The management of goods that are rival and non-excludable gives rise to the famous tragedy of the commons – or the tragedy of open access resources, as it is more accurately called. Now, the other problematic category consists of goods that are non-rival and excludable. If I use the Pythagorean theorem, I do not prevent you from using it at the same time. Knowledge is non-rival, but it often is made excludable through intellectual property and patent rights. So those are two difficult categories that create problems. One is the tragedy of open access to the rival commons, and the other we could call the tragedy of enclosure of the non-rival commons (artificial scarcity).

	Does use by one person physically preclude use by others?	
	Yes **Rival**	**No** **Non-rival**
Yes **Excludable**	**Market Goods** (for example automobiles and fishing reels) *Let the market allocate these goods.*	**Tragedy of Artificial Scarcity** (for example patented meds and knowledge in heads) *Reduce patent monopolies and intellectual property rights – share these goods.*
No **Non-excludable**	**Tragedy of the Commons** (for example old growth trees and fish in the seas) *Designate property rights and use cap–auction–trade to allocate these goods.*	**Public Goods** (for example national security and roads that are free) *Collect depletion and pollution taxes so that government can provide these goods.*

(Left axis: Do laws prohibit access to these goods?)

Figure D18.1   Different types of goods and policies to achieve a sustainable, fair and efficient economy

The Commonwealth of Nature

Fish in the ocean are an example of the commonwealth of nature. I will argue that natural goods and services that are rival and have so far remained non-excludable should be enclosed in the market in order to avoid unsustainable use. Excludability can take the form of individual property rights or social property rights – what needs to be avoided is open access. For dealing with the broad class of rival but, up to now, non-excludable goods, the so-called cap–auction–trade system is a market-based institution that merits consideration.

In addition to its practical value, the cap–auction–trade system also sheds light on a fundamental issue of economic theory: the logically separate issues of scale, distribution, and allocation. Neoclassical economics deals mainly with the question of allocation. Allocation is the apportionment of resources among competing uses: how many resources go to produce beans, how many to cars, how many to haircuts. Properly functioning markets allocate resources efficiently, more or less. Yet the concept of efficient allocation presupposes a given distribution. Distribution is the apportionment of goods and resources among different people: how many resources go to you, how many to somebody else. A good distribution is one that is fair or just – not efficient, but fair. The third issue is scale: the physical size of the economy relative to the ecosystem that sustains it. How many of us are there and how large are the associated matter-energy flows from producing all our stuff, relative to natural cycles that maintain the biosphere. In neoclassical economics, the issue of scale is completely off the radar screen.

The cap–auction–trade system works like this. Some environmental assets, say fishing rights or the rights to emit sulfur dioxide, have been treated as non-excludable free goods. As economic growth increases the scale of the economy relative to that of the biosphere, it becomes recognized that these goods are in fact physically rival. The first step is to put a cap – a maximum – on the scale of use of that resource, at a level that is deemed to be environmentally sustainable. Setting that cap – deciding what it should be – is not a market decision, but a social and ecological decision. Then, the right to extract that resource or emit that waste, up to the cap, becomes a scarce asset. It was a free good. Now it has a price. We have created a new valuable asset, so the question is: Who owns it? This also has to be decided politically, outside the market. Ownership of this new asset is initially public, and then is auctioned to the highest bidder, with the proceeds entering the public treasury. Sometimes rights are simply given to the historical private users – a bad idea, I think, but frequently done under the misleading label of 'grandfathering'. The cap–auction–trade system is not, as often called, 'free-market environmentalism'. It is really socially constrained market environmentalism. Someone must own the assets before they can be traded in the market, and that is an issue of distribution. Only after the scale question is answered, and then the distribution question, can we have market exchange to answer the question of allocation.

Another good policy for managing the commonwealth of nature is ecological tax reform. This means shifting the tax base away from income earned by labor and capital and onto the resource flow from nature. Taxing what we want less of, depletion and pollution, seems to be a better idea than taxing what we want more of, namely income. Unlike the cap–auction–trade system, ecological tax reform would exert only a very indirect and uncertain limit on the scale of the economy relative to the biosphere. Yet, it would go a long way toward improving allocation and distribution.

The Commonwealth of Knowledge

If you stand in front of the McKeldin Library at the University of Maryland, you will see a quotation from Thomas Jefferson carved on one of the stones: 'Knowledge is the common property of mankind'. Well, I think Mr. Jefferson was right. Once knowledge exists, it is non-rival, which means it has a zero opportunity cost. As we know from studying price theory, price is supposed to measure opportunity cost, and if opportunity cost is zero, then price should be zero. Certainly, new knowledge, even though it should be allocated freely, does have a cost of production. Sometimes that cost of production is substantial, as with the space program's discovery that there's no life on Mars. On the other hand, a new insight could occur to you while you are lying in bed staring at the ceiling and cost absolutely nothing, as was the case with Rene Descartes' invention of analytic geometry. Many new discoveries are accidental. Others are motivated by the joy and excitement of research, independent of any material motivation. Yet the dominant view is that unless knowledge is kept scarce enough to have a significant price, nobody in the market will have an incentive to produce it. Patent monopolies and intellectual property rights are urged as the way to provide an extrinsic reward for knowledge production. Even within that restricted vision, keeping knowledge scarce still makes very little sense, because the main input to the production of new knowledge is existing knowledge. If you keep existing knowledge expensive, that is surely going to slow down the production of new knowledge.

In Summary

Managing the commonwealth of nature and knowledge presents us with two rather opposite problems and solutions. I have argued that the commonwealth of nature should be enclosed as property, as much as possible as public property, and administered so as to capture scarcity rents for public revenue. Examples of natural commons include: mining, logging, grazing rights, the electromagnetic spectrum, the absorptive capacity of the atmosphere, and the orbital locations of satellites. The commonwealth of knowledge, on the other hand, should be freed from enclosure as property and treated as the non-rival good that it is. Abolishing all intellectual property rights tomorrow is draconian, but I do think we could grant patent monopolies for fewer 'inventions' and for shorter time periods.

19. UNECONOMIC GROWTH DEEPENS DEPRESSION

The United States and Western Europe are in a recession threatening to become a depression as bad as that of the 1930s. Therefore, we look to Keynesian policies as the cure, namely stimulate consumption and investment – that is, stimulate growth of the economy. It seemed to work in the past, so why not now? Should not ecological economics and steady-state ideas give way to Keynesian growth economics in view of the present crisis?

Certainly not! Why? Because we no longer live in the empty world of the 1930s – we live in a full world. Furthermore, in the 1930s the goal was full employment and growth was the means to it. Nowadays, growth itself has become the goal and the means to it are off-shoring of jobs, automation, mergers, union busting, importing cheap labor, and other employment-cutting policies. The former goal of full employment has been sacrificed to the modern ideology of 'growth in shareholder value'.

Growth has filled the world with us and our products. I was born in 1938, and in my lifetime world population has tripled. That is un-precedented. But even more unprecedented is the growth in populations of artifacts – 'our stuff' – cars, houses, livestock, refrigerators, TVs, cell phones, ships, airplanes, and so on. These populations of things have vastly more than tripled. The matter-energy embodied in these living and nonliving populations was extracted from the ecosystem. The matter-energy required to maintain and replace these stocks also comes from the ecosystem. The populations or stocks of all these things have in common that they are what physicists call 'dissipative structures' – in other words, their natural tendency, thanks to the entropy law, is to fall apart, to die, to dissipate. The dissipated matter-energy returns to the ecosystem as waste, to be reabsorbed by natural cycles or accumulated as pollution. All these dissipative structures exist in the midst of an entropic throughput of matter-energy that both depletes and pollutes the finite ecosphere of which the economy is a wholly contained subsystem. When the subsys-tem outgrows the regenerative capacity of the parent system then further growth becomes biophysically impossible.

But long before growth becomes impossible it becomes uneconomic – it begins to cost more than it is worth at the margin. We refer to growth in the economy as 'economic growth' – even after such growth has become uneconomic in the more basic sense of increasing illth faster than wealth. That is where we are now, but we are unable to recognize it.

Why this inability? Partly because our national accounting system, GDP, only measures 'economic activity', not true income, much less welfare. Rather than separate costs from benefits and compare them at the margin we just add up all final goods and services, including anti-bads (without subtracting the bads that made the anti-bad necessary). Also depletion of natural capital and natural services are counted as income, as are financial transactions that are nothing but bets on debts, and then further bets on those bets.

Also, since no one wants to buy illth, it has no market price and is often ignored. But illth is a joint product with wealth and is everywhere: nuclear wastes, the dead zone in the Gulf of Mexico, gyres of plastic trash in the oceans, the ozone hole, biodiversity loss, climate change from excess carbon in the atmosphere, depleted mines, eroded topsoil, dry wells, exhausting and dangerous labor, exploding debt, and so on. Standard economists claim that the solution to poverty is more growth – without ever asking if growth still makes us richer, as it did back when the world was empty and the goal was full employment, rather than growth itself. Or has growth begun to make us poorer in a world that is now too full of us, and all our products, counted or not in GDP?

Does growth now increase illth faster than wealth? This is a threatening question, because if growth has become uneconomic then the solution to poverty becomes sharing now, not growth in the future. Sharing is frequently referred to as 'class warfare'. But it is really the alternative to the class warfare that will result from the current uneconomic growth in which the dwindling benefits are privatized to the elite, while the exploding costs are socialized to the poor, the future, and to other species.

Finally, I eagerly submit that even if we limit quantitative physical throughput (growth) it should still be possible to experience qualitative improvement (development) thanks to technological advance and to ethical improvement of our priorities. I think therefore we should urge policies to limit the quantitative growth of throughput, thereby raising resource prices, in order to increase resource efficiency, to force the path of progress from growth to development, from bigger to better, and to stop the present folly of continuing uneconomic growth. A policy of quantitative limits on throughput (cap–auction–trade) will also block the erosion of initial resource savings resulting from efficiency improvements (the rebound effect or Jevons paradox). In addition the auction will raise much revenue and make it possible to tax value added (labor and capital) less because in effect we will have shifted the tax base to resource throughput. Value added is a good, so stop taxing it. Depletion and pollution, the two ends of the throughput, are bads, so tax them. If you are a technological optimist, please have the courage of your convictions and join us in advocating policies that give incentive to the resource-saving technologies that you believe are within easy reach. You may be right – I hope you are. Let us find out. If you turn out to be wrong, there is really no downside, because it was still necessary to limit throughput to avoid uneconomic growth.

E.

Population

20. THE BIG POPULATION QUESTION

More people are better than fewer – as long as they are not all alive at the same time! Sustainability means longevity for the human race – more people enjoying a sufficient level of consumption for a good life over more generations – not more simultaneously living people elbowing each other off the planet. Nor does it mean a perpetual sequence of generations. Nothing is forever in the present Creation – both science and Christianity agree on that, and perhaps other religions do as well. Christianity hopes for a New Creation free from death, sin, and decay. Science is not in the business of hope, although scientism peddles cheap optimism as a substitute. I share the Christian hope, but also accept the scientific description of the present Creation and its subjugation to entropy and finitude. Economist Georgescu-Roegen criticized sustainability and the steady-state economy as advocacy of perpetuity (or 'eternal life for the species') rather than longevity. Maybe some people confused the two, but it is a confusion easily corrected. As creatures of the present Creation we must do the best we can with what we have for however long it lasts, even while we may hope for the New Creation as an eschatological faith.

In the past 'doing the best we can' seems to have meant a larger and larger population consuming more and more stuff. Now we see that too many people alive at one time, and consuming too much per capita, reduce the carrying capacity of the earth for all life. This will mean fewer people and/or lower consumption per capita in the future, and a lower cumulative population ever to live at a level of consumption sufficient for a good life. If our ethical understanding of the value of longevity ('sustainability') is to maximize cumulative lives ever to be lived, subject to a per capita consumption level sufficient for a good life, then we must limit the load we place on the earth at any one time. Fewer people, and lower per capita resource consumption, facilitated by more equitable distribution today, mean more, and more abundant lives for a longer, but not infinite, future. There is no point in maximizing the cumulative number of lives lived in misery, so the qualification 'sufficient for a good life' is important, and requires deep rethinking of economics, and a shift of focus from growth to sufficiency.

The population problem should be considered from the point of view of all populations – populations of both humans and their artifacts (cars, houses, livestock, cell phones, and so on) – in short, populations of all 'dissipative structures' engendered, bred, or built by humans; in other words, the populations of human bodies and of their extensions. Or in yet other words, the populations of all organs that support human life and the enjoyment thereof, both endosomatic (within the skin) and exosomatic (outside the skin) organs.

All of these organs are capital equipment that support our lives. The endosomatic equipment – heart, lungs, kidneys – support our lives quite directly. The exosomatic organs – farms, factories, electric grids, transportation networks – support our lives indirectly. One should also add 'natural capital' (for example, the hydrologic cycle, carbon cycle, and so on) which is exosomatic capital comprised of structures complementary to endosomatic organs, but not made by humans (forests, rivers, soil, atmosphere).

The reason for pluralizing the 'population problem' to the populations of all dissipative structures is two-fold. First, all these populations require a metabolic throughput from low-entropy resources extracted from the environment and eventually returned to the environment as high-entropy wastes, encountering both depletion and pollution limits. In a physical sense the final product of the economic activity of converting nature into ourselves and our stuff, and then using up or wearing out what we have made, is waste. Second, what keeps this from being an idiotic activity, grinding up the world into waste, is the fact that all these populations of dissipative structures have the common purpose of supporting the maintenance and enjoyment of life.

As A.J. Lotka pointed out, ownership of endosomatic organs is equally distributed, while the exosomatic organs are not. Ownership of the latter may be collective or individual, equally or unequally distributed. Control of these external organs may be democratic or dictatorial. Owning one's own kidneys is not enough to support one's life if one does not have access to water from rivers, lakes, or rain, either because of scarcity or monopoly ownership of the complementary exosomatic organ. Likewise our lungs are of little value without the complementary natural capital of green plants and atmospheric stocks of oxygen. Therefore all life-supporting organs, including natural capital, form a unity. They have a common function, regardless of whether they are located within the boundary of human skin or outside that boundary. In addition to being united by common purpose, they are also united by their role as dissipative structures. They are all physical structures whose default tendency is to dissipate or fall apart, in accordance with the entropy law.

Our standard of living is roughly measured by the ratio of outside-skin to inside-skin capital – that is, the ratio of human-made artifacts to human bodies, the ratio of one kind of dissipative structure to another kind. Within-skin capital is made and maintained overwhelmingly from renewable resources, while outside-skin capital relies heavily on non-renewable resources. The rate of evolutionary change of endosomatic organs is exceedingly slow; the rate of change of exosomatic organs has become very rapid. In fact the evolution of human beings is now overwhelmingly centered on exosomatic organs. This evolution is goal-directed, not random, and its driving purpose has become 'economic growth', and that growth has been achieved largely by the depletion of non renewable resources.

Although human evolution is now decidedly purpose-driven we continue to be enthralled by neo-Darwinist aversion to teleology and devotion to random. Economic growth, by promising 'more for everyone eventually', becomes the de facto purpose, the social glue that keeps things from falling apart. What happens when growth becomes un-economic, increasing costs faster than benefits? How do we know that this is not already the case? If one asks such questions one is told to talk about something else, like space colonies on Mars, or unlimited energy from cold fusion, or geo-engineering, or the wonders of globalization, and to remember that all these glorious purposes require growth now in order to provide still more growth in the future. Growth is good, end of discussion, now shut up!

Let us reconsider in the light of these facts, the idea of demographic transition. By definition this is the transition from a human population maintained by high birth rates equal to high death rates, to one maintained by low birth rates equal to low death rates, and consequently from a population with low life expectancy to one with high life expectancy. Statistically such transitions have been observed as standard of living (ratio of exosomatic to endosomatic capital) increases. Many studies have attempted to explain this fact, and much hope has been invested in it as an automatic cure for overpopulation. 'Development is the best contraceptive' is a related slogan, partly based in fact, and partly in wishful thinking.

There are a couple of thoughts I would like to add to the discussion of demographic transition. The first and most obvious one is that populations of artifacts can undergo an analogous transition from high rates of production and depreciation to low ones. The lower rates will maintain a constant population of longer-lived, more durable artifacts.

Our economy has a growth-oriented focus on maximizing production flows (birth rates of artifacts) that keeps us in the pre-transition mode, giving rise to growing artifact populations, low product lifetimes, high GDP, and high throughput, with consequent environmental destruction. The transition from a high-maintenance throughput to a low one applies to both human and artifact populations independently. From an environmental perspective, lower throughput is desirable in both cases, at least up to some distant limit.

The second thought I would like to add to the discussion of demographic transition is a question: does the human transition, when induced by rising standard of living, as usually assumed, increase or decrease the total load of all dissipative structures on the environment? Specifically, if Indian fertility is to fall to the Swedish level, must Indian per capita possession of artifacts (standard of living) rise to the Swedish level? If so, would this not likely increase the total load of all dissipative structures on the Indian environment, perhaps beyond capacity to sustain the required throughput?

The point of this speculation is to suggest that 'solving' the population problem by relying on the demographic transition to lower birth rates could impose a larger burden on the environment rather than the smaller burden that would be the case with direct reduction in fertility. Of course, reduction in fertility by automatic correlation with rising standard of living is politically easy, while direct fertility reduction is politically difficult. But what is politically easy may be environmentally destructive.

To put it another way, consider the I = PAT formula. P, population of human bodies, is one set of dissipative structures. A, affluence, or GDP per capita, reflects another set of dissipative structures – cars, buildings, ships, toasters, iPads, cell phones, and so on (not to mention populations of livestock and agricultural plants). In a finite world some populations grow at the expense of others. Cars and humans are now competing for land, water, and sunlight to grow either food or fuel. More nonhuman dissipative structures will at some point *force* a reduction in other dissipative structures, namely human bodies. This forced demographic transition is less optimistic than the voluntary one induced by chasing a higher standard of living more effectively with fewer dependents. In an empty world we saw the trade-off between artifacts and people as induced by desire for a higher standard of living. In the full world that trade-off seems forced by competition for limited resources.

The usual counter to such thoughts is that technology can improve the efficiency by which throughput maintains dissipative structures (T in the formula, measured as throughput per unit of GDP). For example, a car that lasts longer and gets better mileage is still a dissipative structure, but with a more efficient metabolism that allows it to live on a lower rate of throughput.

Likewise, human organisms might be genetically redesigned to require less food, air, and water. Indeed smaller people would be the simplest way of increasing metabolic efficiency (measured as number of people maintained by a given resource throughput). To my knowledge no one, including me, suggests breeding smaller people as a way to avoid limiting births. We have, however, been busy breeding and genetically engineering larger and faster-growing plants and livestock. So far, the latter dissipative structures have been complementary with populations of human bodies, but in a finite and full world, the relationship will soon become competitive.

Indeed, if we think of population as the cumulative number of people ever to live over time, then many artifact populations are already competitive with the human population. That is, more consumption today of terrestrial low entropy in non-vital uses (Cadillacs, rockets, weapons) means less terrestrial low entropy available for capturing solar energy tomorrow (plows, solar collectors, ecosystem regeneration). The solar energy that will still fall on the earth for millions of years after the material structures needed to capture it are dissipated, will be wasted, just like the solar energy that shines on the moon.

There is a limit to how many dissipative structures the ecosphere can sustain – more endosomatic capital must ultimately displace some exosomatic capital and vice versa. Some of our exosomatic capital is critical – for example, that part which can photosynthesize, the green plants. Our endosomatic capital cannot long endure without the critical exosomatic capital of green plants (along with soil and water, and of course sunlight). In sum, demographers' interest should extend to the populations of all dissipative structures, their metabolic throughputs, and the relations of complementarity and substitutability among them. Economists should analyse the supply, demand, production, and consumption of all these populations within an ecosphere that is finite, nongrowing, entropic, and open only to a fixed flow of solar energy. This reflects a paradigm shift from the empty-world vision to the full-world vision – a world full of human-made dissipative structures that both depend upon and displace natural structures. Growth looks very different depending on from which paradigm it is viewed.

Demands on carrying capacity come from dissipative structures of all kinds. Some will say to others, 'You cannot have a glass of wine and piece of meat for dinner because I need the grain required by your fine diet to feed my three hungry children'. The answer will be, 'You cannot have three children at the expense of my and my one child's already modest standard of living'. Both have a good point. That conflict will be difficult to resolve, but we are not yet there.

Rather, now some are saying, 'You cannot have three houses and fly all over the world twice a year, because I need the resources to feed my eight children'. And the current reply is, 'You cannot have eight children at the expense of my small family's luxurious standard of living'. In the second case, neither side elicits much sympathy, and there is great room for compromise that limits both excessive population and per capita consumption. Better to face limits to both human and artifact populations before the terms of the trade-off get too harsh.

21. OPEN BORDERS AND THE TRAGEDY OF OPEN ACCESS COMMONS

'Open borders' refers to a policy of unlimited or free immigration. I argue here that it is a bad policy. If you are poor and your country provides no social safety net, you move to one that does. If you are rich and your country makes you pay your taxes, you move (or at least move your money) to one that does not. Thus safety nets, and public goods in general, disappear as they become both overloaded and underfunded. That is the 'world without borders', and without community. That is the tragedy of open access commons.

Some will think that I am attacking a straw man, because, they will say, no sensible person really advocates open borders. They simply advocate, it will be said, 'more generous levels of immigration, and a reasonable amnesty for existing illegal immigrants'. I agree that some form of strictly conditional amnesty is indeed necessary as the lesser evil, given the impasse created by past non-enforcement of our immigration laws. Deporting 12 million long-settled residents is too drastic and would create more injustices than it would rectify. But unless we enforce immigration laws in the future there will soon be need for another amnesty (the first, often forgotten, was in 1986), and then another – a de facto open-borders policy. Nevertheless, the policy of open borders should be fairly discussed, not only because some people explicitly advocate it, but also because many others implicitly accept it by virtue of their unwillingness to face the alternative.

Immigration is a divisive issue. A good unifying point to begin a discussion is to recognize that every country in the world has a policy of limiting immigration. Emigration is often considered a human right, but immigration requires the permission of the receiving country. Some countries allow many legal immigrants. Others allow few. As the World Bank reported in its *Global Bilateral Migration Database*: 'The United States remains the most important migrant destination in the world, home to one fifth of the world's migrants and the top destination for migrants from no less than 60 sending countries. Migration to Western Europe remains largely from elsewhere in Europe'.

There are also arguments about the emigration side of open borders – even if emigration is a human right, is it unconditional? Might 'brain-drain' emigrants have some obligation to contribute something to the community that educated and invested in them, before they emigrate to greener pastures?

Immigrants are people, and deserve to be well treated; immigration is a policy, and deserves reasoned discussion in the public interest. It seems that neither expectation is fulfilled, perhaps partly because the world has moved from largely empty to quite full in only one lifetime. What could work in the world of two billion people into which I was born, no longer works in today's world of seven billion. In addition to people, the exploding populations of cars, buildings, livestock, ships, refrigerators, cell phones, and even corn stalks and soybean plants, contribute to a world full of 'dissipative structures' that, like human bodies, require not only space but also a metabolic flow of natural resources beginning with depletion and ending with pollution. This growing entropic throughput already exceeds ecological capacities of regeneration and absorption, degrading the life-support capacity of the ecosphere.

The United States is indeed a 'country of immigrants', although for American Indians this frequent refrain reflects a less positive historical experience than it does for European settlers. Nor does the term resonate positively with those African Americans whose recent ancestors were brought here as involuntary immigrants. Many Americans, including me, think that heirs of slavery deserve priority in the US job market (including job training) over new immigrants, especially illegal immigrants. Likewise for the many Americans of all races living in poverty. Some other Americans, unfortunately, seem to feel that if we cannot have slaves, then the next best thing is abundant cheap labor.

We have in the United States a strong cheap labor lobby that uses immigration (especially illegal immigration) to force down wages and break labor unions, as well as weaken labor safety standards. This is less the fault of the immigrants than of our own elite employing class and pandering politicians. The immigration issue in the United States is largely an internal class battle between labor and capital, with immigrants as pawns in the conflict. Class division is more basic than the racial and ethnic divide in current US immigration politics, although the latter is not absent. Progressives in the United States, with their admirable historical focus on racial justice, have been slow to see the increasing dominance of the class issue in immigration. *The Wall Street Journal*, the Chamber of Commerce, and big corporations in general, do not mind seeing the class question submerged by racial and ethnic politics favoring easy immigration because it provides a domestic cheap labor supplement to off-shoring. It feeds the myth that we are a classless society, even as it contributes to increasing income inequality. Also, given the closeness of recent elections, a bit of ethnic pandering can be politically decisive.

The United States is also a country of law, or at least strives to be. Illegal immigration falls outside the rule of law, and renders moot all democratic policy deliberations about setting immigration policy for the common good. It is hardly democratic to refuse to enforce democratically enacted laws, even though difficult individual cases arise, as with any law. Humane provisions for difficult cases must be worked out, for example, children brought here illegally by their parents 20 years ago. We have judges to deal with difficult cases, as well as statutes of limitation regarding the time period within which certain laws must be enforced, and this principle could be applied to immigration laws.

Which democratically enacted laws will the open-borders lobby not enforce next? How about laws against financial fraud? We have apparently already quit enforcing those, partly abetted by globalization and foreign tax havens as well as too big to fail or jail banks. Acceptance of illegal immigration is only one part of the broader trend toward impunity connected to the blurring of borders. While impunity for banksters is arguably worse than for illegal immigrants and their employers, the latter still play a part in undermining the general respect for law.

Surely our immigration laws could be improved. Indeed, the 1995 US Commission on Immigration Reform, chaired by the late Texas Congresswoman Barbara Jordan, made a good start, but was ignored for reasons already suggested. Her Commission called for lower legal immigration quotas, stricter family reunification criteria, and enhanced border control, as well as stricter sanctions against employers of illegal immigrants. The last embraced the caveat that ethnic profiling would likely result without a secure national identification system, since employers are not able to adjudicate false documents. A secure identification system would of course make it easier to identify illegal immigrants and is often opposed by open-borders advocates and libertarians. The present Congress should build on the good work of the Jordan Commission, but they seem to have forgotten it.

Would open borders be good for Japan, or China, or Greece, or for an independent Catalonia, if that should come about? Do any political parties in member countries advocate open borders for the European Union with respect to the rest of the world? Should the areas of the Amazon reserved for indigenous people be open to free immigration? Should Bhutan, bordered by the world's two most populous countries and trying to preserve its culture and ecosystems, declare a policy of open borders? Or are open borders only advocated for the United States?

In developed countries immigration boosters are especially interested in opening borders to young workers to help cover social security shortfalls resulting from the older age structure caused by slower natural population growth. The cheap labor lobby is joined by the cheap retirement lobby. Apparently the immigrants are expected to die or go home as soon as they reach retirement age and would start receiving rather than paying into social security. Also, while working they are expected to boost fertility and population growth sufficiently to postpone the necessity of raising the retirement age or lowering benefits. Population growth is expected, indeed required, to continue indefinitely.

In addition to the cheap labor and cheap retirement lobbies, advocacy of open borders comes both from the politically correct faction of left-wing economists, and from the libertarian faction of right-wing economists. The former consider any limits on total number of immigrants as 'thinly disguised racism'. All evil is reduced to racism, often 'in disguise'. The libertarian economists label any restriction on immigration as a 'market distortion', their synonym for regulation.

We already have open borders for capital (as well as goods), so that open borders for labor would complete the global integration agenda – deregulation taken to the limit. This is not 'free trade' or reasonable recognition of interdependence among many separate trading economies, as embodied in the 1945 Bretton Woods Treaty. Rather it is a single global economy tightly integrated on the principle of absolute, not comparative, advantage. It is being imposed top-down by transnational corporations via the undemocratic World Trade Organization.

Net immigration is the overwhelming cause of US population growth. How big should the US population be? We are currently the third most populous country in the world. Do we aspire to overtake China and India? What numbers define a 'more generous immigration policy', and exactly who is being generous to whom, and at whose expense? Our elite is being generous to itself at the expense of the US working class, which let us not forget, includes many legal immigrants.

Any limitation of the number of new immigrants still requires selectivity and enforcement of immigration laws. It requires saying 'no' to many worthy applicants, which is difficult, and is why some humanitarians are tempted to favor open borders. Community is both inclusive and exclusive, it requires borders, while individualism, writ large as 'globalism', does not. Never mind that growth in the United States has, at the margin, become uneconomic, increasing social and environmental costs faster than benefits. The idea of a community organized around a steady-state economy goes out the window, and customary growthmania is reaffirmed.

If the United States could just set an example of how a country can live justly and sustainably within its ecological limits (in other words, in a steady-state economy) that would be a splendid contribution to the rest of the world. We are far from setting such an example – indeed we are not even trying.

22. ELITIST GROWTH BY CHEAP LABOR POLICIES

A front-page story in the *Washington Post* might have considered other reasons why growth has not led to more employment, besides simply claiming that growth has been 'too slow'. First, the jobs that workers would have gone back to have largely been off-shored as employers sought cheap foreign labor. Second, cheap foreign labor by way of illegal immigration seems to have been welcomed by US employers trying to fill the remaining jobs at home. And third, jobs have been 'outsourced' to the consumer (the ultimate source of cheap labor), who is now his own checkout clerk, travel agent, baggage handler, bank teller, gas station attendant, and so on.

These obvious but unmentioned facts suggest other policies for increasing employment beside the mindless call for more 'growth', gratuitously labeled 'economic growth' when on balance it has become uneconomic.

Let us consider each of the three reasons and related policy implications a bit more.

First, off-shoring production is not 'trade'. The good whose production has been off-shored is sold in the United States to satisfy the same market that its domestic production used to satisfy. But now, thanks to cheap foreign labor, profit is greater and/or prices are lower, mainly the former. Off-shoring increases US imports, and since no product has been exported in exchange, it also increases the US trade deficit. Because the production of the good now takes place abroad, stimulus spending in the US simply stimulates US imports and employment abroad. Demand for US labor consequently declines, lowering US employment and/or wages. It is absurd that off-shoring should be defended in the name of 'free trade'. No goods are traded. The absurdity is compounded by the fact that off-shoring entails moving capital abroad, and international immobility of capital is one of the premises on which the doctrine of comparative advantage rests – and the policy of free trade is based on comparative advantage! If we really believe in free trade, then we must place limits on capital mobility and off-shoring. Budget deficits, printing money, and other measures to stimulate growth no longer do much to raise US employment.

Second, for those jobs that have not yet, or cannot easily be off-shored (for example, services such as bartending, waiting tables, gardening, home repairs, and so on), cheap foreign labor has become available via illegal immigration. US employers seem to welcome illegal immigrants. Most are good and honest workers, willing to work for little, and unable to complain about conditions given their illegal status. What could be better for union busting and driving down wages of the American working class? The federal government, ever sensitive to the interests of the employing class, has done an obligingly poor job of enforcing our immigration laws. Immigration reform requires deciding how many immigrants to accept and who gets priority. All countries do that. Most are far more restrictive than the United States. Whatever reforms we make, however, will be moot unless we control the border and actually enforce the laws we will have democratically enacted. Ironically our tolerance for illegal immigration seems to have caused a compensatory tightening up on legal immigrants – longer waiting periods and more stringent requirements. It is cheaper to 'enforce' our immigration laws against those who obey them than against those who break them – but quite unfair, and perceived as such by many legal immigrants and people attempting to immigrate legally. This is a very perverse selection process for new residents.

Third, the automation of services of bank tellers, gas station attendants, and so on, is usually praised as labor-saving technical progress. To some extent it is that, but it also represents labor-shifting to the consumer. The consumer does not even get the minimum wage for his extra work, even considering the dubious claim that he enjoys lower prices in return for his self-service. Ordinary human contacts are diminished and commerce becomes more sterile and impersonally mechanical. In particular inter-action between people of different socio-economic classes is reduced. I remember at the World Bank, for example, that the mail clerks were about the only working class folks that professional bank staff came into daily contact with on the premises. Even that was eliminated by automated carts that delivered mail to each office cubicle. While not highly productive, such jobs do provide a service, and also an entry into the work force, and help distribute income in a way more dignified than a dole. Reducing daily contact of World Bank staff with working class people does nothing to increase sensitivity and solidarity with the poor of the world. And of course this does not only apply to the World Bank. The idea that it is degrading to be a gas station attendant or mail handler, and that we will re-educate them to become petroleum engineers or invest-ment bankers, is delusional.

Excuse my populism, but the working class in the United States, as well as in other countries, really exists and is here to stay. Cheap labor policies in the name of 'growth and global competitiveness' are class-based and elitist. Even when dressed in the emperor's new wardrobe of free trade, globalization, open borders, and automation, they remain policies of growth by cheap labor, pushing employment and wages down and profits up. And we wonder why the US distribution of income is becoming more unequal? Obviously it must be because growth is too slow – the single cause of all our problems!

That we would be better off if we were richer is a definitional truism. The question is, does further growth in GDP really make us richer, or is it making us poorer by increasing the uncounted costs of growth faster than the measured benefits? That simple question is taboo among economists and politicians.

F.

Monetary reform

23. COMMODITY MONEY, FIAT MONEY AND SEIGNIORAGE

Historically money has evolved through three phases: (1) commodity money (for example, gold); (2) token money (certificates tied to gold); and (3) fiat money (certificates not tied to gold).

1. Gold has a real cost of mining and value as a commodity in addition to its exchange value as money. Gold's money value and commodity value tend to equality. If gold as commodity is worth more than gold as money then coins are melted into bullion and sold as commodity until the commodity price falls to equality with the monetary value again. The money supply is thus determined by geology and mining technology, not by government policy or the lending and borrowing by private banks. This keeps irresponsible politicians' and bankers' hands off the money supply, but at the cost of a lot of real resources and environmental destruction necessary to mine gold, and of tying the money supply not to economic conditions, but to extraneous facts of geology and mining technology. Historically, the gold standard also had the advantage of providing an international money. Trade deficits were settled by paying gold; surpluses by receiving gold. But since gold was also national money, the money supply in the deficit country went down, and in the surplus country went up. Consequently the price level and employment declined in the deficit country (stimulating exports and discouraging imports) and rose in the surplus country (discouraging exports and stimulating imports), tending to restore balanced trade. Trade imbalances were self-correcting, and if we remember that gold, the balancing item,

was itself a commodity, we might even say imbalances were nonexistent. But of course the associated increases and decreases in the national price levels and employment were disruptive.

2. Token money would function pretty much like the gold standard if there were a one-to-one relation between gold and tokens issued. But with token money came fractional reserve banking. Goldsmiths used to loan gold to people, but gold is heavy stuff and awkward to carry around. Token money was created when a goldsmith gave a borrower a document entitling the bearer to a stated quantity of gold. If the goldsmith were widely trusted, the token would circulate with the same value as the gold it represented. As goldsmiths evolved into banks they began to make loans by creating tokens (demand deposits) in the name of the borrower in excess of the gold they held in reserve. This practice, profitable to banks, was legalized. Statistically it works as long as most depositors do not demand their gold at the same time – a run on the bank. Bank failures in the United States due to such panics led to insuring deposits by the FDIC. But insurance also has a moral hazard aspect of reducing the vigilance of depositors and stockholders in reviewing risky loans by the bank. Fractional reserves allow the banking system to multiply the money tokens (demand deposits that function as money) far beyond the amount of gold 'backing'.

3. Fiat money came when we dropped any pretense of gold 'backing' and paper tokens were declared to be money by government fiat. Currency is printed by the government at negligible cost of production, unlike gold. As the issuer of fiat money the government makes a profit (called seigniorage) from the difference between the commodity value of the token (nil) and its monetary value ($1, $5, ... , $100 ... depending on the denomination of the paper note). Everyone has to give up a dollar's worth of goods or services to get a dollar – except for the issuer of the money who gives up practically nothing for a full dollar's worth of wealth.

Nowadays, the fractional reserve banking system counts fiat currency instead of gold as reserves against its lending. The demand deposit money created by the private banking sector is a large multiple of the amount of fiat money issued by the government. Who earns the seigniorage on the newly created demand deposits? The private banks in the first instance, but some is competed away to customers in the form of higher interest rates on savings deposits and lower service charges (at least that used to happen!). It is difficult to say just what happens to seigniorage on demand deposits, but clearly that on fiat currency goes to the government. (With commodity money seigniorage is zero because commodity value equals monetary value – except when the mint purposely debased gold coins). Under our present system, money is currency plus demand deposits. Currency is created out of paper by the government, and no interest is charged for it; demand deposits are created by banks out of nothing (up to a large limit set by small reserve requirements) and interest is charged for it.

For example, when you take out a mortgage to buy a house, you are not borrowing someone else's money deposited at the bank. The bank is in fact loaning you money that did not exist before it created a new deposit in your name. When you repay the debt, it in effect destroys the money the bank initially loaned into existence. But over the next 30 years, you will pay back several times what the bank initially loaned you. Although demand deposits are constantly being created and destroyed, at any given time over 90 percent of our money supply is in the form of demand deposits. But the deposit multiplier is only part of the story. Also important is the amount of reserves that enter the deposit multiplier chain. That is determined by the Fed mainly by buying treasury bonds in the open market (paying with newly created reserves) when it wants to increase the money supply and drive down interest rates, as it has done under the so-called 'quantitative easing'. The Fed can also lend reserves directly to banks at a variable interest rate (usually called a discount rate). When the Fed buys treasury bills the government is simply purchasing its own debt with newly created reserves. This is equivalent to printing new money, which then enters the banking systems deposit multiplier chain. The Fed incidentally is owned by the very commercial banks that it is so lavishly subsidizing. A better system is suggested in 'Nationalize money, not banks', essay 24.

24. NATIONALIZE MONEY, NOT BANKS

If our present banking system, in addition to fraudulent and corrupt, also seems 'screwy' to you, it should. Why should money, a public utility (serving the public as medium of exchange, store of value, and unit of account), be largely the by-product of private lending and borrowing? Is that really an improvement over being a by-product of private gold mining, as it was under the gold standard? The best way to sabotage a system is to hobble it by tying together two of its separate parts, creating an unnecessary and obstructive connection. Why should the public pay interest to the private banking sector to provide a medium of exchange that the government can provide at little or no cost? And why should seigniorage (profit to the issuer of fiat money) go largely to the private sector rather than entirely to the government (the commonwealth)?

Is there not a better way? Yes, there is. We need not go back to the gold standard. Keep fiat money, but move from fractional reserve banking to a system of 100 percent reserve requirements on demand deposits. Time deposits (savings accounts) would have zero or minimal reserve requirements and would be available to lend to borrowers. The change need not be abrupt – we could gradually raise the reserve requirement to 100 percent. Already the Fed has the authority to change reserve requirements but seldom uses it. This would put control of the money supply and seigniorage entirely with the government rather than largely with private banks. Banks would no longer be able to live the alchemist's dream by creating money out of nothing and lending it at interest. All quasi-bank financial institutions should be brought under this rule, regulated as commercial banks subject to 100 percent reserve requirements for demand deposits.

Private banks cannot create money under 100 percent reserves (the reserve deposit multiplier would be unity), and banks would earn their profit by financial intermediation only, lending savers' money for them (charging a loan rate higher than the rate paid to savings or 'time-account' depositors) and charging for checking, safekeeping, and other services. With 100 percent reserves every dollar loaned to a borrower would be a dollar previously saved by a time-account depositor (and not available to the depositor during the period of the loan). This reestablishes the classical balance between abstinence and investment. With credit limited by saving (abstinence from consumption) there will be less lending and borrowing and it will be done more carefully – no more easy credit to finance the leveraged purchase of 'assets' that are nothing but bets on dodgy debts. Rather than trust the Fed not to subvert this limitation by quantitative easing, it would be better to abolish the Fed and allow the Treasury to directly control the money supply by spending newly created money for public purposes, and taxing the public when inflation threatens.

To make up for the decline and eventual elimination of bank-created, interest-bearing money, the Treasury can, as suggested above, pay some of its expenses by issuing more non-interest-bearing fiat money. However, it can only do this up to a strict limit imposed by inflation. If the government issues more money than the public voluntarily wants to hold, the public will trade it for goods, driving the price level up. As soon as the price index begins to rise the government must print less and tax more. Thus a policy of maintaining a constant price index would govern the internal value of the dollar.

The external value of the dollar could be left to freely fluctuating exchange rates. Alternatively, if we instituted Keynes' international clearing union, the external value of the dollar, along with that of all other currencies, could be set relative to the bancor, a common denominator accounting unit used by the payments union. The bancor would serve as an international reserve currency for settling trade imbalances – a kind of 'gold substitute'.

The United States opposed Keynes' plan at Bretton Woods precisely because under it the dollar would not function as the world's reserve currency, and the United States would lose the enormous international subsidy that results from all countries having to hold large transaction balances in dollars. The payments union would settle trade balances multilaterally. Each country would have a net trade balance with the rest of the world (with the payments union) in bancor units. Any country running a persistent deficit would be charged a penalty, and if continued would have its currency devalued relative to the bancor. But persistent surplus countries would also be charged a penalty, and if the surplus persisted their currency would suffer an appreciation relative to the bancor. The goal is balanced trade, and both surplus and deficit nations would be expected to take measures to bring their trade into balance. With trade in near balance there would be little need for a world reserve currency, and what need there was could be met by the bancor. Freely fluctuating exchange rates would also in theory keep trade balanced and reduce or eliminate the need for a world reserve currency. Which system would be better is a complicated issue not pursued here. In either case the IMF could be abolished since there would be little need for financing trade imbalances (the IMF's main purpose) in a regime whose goal is to eliminate trade imbalances.

Returning to domestic institutions, the Treasury would replace the Fed (which is owned by and operated in the interests of the commercial banks). The interest rate would no longer be a target policy variable, but rather left to market forces. The target variables of the Treasury would be the money supply and the price index. The Treasury would print and spend into circulation for public purposes as much money as the public voluntarily wants to hold. The Treasury has the power to create money, and therefore does not face a traditional budget constraint. But it does face the discipline of maintaining a stable price level. When the price index begins to rise it must cease printing money and finance any additional public expenditures by taxing or borrowing from the public (not from itself). The policy of maintaining a constant price index effectively gives the fiat currency the 'backing' of the basket of commodities in the price index.

In the 1920s the leading academic economists, Frank Knight of Chicago and Irving Fisher of Yale, along with others including underground economist and Nobel Laureate in Chemistry, Frederick Soddy, strongly advocated a policy of 100 percent reserves for commercial banks. Why did this suggestion for financial reform disappear from discussion until recently? The best answer I have found is that the Great Depression and subsequent Keynesian emphasis on growth swept it aside, because limiting lending (borrowing) to actual savings (a key feature of 100 percent reserves) was considered too restrictive on growth, which had become the big panacea. Saving more, even with the intent to invest more, would require reduced present consumption, and that too has been deemed an unacceptable drag on growth. As long as growth is the *summum bonum* then we will find ways to borrow against future wealth in order to finance the present investment needed to maximize growth.

Why would full reserve banking not crash on the rock of the growth obsession again, as it did before? One answer is that we might recognize that aggregate growth today increases unmeasured illth faster than measured wealth, thereby becoming uneconomic growth. How can loans be repaid out of the net illth they generate? Should we not welcome full reserve banking as a needed financial restraint on growth (uneconomic growth)? Another answer is that, thanks to financial meltdowns, the commercial banks' private creation of money by lending it at interest has now become more obvious and odious to the public. More than in the 1930s, fractional reserve banking has become a clear and present danger, as well as a massive subsidy to commercial banks.

Real growth has encountered the biophysical and social limits of a full world. Financial growth is being stimulated ever more in the hope that it will pull real growth behind it, but it is in fact pushing uneconomic growth – net growth of illth. Quantitative easing of the money supply does nothing to counteract the quantitative tightening of resource limits on the growth of the real economy.

The original 100 percent reserve proponents mentioned above were in favor of aggregate growth, but wanted it to be steady growth in wealth, not speculative boom and bust cycles. One need not advocate a steady-state economy to favor 100 percent reserves, but if one does favor a steady state then the attractions of 100 percent reserves are increased. Soddy was especially cautious about uncontrolled physical growth, but his main concern was with the symbolic financial system and its disconnect from the real system that it was supposed to symbolize. As he put it: 'You cannot permanently pit an absurd human convention, such as the spontaneous increment of debt [compound interest], against the natural law of the spontaneous decrement of wealth [entropy]'. Wealth has a physical dimension and is subject to physical limits; debt is a purely mathematical quantity and is unlimited.

How would the 100 percent reserve system serve the steady-state economy?

First, as just mentioned it would restrict borrowing for new investment to existing savings, greatly reducing speculative growth ventures – for example the leveraging of stock purchases with huge amounts of borrowed money (created by banks *ex nihilo* rather than saved out of past earnings) would be severely limited. Down payment on houses would be much higher, and consumer credit would be greatly diminished. Credit cards would become debit cards. Long-term lending would have to be financed by long-term time deposits, or by carefully sequenced rolling over of shorter-term deposits. Equity financing would increase relative to debt financing. Growth economists will scream, but a steady-state economy does not aim to grow, for the very good reason that aggregate growth has become uneconomic.

Second, the money supply no longer has to be renewed by new loans as old loans are repaid. A continuing stream of new loans requires that borrowers expect to invest in a project that will grow at a rate greater than the rate of interest. Unless that expectation is sustained by growth, they will not borrow, and in a fractional reserve system the money supply will shrink. With 100 percent reserves a constant money supply is neutral with respect to growth; with fractional reserves a constant money supply imparts a growth bias to the economy because it requires a continuing stream of new loans to replace the money lost by repayment of old loans.

Third, the financial sector will no longer be able to capture such a large share of the nation's profits (around 40 percent!), freeing some smart people for more productive, less parasitic, activity.

Fourth, the money supply would no longer expand during a boom, when banks like to loan lots of money, and contract during a recession, when banks try to collect outstanding debts, thereby reinforcing the cyclical tendency of the economy.

Fifth, with 100 percent reserves there is no danger of a run on a bank leading to a cascading collapse of the credit pyramid, and the FDIC could be abolished, along with its consequent moral hazard. The danger of collapse of the whole payment system due to the failure of one or two 'too big to fail' banks would be eliminated. Congress then could not be frightened into giving huge bailouts to some banks to avoid the 'contagion' of failure because the money supply is no longer controlled by the private banks. Any given bank could fail by making imprudent loans in excess of its capital reserves (as opposed to 100 percent demand deposit reserves), but its failure, even if a large bank, would not disrupt the public utility function of money. The club that the banks used to beat Congress into giving bailouts would have been taken away.

Sixth, the explicit policy of a constant price index would reduce fears of inflation and the resultant quest to accumulate more as a protection against inflation. Also it in effect provides a multi-commodity backing to our fiat money.

Seventh, a regime of fluctuating exchange rates automatically balances international trade accounts, eliminating big surpluses and deficits. US consumption growth would be reduced without its deficit; Chinese production growth would be reduced without its surplus. By making balance of payments lending unnecessary, fluctuating exchange rates (or Keynes' international clearing union) would greatly shrink the role of the IMF and its 'conditionalities'.

To dismiss such sound policies as 'extreme' in the face of the repeatedly demonstrated colossal fraudulence of our current financial system is quite absurd. *The idea is not to nationalize banks, but to nationalize money, which is a natural public utility in the first place.* The fact that this idea is hardly discussed today, in spite of its distinguished intellectual ancestry and common sense, is testimony to the power of vested interests over good ideas. It is also testimony to the veto power that our growth fetish exercises over the thinking of economists today. Money, like fire and the wheel, is a basic invention without which the modern world is unthinkable. But today out-of-control money is threatening to 'burn and run over' more people than both out-of-control fires and wheels.

25. THE CRISIS: DEBT AND REAL WEALTH

The current (2008) financial debacle is really not a 'liquidity' crisis as it is often euphemistically called. It is a crisis of overgrowth of financial assets relative to growth of real wealth – pretty much the opposite of too little liquidity. Financial assets have grown by a large multiple of the real economy – paper exchanging for paper is now 20 times greater than exchanges of paper for real commodities. It should be no surprise that the relative value of the vastly more abundant financial assets has fallen in terms of real assets. Real wealth is concrete; financial assets are abstractions. Real wealth carries a lien on it in the amount of future debt. The value of present real wealth is no longer sufficient to serve as a lien to guarantee the exploding debt. Consequently the debt is being devalued in terms of existing wealth. No one any longer is eager to trade real present wealth for debt even at high interest rates. This is because the debt is worth much less, not because there is not enough money or credit, or because 'banks are not lending to each other' as commentators often say.

Can the economy grow fast enough in real terms to redeem the massive increase in debt? In a word, no. As Frederick Soddy (1926 Nobel Laureate chemist and underground economist) pointed out long ago, 'you cannot permanently pit an absurd human convention, such as the spontaneous increment of debt [compound interest] against the natural law of the spontaneous decrement of wealth [entropy]'. The population of 'negative pigs' (debt) can grow without limit since it is merely a number; the population of 'positive pigs' (real wealth) faces severe physical constraints. The dawning realization that Soddy's common sense was right, even though no one publicly admits it, is what underlies the crisis. The problem is not too little liquidity, but too many negative pigs growing too fast relative to the limited number of positive pigs whose growth is constrained by their digestive tracts, their gestation period, and places to put pigpens. Also there are too many two-legged Wall Street pigs, but that is another matter.

Growth in US real wealth is restrained by increasing scarcity of natural resources, both at the source end (oil depletion), and the sink end (absorptive capacity of the atmosphere for CO_2). Further, spatial displacement of old stuff to make room for new stuff is increasingly costly as the world becomes more full, and increasing inequality of distribution of income prevents most people from buying much of the new stuff – except on credit (more debt). Marginal costs of growth now likely exceed marginal benefits, so that real physical growth makes us poorer, not richer (the cost of feeding and caring for the extra pigs is greater than the extra benefit). To keep up the illusion that growth is making us richer we deferred costs by issuing financial assets almost without limit, conveniently forgetting that these so-called assets are, for society as a whole, debts to be paid back out of future real growth. That future real growth is very doubtful and consequently claims on it are devalued, regardless of liquidity.

What allowed symbolic financial assets to become so disconnected from underlying real assets? First, there is the fact that we have fiat money, not commodity money. For all its disadvantages, commodity money (gold) was at least tethered to reality by a real cost of production. Second, our fractional reserve banking system allows pyramiding of bank money (demand deposits) on top of the fiat government issued currency. Third, buying stocks and 'derivatives' on margin allows a further pyramiding of financial assets on top of the already multiplied money supply. In addition, credit card debt expands the supply of quasi-money as do other financial 'innovations' that were designed to circumvent the public interest regulation of commercial banks and the money supply. I would not advocate a return to commodity money, but would certainly advocate 100 percent reserve requirements for banks (approached gradually), as well as an end to the practice of buying stocks on the margin. All banks should be financial intermediaries that lend depositors' money, not engines for creating money out of nothing and lending it at interest. If every dollar invested represented a dollar previously saved we would restore the classical economists' balance between investment and abstinence. Fewer stupid or crooked investments would be tolerated if abstinence had to precede investment. Of course the growth economists will howl that this would slow the growth of GDP. So be it – growth has become uneconomic at the present margin as we currently measure it.

The agglomerating of mortgages of differing quality into opaque and shuffled bundles should be outlawed. One of the basic assumptions of an efficient market with a meaningful price is a homogeneous product. For example, we have the market and corresponding price for number 2 corn – not a market and price for miscellaneous randomly aggregated grains. Only people who have no understanding of markets, or who are consciously perpetrating fraud, could have either sold or bought these negative pigs-in-a-poke. Yet the aggregating mathematical wizards of Wall Street did it, and now seem surprised at their inability to correctly price these idiotic 'assets'.

And very important in all this is our balance of trade deficit that has allowed us to consume as if we were really growing instead of accumulating debt. So far our surplus trading partners have been willing to lend the dollars they earned back to us by buying treasury bills – more debt 'guaranteed' by liens on yet-to-exist wealth. Of course they also buy real assets and their future earning capacity. Our brilliant economic gurus meanwhile continue to preach deregulation of both the financial sector and of international commerce (in other words, 'free trade'). Some of us have for a long time been saying that this behavior was unwise, unsustainable, unpatriotic, and probably criminal. Maybe we were right. The next shoe to drop will be repudiation of unredeemable debt either directly by bankruptcy and confiscation, or indirectly by inflation.

G.

Employment

26. FULL EMPLOYMENT VERSUS JOBLESS GROWTH

The Full Employment Act of 1946 declared full employment to be a major goal of US policy. Economic growth was then seen as the means to attain the end of full employment. Today that relation has been inverted. Economic growth has become the end, and if the means to attain that end – automation, off-shoring, excessive immigration – result in unemployment, well that is the price 'we' just have to pay for the glorified goal of growth in GDP. If we really want full employment we must reverse this inversion of ends and means. We can serve the goal of full employment by restricting automation, off-shoring, and easy immigration to periods of true domestic labor shortage as indicated by high and rising wages. In addition, full employment can also be served by reducing the length of the working day, week, or year, in exchange for more leisure, rather than more GDP.

Real wages have been falling for decades, yet our corporations, hungry for cheaper labor, keep bleating about a labor shortage. What the corporations really want is a surplus of labor. With surplus labor, wages generally do not rise and therefore all the gains from productivity increase will go to profit, not wages. Hence the elitist support for automation, off-shoring, and lax enforcement of democratically enacted immigration laws.

Traditional stimulus policies do little to reduce unemployment, for several reasons. First, the jobs that workers would have gone back to have largely been off-shored as employers sought cheap foreign labor. Second, cheap foreign labor by way of illegal immigration seems to have been welcomed by domestic employers trying to fill the remaining jobs at home. Third, jobs have been 'outsourced' to automation – to robots in the factory and to the consumer, who is now her own checkout clerk, travel agent, baggage handler, bank teller, gas station attendant, and so on. And fourth, quantitative easing has kept interest rates low and bond prices high to the benefit of banks' balance sheets more than employment. The public benefits from lower mortgage rates, but loses more from reduced interest earnings on savings.

These facts argue for a return to the original intent of the Full Employment Act of 1946 – specifically that full employment, not growth, should be the goal. Let us consider four further reasons for this return.

First, off-shoring production and jobs cannot be justified as 'trade'. The good whose production has been off-shored is sold in the United States to satisfy the same market that its domestic production used to satisfy. Off-shoring increases US imports, and since no product has been exported in exchange, it also increases the US trade deficit. Because the production of the good now takes place abroad, stimulus spending in the United States largely stimulates US imports and employment abroad. Demand for US labor consequently declines, lowering US employment and/or wages. It is absurd that off-shoring should be defended in the name of 'free trade'. No goods are traded. The absurdity is compounded by the fact that off-shoring entails moving capital abroad, and international immobility of capital is one of the premises on which the doctrine of comparative advantage rests – and the policy of free trade is based on comparative advantage! If we really believe in comparative advantage and free trade then we must place limits on capital mobility and off-shoring.

Second, for those jobs that have not yet, or cannot easily be off-shored (for example, services such as bartending, waiting tables, gardening, medical care, and so on), cheap foreign labor has become available via illegal immigration. Many US employers seem to welcome illegal immigrants. Most are good and honest workers, willing to work for little, and unable to complain about conditions given their illegal status. What could be better for union busting and driving down wages of the American working class, which, by the way, includes many legal immigrants? The federal government, ever sensitive to the interests of the employing class, has done an obligingly poor job of enforcing our immigration laws.

Third, the automation of factory work, services of bank tellers, gas station attendants, and so on, is usually praised as labor-saving technical progress. To some extent it is that, but it also represents substitution of capital for labor and labor-shifting to the consumer. The consumer does not even get the minimum wage for her extra work, even considering the dubious claim that she enjoys lower prices in return for her self-service. Ordinary human contacts are diminished and commerce becomes more sterile and impersonally digitized. In particular daily interaction between people of different socio-economic classes is reduced.

Fourth, a 'Tobin tax', a small percentage tax on all stock market, bond market, and foreign exchange transactions would slow down the excessive trading, speculation, and gambling in the Wall Street casino, and at the same time raise a lot of revenue for public purposes. This could be enacted quickly. In the longer run, we should move to 100 percent reserve requirements on demand deposits and end the commercial banks' alchemy of creating money out of nothing and lending it at interest. Every dollar loaned by a bank would be a dollar previously saved by the owner of a time deposit, respecting the classical economic balance between abstinence from consumption and new investment. Most people mistakenly believe that this is how banks work now. Our money supply would move from being mainly interest-bearing debt of private banks, to being non-interest-bearing government debt. Money should be a public utility (a unit of account, a store of value, and a medium of exchange), not an instrument by which banks extort unnecessary interest payment from the public – like a private toll booth on a public road.

Cheap labor and funny money policies in the name of 'growth and global competitiveness' are class-based and elitist. Even when dressed in the emperor's fashionable wardrobe of free trade, globalization, open borders, financial innovation, and automation, they remain policies of growth by cheap labor and financial delusion. And we wonder why the US distribution of income has become so unequal? We are constantly told it is because growth is too slow – the single cause of all our problems! That we would be better off if we were richer is a definitional truism. The question is, does further growth in GDP really make us richer, or is it making us poorer by increasing the uncounted costs of growth faster than the measured benefits? That simple question is taboo among economists and politicians, lest we discover that the falling benefits of growth are all going to the top 1 percent, while the rising costs are 'shared' with the poor, the future, and other species.

27. GROWTH AND FREE TRADE: BRAIN-DEAD DOGMAS STILL KICKING HARD

There are two dogmas that neoclassical economists must never publicly doubt lest they be defrocked by their professional priesthood: first, that growth in GDP is always good and is the solution to most problems; second, that free international trade is mutually beneficial thanks to the growth-promoting principle of comparative advantage. These two cracked pillars 'support' nearly all the policy advice given by mainstream economists to governments.

Even such a clear thinker as Paul Krugman never allows his usually admirable *New York Times* column to question these most sacred of all tenets. And yet in less than 1000 words the two dogmas can easily be shown to be wrong by just looking at observable facts and the first principles of classical economics. Pause, and calmly consider the following:

1. Growth in all microeconomic units (firms and households) is subject to the 'when to stop rule' of optimization, namely stop when rising marginal cost equals declining marginal benefit. Why does this not also apply to growth of the matter-energy throughput that sustains the macroeconomy, the aggregate of all firms and households? And since real GDP is the best statistical index we have of aggregate throughput, why does it not roughly hold for growth in GDP? It must be because economists see the economy as the whole system, growing into the void – not as a subsystem of the finite and nongrowing ecosphere from which the economy draws resources (depletion) and to which it returns wastes (pollution). When the economy grows in terms of throughput, or real GDP, it gets bigger relative to the ecosystem and displaces ever more vital ecosystem functions. Why do economists assume that it can never be too big, that such aggregate growth can never at the margin result in more illth than wealth? Perhaps illth is invisible because it has no market price. Yet, as a joint product of wealth, illth is everywhere: nuclear wastes, the dead zone in the Gulf of Mexico, gyres of plastic trash in the oceans, the ozone hole, biodiversity loss, climate change from excess carbon in the atmosphere, depleted mines, eroded topsoil, dry wells, exhausting and dangerous labor, exploding debt, and so on. Economists claim that the solution to poverty is more growth – without ever asking if growth still makes us richer, as it did back when the world was empty, or if it has begun to make us poorer in a world that is now too full of us and our stuff. This is a threatening question, because if growth has become

uneconomic then the solution to poverty becomes sharing now, not growth in the future. Sharing is now called 'class warfare'.

2. Countries whose growth has pushed their ecological footprint beyond their geographic boundaries into the ecosystems of other countries are urged by mainline economists to continue to do so under the flag of free trade and specialization according to comparative advantage. Let the rest of the world export resources to us, and we will pay with exports of capital, patented technology, copyrighted entertainment, and financial services. Comparative advantage guarantees that we will all be better off (and grow more) if everyone specializes in producing and exporting only what they are relatively better at, and importing everything else. The logic of comparative advantage is impeccable, given its premises. However, one of its premises is that capital, while mobile within nations, does not flow between nations. But in today's world capital is even more mobile between countries than goods, so it is absolute, not comparative advantage that really governs specialization and trade. Absolute advantage still yields gains from specialization and trade, but they need not be mutual as under comparative advantage – in other words, one country can lose while the other gains. 'Free trade' really means 'deregulated international commerce' – similar to deregulated finance in justification and effect. Furthermore, specialization, if carried too far, means that trade becomes a necessity. If a country specializes in producing only a few things then it *must* trade for everything else. Trade is no longer voluntary. If trade is not voluntary then there is no reason to expect it to be mutually beneficial, and another premise of free trade falls. If economists want to keep the world safe for free trade and comparative advantage they must limit capital mobility internationally; if they want to keep international capital mobility they must back away from comparative advantage and free trade. Which do they do? Neither. They seem to believe that if free trade in goods is beneficial, then by extension free trade in capital (and other factors) must be even more beneficial. And if voluntary trade is mutually beneficial, then what is the harm in making it obligatory? How does one argue with people who use the conclusion of an argument to deny the argument's premises? Their illogic is invincible!

Like people who cannot see certain colors, maybe neoclassical economists are just blind to growth-induced illth and to destruction of national community by global integration via free trade and free capital mobility. But how can an 'empirical science' miss two red elephants in the same room? And how can economic theorists, who make a fetish of advanced mathematics, persist in such elementary logical errors?

If there is something wrong with these criticisms then some neo-classical colleague ought to straighten me out. Instead they lamely avoid the issue with attacks on nameless straw men who supposedly advocate poverty and isolationism. *Of course* rich is better than poor – the question is, does growth any longer make us richer, or have we passed the optimum scale at which it begins to make us poorer? *Of course* trade is better than isolation and autarky. But deregulated trade and capital mobility lead away from reasonable interdependence among many separate national economies that mutually benefit from voluntary trade, to the stifling specialization of a world economy so tightly integrated by global corporations that trade becomes, 'an offer you cannot refuse'.

Will standard economists ever pull the plug on brain-dead dogmas?

28. THE NEGATIVE NATURAL INTEREST RATE AND UNECONOMIC GROWTH

In a recent speech to the IMF (http://www.businessinsider.com/larry-summers-imf-speech-on-the-zero-lower-bound-2013-11), economist Larry Summers argued that since near zero interest rates have not stimulated GDP growth sufficiently to reach full employment we probably need a negative interest rate. By this he means a negative monetary rate set by the Fed to equal the negative natural rate that would equalize planned saving with planned investment. With near zero monetary rates, current inflation already pushes us to a negative real rate of interest, but that is still insufficiently negative, in Summers' view, to equalize planned investment with planned saving and thereby stimulate GDP growth sufficient for full employment.

Suppose for a moment that GDP growth, *economic* growth as we gratuitously call it, entails *uneconomic* growth by a more comprehensive measure of costs and benefits – that GDP growth has now begun to increase counted plus uncounted costs by more than counted plus uncounted benefits, making us inclusively and collectively poorer, not richer. If that is the case, and there are good reasons to believe that it is, would it not then be reasonable to expect, along with Summers, that the natural rate of interest would be negative? To keep the GDP growing (even as its associated throughput diminishes real wealth), we would need a growing monetary circular flow, which would require more investment, which, in turn, would only be forthcoming if the monetary interest rate were negative (in other words, if you lost less by investing the money than by holding it). A negative interest rate 'makes sense' if the goal is to keep on increasing GDP even after it has begun to make us poorer at the margin – that is after growth has already pushed us beyond the optimal scale of the macroeconomy relative to the containing ecosphere, and thereby become uneconomic.

Summers (along with other mainstream economists), does not accept the concept of optimal scale of the macroeconomy, nor the possibility of uneconomic growth in the sense that growth in resource throughput could reduce net wealth and wellbeing. Nevertheless, it is at least consistent with his view that the natural rate of interest is negative.

A positive interest rate restricts the volume of investment but allocates capital to the most productive projects. A negative interest rate increases volume, but allows investment in practically anything, increasing the probability that growth will be uneconomic. Shall we become hyper-Keynesians and push GDP growth to maintain full employment, even after growth has become uneconomic? (Remember that GDP, among other things, is also our best index of throughput.) Or shall we back off from growth and seek full employment and distributive equity by job sharing and reallocation toward leisure and public goods?

Why would we allow growth to carry the macroeconomy beyond the optimal scale? Because growth in GDP is considered the *summum bonum* and it is heresy not to advocate increasing it. If increasing GDP makes us worse off we will not admit it, but will adapt to the experience of increased scarcity by pushing GDP growth further. Non growth is viewed as 'stagnation', not as a sensible steady-state adaptation to objective limits. Stimulating GDP growth by increasing consumption and investment, while cutting savings, is the only way that hyper-Keynesians can think of to serve the worthy goal of full employment. There really are other ways, and people really do need to save for security and old age. Yet the Fed is advised to penalize saving with a negative interest rate. The focus is on what the growth model requires, not on what people need.

A negative interest rate seems also to be the latest advice from Paul Krugman (http://krugman.blogs.nytimes.com/2013/11/16/secular-stagnation-coalmines-bubbles-and-larry-summers/), who praises Summers' insights. It is understandable from their viewpoint because in their vision the economy is not a subsystem, or if it is, it is infinitesimal relative to the total system. The economy can expand forever, either into the void or into a near infinite environment. It does not grow into a finite ecosphere, and therefore has no optimal scale relative to any constraining and sustaining environment. Its aggregate growth incurs no opportunity cost and can never be uneconomic. Unfortunately, this tacit assumption of the growth model is seriously wrong.

A negative monetary interest rate means that citizens will spend rather than save, so savings will not be available to finance the unproductive investments that produce uneconomic growth. The new money for investment comes from the Fed. Quantitative easing will likely be increased, in spite of occasional 'tapering'. The faith is that an ever-expanding monetary circulation will pull the real economy along behind it, providing growth in real income and jobs as previously idle resources are employed. But the resulting GDP growth is uneconomic because in the full world the 'idle' resources are not really idle – they are providing vital ecosystem services. Redeploying these resources to GDP growth has environmental and social opportunity costs that are greater than production benefits. Although hyper-Keynesian macroeconomists do not believe this, the micro actors in the real economy experience it, and consequently find it difficult to follow the unlimited growth recipe.

Welcome to the full-world economy. In the old empty-world economy, assumed in the macro models of Summers and Krugman, growth always remains economic, so they advocate printing more and more dollars to expand the economy to take over ever more of the 'unemployed' sources and sinks of the ecosystem. If a temporary liquidity trap or zero lower bound on interest rates keeps the new money from being spent, then negative monetary interest rates will open the spending spigot. The empty-world assumption guarantees that the newly expanded production will always be worth more than the natural wealth it displaces. But what may well have been true in yesterday's empty world is no longer true in today's full world.

This is an upsetting prospect for growth economists – growth is required for full employment, but growth now makes us poorer. Without growth we would have to cure poverty by redistributing wealth and stabilizing population, two political anathemas, and could only finance investment by reducing present consumption, a third anathema. There remains the microeconomic policy of reallocating the same GDP to a more efficient mix of products by internalizing external costs (getting prices right). While this certainly should not be neglected, it is not macroeconomic growth as pursued by the Fed.

These painful choices could be avoided if only we were richer. So let us just focus on getting richer. How? By growing the aggregate GDP, of course! What? You repeat that GDP growth is now uneconomic? That cannot possibly be right, they say. OK, that is an empirical question. Let us separate costs from benefits in the existing GDP accounts, and develop more inclusive measures of each, and then see which grows more as GDP grows. This has been done (Index of Sustainable Economic Welfare (ISEW), Genuine Progress Indicator (GPI), Ecological Footprint) and results support the uneconomic growth view. If economists think these studies were done badly they should do them better rather than ignore the issue.

Although economists think quantitative easing will stimulate demand they are disappointed even in terms of their own model because the banks, who are supposed to lend the new money, encounter a 'lack of bankable projects', to use World Bank terminology. This, of course, should be expected in the new era of uneconomic growth. The new money, rather than calling forth new wealth by employing all these hypothetical idle resources from the empty-world era, simply bids up existing asset prices in the full world. Most asset prices are not counted in the consumer price index (not to mention exclusion of food and energy), so economists unconvincingly claim that quantitative easing has not been inflationary and therefore they can keep doing it. And even if it causes some inflation that would help make the interest rate negative.

People will not immediately revert to barter even with negative interest rates. Barter is so inconvenient that money remains more efficient even if it loses value at a rapid rate, as we have seen in several hyperinflations. But transactions balances will be minimized, and speculative and store of value-balances will be diverted to real estate, gold, works of art, tulip bulbs, Bitcoins, and beanie babies, creating speculative bubbles. But not to worry, say Summers and Krugman, bubbles are a necessary, if regrettable, means to boost spending and growth in the era of newly recognized negative natural interest rates – and still unrecognized uneconomic growth.

A silver lining to this cloud is that the recognition of a negative natural interest rate may be the prelude to recognition of the underlying uneconomic growth. For sure this has not yet happened because so far the negative natural interest rate is seen as a reason to push growth with a negative monetary rate, rather than as a signal that growth has become a losing game. But such a realization is a reasonable hope. Perhaps a step in this direction is Summers' suggestion that the old Alvin Hansen thesis of secular stagnation might deserve a new look.

The logic that suggests negative interest also suggests negative wages as a means of increasing investment by lowering costs. To maintain full employment via GDP growth not only must the interest rate now be negative, but wages should become negative as well. No one yet advocates negative wages because subsistence provides an inconvenient lower positive bound below which workers die. But the logic of uneconomic growth pushes us in the direction of a negative 'natural' wage, just as with a negative 'natural' rate of interest. So we artificially lower the wage costs to 'job creators' by subsidizing below-subsistence wages with food stamps, housing subsidies, and unpaid internships as a customary cost of entry into the paid job market. Negative interest rates also subsidize investment in job-replacing capital equipment, further lowering wages. Negative interest rates and below-subsistence wages subsidize uneconomic growth.

The hyper-Keynesians tell us, reasonably enough, that paying people to dig holes in the ground and then fill them up, is better than leaving them unemployed with no income. But paying people to deplete and pollute the Creation on which our lives and welfare ultimately depend, in order to expand the macroeconomy beyond its optimal or even sustainable scale, is surely worse than just giving them a minimum income, and some leisure time, in exchange for doing no harm.

An artificial monetary rate of interest forced down by quantitative easing to equal a negative natural rate of interest resulting from uneconomic growth is not a solution. It is just baling wire and duct tape. But it is all that even our best and brightest economists can come up with as long as they are imprisoned in the empty-world growth model. The way out of this trap is to recognize that the growth era is over, and that instead of forcing growth into uneconomic territory we must seek to maintain a steady-state economy at something approximating the optimal scale. Since we have overshot the optimal scale of the macroeconomy, this will require a period of retrenchment to a reduced level, accompanied by much more equal sharing, frugality, and efficiency. Sharing means putting limits on the range of inequality that we permit; frugality means using less resource throughput; efficiency means squeezing more life-support and want-satisfaction from a given throughput. Economists need to replace the Keynesian–neoclassical growth synthesis with a new version of the classical stationary state.

H.

Tax policy

29. WHAT SHOULD WE TAX?

For some time a small group of ecological economists has been suggesting that we switch the tax base from income (value added to natural resources by labor and capital), and on to natural resources themselves. Value added to resources is something we want more of, so do not tax it (either at each stage of production as in Europe, or at the final stage as income as in the United States). The resource throughput, beginning with depletion and ending with pollution (both real costs), is something we want less of in a full-world economy, so let us tax it. Even though resources in the ground and waste absorption services are free gifts of nature in the cost of production sense, they are nevertheless increasingly scarce in a full world. They need a price to be efficiently allocated and not overused. So let us give them the needed price by taxing them, and use the revenue from the tax (or equivalent cap–auction–trade system) to substitute for the revenue lost from no longer taxing value added. The resource tax should be levied at the point of extraction (severance) so that the higher price will stimulate increased efficiency of use at all upstream stages of production, as well as in the final stages of consumption and recycling. Also depletion is spatially more concentrated than pollution, so in most cases a depletion tax is easier to monitor than a pollution tax.

In addition to this economic argument there is a political one. People do not like to see value that they added taxed away. They resent it, even while accepting it as necessary to fund public goods. But value that no one added, the original *in situ* value of natural resources and services, many people think should be common property, and most people think

should at least be taxed for public purposes. If there is popular resentment it is against the resource owners who receive an unearned income
(scarcity rent) over and above the value they truly add to the *in situ*
resource by extraction and purification (echoes of Henry George). Of
course, oil and coal companies, and other extractive industries, will resist
resource taxation (they currently enjoy government subsidies in addition
to scarcity rents!), even though they would be expected to legitimately
pass the tax on to consumers to the extent that markets allow. It is
necessary that consumers, as well as producers, also get the higher price
signal and become more efficient and frugal in consumption.

I have been told that we could not substitute resource taxes for
value-added taxes because resource rents are a small portion of GDP
while value added accounts for nearly all of GDP. You have to put the tax
where the money is, I am told. But this is confusion between what is
taxed and what the tax is paid with. All taxes are paid out of total income
(money is fungible). But the question is, what is the tax proportional to –
income or resource use? It makes much more sense for taxes to be
proportional to resource use than to income. A resource tax falls on all
citizens in proportion to their resource consumption, how much of a
burden they impose on the biosphere, and not according to how much
value they add to the resources necessarily extracted. Also, resource taxes
are harder to evade than income taxes because, unlike resource depletion,
income is not an easily measured physical quantity, but an abstract
concept subject to manipulation by lawyers and accountants.

As to the reasonable objection that a resource tax is regressive with
respect to income, that can easily be remedied by some combination of
the following: (1) retaining an income tax on higher incomes, (2)
spending the tax revenue progressively, including by abolishing existing
regressive income taxes such as the payroll tax, (3) instituting a significant and progressive inheritance tax. Some object, less reasonably, that
higher resource prices due to a resource tax will put us at a competitive
disadvantage in international trade. But then so does an income tax, and
it is not clear that there would be any net difference between the two in
terms of competitive advantage. In fact, *any* internalization of environmental and social costs would also raise prices and thereby create a trade
disadvantage relative to countries that did not internalize those costs.
However, the first rule of efficiency is to count all costs, not to run a
trade surplus based on standards-lowering competition to externalize
costs.

So why not shift the tax base from value added (earned income) and on
to that to which value is added (natural resource throughput)? This would
help us to count all costs and minimize depletion and pollution. It would

stop penalizing the desired creation of value added by taxing it. It would reduce unemployment. It would use the revenue from natural resource taxes to substitute that from the eliminated value-added taxes. The first value-added taxes to be eliminated would be the most regressive ones, thereby serving both efficiency and equity. This seems such an obvious improvement that one wonders why economists remain so in thrall to value-added taxation?

30. MODERNIZING HENRY GEORGE

Economists have traditionally considered nature to be infinite relative to the economy, and therefore not scarce, and therefore properly priced at zero. But the biosphere is now scarce, and becoming more so every day as a result of growth of its large and dependent subsystem, the macroeconomy. As the macroeconomy expands into the ecosystem it displaces what was there before, namely habitat of other species (and of indigenous and poor members of our own species). Consequently, biodiversity decline is a salient index of the increasing scarcity of nature, as is involuntary resettlement of people to make way for dams, mines, soybeans, and cattle; and, of course, increasing depletion and pollution. Sacrifice of nature's scarce services constitutes an increasing opportunity cost of growth, and that in turn means that nature must be priced, either explicitly or implicitly.

But to whom should this price be paid? Nature would prefer not to sell herself, but if forced to it by growth, would at least like to divide equally among her children the revenue from the forced sale of her previous gifts. From the point of view of efficiency it does not matter who receives the price, as long as it is counted and paid by the users. But from the point of view of equity it matters a great deal who receives the price for nature's increasingly scarce services. Such payment is the ideal source of funds with which to finance public goods, and to redistribute to the poor.

'Value added' belongs to whoever added it. But the original value of that to which further value is added by labor and capital, the value of scarce natural resources and natural services, should belong to everyone. It is the original commonwealth. These 'payments to nature' should be the focus of redistributive efforts. Payment for what is now too scarce to be treated as a free gift is measured and appropriated by markets as a rent (payment in excess of necessary supply price). Rent is unearned income to the recipient. But allocative efficiency requires that payment by the user of the resource. Taxation of value added by labor and capital is certainly legitimate. But it is both more legitimate and less necessary after we have, as much as possible, captured natural resource rents for public revenue.

The above seems to be the basic insight of early American economist Henry George (1839–1897) who applied it specifically to rent on the scarcity of desirable locations of land, rather than to rents on natural resource scarcity in general. Could we not extend Henry George's logic to resources in general? For resources the necessary supply price is the cost of extraction – so any payment above cost of extraction is rent. Since land has no cost of extraction all payment for land is rent. If no rent is paid, land does not cease to exist. Neoclassical economists accept this definition of rent but resist Henry George's ethical emphasis on rent as *unearned* income.

The modern form of the Georgist insight is to tax the rent from land, and by extension from natural resources and services of nature, and to use these funds for fighting poverty and for financing public goods. Or we could simply create a trust fund from these rents, and disburse the earnings from it to all citizens, as in the Alaska Permanent Fund. Our present practice of taxing away a lot of the value added by individuals from applying their own labor and capital creates resentment, and discourages the supply of labor and capital. Taxing away value that no one added, scarcity rents on nature's contribution, does not create as much resentment, and the resentment it does cause is less justified. In fact, failing to tax away the scarcity rents to nature and letting them accrue as *unearned* income to a landlord class has long been a primary source of resentment and social conflict. Furthermore, taxing land and resource rent does not diminish their quantity. Soviet communists tried for a while to abolish the category of rent because it represented unearned income – a part of 'surplus value' like profit and interest. They jumped to the conclusion that therefore resources and land should be free. But that makes it impossible to allocate resources efficiently. Better to follow Henry George and retain rent as a necessary price for measuring opportunity cost, but to then tax it away as unearned income to the landlords. The more we tax away rent the less we have to tax the value added by human labor and capital.

Charging scarcity rents on natural resources and redistributing them to the commonwealth can be effected either by ecological tax reform, or by quantitative cap–auction–trade systems. In differing ways each would limit expansion of the scale of the economy into the biosphere, thereby preserving biodiversity and also providing revenue to run the commonwealth. I will not discuss their relative merits here, but rather emphasize the advantage that both have over the currently favored strategy. The currently favored strategy might be called 'efficiency first' in distinction to the 'frugality-first' principle embodied in each of the policies mentioned above.

'Efficiency first' sounds good, especially when referred to as 'win–win' strategies, or more picturesquely as 'picking the low-hanging fruit'. But the problem of 'efficiency first' is with what comes second. An improvement in efficiency by itself is equivalent to having an increased supply of the resource whose efficiency increased. The price of that resource will decline. More uses for the now cheaper resource will be made. We will end up consuming perhaps as much or more of the resource than before, albeit more efficiently, as pointed out in the nineteenth century words of economist William Stanley Jevons: 'It is wholly a confusion of ideas to suppose that the economical [efficient] use of fuel is equivalent to a diminished consumption. The very contrary is the truth' (*The Coal Question*, 1866, p. 123).

We need frugality (diminished consumption) more than efficiency. 'Frugality first' induces efficiency as a secondary consequence, an adaptation; efficiency first does not induce frugality – it makes frugality less necessary, and it does not give rise to a scarcity rent that can be redistributed. Let us put frugality first by reducing physical throughput with ecological tax reform and/or cap–auction–trade systems for basic resources, and by so doing both avoid the Jevons effect and collect the scarcity rents on nature for the commonwealth rather than the elite.

If we could directly limit population and per capita resource use (scale of the macroeconomy) to a level that nature could easily sustain, then nature's services could remain free. But if we insist that population and per capita consumption must be free to grow, then the rising cost of natural resources must indirectly limit growth, and the question of who receives the increasing rent (who owns nature) will become ever more pressing, and Henry George's thinking ever more relevant. Alternatively, our increasing takeover of nature will, beyond some point, render moot the question of distribution of rents by eliminating all potential claimants! When an overloaded ship sinks all aboard drown – even if the overload is justly distributed and efficiently allocated!

I.

Miscellaneous

31. FITTING THE NAME TO THE NAMED

There may well be a better name than 'steady-state economy', but both the classical economists (especially John Stuart Mill) and the past few decades of discussion, not to mention the good work of the Center for the Advancement of the Steady-State Economy, have given considerable currency to 'steady-state economy' both as a concept and name. Also both the name and concept of a 'steady state' are independently familiar to demographers, population biologists, and physicists. The classical economists used the term 'stationary state' but meant by it exactly what we mean by steady-state economy – briefly, a constant population and stock of physical wealth. We have added the condition that these stocks should be maintained constant by a low rate entropic throughput, one that is well within the regenerative and assimilative capacities of the ecosystem. Any new name for this idea should be sufficiently better to compensate for losing the advantages of historical continuity and interdisciplinary familiarity. Also, steady-state economy conveys the recognition of biophysical constraints and the intention to live within them economically – which is exactly why it cannot help evoking some initial negative reaction in a growth-dominated world. There is an honesty and forthright clarity about the term 'steady-state economy' that should not be sacrificed to the short-term political appeal of vagueness.

A confusion arises with neoclassical growth economists' use of the term 'steady-state growth' to refer to the case where labor and capital grow at the same rate, thus maintaining a constant labor to capital ratio, even though both absolute magnitudes are growing. This should have been called 'proportional growth', or perhaps 'steady growth'. The term 'steady-state growth' is inept because growth is a process, not a state, not even a state of dynamic equilibrium.

Having made my terminological preference clear, I should add that there is nothing wrong with other people using various preferred synonyms, as long as we all mean basically the same thing. Steady state, stationary state, dynamic equilibrium, microdynamic–macrostatic economy, development without growth, degrowth, post-growth economy, economy of permanence, new economy, mature economy. These are all in use already, including by me at times. I have learned that English usage evolves quite independently of me, although like others I keep trying to 'improve' it for both clarity and rhetorical advantage. If some other term catches on and becomes dominant then so be it, as long as it denotes the reality we agree on. Let a thousand synonyms bloom and linguistic natural selection will go to work. Also it is good to remind sister organizations that their favorite term, when actually defined, is usually a close synonym to steady-state economy. If it is not, then we have a difference of substance rather than of terminology.

Out of France now comes the 'degrowth' (*decroissance*) movement. This arises from the recognition that the present scale of the economy is too large to be maintained in a steady state – its required throughput exceeds the regenerative and assimilative capacities of the ecosystem of which it is a part. This is almost certainly true. Nevertheless 'degrowth', just like growth, is a temporary process for reaching an optimal or at least sustainable scale that we then should strive to maintain in a steady state.

Some say it is senseless to advocate a steady state unless we first have attained, or can at least specify, the optimal level at which to remain stationary. On the contrary, it is useless to know the optimum unless we first know how to live in a steady state. Otherwise knowing the optimum level will just allow us to wave goodbye to it as we grow beyond it – or as we 'degrow' below it. Optimal level is one thing; optimal growth rate is something else. Once we have reached the optimal level then the optimal growth rate is zero; if we are below that level the temporary optimal growth rate is at least known to be positive; if we are above the optimal level we at least know that the temporary growth rate should be negative. But the first order of business is to recognize the long-run necessity of the steady state, and to stop positive growth. Once we have done that, then we can worry about how to 'degrow' to a more sustainable level, and how fast.

There is really no conflict between the steady-state economy and 'degrowth' since no one advocates negative growth as a permanent process; and no one advocates trying to maintain a steady state at the unsustainable present scale of population and consumption. But many people do advocate continuing positive growth beyond the present excessive scale, and they are the ones in control, and who need to be confronted by a united opposition!

Nicholas Georgescu-Roegen, adopted by the 'degrowth' movement as its posthumous founder, indeed recognized that the very long-run growth rate must be negative given the entropy law and the final dissolution of the universe. But he did not advocate speeding up that cosmic result by negative growth as an economic policy, nor for that matter did he in the least advocate a steady-state economy! In fact he speculated that the destiny of mankind might be to have a short, fiery, and exciting life rather than a long and uneventful one. He did, however, tentatively suggest a 'minimal bio-economic program'[1] that would surely reduce growth. In general he was interested in what is possible more than in what is desirable. The question – given the limits of the possible, what is the most desirable policy for mankind? – was not his main focus, although he did not entirely ignore it. The closest he came to explicitly dealing with that question was in the following footnote,[2] 'Is it not true that mankind's problem is to economize S (a stock) for as large an amount of life as possible, which implies to minimize s_j (a flow) for some "good life"?' In other words, should we not strive to maximize cumulative lives ever to be lived over time by depleting S (terrestrial low-entropy stocks) at an annual rate s_j that is low, but sufficient for a 'good life'? There is no point in maximizing years lived in misery, so the qualification 'for a good life' is important. I have always thought that Georgescu-Roegen should have put that question in bold in the text, rather than hiding it in a footnote. True enough, eventually S will be gone and mankind will revert to what he called 'a berry-picking economy' until the sun burns out, if not driven to extinction sooner by some other event. But in the meantime, striving for a steady state at a resource-use rate sufficient for a good (but not luxurious) life, seems to me a worthy goal, a goal of maximizing the cumulative life satisfaction possible under limited total resource constraints. This puts at the very center of economics the questions:

- How much resource use per capita is sufficient for a good life?
- How do we ensure that everyone gets that amount?
- How large a population can be supported at that standard of consumption without sacrificing carrying capacity and future life?

Needless to say these questions have not been central to modern economics – indeed, not even peripheral!

Georgescu-Roegen did not like the idea of 'sustainability' any more than that of a steady-state economy because he interpreted both to mean 'ecological salvation' or perpetual life for our species on earth – which of course flies in the teeth of the entropy law. And he was right about that. So sustainability should be understood as longevity, not eternal species-life in the sense of perpetuity. Clear scientific thinking about 'forever' seems, interestingly, to lead to the religious model of death and resurrection, new creation, not perpetual continuation of this creation. Perpetuity in this world is just a glorified perpetual motion machine! To think about forever we must cross from science into theology. But longevity (a long and good life for both individual and species), even if it falls short of forever, or 'ecological salvation', is still a worthy goal both for scientists and theologians, not to mention economists. A steady-state economy is arguably the best strategy for achieving longevity – regardless of what we call it.

NOTES

1. N. Georgescu-Roegen (1993), Energy and economic myths, reprinted in H. Daly and K. Townsend, *Valuing the Earth*, Cambridge, MA: MIT Press, pp. 103–4.
2. Ibid. p. 107, fn 11.

32. THE FRACKING OF *THE LIMITS TO GROWTH*

One tends to read the obituary column more attentively as one gets older. That is probably what led me to notice the death of George P. Mitchell, age 94 – that plus the fact that he was from the Texas Gulf Coast (Galveston and Houston), the part of the country where I grew up. The obituary credited Mr. Mitchell, highly successful oil mogul and geologist, with having been the major developer of the technology of 'fracking', and praised him for thereby having guaranteed energy independence and continued economic growth for the United States.

Wait a minute, I thought – could this be the same George Mitchell who organized the 1975 Woodlands Conference on *Limits to Growth*, and did so much to promote serious discussion of that book? Yes it was. How strange! On the one hand, he was actively concerned about the likelihood that growth would wreck the planet, and on the other hand he was the major developer of the most growth-pushing and planet-wrecking technology of recent decades!

My first thought was that such a contradiction was irreconcilable. But, on second thought, I began to think of a possible reconciliation. It is a matter of sequencing. Does a new extractive technology arrive before or after limits to growth in resource throughput are in place? If we were to first enact limits to growth in resource throughput, then even a violent extractive technology such as fracking would be constrained in its ability to wreck the planet on a large scale. The lower carbon content of natural gas might reduce global warming enough to make up for additional extraction damage to the environment. However, if we insist that unlimited growth must remain our first goal, then fracking will just increase total greenhouse gas emissions, not to mention groundwater depletion and pollution. With growth in first place, even soft technologies, those that increase efficiency of resource usage, are likely (thanks to the Jevons paradox) to promote growth in resource throughput to a scale that is on balance harmful.

A charitable understanding of this contradiction in Mitchell's life is that perhaps he tried to gain acceptance of limits to growth before he developed fracking, but the effort failed. Or, maybe more likely, he saw no contradiction and pursued each activity independently – growth as a private entrepreneur; limits to growth as a public citizen. Subsequently he was at least a proponent of strong environmental regulations on fracking. But, with growth in first place, such regulations will be no more successful in limiting damage done by fracking than the Woodlands Conferences ultimately were in promoting limits to growth.

What happened at the Woodlands? Mitchell was inspired by Dennis and Donella Meadows' book, *The Limits to Growth*, to fund and organize a series of five biennial conferences to be held at the Woodlands, a planned community developed by Mitchell just north of Houston. The first Woodlands Conference in 1975 was a great success. Its theme was 'Alternatives to Growth'. In addition to the Meadows, speakers included E.F. Schumacher, Jay Forrester, Wendell Berry, Lester Brown, Amory Lovins, Bruce Hannon, Gerald Barney, and many others including yours truly. The anti-limits position was led by Herman Kahn. The idea of a steady-state economy got a respectful hearing. It was an excellent beginning, to be followed by four more conferences on the same theme.

Somehow by the third conference the theme had mutated from 'limits and alternatives to growth' to 'management of sustainable growth'. The leadership passed from Meadows and Meadows to the Aspen Institute and the University of Houston. Instead of challenging business as usual, the emphasis shifted to sucking up as usual to business interests. The new, 'more balanced' view was that we really must not limit growth, just focus on good growth rather than bad growth. Growth had somehow become 'sustainable', contrary to the main conclusion of *The Limits to Growth*. The reasoning behind this reversal was kept vague. There was an utter failure of nerve on the part of scientists and especially economists to confront the continuing challenge that George Mitchell and the Meadows had initially set up. Indeed, practically no economists attended the conference. The very idea of limiting growth was too big a pill for economists, politicians, and most scientists to swallow. They coughed it up and silently spit it into their napkin at the conference banquet.

I briefly met George Mitchell but did not know him personally. Maybe he changed his mind about limits to growth; maybe he thought that more energy would always overcome any limits; or maybe he figured he had given the issue of limits his best shot with disappointing results, and it was time to move on. Compared to other leaders in the fossil fuel industry George Mitchell was a beacon of light, as well as a civic leader and philanthropist. Since 1975 there has been serious retrogression in leadership of the fossil fuel industry. Just compare George Mitchell to the Koch brothers!

The bad news is that evidently things still have to get much worse before we will muster the courage and clarity to try to make them better. The 'good news' is that things are indeed getting worse – thanks to our mistaken belief that growth in GDP and its close correlate, resource throughput, must, even in a full world, always increase wealth faster than illth.

33. A MEDICAL MISSIONARY'S ENVIRONMENTAL EPIPHANY

Dr. Paul Brand was the son of British missionary parents in South India where he grew up. He returned to England to study medicine, then went back to take care of people with leprosy in India, mainly doing reconstructive hand and foot surgery – some 3000 operations over many years. He also spent some time in Ethiopia doing similar things, and finally ended up as director of the only leprosy hospital in the United States, located in Carville, Louisiana. I believe that hospital closed about 10 years ago, after Dr. Brand retired. He died in 2003. His son happened to be a student of mine at Louisiana State University (LSU), so that is how I met him. Medically he is credited with having established that leprosy is not the direct cause of decay or necrosis of the hands and feet universally observed in people with leprosy. Rather the damage to extremities is self-inflicted, resulting from the loss of sensation and inability to feel pain. Without pain there is no feedback to tell you that you are damaging yourself. Brand developed routines and practices to help avoid self-inflicted injuries, and wrote a book entitled *Pain: the Gift Nobody Wants*. He also wrote the standard medical textbook on hand and foot surgery.

LSU is a big football school, and an assistant coach invented a super-cushioned helmet that much reduced head pain on impact. This was thought a great thing until Dr. Brand pointed out that head pain was what kept football players from breaking their necks. Would you rather have a headache or a broken neck?

So much for background. I want to focus on a paragraph that Dr. Brand wrote in 1985:

> I would gladly give up medicine tomorrow if by so doing I could have some influence on policy with regard to mud and soil. The world will die from lack of pure water and soil long before it will die from a lack of antibiotics or surgical skill and knowledge. But what can be done if the destroyers of our earth know what they are doing and do it still? What can be done if people really believe that free enterprise has to mean absolute lack of restraint on those who have no care for the future?

What led him to such a statement? Living in India, Ethiopia, and Louisiana – and witnessing the same thing in each place.

In India he received his first lesson in soils management at age six, from an old Indian farmer who reprimanded him and some other boys who carelessly broke the little turf dams on the terraced rice paddies along the mountain side while chasing frogs in the wet level terraces. The old man scooped up a handful of mud and said, 'This soil will feed my family year after year. But the soil has to stay up here. The water wants to carry the soil down the mountain to the river, and then to the sea. Do you think the water will bring it back up?'

'No,' they answered.

'Will you be able to bring it back up?'

'No, grandfather.'

'Will rocky hillsides without soil feed my family?'

'No.'

'Well, that is why the dams must be cared for. Do you understand?'

'Yes, grandfather, we are sorry'. Returning to this area many years later Brand observed barren rocky hillsides – the result of government programs to use ex-prisoners to grow potatoes, but without first teaching them the wisdom of the old farmer.

In Ethiopia most of his leprosy patients were farmers, and that brought him again to the farms where he witnessed terrible erosion where there had once been trees and grasses. The Nile carried Ethiopian soil to Egypt. Farms grew poor crops, and the fields were full of large stones. But the stones were not so large that they could not be levered up and rolled to the edge of the field where they could have made useful walls instead of obstacles to tilling and harvesting. Why were such simple improvements not made, Brand asked. The peasants explained that if they made their fields look good and productive they would lose them to the ruling class. Someone from the city would claim that his ancestors had owned it, and the peasants had no chance in court. So injustice, as well as water and wind, contributed to erosion of the soil. People with leprosy who returned to the eroded farms did not have a good prognosis even if their leprosy was now under control.

The leprosarium at Carville, Louisiana, was just a stone's throw from the Mississippi River. It dated from before levees had been built to contain the river. Therefore all the buildings and houses were built on stilts – maybe 4–8 feet high. For a week or so each year, water swirled under your house, but you got around in a skiff or pirogue. (Nowadays, a fiberglass bass boat with a 200 horsepower Mercury outboard engine is the standard mode of transportation in Louisiana bayous.) Meanwhile the water deposited its silt before returning to its banks, transferring Midwestern topsoil to the Louisiana delta or rebuilding the eroding marshlands or barrier islands. Now the river is contained between levees to eliminate annual floods, so the silt is deposited in the river bottom rather than on the land, necessitating higher levees. Or the silt flows all the way out into the Gulf of Mexico and over the continental shelf, no longer rebuilding coastal marshlands that are now disappearing – and would have served New Orleans as a buffer against Hurricane Katrina. In addition to silt, the Mississippi carries fertilizer and pesticide runoff from Midwestern farms into the Gulf, creating a dead zone the size of New Jersey. 'Cheap' corn and soybeans do not include the costs of lost seafood in the Gulf.

So in light of these experiences in Dr. Brand's life, let us reread the first part of his statement:

> I would gladly give up medicine tomorrow if by so doing I could have some influence on policy with regard to mud and soil. The world will die from lack of pure water and soil long before it will die from a lack of antibiotics or surgical skill and knowledge.

A physician treats our internal organs – heart, lungs, liver, kidneys, and so on – in order that we may live longer and better. But our lives depend on external organs as well, environmental life-support systems. What good are our lungs if there are no trees and grasses capable of photosynthesis? What good is our digestive tract if the land will not grow food? What good are our kidneys if the rivers run dry, or are toxic? I think it is not much of a stretch for a good physician to realize that health and wellness now depend as much on care of our collective external organs as on our individual internal organs. Reconstructing a patient's hands and feet, and then sending him to slowly starve on eroded farmland is at best a partial cure.

The other part of Dr. Brand's statement, his questions, is also important:

> But what can be done if the destroyers of our earth know what they are doing and do it still? What can be done if people really believe that free enterprise has to mean absolute lack of restraint on those who have no care for the future?

Environmental destruction, like other sins, is not just the result of ignorance. There is ignorance to be sure, but mostly we know what we are doing. We are caught up in structures that demand fast growth, rapid turnover, and quick profits. And that is facilitated both by ignorance of environmental costs, and by willingness to shift those costs on to others. Simple denial also plays a role – pie-in-the-sky savior fantasies of space colonization and belief in perpetual motion schemes – technological Gnosticism, I call it.

We all seem to suffer from a symptom of leprosy, we do not feel pain in our external organs and structures (our environmental extremities), and therefore do not stop the behavior that is damaging them. In part this is because often the benefits of the damaging behavior go to the people responsible for the behavior while the costs fall on others – the painful feedback is diverted to people who did not cause the damage. The fishermen in the Gulf of Mexico pay the cost of pesticide and fertilizer runoff caused by careless farming. Environmental costs have been shifted from those who caused them to those who did not.

It would be easy to say, 'Well this is nothing new, just the same old prophets of doom in modern dress – there is nothing new under the sun'. But there is something new – the earth is now relatively full of us and all our stuff. In my lifetime world population has tripled, and the populations of livestock, automobiles, and refrigerators have vastly more than tripled. Meanwhile the size of the earth has stayed the same – so it is a lot more full. And the growing scale of the economy means that environmental and social cost-shifting is ever larger and more dangerous.

Consequently there are many more environmental problems than soil erosion. I focused on that because it was what led Dr. Brand to his realization. Other, newer environmental problems, many of them inter-related, include climate change, biodiversity loss, ozone layer depletion, overpopulation, oil depletion, and so on. Not to mention modern warfare. I will spare you a complete litany.

Many environmentalists look at this list and despair. Humans, after all, they say, are just one more animal species and will over-consume and over-reproduce until they provoke a collapse – just like deer on an island or bacteria in a flask. But Christians like Dr. Brand, and other thoughtful people as well, cannot take that attitude. Yes, we are a part of the Creation, and share many commonalities with our fellow creatures, and we are kin to them by evolution. But we are inescapably the creature in charge – the one that bears the capability and responsibility of the *imago Dei*. Dr. Brand was an example and witness to that truth.

Index

Weiskopf, W.A. 18
welfare 64–5, 90, 98, 140, 159–60, 179
  GNP as measure of 22–4
  and wealth and illth 135–7
Western Europe, immigration 195
Wheeler, John 87
Whitehead, Alfred North 74, 86,
  119–21, 149, 162–3, 165
Wiesltier, Leon 118–19
willingness to pay 70, 98, 105, 121,
  135–6, 164
within-skin capital 191
Woodlands Conference on *Limits to
  Growth* 237–8
work–leisure balance 23, 68, 81, 215,
  222, 224
World Bank 5, 47–50, 59–60, 69, 177,
  200, 223

'bankable projects' 47–9
Commission on Growth and
  Development 59–62, 106,
  114–15, 124–5
country development teams 47, 49
downgrading 82
Global Bilateral Migration Database
  195
negative payment flows 49–50
World Trade Organization (WTO) 69,
  198
downgrading 82
Wright, N.T. 122

young ecosystems 24
youth culture and gerontocracy 33

zero growth 18, 21